Announcing the Most Pract
Vocational Astrology in

Improve your astrological skills wi
tools for vocational and business analysis! Not since the work of
Charles Luntz in 1942 has the subject of Vocational Astrology been
so thoroughly explored. Now, in *How to Use Vocational Astrology for
Success in the Workplace*, edited by Noel Tyl, seven respected astrologers provide their well-seasoned modern views on that great issue
of personal life—Work. Their expert advice will prepare you well
for those tricky questions clients often ask: "Am I in the right job?"
"Will I get promoted?" or "When is the best time to make a career
move?"

With an introduction by Noel Tyl in which he discusses the
startling research of the Gauquelins, this ninth volume in Llewellyn's New World Astrology Series features enlightening counsel
from the following experts:

- **Jayj Jacobs:** The Transits of Experience/Career Cycles, Job
  Changes and Rewards

- **Gina Ceaglio:** Money Patterns in the Horoscope

- **Donna Cunningham:** Attitudes and Aptitudes in the Chart

- **Anthony Louis:** Void-of-Course Moon Strategies for Doing
  Business, Retrograde Planets, and Electional Astrology

- **Noel Tyl:** Special Measurements for Vocational Guidance, and
  How to Evaluate Personnel for Profit

- **Henry Weingarten:** 12 Principles of Modern Astro-Vocational
  Guidance, Planetary Rulership and Career Guidance, and The
  21st Century Astrologer

- **Bob Mulligan:** How to Advance *Your Own* Career as a Professional Astrologer!

Read How to Use Vocational Astrology today, and add "Vocational Counselor" to your resume tomorrow!

TWO BOOKS IN ONE!
Includes the complete 1942 classic by Charles E. Luntz
Vocational Guidance by Astrology

To Write to Llewellyn Authors

We cannot guarantee that every letter written to the authors can be answered, but all will be forwarded. Both the authors and the publisher appreciate hearing from readers, learning of your enjoyment and benefit from this book.

Llewellyn also publishes a bimonthly news magazine with news and reviews of practical esoteric studies and articles helpful to the student, and some readers' questions and comments to the authors may be answered through this magazine's columns if permission to do so is included in the original letter.

The authors sometimes participate in seminars and workshops, and dates and places are announced in *The Llewellyn New Times*. To write to the authors, or to ask a question, write to:

THE LLEWELLYN NEW TIMES
P.O. Box 64383-387, St. Paul, MN 55164-0383, U.S.A.
Please enclose a self-addressed, stamped envelope for reply, or $1.00 to cover costs.

Llewellyn's New World Astrology Series
Book 9

How to Use Vocational Astrology For Success in the Workplace

Modern, Practical Techniques
Presented by Seven Expert Astrologers

Edited by Noel Tyl

1992
Llewellyn Publications
St. Paul, Minnesota, U.S.A. 55164-0383

FIRST EDITION

Cover Design: Christopher Wells and Terry Buske

Library of Congress Cataloging-in-Publication Data

How to use vocational astrology for success in the workplace : modern, practical techniques presented by seven expert astrologers / edited
    by Noel Tyl.
      p. cm. -- (Llewellyn's new world astrology series)
  Includes bibliographical references.
  ISBN 0-87542-387-6
    1. Astrology and vocational guidance. I. Tyl, Noel. II. Series.
BF1729.V63H69 1991
133.5'8331702--dc20   91-47051
                                                CIP

Llewellyn Publications
A Division of Llewellyn Worldwide, Ltd.
P.O. Box 64383, St. Paul, MN 55164-0383

THE NEW WORLD ASTROLOGY SERIES

This series is designed to give all people who are interested and involved in astrology the latest information on a variety of subjects. Llewellyn has given much thought to the prevailing trends and to the topics that would be most important to our readers.

Future books will include such topics as the outer planets, various relationships and astrology, electional astrology, astrology and past lives, and many other subjects of interest to a wide range of people. This project has evolved because of the lack of information on these subjects and because we wanted to offer our readers the viewpoints of the best experts in each field in one volume.

We anticipate publishing approximately four books per year on varying topics and updating previous editions when new material becomes available. We know this series will fill a gap in your astrological library. We look for only the best writers and article topics when planning the new books and appreciate any feedback from our readers on subjects you would like to see covered.

Llewellyn's New World Astrology Series will be a welcome addition to the novice, student and professional alike. It will provide introductory as well as advanced information on all the topics listed above—and more.

Enjoy, and feel free to write to Llewellyn with your suggestions or comments.

Other Books in This Series

Forthcoming

Contents

Noel Tyl

For over 20 years, Noel Tyl has been one of the most prominent astrologers in the Western world. His 17 textbooks, built around the 12-volume *Principles and Practice of Astrology*, were extraordinarily popular throughout the 1970s, teaching astrology with new and practical sensitivity to modern psychotherapeutic methodology.

At the same time, Noel presented lectures and seminars throughout the United States, appearing in practically every metropolitan area and on well over 100 radio and televison shows. Additionally, he founded and edited the legendary *Astrology Now* magazine.

His book, *Holistic Astrology: The Analysis of Inner and Outer Environments*, distributed by Llewellyn Publications, has been translated into German and Italian. His international lectures are very popular throughout Denmark, Norway, Germany, and Switzerland where for the last three World Congresses of Astrology he has been a keynote speaker.

Most recently, Noel wrote *Prediction in Astrology* (Llewellyn Publications), a master volume of technique and practice.

Noel is a graduate of Harvard University with a degree in psychology, and lives in McLean, VA.

Introduction

Noel Tyl

• **Vocational Profiles** • **Success** • **Temperaments** • **Relocation**
• **Alarming Research: the Gauquelin findings**

"What do you do for a living?"—That question is asked so often; even before someone knows our name or remembers it from an introduction in a crowded, noisy social setting. The answer to the question is revelatory.

Besides probing into what we actually do to stay alive, the question asks how much general or specialized education we have had, what level of income we have achieved, what kinds of friends we have, how we dress, what magazines we read, how trustworthy we are, on which side of our brain we rely, where we stand politically, how romantic we might be, and on and on and on. What we do and where we work influence enormously whom we meet, socialize with, and marry. *Our work puts us into society more than does any other facet of our life.*

Imagine answering the question with the job label "astrologer, lawyer, model, airline pilot, cook, mailperson, waiter, accountant, or politician." Each one of these labels *instantly* calls up into consciousness an enormous amount of different personal experiences, value judgments, and expectations of behavior. Going one step further, after the answer "lawyer," for example, there is the follow-up question "What kind?" The next answer, "corporate, tax, trial, or divorce" then adds *even more* personal experience, value judgment, and behavioral expectancy to the social interaction!

All of this tells us two things in the main: our job is so important in the frame of society, stratifying who we are, that it is an actual ex-

1

tension of personal identity; and second, since it *is* so much of who we are, as much as possible of who we *really* are should be involved with it. With so much social stratification, even our name is frequently inadequate in a business discussion since our social security number or some other such account number is more telling, more important! *Without* such numbers, *i.e.,* without involvement with the workplace, we experience the painful loss of social contact, the loss of the challenges and rewards of working together with others, and an overall loss of credibility and personal significance.

"What sign are you?" That question is also asked so often; even before someone knows our name. Astrologers think the answer to the question is revelatory.

Do job and sign get together? *We certainly think they should!* If our job is such an enormous part of our life, and life reflects our astrology, shouldn't vocational astrology literally be a Godsend? Shouldn't we all want to feel right with our job as we feel right with our astrology?

Surely every practicing astrologer will acknowledge that the two most common questions heard from clients are about job and love. Indeed, throughout the history of astrology, we find these questions as well: "Will my son be successful? Will my daughter marry a wealthy man?" Practically every astrology writer has presented job profiles aligned with strong planetary positions and reinforced zodiacal signs. For example, Morin de Villefranche, official astrologer to the courts of Louis XIII and XIV and a prolific writer in astrology, suggested groups of professions for well-situated planets. But planets cannot be all things to each of us, *i.e.,* with a strong Saturn, I cannot easily be a theologian, sculptor, *and* mining engineer. If we are to follow these listings, our question becomes, "How do we make a choice among astrologers' options and guidelines?" We need more measurements, more indications. With a strong Moon, we read the incompatible suggestions of queens, princesses, hunters, and the common people! Among those professions listed under Mars, we have soldiers and hunters, doctors and iron merchants. And aligned with the Sun? Nothing but potentates, from ambassadors to popes!

This is not a glib criticism of astrological deduction or of astrologers who offered their deductions as guidelines throughout history. It is all very clear from the rich stores of our eternal symbolisms *why* these deductions are made. And indeed, throughout so many centuries there *has been* enough corroboration in life experience *to preserve* the guidelines *and* our expectancy for there someday to be astrological signatures for professions. But the fact is that what we expect to be cut-and-dried and simple definitely is not.

In 1942, a fine astrologer and writer, Charles E. Luntz, wrote the landmark book *Vocational Guidance by Astrology*. Luntz revised the book in 1962, and it is still a valuable guidebook today.* Luntz formally listed some 360 professions with accompanying planet-keys and made textual reference to many others. Princesses, queens, and popes are no longer listed as viable professions, but we do have "Cheese Manufacturers (Moon) and Furniture Dealers (Venus)" and many other fascinating and practical extensions of astrological symbology.

There are reasons behind and eye-opening corroboration for the work Morin, Luntz, and many other astrologers have shared with regard to vocational astrology. Each of our two brief examples was conceived in the style of an expert astrologer reflecting his own time, using what was known then to guide the practice of astrology into the future. These astrologers were also reflecting the work and ways of their society.

And that is precisely what we authors are doing in this volume you read now: this is a 50-year update since Luntz's work. It is not an historical perspective; rather, it presents new thoughts with ageless tools.

The ideas and practices in this volume are modern for one very important reason beyond the fact that they are presented in the now. Within vocational analysis, the authors go beyond a job or profession that is taken on by inheritance, family pressure, or routine: *they take into consideration the whole person.*

Astrology and vocation do get together, not simplistically, but in a dynamic and decidedly holistic way that reflects our reality. Instead of job signatures, we see *an astrological process* accompanying an individual's relationship with society through vocation. Although our expectations of hand-in-glove congruence are denied, we can now gain greater perspective socially and a more practical methodology for our astrology than ever before.

---

* Because we think it's still as vital and timely, we are including the text of Luntz's book as an appendix to this volume.

ALARMING RESEARCH

In the late 1950s and 1960s, Michael Gauquelin and his wife Francoise accomplished an enormous program of research into astrology, with a specific focus on vocations and temperament, character and success. Dr. Gauquelin, whose work at the Sorbonne was in psychology and statistics, devoted some 40 years in research to the question of astrology. He was an active lecturer as well, internationally, until his death in May, 1991.

The Gauquelin data and results of the research that concerns us here originally filled some 13 volumes! An overview of the findings is presented in the tidy volume *Cosmic Influences on Human Behavior*, published by Stein and Day, New York.

Many people—astrologers and non-astrologers—think that Gauquelin disproved astrology. This is not so. He did not prove it either. The clarification of what Gauquelin *did* do is presented in the Foreword (by astronomer J. Allen Hynek) as "disproved and disposed of much of the astrologer's foolishness ... the astrology of the masses." Even within this perspective, astrologers can be proud of the Gauquelin findings. They tell us much—but, indeed, they were/ are alarming!

Gauquelin used some 27,000 painstakingly researched birth records of professionals as his sample, with about 60 percent of the group being well-known and very successful and about 40 percent being in the same professions but average in performance rating. The professions were chiefly sports, acting, science, and writing, which Gauquelin keyed to the planets Mars, Jupiter, Saturn, and the Moon, respectively.

Gauquelin qualified the samples with carefully denoted lists of character traits and temperaments; the thrust was to determine if there were correlations among well-known successful professionals, temperament, and astrology.

The Zodiac—Gauquelin calculated the frequency of occurrence of the Sun, Moon, and planets in each sign of the zodiac. Using a sub-set sample of 3,439 well-known military men, Gauquelin found no predominant sign emphasis or conspicuous sign indication. He found nothing beyond the average in terms of Ascendant distribution. The study was extended to 16,000 cases of professional celebrities, and still there were no significant results.

The Aspects—After some 100,000 specific coordinates were evaluated, nothing significant could be found. There was no way to prove the validity of astrology's aspects to "explain" success, character type, or temperament among the professionals.

The Houses—Again there were no correlations.

Now, it is with the houses that we have much to understand here. Gauquelin's chief discovery was that *there is conspicuous significance with planetary positions in the sky*, i.e., marked by astrology's house references. There were two key positions: just above the Ascendant in the 12th House and just past culmination at the Midheaven in the 9th House. The outstandingly successful professional had the vocationally keyed planet in these zones extraordinarily more often than not.

- For sports champions, Mars dominated as rising or just after culmination. The probability of chance being responsible was one in five million.

- Among famous actors, Jupiter was recorded in either of the two special zones, with a probability of chance being one in 1,000.

- Among writers, the Moon was key, and the probability of chance was one in 100,000.

There is so much more, of course, but in this volume we can only introduce the tip of the iceberg for our immediate orientation to Gauquelin's work. What was upsetting—and that is the apt word—to the astrological community was the fact that these planetary positions were in so-called "weak" houses! The 12th House placement or the 9th House placement simply did not correlate with astrology's knowledge. These two houses are Cadent, reactant; how could they "compete" in importance with the mighty Angles of the Ascendant and Midheaven?

We must understand here that having Mars just rising or just having culminated *does not profile* a sports champion. It does mean that *very successful* sports champions will have Mars in either of the two positions so often, where, by chance, the probability would be one in five million!

Fascinatingly, Gauquelin correlates these findings with temperament. He describes statistically that a "classical introverted scientist" will have *Saturn* positioned in the special Cadent zones, much, much more often than will an "eccentric, extroverted scientist." Does this tell us something important, say, with regard to Richard M. Nixon's temperament, a politician with Saturn just past culmination?

Gauquelin shows statistical models for "immodest actors" with much, much higher incidence of Jupiter in the special zones than for "modest actors." Are the immodest actors more well-known because they promote themselves more? Does this tell us something important about the temperaments of Theodore Roosevelt and Franklin Roosevelt—both very self-promoting, bigger-than-life politicians—who had Jupiter just rising above the Ascendant?

What Gauquelin did discover through the enormous research effort (which has been duplicated on a smaller scale by a team of Belgian scientists) alerts us to a major analytical insight: the specially sensitive zones just above the Ascendant and just after the Midheaven—and, unfortunately, Gauquelin did not define the size of the area, but astrologers over the years measure the special areas up to about 10 degrees—do suggest success and temperamental coloration of behavior in terms of the planet involved.

It matters not to feel betrayed somehow about the alarming news that the supposedly "weaker" houses have extraordinary new significance. We could say that when a key planet is placed there natally *it will progress back over the Angle with great significance during the early, crucially formative years of life*. The person will start to take on individuality, keyed significantly by the nature of the arcing planet. Our psychology study has proved dramatically how important the early years of development are. Our astrology is keeping pace with all these person-centered findings. Perhaps now, thanks to the Gauquelin discoveries, we can confidently modernize our understandings of the Cadent Houses, the 12th and 9th in particular. Perhaps the key to more realistic and complete interpretation guidelines is with the Cadent sense of "reaction" within the frame of "development," *i.e.*, as the Angle and the entire angular House become involved in time as life develops.

Most interestingly, Gauquelin presents research gathered about success, chiefly by Alain Girard: most men who have been successful in life came from families in privileged social positions. In general terms, according to studies done in France and the United

States, two-thirds of famous people originate from 5 percent of the population comprised primarily of the wealthiest and most intellectual people. Again, this highlights the parental significance of the Midheaven axis *and* the Ascendant axis which in turn relates to the parents as the *derived* Midheaven axis.

Gauquelin presents findings supporting a second factor for success: an inner drive, a psychological bond we have with the hour of our birth and the positions of key planets in or out of the special zones. He showed that winning requires a "complete mobilization of one's personality," and that it is a "character difference" that separates the successful athlete, for example, from the unsuccessful. And all of this is related to planetary position—singular ones, to be sure—a dramatic fix on key planets at key positions.

So we return from the statistics to the holistic, to awareness of people mobilizing all of themselves to be all they can be. It seems to me that Gauquelin's work is not an end but a grand beginning in research made possible by modern technology and analytical sophistication. So much more needs to be done. Our astrology still develops in a richness that reflects one unavoidable truth: as we grow to be who we can be, *all of us* speaks to the task. Astrology shows this process. Astrologers learn to see it.

RELOCATION

In addition to questions about job success and love success, astrologers so very often hear questions about where to live. We want to leave a location because we may have a pervasive sense of being in the wrong place, of having used up opportunities, of wanting to flee a "bad scene," of wanting to start over someplace else. Escape is usher to opportunity. This is a classic fight-or-flight instinct.

But, within the frame of our study here, what does relocation do? *Relocation changes the Angles of our horoscope!* By taking up residence in a new geographic location (especially a longitudinal shift), our natal horoscope redrawn for the exact birth moment as it would have been timed in the new time zone and at the new location shows new Angles, and the planets, while still in the exact sign-degree positions of the birth moment, take up new positions in the sky. What would a professional athlete gain, say, by taking up new residence and training activity in a place that brought natal Mars to one of the special zones Gauquelin uncovered? How would a business executive's temperament change if a new residence and work location brought natal Jupiter into one of the very powerful Cadent House placements?

Indeed, relocation astrology has steadily grown in fascination as people have gained the facility for travel. As the world has become busier and smaller, people are on-the-move in enormous numbers. Astrologers know that major progression, arc, and transit activity to natal Angles, especially involving Pluto, Uranus, and Saturn, promises high probability of relocation, of new starts that more than likely will be accompanied by a change of location.

Astrologer Jim Lewis is an expert authority on relocation. His Astro*Carto*Graphy techniques and services are used around the world, and his Llewellyn book (with Ariel Guttman), *The Astro*Carto*Graphy Book of Maps,* brings the concept personally to your desk. Lewis' maps show the shift of Angles for an individual's horoscope everywhere on earth. But, we have always looked hard at the Ascendant and Midheaven and not to the other side, if you will. If we pay more attention to what we are learning about vocation, temperament, and development, measurements that have not yet occurred to us will continue to rise to practical prominence. Observation will open the door more.

Gauquelin mentions the outer planets only fleetingly and specifically only in relation to "cosmic genetics," to inheritance factors seen through planetary placements. He determined that the planetary effect of inheritance is "partially related to the distance of the planet from the earth." There is a complete fall-off of significance beginning with Uranus and including Neptune and Pluto. But here Gauquelin was *not* discussing temperament, how a person behaves in relation to planetary placement, specifically through vocation. On that subject, as we have seen, his research had been confined in the main to the planets Mars, Jupiter, Saturn, and the Moon. Yet, we must note that it is analytically, undeniably significant that Richard Nixon's relocation from his Yorba Linda, California birthplace to Washington D.C.—a major longitudinal shift—shifted the Angles of his horoscope to the extent that his critically important Neptune (opposed his Sun) was brought *just past culmination,* four degrees past his Midheaven into the 9th House in Washington D.C.

What a fascinating subject! What do *you* do for a living? What sign are *you*? What are we learning about ourselves every day of our life? What are we, who are we in the workplace? What further development can we expect from ourselves? When? Are we really in the right career, the right job?

Yes, astrologers, these are the questions, for us and from our clients. And here in this volume are fresh guidelines to many answers, shared by experts, all with a well-seasoned modern view.

And to these authors, I give personal thanks and applause for joining in the quest and doing such fine work.

Donna Cunningham

Donna became interested in astrology in the late 60s and quickly saw that it was the *real* vocation for her. She had already received her master's degree in social work in 1967 and seen in astrology a stunning tool for quick, specific, and yet deep diagnosis of issues in people's lives.

For many years, Donna's dual career continued as a private practice astrologer and psychotherapist, and as a caseworker in such settings as hospitals, clinics, women's health, alcoholism, psychiatric facilities, and addiction treatment. In addition, Donna has written hundreds of articles and nine books, generally with a psychological perspective. Her writing, lectures, and work with clients reflect her growing interest in spiritual studies and healing tools such as flower remedies, color meditation, and affirmations.

Donna has been certified as a professional astrologer by the AFA and PAI, and was given PAI's 1986 award for outstanding contributions to the art and science of astrology.

Donna has led workshops throughout the United States and abroad, focusing on professional training in counseling principles for astrologers and advanced students.

Updating the Tradition— Attitudes Brought to the Workplace

Donna Cunningham

To know how to use astrology for success in the workplace, we need to know more than vocational astrology: we need to know about careers themselves. We must assess such reality-based concerns as the practical demands of any given profession, the educational requirements, and the earning potentials. To advise clients well, we need answers to questions like the following: what is the shape of a particular vocation today? How are the traditional professions changing? What are the growth careers, and what careers are overcrowded or dying out?

You may reply that we astrologers are not counselors and that we are not trained to do vocational counseling. Yet, that is what a good proportion of our clients are going to pay us to do, and we must be able to apply our personal talents and our astrological intelligence to this extremely important specialization within our field.

Most definitely, the birth chart is the beginning of a rich, personal professional profile. For example, *attitudes* toward work, authority, and money do not readily show up in traditional vocational tests, yet they *are* clear in the horoscope. When these attitudes are clarified, it is easier for us to match job choices with temperament. In addition, astrology provides what no test instrument can, which is an indication of timing in career moves. Timing is everything, and though many clients seem to have excellent instincts in

11

terms of such moves, others do not. Many are driven by frustration to make the right moves at the wrong times.

WHERE TO GET INFORMATION ON CAREERS

It would be wonderful if we could all go back to school and study counseling. However, if you were only able to take one or two courses, the most practical credits would be in the area of modern vocational realities and how to do vocational counseling. It would be an excellent investment in terms of increasing both your professional skills and your income. Courses of this nature are often included in M.B.A. programs or in the fields of personnel or vocational rehabilitation.

Short of taking classes, there are excellent reference books available which can help answer our special questions. In the bibliography presented at the end of this chapter, there are several excellent career directories that get updated every year or two. Most of these publications have 800 numbers and will ship the directory to you. For the same price as still another astrology book, you could own one of these guidebooks and look up occupations that clients are considering. For example, one called *Occufacts: Information on 565 Careers in Outline Form* has information on working conditions, job duties, physical demands, temperament, aptitudes required, and earnings. Short of owning one of these informative reference books, if you went to the library and checked out several up-to-date books about careers, you would immediately be better prepared to serve your clients.

One listing in the bibliography which deserves special mention is Barry and Linda Gale's *Discover What You're Best At*. Although not intended to replace full-scale testing and individual interpretation by a certified career counselor, this book contains a series of tests that measure vocational aptitudes. It sorts 1,100 vocations into 41 career clusters, identifies the clusters into which the person fits, and gives brief descriptions of the variety of lines of work in each cluster. At $10.95, the book is affordable and could easily become part of your offerings to clients who are searching for a good career fit.

Even informally, you can make it your business to learn about different vocations. At social gatherings, when you ask the inevitable question, "What do you do," follow it up with questions about *exactly* what that line of work involves. Remember, you may have known what it was like to be a nurse *ten years ago*, but what it is like to be a nurse today is very different.

THE CHART AS POTENTIAL—LIFE AS REALITY

To give sound astrological advice, we must assess reality. We need information that the astrological chart does not give us. We must ask our clients important questions: what level of education have they reached? In what specific studies? What kinds of financial and environmental supports do they have? What has pleased them in their work experience? What other kinds of careers have they considered?

We must use our skills of observation to get an idea of the client's intelligence and verbal and social skills. When it comes to intelligence, however, it is important to distinguish between "Air smart" and "Earth smart." For example, the person who is only Air smart may have brilliant ideas yet lack the practicality to make anything of them. The person who is Earth smart, on the other hand, may have only one original idea in a lifetime and yet have the business skills to parlay that idea into a fortune. (An Earth-smart individual would have strong Earth accents in the horoscope, involving Mercury and the Ascendant, especially. An Air-smart person would have much emphasis in the Air signs, but not much going on in Earth.)

Suppose you do a reading for a woman in her early thirties whose chart indicates very fine counseling skills. (She may have a strong and well-aspected Pluto and maybe the Moon or other placements in Libra.) Before you suggest that she go for a Master's degree in social work or counseling, find out more about her situation. Suppose she only has a high school education: is she up to four years of college for a B.A. and two for a Master's? Is money for tuition and expenses available from savings, a mate, or family? Do you personally have any idea what tuition would amount to for the career you are recommending? Were her grades good enough to get a scholarship? With all the cutbacks in government funding, what is actually available now in terms of financial aid? Where would you find that out? Or, where would the woman herself find that out?

Suppose you discover that she is separated, has two little children, does not get child support, and her family is poor. Are you still ready to recommend a Master's degree? What about the child-care concerns while the woman would be in class? Perhaps there are paraprofessional careers requiring only a *two*-year degree in which those same counseling skills would be an asset. If you look through a career directory like those given in the bibliography, you might come up with some alternatives. My point is that there are many important dimensions of career counseling with which we need to become familiar in order for our astrological analysis to be practical.

Often, people come with strong chart indicators for a creative talent such as writing, music, or acting. They want to know if they are going to be famous for this gift that three or four astrologers and their own dear mother have recognized. When clients ask if I think they can make it big as a musician or a singer, I ask, "How many hours a day do you practice?" Of would-be actors, I ask, "How many auditions did you go on this week?" That's what it takes to make it in these kinds of careers: discipline, hard work, and putting yourself out there. Even then you may or may not make it, depending on luck—but you cannot wait for luck to strike. Jupiter works *if you work it*—and working it is Saturn.

FINDING APTITUDES AND ATTITUDES IN THE CHART

In preparing for a reading, you might ask for three choices of careers the client has considered. Naturally, you are not limited to those choices, since the chart will surely suggest more possibilities, but the client's list will show you the person's line of thought. Then analyze the chart to see how those choices fit. Traditionally, we have learned to look for some combination of the 2nd, 6th, and 10th Houses; the planets placed in those houses weighing most heavily, and then the signs.

In those houses, you can read not only the client's aptitudes for success but the attitudes toward work as well. *Attitude often has more to do with success than aptitude.* Many intelligent, competent, or talented people sabotage themselves in their work because of negative attitudes, such as believing they will fail, or wearing a chip on their shoulder. On the other hand, a set of constructive work attitudes and habits can serve even a moderately talented individual in good stead. It is the old story of the tortoise and the hare: the hare had the aptitude for racing, but the tortoise had the winning attitude.

To illustrate how both attitude and aptitude contribute to vocational choice, let us suppose that someone has Uranus or Aquarius in the 6th House. The aptitudes suggested would be in modern, technical fields such as computers; or offbeat, nontraditional professions such as astrology or biofeedback. However, the underlying attitudes could be that this person resents supervision and functions better unsupervised. When unsupervised, there would be highly independent and self-motivated behavior; whereas when closely supervised, there could be a rebellious, erratic, and somewhat contemptuous temperament. The *ideal* work might be *self*-employment, consulting, or in chaotic, rapidly changing lines of work where personal initiative pays off.

Let us suppose a client has Leo on the Midheaven or planets in Leo in the 10th House. The desire to shine and "to be somebody" is very strong, and there probably is an aptitude for acting. Whether the person can, in fact, make it on stage depends a great deal on attitudes. The individual may remain a frustrated actor, given the Leonine wish to be loved and adored just because one is. Such beliefs need to be offset by attitudes that produce hard work, patience, and the willingness to expose oneself to auditions time after fruitless time. Without attitudes like these, people with Leo-emphasized Midheavens may be reduced to creating drama and uproar at the straight jobs they get while endlessly waiting "to be discovered."

It is important to distinguish among the 2nd, 6th, and 10th Houses, however, even though the actual occupation may be keyed by any one of them. The 2nd House shows skills and personal resources which the individual can draw on to earn a living. When the 2nd House or the sign Taurus is strong, while the 6th and 10th are unoccupied, then *earning money is a primary concern*, rather than a career path.

In the 2nd House, you will also discern attitudes toward money that can either enhance or block the career. Review the chosen vocation to see how financial attitudes or practices suggested by the client's 2nd House could affect success. For instance, with Neptune or Pisces in the 2nd, the individual may be very dedicated and work hard, but be self-sabotaging in terms of earnings. For a salaried employee, there is a degree of protection, but a self-employed person with Neptune in the 2nd could be courting disaster.

The 6th House shows work habits, attitudes toward the job, potential types of jobs, and what kind of employee the person would make. Look at the vocational choices to see how work habits and attitudes described by the 6th House match working conditions and job tasks required for the particular line of work. (Here, again, you could refer to a career directory for very helpful information.) With the Sun or Moon in the 6th House, identification with a blue collar background may be a factor the upwardly-mobile would have to work through to allow themselves to be especially successful.

When the 6th House or the sign Virgo is strong, but the 2nd and 10th are not emphasized, then work for its own sake may be the motivation. Depending on the planets involved, these chart dimensions may show people who find work a primary gratification in itself—or, at the very least, a major focus of energy and concern. If there is little satisfaction in their work, their health could suffer. Some are workaholics.

The 10th House shows the long-term career path or the primary source of career recognition for that individual. As we will explore later, attitudes toward authority figures and toward becoming an authority can be seen here. These attitudes can be crucial in assessing the most suitable vocations and any barriers that can get in the way. When the 10th House or the sign Capricorn is strong and the 6th and 2nd are not, people are strongly motivated toward some vocation or calling. We are not looking at work for its own sake, nor is money the primary motivation; rather their drive toward significance is strong—they want to be somebody. The means may be less important than the end.

In short, in vocational astrology we must assess attitudes and motivation as carefully as we do aptitudes. Fortunately, both can be seen in the signs and planets in the vocational houses. When Gemini is involved in the 6th or 10th, for example, ask yourself what would be a Gemini *modus operandi* on the job? Specifically, how would Gemini operate in the current work situation or within the proposed change? If Gemini would be bored, restless, and lonely, it is surely not a good match. What would be the Cancerian *modus operandi*? Or the Sagittarian one? By thinking through the things that motivate and satisfy the sign in question, you will come up with a strong vocational sense about the client. Then, discussing precisely how particular attitudes impact on vocational choice becomes enlightening and helpful.

ADDITIONAL VOCATIONAL INDICATORS

Planets in aspect to the Midheaven color the career and show skills and resources the person can draw upon. Many astrologers do not have Uranus in the 10th House, but, instead, many have an *aspect* between Uranus and the Midheaven. The Gauquelin research showed that a planet within ten degrees of the Midheaven is the most powerful vocational significator—even and especially when it is in the 9th House.

The House the Sun is in is also an important indicator. Since the Sun is the center of one's being and an important source of self-discovery and self-expression, one might as well get paid for it. For example, in working in the health fields. I came across many health professionals with the Sun in the 6th House. Any house that has a stellium in it may also play a role in the career, either positively or negatively or both. Someone with a strong 3rd House emphasis will doubtlessly be a communicator, regardless of the actual career.

The strongly occupied houses are especially crucial when you find charts where the 2nd, 6th, and 10th are all vacant. Usually, such people are basically only working to pay the rent and support whatever is really important to them—*i.e.,* their avocation, as shown by the houses where they *do* have planets. If you can find a vocation which matches their avocation, they will be getting paid for doing what they really love.

There are occupations matching each of the 12 houses. If any area of life is outstandingly important, you can bet there is money in it. For instance, the 5th House generates hundreds of kinds of jobs dealing with children, recreation, or romance. The 9th House provides not only jobs in education but also in the travel industry and in law. And so on.

FITTING THE CAREER TO THE WHOLE PERSON

Some people may have a 10th or 6th House that is somewhat favorable for the vocational choices given, but indications elsewhere in the chart make the selections questionable. You would then want to think of similar or related careers which do not have the difficulties suggested by the chart. The book, *Discover What You're Good At*, with its 41 career clusters, is especially helpful in this pursuit.

Looking at some mismatches shows you how to fine-tune career choices. Suppose you have a client with Gemini emphasized, a strong Mercury, or a strong 3rd House, but little Saturn or Pluto, who wants to be a writer. The client will undoubtedly have a gift for words, yet, as Julian Armistead has pointed out, they lack the Saturnian discipline to stay put long enough to complete anything major. Without a strong Saturn, this person could be eager for immediate gratification, whereas the rewards of writing are very long in coming. Pluto gives the ability to spend time alone, needed for writing anything lengthy. In order to capitalize on the verbal skills, such individuals can pursue *other* kinds of work involving communication. For example, they might become teachers, speakers, salespersons, or even journalists writing short pieces. The sign and house emphasized would help you pinpoint the possible focus of the writing or communicating. If it were Virgo, for instance, health education is a possible focus; in Leo, children, the theater, or romance.

On the other hand, let us consider someone who has strong Saturn, Capricorn, or 10th House placements, but has a remote Venus. (The way you can tell is to do the chart preparation and then go

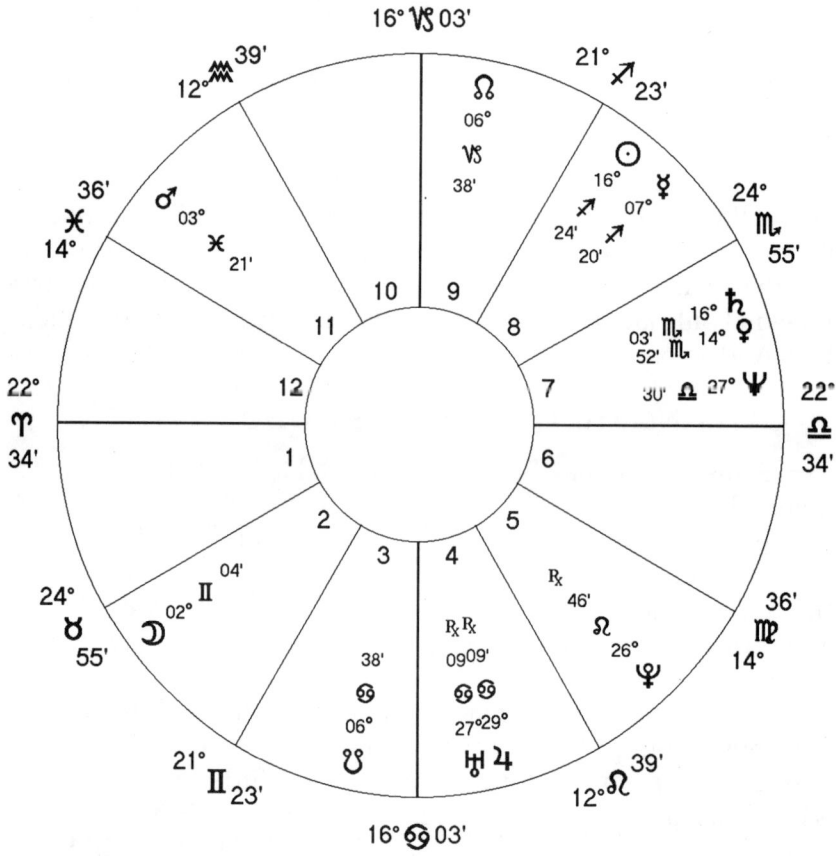

Case #1, Female

away and get busy with something else. Then ask yourself where Venus was in that chart and struggle to remember!) The individual wants to go into business management. Here, you would need to draw the distinction between administration and supervision. We know that Saturn/Capricorn focal points are good for administration, in that paperwork would get handled and activities involving structure, order, and long-range planning would benefit. However, without a pervasive Venus, supervision would not be a good choice; the people skills, like the capacity to motivate others and resolve conflicts, might be lacking. This is not to say that supervisors automatically do have the correct people skills, but it is much harder on everyone when they do not. Fortunately, these skills are learnable to some extent through courses in management, supervision, and employee relations.

A woman who has been a successful professional dancer, appearing in Broadway musicals and other shows, comes to you for a reading. At 35, she feels she does not have many more years left as a dancer, so she wants to begin to prepare now for a career change. Her thought is that perhaps she should go for an M.B.A. and a career in business administration, as that would be lucrative. First, are there any chart features that would cause you to advise her *against* a career in business administration? What kinds of careers would you suggest as an alternative? Think about these questions before reading on: study the horoscope for a while, as though you were preparing for an actual consultation.

Despite the Capricorn Midheaven, her basic nature seemed to mitigate against anything as dry as business administration. With the Gemini Moon and a mutable T-Square among Mars and Moon/ Mercury, I suspected she'd be easily bored with work that did not involve constant change and challenge, stimulation, quick reactions, and public contact. Additionally, the strong Jupiter-Uranus conjunction (which sat on her relocated New York City Ascendant) seemed to mitigate against anything so hierarchical as administration. This conjunction also suggested that excitement and frequent change were necessary for her sense of fulfillment.

Since she intended to go back to school, I suggested she consider a degree in Public Relations to become a publicist or manager for people in show business. She had a great deal of Fire emphasis, with Aries Rising and the Sun in Sagittarius. Therefore, the dynamism that had made her a successful entertainer could easily transfer to promoting others. In addition, the prominent Mercury and Jupiter highlighted the 3rd/9th House axis by rulership, important for publicity and information. The 7th House indicated business partnerships as well as more personal ones, and Venus, the ruler of her 7th, was in the 7th conjunct Saturn, ruler of her Midheaven.

In any midlife career change, you would want *transferability of skills learned in the original career*. All her years of work in show business, plus her connections, would be put to good use in being a publicist. This recommendation was very pleasing to her, since she did not want to give up the glamour of show business, but was merely trying to be practical. The Capricorn Midheaven would be useful in managing creative performers, who are often disorganized.

Personal Liabilities Against the Career

I have found it very important to look at the chart as a whole for character liabilities that might mitigate against career choice or performance. Let's pretend, again, that you are in an actual consultation. The young person in front of you wants to become a doctor. This is a bright individual with no money problems. The Sun and Mercury are in the 6th House and Virgo is rising, which would go along with a career in the health fields. However, you notice a Mars/Uranus conjunction in the 9th House, near the Midheaven. What *three* problems would you see in this placement that might make you advise the client against becoming a doctor? Take a moment and think this question through.

The three problems I see that conjunction presenting are as follows. The first is in getting *through* medical school. How would the person ever finish, when it requires approximately six to eight years of intensive postgraduate study in which all outside interests are put on hold? There would also be a strong tendency for rebelliousness, getting the individual into trouble with teachers and the school itself. When a career requires extensive education, look at the 9th House for sure.

Second, the rigid, conservative hierarchy involved in hospitals and other traditional medical settings would be extremely difficult for this individual to tolerate, both in school and after graduation. And, third, even if the person did complete school and begin to practice, there would be a strong propensity for malpractice suits due to unorthodox methods and a provocative bedside manner, all keyed as well to the intense Mars-Uranus conjunction.

What alternatives would you suggest? What about nursing? Although the education requirements are less arduous, there could be the same problem with the hierarchy, or even worse. A nurse has little power to take independent action, being subject to the physician's orders. Physical therapy, which could be an outlet for the physical side of the Mars energy, would hold similar problems in terms of the medical hierarchy.

What about an alternative health career? The propensity to legal problems—like being accused of practicing medicine without a license—still exists. However, the curriculum in alternative school settings may be more acceptable and thus more likely to be completed. What *type* of alternative health career would you suggest? Possibly energy-oriented work like Reiki or acupuncture would be a place to channel the Mars-Uranus conjunction. Maybe the inventiveness of the Uranus factor could be turned to medical equipment, and the result would be a medical engineer.

With the strong 9th House emphasis, rather than being sued for malpractice, perhaps the person could become a malpractice attorney for the downtrodden. Other possibilities include becoming a lobbyist, activist, or educator for health concerns like AIDS, health hazards in the workplace, or toxic waste. The 9th House conjunction then is addressed and channeled very well into political action, although there are still likely to be rash acts. However, the conjunction also strongly suggests the need to get free of anger toward authority based on childhood experiences—probably in the early school years. Otherwise, there would be the propensity to act in explosive, rebellious ways that would be damaging personally and to the cause.

With a Uranian client like this one, the astrologer needs to discuss the desirability of healing the rage and addressing it in a detached, logical manner. You are not doing it to pry into personal childhood and emotions, which could arouse resentment: rather, you are pointing out exactly how the temperament could interfere with current, stated concerns, *i.e.*, choosing a career. Sermonizing and generally acting like a disapproving parent will only provoke the client to rebel, possibly very angrily. In less extreme reactions, the client might automatically reject what you have to say.

In order to be effective, you will probably have to listen to—and maybe even draw out—the anger against educators and other authority figures. You need to *accept* the anger, perhaps agreeing with how terribly unfair it all was. Do not justify or rationalize the authority's actions. You would want to examine any difficulties of your own about conflict, such as a fear of anger and a need to suppress it in yourself and others.

You would be on particularly shaky ground if you attempted to bring in sweet reason, the karmic necessity for forgiveness, or the spiritual lessons to be learned. ("After all, you chose this set of parents.") As an authority figure with Divine overtones, your *acceptance* of the anger can in itself be healing. It allows the person to move on from there and finish school to have the ability to change the things that are bothersome.

Let's look at another example. (Please note that the following is not a real chart, I just made it up. Any resemblance to persons living or dead is purely coincidental.) Suppose that a young person wants to pursue a career in financial planning or maybe the stock market. There is a Sun-Mercury conjunction in Taurus in the 8th House. It trines Pluto in Virgo. Looking good, right?

However, as you look further, the Sun and Mercury oppose Mars and Neptune in Scorpio in the 2nd. Oops! Would you entrust your trust fund to this person? What would you say? I might begin by exploring how the client handles personal finances and I would look for any problems there. Tactfully, I would point out that handling large sums of other people's money might get frustrating, and there could be temptations to cut corners or adopt get-rich-quick schemes. If I heard defensive protest, I would offer the reminder that there would be the challenge of continually managing millions of dollars. In other words, I would test the career waters, the attitudes signaled by outstanding planetary placements.

So, then, what would you suggest as a possible career for this person? I have to confess I cannot think of a good one. Anything to do with handling other people's money faces the same temptation and vulnerability. Even fund raising for a worthy cause has that possibility. Healing is another 8th House activity and, again, the person might be very good at it, but the money end of it could become too fascinating. You would have to assess the spiritual quality of the person—and yet, even fire and brimstone preachers are not immune to the pull of money.

Look at the rest of the chart, especially the vocational houses, to see what else you could come up with. This same combination in other houses would not be so difficult. For example, moving the opposition to the 3rd/9th House axis might suggest a dynamic yet down-to-earth teacher, an evangelist, or a crusading albeit conservative journalist—a Ralph Nader type. What would be potentially corrupting would be the 2nd/8th House axis.

The examples we have been looking at are extreme, of course. Yet, the reasoning we have explored is what takes place in any vocational reading. While the traditional career Houses are your starting point, you do need to scan the chart as a whole. Are there any character traits that counter-indicate the fields the client is considering? Does the work rely heavily on logic, for instance, and yet the person has a stellium in Pisces in the 3rd House and a Mercury-Neptune conjunction? Your analysis would not only include the astrological factors but also the specific kinds of tasks involved. If you don't know what those tasks are, check the vocational reference books. The choice of a career is such a serious matter that it merits a complex and thoughtful analysis.

WHY VOCATIONAL ASTROLOGY IS NOT PSYCHOTHERAPY

It is important to understand that a vocational reading is not psychoanalysis. That statement may sound strange from an astrologer who is also a psychotherapist, but consider where clients who ask for vocational advice are coming from. They are in a business frame of mind, a bottom-line mood, even a Saturn sensibility. They are probably having Saturn transits or transits to the Midheaven or they would not be coming for this particular session in the first place. They are future-oriented and want to get on with their lives, not rummage around in the garbage of the past. They are not paying you for that, so any rummaging you do had better be *relevant to the question at hand*. You need to be able to demonstrate, clearly and logically, just how any emotional and historical questions impinge on their potentials for success.

To do otherwise would be intrusive. I believe strongly in a non-intrusive approach to the chart analysis, one in which you focus on clients' concerns and, in other matters, respect their right to privacy. If you can show precisely why a problem with Dad causes the client to do self-defeating things on the job, then you are providing useful information. If you are skillful in this, you can go a long way toward motivating the client to seek help with the problem. The client now would have a practical reason to spend all that money on therapy or healing or to invest precious time in a self-help group.

Proving the relevancy of the past to the present is not even that hard to do. Consider that the 10th House, which shows the parents as authority figures, is related to how people handle authority figures as adults. Suppose they are having a difficult relationship with the boss or, especially, a pattern of difficulties with supervisors. You can delineate with a good deal of accuracy what the primary authority figure at home was like. It is then easy to lead the client to make connections between reactions to that authority figure and habitual reactions to bosses.

Incidentally, that tired old 4th/10th House debate about which house represents the mother and which is the father is a false one to my way of thinking. The 10th is the primary authority figure, but also depicts both parents in their authority function, while the 4th is the nurturing function. The Moon at the Midheaven suggests a mother-dominated home, but also generally describes the father as a lunar type.

In showing how issues with parents get transferred to supervisors, it is also powerful to point out that the expectations and needs that the inner child is still trying to have met are *not appropriate to the workplace*. Bosses are not parents, and it is no use being mad because they are not taking care of you. Speaking as one who has supervised, when you hire an employee, you are not looking to adopt a child, you just want to get the job done. And, yet, it is very common for residues of unmet or frustrated needs to be transferred onto the employer—especially where parents have been dysfunctional. Even when the boss is different by nature than the parent was, the behaviors and attitudes of the employee can recreate family dynamics, setting up conflict. For instance, with the Moon on the Midheaven, there may have been a strong codependency with the mother. By being highly responsive and sensitive to the supervisor's emotions and needs, the employee may set up a codependent relationship at work, time after time.

An examination of the 10th House and parental authority is also relevant at another stage of the career. That is when the person crosses the line into supervision or management—from *having* a boss to *being* a boss. This is an important developmental stage in the career, and one which is fraught with potential stumbling blocks. If you cannot master this task, you limit your success potential. Even if you are in business for yourself, you can only go so far without eventually having to hire some employees.

Parental modeling is likely to creep in at this stage, without conscious awareness, as a model for now becoming an authority. Or, people in this position may bend over backward *not* to be like their parents were and thus avoid the boundary issues that being a boss entails. Similarly, people who function well as single adults or even in marriage get tripped into acting like their parents when they become parents themselves. We live what we learn. Thus, in order to be successful in an administrative or supervisory capacity, the person may well need to resolve any remaining authority problems.

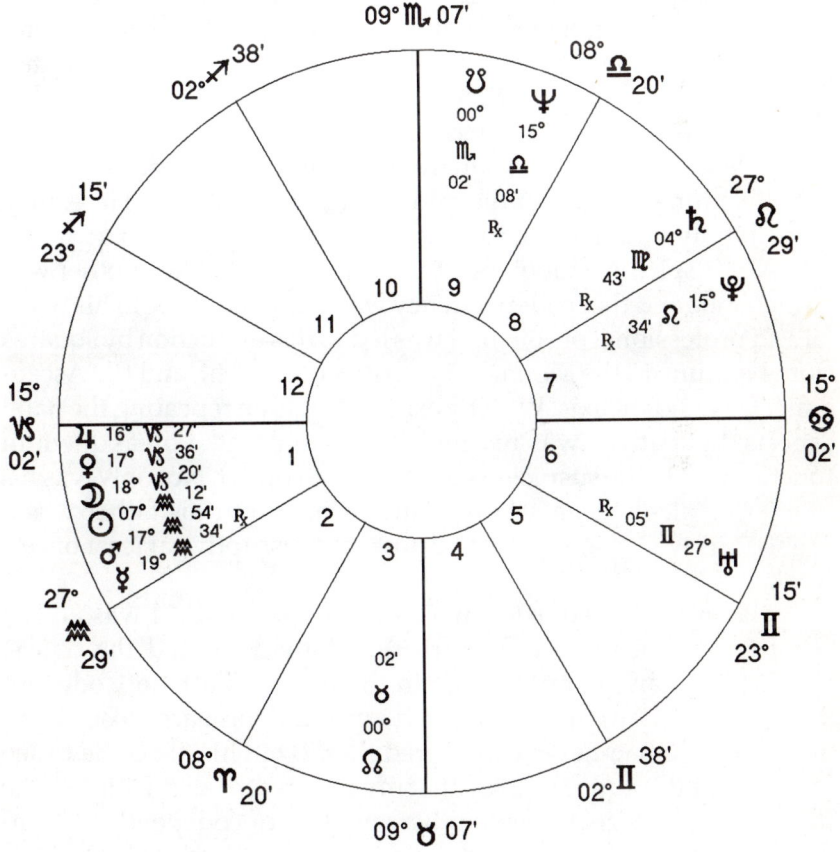

Case #2, Male

HOW PERSONAL HISTORY AFFECTS VOCATION

This man came to me in the midst of a career crisis, having recently been demoted out of a management position. He was a conservative businessman who did "benefits consulting," *i.e.*, he planned benefits like insurance and pension plans for major corporations. At the same time, his wife was thinking of leaving their long, committed marriage.

You might like to take a look at the transits for the original consultation, which took place in late June, 1989, and the follow-up in February, 1991. The most important transits were that Neptune and Saturn in Capricorn were beginning to set off his Capricorn Ascendant and 1st House planets, while squaring natal Neptune. This repeated a natal Neptune square to his Capricorn Ascendant, Jupiter, Venus, and Moon. In addition, transiting Pluto in the 10th was beginning to set off the natal opposition between Pluto and Mars-Mercury. The transits of Pluto square natal Pluto and Neptune square natal Neptune are part of the midlife crisis for all of us. Here, they were doubly difficult due to their strength in the birth chart.

My suspicion, in looking at the chart, was that his mother was an alcoholic and that codependency was at the root of both his marital and professional problems. I was led to this deduction by squares from Neptune to the Moon, Venus (ruler of the 4th), and the Ascendant/Descendant axis. With transiting Neptune repeating the natal aspects, the pattern was reaching a critical point, a breakdown in functioning. These suspicions proved to be correct. Not only was his mother an alcoholic, a steady, daily drinker, but his father was a problem as well, coming home drunk and disruptive at least once a week.

Having just read extensively on codependency, I was at that point crusading for people with this pattern to read the books, watch Bradshaw marathons, go to therapy, and attend Codependency Anonymous meetings. Yet, how would this hard-nosed businessman who had never considered therapy in his life come to see the need for it? Suffice it to say that my own recent acquisition of the material and my zeal to help others get free of codependency rendered me both knowledgeable and articulate. I was able to show specific ways this history affected both his functioning in his career and his shaky relationship with his wife. He was also beaten and ready to listen. He was at a crisis point in the two areas of life that had the most meaning for him—his career and his marriage. He had suffered what had to be unbearable for one with so much Capricorn energy—the humiliation of demotion and the possibility of losing the job altogether. I did have his ear!

In February 1991, he returned for a repeat reading—or, for what he called, in his inimitably Capricornian fashion, a "midcourse correction." He had just re-listened to the tape of our original session. Thus, all the material we had discussed was fresh in his mind, and he could see that he had made substantial progress in that year and a half. He had not gone to therapy—that was just too much for him to contemplate—but he had read a variety of books about codependency and adult children of alcoholics.

With Sun, Mars, and Mercury in Aquarius, he had to put the books down as simplistic, of course. Yet he seemed to have fully absorbed the ideas and worked hard at applying them. This was shown by marked changes in behavior, with a tougher approach to conflict—direct and honest. He had recently taken some very assertive, courageous, and effective stances with his bosses and his wife. Future transits by Neptune to his Capricorn planets, followed by Uranus, suggested that he was far from out of the woods. He had faced the fact that both the job and the marriage might end. However, he was prepared to continue growing and felt he could not go back to the old patterns at work and at home.

In this example, we see how *psychological interpretations need to be couched in career-relevant terms* when you are doing a vocational astrology reading. Many of the same critical issues will doubtlessly come up as if the client had come for a psychologically-oriented reading, and yet the focus is very different. You would endeavor to show exactly how long-standing emotional and behavioral patterns affect the client's success. In doing so, you are more likely to be heard with less resistance and to be able to motivate the client to change.

THE ACA ASTROLOGER AND VOCATIONAL ADVICE

In my chapter in the Llewellyn New World Astrology Series volume, *Astrological Counseling,* I discussed the reasons so many astrologers—and so many of our clients—are Adult Children of Alcoholics (ACAs) or members of dysfunctional families. If this applies to you, it would be worthwhile reading, as the effects on our practice and approach to clients are profound. There is no space in this article to cover this topic in detail, but it is an important one to raise, because this background has an especially strong impact on the area of career and relationships to authority figures. Where the alcoholic parent (and often the sober parent as well) has been erratic or destructive, the child's reaction pattern to authority may be carried over into adulthood. Since much of our conditioning about authority happens before the age of five, the now-adult offspring may react to bosses with the same resentment, codependency, or intimidation that went on in relationship to the parent(s).

In my experience, at least one in four of the clients who come for vocational advice are struggling with this syndrome. In order to make sense of what is happening to sabotage the client's career, the astrologer would do well to be familiar with the after-effects of alcoholic and other dysfunctional backgrounds. Not all clients express it in the way the person in the example above did.

There are a number of well-established roles children in alcoholic families fall into, such as the Family Hero, the Lost Child, and the Scapegoat. Until awareness and de-conditioning are achieved, these roles often get played out over and over in adult life, *including on the job*. Other primary characteristics of alcoholics and many of their offspring which carry over to vocation are grandiosity and defiance—Neptune and Uranus. Due to modeling the parent's lack of grounding and dysfunctional behavior, even a completely sober ACA can lack certain survival skills needed for success.

Astrologers who are ACAs may mirror the grandiosity, defiance, lack of grounding, and low self-esteem of their ACA clients. This may affect the soundness of the vocational advice they give— possibly egging clients on in grandiose schemes, unsound financial practices, or unrealistic career choices. For the sake of clients, as well as ourselves, we astrologers who come from dysfunctional backgrounds like these would do well to soak up all the recovery literature we can, to belong to groups for ACAs, and in other ways do everything possible to deprogram ourselves and our clients from our upbringing.

OUTER PLANET PEOPLE AND CAREERS

The clients for whom I have the most difficult time finding a satisfactory career match are what I call "Outer Planet People." These are people with at least one of the outer planets—Uranus, Neptune, or Pluto—aspecting the Sun, Moon, Ascendant or Midheaven, part of a T-Square, or forming many aspects to personal planets. A true OPP has more than one of the outer planets in high focus. The adult children we have just been talking about often have Neptune and Pluto in high focus, but there are many other spawning grounds for OPPs.

The individual with outer-planet emphasis in the 10th House is often reduced to earning a living through the 2nd House and the skills and resources shown there. Our society does not tend to validate or reward the callings denoted by the outer planets. (OPPs are likely to regard their true vocation as a calling—not as something *they* chose but as something which chose them.) They are other-worldly rather than worldly, visionary rather than practical. These would include nontraditional careers like New Age practitioners, creative artists, or political or environmental activists—alternate lifestyles. Traditional vocational testing is likely to be useless—probably 90 percent would register as poets or artists.

Briefly, Uranian fields of work might involve any state of the art or leading-edge endeavor, such as those in science and technology, computers and other electronic media, astrology, working with groups or adolescents, political activism and social change. Neptunian careers could be in the creative arts, performing, work in prisons, hospitals or chronic care, addictions, and other service agencies. Plutonian fields include counseling, healing work of various sorts, work with death and dying, investigation, research, or financial services. Within any one of the areas given for an outer planet, there is a large variety of jobs, at various levels of skill and education. Again, a vocational directory would help you sort out where within a given field a client might fit.

OPPs tend to meander and have a history of false career starts until the time period of the Saturn return or later. They often feel like miserable failures and wonder why they are not as well-established as their contemporaries. There is a good reason for this, in that it takes well-seasoned, mature individuals to handle these planets' energies well. Finally, after years of meandering, some transit sets off their 10th or 6th House or the Midheaven, and they find their calling. This transit often coincides with a re-evaluation of the life path, in which the individual changes to a nontraditional career.

You may find rather extreme examples of authority problems with people who have outer planet emphasis in the 10th House. This is especially true when these planets fall into the Gauquelin sector, ten degrees from the Midheaven on either side, especially in the 9th. These people come by this authority complex honestly, based on a history with a seriously dysfunctional parent or some unfortunate loss of a parent. When these planets are emphasized in the 6th House, a similar line of work is indicated, but authority problems are not so clear, except when Uranus is involved. Instead, you may be looking at how low self-esteem gets in the way.

Often the parent was also an OPP who never got to do anything with his or her personal gifts or visions of achievement. This is especially true with Neptune, and there may be important consequences of the parent's failed dream placed on the career of the offspring. On the one hand, the person struggles to live out the parent's dream for the child, so the parent can have vicarious achievement. On the other hand, it would not do to succeed, which would be showing the parent up. Thus, the person tends to do and not do—for instance, to be the artist or musician or writer the parent wanted to be, yet to live from hand to mouth. None of this needs to operate on the conscious level—with Neptune, what is? The parent may appear to be proud, supportive, and sympathetic. Yet, I see this dynamic so often that I am forced to conclude that it is a rare child who dares to live out the parent's dream and succeed at it.

Looking at Uranus or Pluto in the 10th or in hard aspect to the Midheaven, you may say that such people are better off working for themselves, and that is probably so. However, unresolved authority problems continue to operate even when you do not have a boss. When you are self-employed in a service function, your client is your boss, if only for the hour or two that they hire you. As most astrologers fit into this category, it would be worthwhile to notice how authority issues play themselves out in your sessions and how attached you are to being considered an authority or guru by your clients.

Fairly often, the conflicts that exist simply get projected onto *them*, onto others. The visual artist with Neptune in the 10th, for example, feels victimized by The Art Establishment, the musician by Show Biz. (For Neptune in the 10th, also read Pisces on the Midheaven, Neptune aspects to the Midheaven, and so on.) The astrologer with Uranus in the 10th rebels against the constraints of society and The Astrological Community in particular. The sometimes gnarly 10th House-Pluto healer can be resentful and paranoid against a variety of "thems" but especially the all-powerful AMA.

Vocational Counseling with an OPP

Let's look at an example of a career reading for an Outer-Planet Person. The man came for a reading the week of his Saturn return, in April 1990. He was a salesman of pharmaceuticals and was doing well, but he had begun to feel he wanted more out of himself than that. He had a long-standing interest in yoga and other spiritual practices.

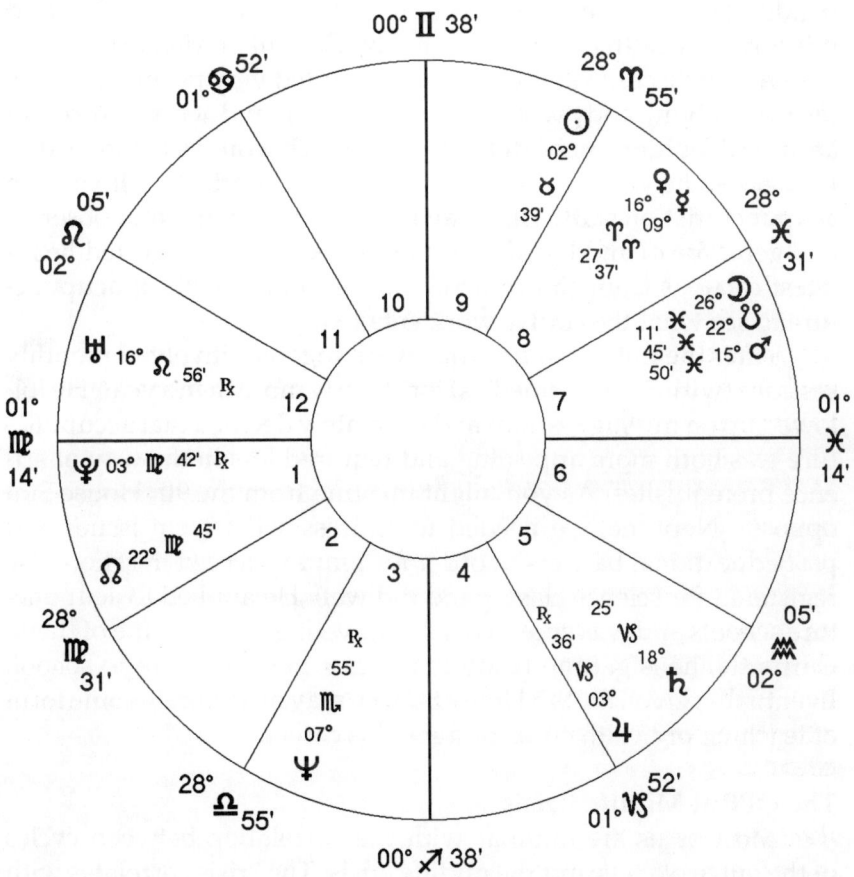

Case #3, Male

The client qualified as an OPP: Pluto in Virgo was on the Ascendant, part of a Grand Trine including his Sun. Neptune and Pisces were prominent, with the Moon and Mars in Pisces and

Neptune opposing his Sun. Uranus, in the 12th, was the apex of a Yod configuration (Uranus-Mars/Saturn).

As an outer-planet person, the likelihood of an unusual or non-traditional profession seemed likely. Healing work of some kind seemed indicated by Pluto Rising and the strong 8th House. With Virgo on the Ascendant, a physical or body-work approach rather than counseling seemed likely. While the Gemini Midheaven did suggest his ability at sales, it could also indicate working with his hands. Having done the charts of many chiropractors, I often find this form of health care represented by Gemini or Mercury.

As we discussed his chart, he responded very positively to the idea of studying body work. Both chiropractic and acupuncture had an appeal for him, but he did not know which would suit him better. I suggested he visit a chiropractor in the neighborhood who had an acupuncturist on staff. That way he could talk with both, observe, and get more of an idea of which appealed. I also suggested he request catalogs from chiropractic colleges and schools of acupuncture to see what the course work entailed.

After the initial reading, our work together involved monthly sessions (with flower remedies) for slightly more than a year. He followed up on my suggestions and ultimately decided that accupuncture was both more appealing and required less in the way of science prerequisites. As you might imagine from the 9th House Sun opposite Neptune, we needed to address self-esteem issues and past educational barriers in order for him to succeed in school. He registered for science classes and did well. He applied to acupuncture schools and was accepted, after traveling to visit some of them. Currently, he is getting ready to relocate in order to go to school. Eventually, given the 9th House Sun, he may incorporate some form of teaching or health education into his career.

The OPP at Midlife Crisis

Most of us are familiar with the correlation between cycles of the outer planets and the midlife crisis. The crisis correlates with the following series of aspects: Uranus opposite natal Uranus, Neptune square natal Neptune, Pluto square natal Pluto, and Saturn opposite natal Saturn. Though everyone of that age goes through the crisis, it tends to be more intense for Outer-Planet People. They have the Sun, Moon, Ascendant, or Midheaven involved with one or more of these planets natally. At midlife, we all have the opportunity to resolve whatever dysfunctional ways we are using these outer planets and to heal the barriers to personal fulfillment they represent. Put more succinctly, it is a big chance to clean up our act with these planets.

When Uranus, Neptune, or Pluto is connected with the vocational houses natally, the midlife crisis is likely to result in a midlife career change. Many people with outer planets in these Houses have failed to find a true vocation due to a lack of opportunity to express these planets constructively and creatively earlier. Perhaps society was not ready when they entered the work force. The opportunities for such vocations were limited, or careers involving such abilities are only now developing. Or, perhaps, the need to please a parent—or family responsibilities—kept them from pursuing their true path. Many outer-planet vocations are not easy to manifest or to do well at until you are a seasoned individual with some experience in the real world.

With outer planets in the vocational houses, the yearning for a true vocation may emerge sharply at midlife. The person may contemplate a new career. With any such major change, there is great resistance. It may seem easier, safer, and more secure to continue to follow the same old path. Yet, the outer planets repeat natal aspects over the course of two years or longer. The pain of resisting change grows until the individual virtually has no choice but to pursue a new path. The alternative is stagnation—merely marking time for the rest of one's life.

By this time the individual has had to pay some dues, so some of the original barriers may be gone. The children may be grown. The disapproving parent may have died. The Outer-Planet Person who has been dysfunctional may have sobered up or grown up. Or, for the female client, maybe society accepts women doing the particular job now, when it was unthinkable in her youth. Over the years, the person may have saved up enough money to go back to school. Even better, some of the newer careers may match the person's original life purpose and abilities—careers that were unheard of when he or she first went out into the world. Not just love, but *many* things are better the second time around.

WORKING UNDER THE
URANUS-NEPTUNE CONJUNCTION

Since Capricorn is the sign most connected with professions and big business, changes in the shape of careers have been accelerating during the entire time the outer planets have been in Capricorn. Large numbers of clients will be asking for career advice as that Neptune-Uranus fogbank rolls in, due to the confusion and uncertainty these planets bring with them. It is all too, too easy for us to be Neptunian and to deal in wish fulfillment and in clients' fantasies rather than vocational realities. Those realities are going to get increasingly more vivid over the time that the Capricorn lineup is in effect and the Recession settles in. Thus, we would do well to get more real in our advice by becoming informed about what is actually happening to various professions. Again, the vocational directories listed on the next page can help us keep up-to-date on how various occupations are changing.

The expansive, affluent era of unlimited possibilities heralded by Neptune and Uranus in Sagittarius is over. We are not in the 1980s any more. As Uranus and Neptune, jointly and separately, continue to affect the sign Capricorn, professions and business will be profoundly altered. Our knowledge of astrology may well give us some foresight that economists and other "scientific" prognosticators will not have. However, we do need to become more informed about various vocations, as the cost of education and wrong career moves is becoming ruinous.

The opportunity exists for many OPPs to come into their own, finally, during this unusual period of history when outer-planet skills and mind-sets are the only things likely to save us. I have often noted that when a major aspect between Saturn, Uranus, Neptune, or Pluto forms in the sky, *people born with those planets in aspect seem to flourish*. Particularly, while Uranus and Neptune are near one another in Capricorn, it would be a significant era for the generation born with Uranus square Neptune during parts of 1952-59. There were also many born with Uranus trine Neptune during the mid-1940s who have special abilities to meet the needs of our era.

The other consideration with this lineup is that when Uranus and Neptune transit the career houses or aspect the Midheaven, the person's career is very likely to be affected by rapidly-changing *world* conditions. The price of oil in Kuwait or the shrinking of the rain forest or the changes in Russia may well have direct impact on the career of the individual in question. The global uncertainties, shakeups, and confusion heralded by this combination are some-how likely to affect the choices and potentials available to the client. Thus, it is important for us to know what is going on in the world and to question our clients about precisely what connection world conditions may have with their business.

With so much rapid, confusing change everywhere, it is harder than ever before to make definite predictions and to achieve a high degree of accuracy in the chart reading. It is nearly impossible to foresee the wild cards and jokers in the deck that may occur under this conjunction of Uranus and Neptune. Although we will con-tinue to predict—and although clients' demands for predictions are likely to increase as the fog gets thicker—we would do well to be cautious and conservative in our prognostications. That attitude helps to free our aptitude in vocational guidance to be helpful to others.

CAREER BIBLIOGRAPHY FOR VOCATIONAL ASTROLOGY

A Do-It-Yourself Vocational Test

Gale, Barry, and Linda. *Discover What You're Best At*. NY: Simon and Schuster, 1990 edition; Paperback, $10.95. An excellent self-test, designed by two vocational counselors, that clients can use to determine which types of careers suit them best. Order from (201)767-5937.

Career Directories

The following directories are printed as paperbacks and are relatively inexpensive. They are essential tools for vocational read-ings and a good desk reference. (They are updated every other year.) Check your public library under 331.702, perhaps in the refer-ence section, to see which you would like to own.

Harkavy, Michael. *101 Careers: A Guide to the Fastest Growing Oppor-tunities*. NY: John Wiley & Sons, 1990; $12.95. A big, readable, ex-cellent book at 350 pages. Order from 1-800-225-5945.

Jist Works, Inc. *America's Top 300 Jobs: A Complete Career Handbook*. Indianapolis, IN: Jist Works, Inc, 1990; $17.95. Here is detailed information on each of the careers, including the nature of the work, training and education required, working conditions, employment trends, job outlook, and earning potential. Order from 1-800-648-JIST.

Occufacts: *Information on 565 Careers in Outline Form*. Largo, FL: Careers Inc., 1989-90 Edition. An excellent directory that breaks down career information into many categories, including duties, working conditions, physical demands, temperament, aptitudes required, and earnings. Order from Careers Inc., Box 135, Largo, FL 34649-0135.

U.S. Department of Labor, Bureau of Labor Statistics. *Occupational Outlook Handbook*. Orange, CA: Career Publishing, Inc. 1990-91 Edition; $22.50 plus $4 postage and handling. About as dry as they come, but with the true statistics on what's happening to 250 major careers. The books listed earlier were based on this one, but they tend to be more readable. Order from 1-800-854-4014.

Special Measurements for Vocational Guidance

Noel Tyl

**• The Moon and Need Fulfillment • The Oriental Planet
• Peregrination • The Final Dispositor • Mutual Reception
• Major Midheaven Aspects and more**

Perhaps the biggest change in astrology over the last 50 years has been its humanization. We, the people, have been recognized within the maze of measurements that defines our horoscopes. Those measurements have taken on psychosensitive potentials that suggest developmental tensions in terms of personal volition as well as astrological law.

This change affects how we look at *vocational* astrology. Where textbooks 50 years ago and earlier—those that were the bedrock of American astrology, imported from turn-of-the-century England— neglected mention of the person almost entirely, today texts put the person front and center. People can actually *choose* the job they go for, rather than follow in their father's footsteps. Women are working! All of us in western culture expect our job *to fulfill* us somehow, more than just paying the rent.

Indeed, the tried-and-true measurements for vocational analysis still prevail. There is no escaping the importance of the 10th House (our place in the Sun), the 2nd House (money, self-worth), and the 6th (actual employment, cooperation). In this matrix, astrology's organization of modality comes to the fore through cardinality, fixity, and mutability focused on house zones of experience. In an Angle, we initiate for growth; in a Succedent House, we organize for value; in a Cadent House, we react for development. Specifically in vocational analysis, this is all brought down to earth within the symbolisms of Capricorn, Taurus, and Virgo in the natural distribution of signs.

And so it begins: one measurement leading to another, to another, and still to yet another and more. The dynamism of astrological analysis gets complicated quickly. Until recently, we have had little recourse but to jam our job-life into a rigid set of structural rigging. Yet, we now live in a time of "Do your own thing" philosophies; myriad specializations within newly created professions; vastly increased competition in the job market; social waves of affluence and unemployment; welfare; the pressure for families to have two job-holders producing two incomes; and, always, the self-aware sense of "what's my job doing for me?"

Let's take a new look at some timeless measurements, updating them to these psychosensitive times.

In the preparation for this article, I was going through my files looking for examples that would be particularly interesting for us all. I saw "Betty's" file, pulled it, and scanned her horoscope quickly for the measurements I was planning to write about. I was startled—not as much by the fact that *all* of them applied in Betty's case but by the excitement I felt in discovering something that would help Betty enormously. I phoned her immediately, woke her up, and as she said, "made her day!"

Look at Betty's horoscope. The rising Virgo Sun, ruler of the Ascendant, trines Uranus in Taurus in the 9th. Venus, ruler of the Midheaven is conjunct Neptune, and that conjunction trines the Midheaven from the Ascendant.

The Venus-Neptune conjunction is opposed by Saturn retrograde in the 7th, and that axis is squared by Jupiter in Sagittarius in the 4th, forming a T-Square.

The Moon in Sagittarius squares Saturn and squares Mercury in Virgo, ruler of the 2nd and in the 2nd.

That's enough for general orientation to Betty's horoscope. We can expect a strongly individualistic woman, highly sensitive and artistic, vulnerable to strong depressions in her relationship situation(s).

When Betty came to see me two years ago, she was 53 years old, just divorced from a long marriage, and relocating to start life anew. In our consultation, when I asked about the summer of 1980,

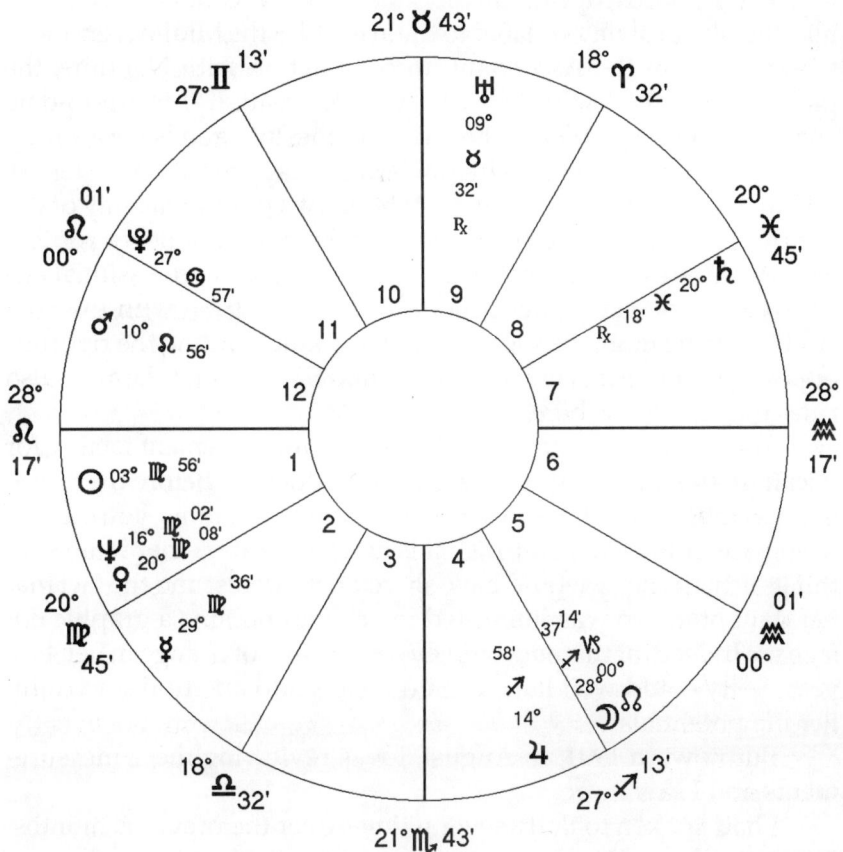

"Betty"

when she was 44 years old, I learned that she had made a total transformation: she had gone back to school to study art and, indeed, had
since become a professional artist, winning prizes, commissions,
and published praise. The measurements that led me to her summer
of 1980 were the transit of Uranus over her fourth cusp, accompanied by Jupiter transiting conjunct her Sun, Neptune square Neptune, and the background Solar Arc measurement of Jupiter opposed Pluto.*

---

* "Establishing new perspectives; building the big picture;" Tyl, Solar Arc Analysis Directory, *Prediction in Astrology.*

Betty's horoscope fits all the old rules for vocational choice: Venus, the planet always related to the arts, rules the Midheaven and is trine to it from the Ascendant, in conjunction with Neptune, the planet also linked with the arts (vision, creativity) in up-to-date analysis. Mercury, ruler of the 2nd, is in the 2nd, and is very strong in its own sign (working with one's hands, appreciation of detail). Uranus, ruler of the 6th, suggests that Betty's individual way of doing things, rebelling perhaps against role expectations—a routine housewife returning to school and succeeding as a professional artist—will work well to her benefit through the trine with the Sun. And that trine might be seen as somehow ameliorating the rigorous opposition between Venus-Neptune and Saturn, since Uranus also rules the 7th House here.

That's about it in terms of traditional measurement facility for vocation. It is very simple to make this deduction. Before the fact of her going back to school to learn art (not relearn, mind you), an astrologer would have had to ask this housewife about her interest in things artistic. Betty would have shared her interest and the fact that her daughter also was interested in art (and became a graphic designer). Indeed, at this enormously strong time of change in her 44th year, Betty could well have been directed into art studies to fulfill her life potentials.

But now, in 1991, in August, I was reviewing these measurements and I saw more

I had spoken to Betty several times over the previous months, learning of her heavy depression over her ex-husband's remarriage. She was really down in the dumps. She had moved to a new home with much space but was not able to bring her art studio into order. She was not exercising. She was lethargic.

My eyes saw that transiting Pluto was going to cross her fourth cusp in two months or so. That cusp had "reacted" strongly with the Uranian transit back in 1980. This would be another powerful new start, another new perspective for Betty. What could she do? What could astrology suggest now, to pick her up out of the doldrums?

- The Moon in Sagittarius: the need to share opinions, to speak one's mind;

- Moon in the 5th House: the need to relate to others, especially children, through teaching, through creativity;

- Jupiter is in its own sign and squares the powerful Venus-Neptune and Saturn opposition: enthusiasm and, again, teaching potential in relation to her art skill; Jupiter is trine to Mars in Leo in the 12th, ruler of the 9th, the house of education, which holds Uranus trining the Sun, ruler of the Ascendant;

- Mars is "oriental," *i.e.,* rising just before the Sun, suggesting the energy of promotion within job capabilities;

- Venus rules Libra on the 3rd, again a mental dimension brought into the artistic profile; Mercury in Virgo, joining Jupiter as final dispositors of the horoscope, making a Quintile aspect (72 degrees; conspicuous creativity) with Jupiter; and Uranus opposes the midpoint of Mercury/Jupiter.

There was little doubt in my mind: now was the time for Betty to promote herself into a position to teach art, whether in her home-studio (Pluto rules the 4th, holding Jupiter) or in some structured program (Sun rules the 12th, holding Mars). I called her, woke her, and, after some preliminary pleasantries, asked her, "Betty—this is a very important astrological question—have you ever thought about *teaching* art?"

Betty's "Yes!!" was so definite: it was as if a large stone were being rolled back from a dark cave. With objective confirmation of a private dream hidden deep within her, astrology had turned on the lights! Betty phoned me later in the day to report her research into the opportunities she had thought through. With great enthusiasm, she told how she was getting her studio into order and then she outlined the steps she was taking to make this new dimension of her career happen.

Along the lines of this case experience, let's add some fresh measurement sensibilities to our traditional structures, some bright brush strokes to the canvas, that can help us with our work in vocational astrology.

FULFILLING NEEDS

Twenty years ago I formulated an overlay scheme to bring psychological need theory and astrological measurements together.* My objective was to take static descriptions of states of being and

---

* Tyl, *Principles and Practice of Astrology*, Volume V; Llewellyn Publications; St. Paul, MN. Tyl, *Holistic Astrology*, TAI Books; distributed by Llewellyn Publications.

convert them into dynamic behavioral images in the process of be-coming. Most simply, by inserting the concept of "need" into the sign descriptions everyone learns in astrology, we can immediately feel *action* and we can begin *to anticipate* behavior. For example, say-ing that Leo energy *needs to be dramatic* actually sets up expectations of what someone will do to fulfill that need, or what will frustrate it.

I postulated that the Moon, using the energy of the Sun in its sign, symbolized *by* its sign the "reigning need" of the personality, that which drives all development. The planets, as symbols of be-havioral faculties, represented special subsidiary needs working to fulfill the reigning need. Mercury in its sign suggests how we *need* to think in order to be most efficient; Mars, what kind of energy we *need* to apply in order to be at our best, and so forth.

Since most of the awake hours in our lifetime (and many of those hours when we sleep!) are occupied with our job . . . close to 60 percent . . . it stands to reason that fulfillment of our personal reign-ing need in life must somehow be abetted by the work atmosphere, pace, energy, growth stimulus, and image trappings of our job, cued by the Moon and its sign. Secondly, it stands to reason that the House placement of the Moon would focus the extraordinarily large need of our life within particular zones of experience and that this House placement would be significant within our sense of job ful-fillment.

With Betty's horoscope, quite simplistically, we felt the Virgo energy flowing into a reigning need symbolism of the Moon in Sag-ittarius—the need to have one's opinions respected and, of course, all the related behaviors connected to that need. We felt how this could be part of an educational thrust, a collaboration-with-others outlet to help with the 7th House pressures under which she was suffering.

With the Moon in Capricorn, in general terms, to give us the feel of this need profile, there is the need to be strategically effective. In Aquarius, the need to be enjoyed and valued for personal idi-osyncrasy and for caring for others; in Pisces, the need to express and be appreciated for sensitivity.

With the Moon in Aries, there will generally be a need to be ego-important, *numero uno*; it will be overtly obvious or hidden away in fantasy and private frustrations. In Taurus, there is the deep need to keep things secure, even to resist change because of a possi-ble threat to security. In Gemini, there is the need for diversification, for communication; the need to be heard.

When the Moon is in Cancer, naturally, there is a grand need for emotional security, for home values. In Leo, there is the king or queen complex, the monarchical need to shine and reign magnanimously; and in Virgo, there is the need to be correct and to gain respect through the accuracy of views and discrimination.

When the Moon is in Libra, there is the need to find ego-prominence through societal reflection, the need to be popular and accepted. In Scorpio, the Moon symbolizes the reigning need to be understood, to be thought deeply significant, to be in control, even feared.

These needs use the personal Sun energy to set up personal life expression. In choosing a profession, in doing a job, the major need must be attended to. *The job environment must accept this need, or intolerable frustration will develop quickly.*

Instantly, we can appreciate the United States Moon in Aquarius, energized by the Cancer Sun. Few extra words are needed when we feel the emotional and security sensibilities coursing through this idiosyncratic, very special, humanitarian need profile. Our Statue of Liberty says it so well, "Give me your tired, your poor, your huddled masses yearning to breathe free..."

Instantly, we can feel George Bush's Libra Moon, using Gemini energies, needing to be fair-and-square, wide open, and popularist in communications. Saddam Hussein's Sagittarian Moon, rationalizing his world views in the name of religion, exploiting propaganda artfully.

These observations are not value judgments. We are simply allowing astrological analysis to commence in terms of a reigning concept, a generalized need that immediately brings into the picture behaviors that will work to fulfill that need. When we see these needs working out in life situations, specifically on the job, we see how important it is, indeed, that the job situation assimilate, support, and/or reward the need fulfillment behaviors.

Marlon Brando may have mumbled his way through a strangely withdrawn career in the movies, after an explosive beginning on the stage, and hidden himself away on a Pacific Island, but he was born with a Moon and Sun conjunction in Aries. His profession allowed the complex ego needs to express themselves. He would have been incarcerated by any other milieu; ostracized for sure. He finally needed his island, so to speak.

Jacqueline Kennedy Onassis was "first lady" throughout her life with the Moon in Aries, using the Sun's Leo energy. Think a moment about the Moon in Pisces fulfilled in the lives of Edgar Allan Poe who died an alcoholic and totally unappreciated for his exquisite creativity; the Duke of Windsor who gave up a kingdom for his love; and Martin Luther King, working to rescue a martyred dream.

Brando and Onassis *had* to make dramatic ego statements in what they did and where they were. The men here with the Moon in Pisces *had* to express themselves the way they did. Each of them was doing something poetical, ultrasensitive, deeply emotional. Give them a different vocation, a different station in life? They would not tolerate it; nor would *they* be tolerated! There is something inexorable about need fulfillment. It reigns supreme in our life expression. Expression through the job is not excepted.

When the Moon is located in the Ascendant, the 1st House, the emphasis is upon individuality, "doing your own thing." The attitude within the work situation is usually going to be—usually must be—highly individualized. All experience is interpreted in personal terms. Reactions are highly individualized.

When the Moon is within the 2nd House, the person will usually need a work structure that emphasizes self-worth, personal excellence. Like a shiny object in a display case, the person needs to be on view while working or, at least, have the work evaluated frequently.

The Moon in the 3rd House emphasizes communication, the sense of the intermediary, the feeling of persuasion and salesmanship. The personality needs to gather, share, and get reactions to information. In the 4th House, the Moon seems to need a work situation that resembles the home environment or actually is in the home itself. In the 5th House, there is a focus on children, creative expression, the dramatization of all experiences.

When the Moon is in the 6th House, there is the suggestion of deep absorption in one's work. Work is easily all-consuming. There may be two jobs to fill all time. The "workaholic" label often fits here.

Above the horizon, the Moon position begins to include the perspectives of others within symbolisms. For example, in the 7th, the work situation is usually tied to public exposure, to partnerships, a keen awareness of public expectations. Often, marriage is important to define security in the work situation. In the 8th House, the Moon takes on the need for a work situation dependent upon others' resources: a stock broker, for example; working as a consultant; reconstructing what others have put together; expediting reforms. Additionally, there can be dimensions of mystery, research, sex, religion.

In the 9th House, individuality seems to lose significance in terms of the job. The self needs to blend with philosophical programs, the ideas and programs of educational institutions, foreign influences, the bigger picture, in order to feel best placed in the job environment.

In the 10th House, the Moon symbolizes a "take charge" need. The individuality is emphasized to such an extent that a subordinate position within work is not tolerated easily. In the 11th, a network of friends is very important to get the job, enjoy the job, keep the job, and evaluate the job. In the 12th, the Moon gains comfort behind the scenes. The stage is given to someone else. Along with the Moon in the 8th House, this is also the position of the consultant.

With these Moon positions and our understanding of need fulfillment, we can quickly add some significant dimensions to horoscope analysis in terms of vocational needs. It simply is *natural* that Howard Hughes had the Moon in the 4th; that Alfred Hitchcock, directing other people's performing resources into mystery dramas, had the Moon in the 8th; that Greta Garbo who wanted to be alone, and Fred Astaire who practically never gave an interview throughout his long, stellar career, had the Moon in the 12th; that John F. Kennedy had the Moon in the 11th; that Bobby Kennedy had the Moon in the 10th, and the United States still does.

In terms of national behavior, it is no surprise to see that the Kingdom of Iraq has its Aries Moon in the 8th House: the need to be extremely prominent and to reconstruct the environment to fulfill that need.

THE ORIENTAL PLANET

The word "oriental" here means eastern, or eastward. It is the adjective that has become attached to the planet that rises just before the Sun over the eastern horizon, *i.e.*, in clockwise motion over the Ascendant. The oriental planet is the planet immediately behind the Sun in celestial longitude. No matter how far apart in distance the planet is behind the Sun in longitude, if it will be the last planet to rise before the Sun, it is the oriental planet.

In Betty's horoscope, at the beginning of this chapter, it is very clear: Mars, which has just risen over the horizon line, at the Ascendant in the East, is the oriental planet. Mars is the planet immediately behind the Sun in celestial longitude. After it rises, the Sun rises. If Mars and Pluto were, for example, in the 5th and 6th Houses in this horoscope, Uranus would be the oriental planet, being the planet immediately behind the Sun in celestial longitude and the last planet to rise before the Sun.

The oriental planet often adds an extra snippet of information to horoscope analysis, especially vocationally. It can quickly suggest the style a person has in working toward need fulfillment in life and on the job. If we were watching a great parade, waiting for the head honcho to appear, we would study the demeanor of the favored aide appearing just before the king, in order to learn what to expect from the all-powerful one. How will the Sun behave toward us? What will be the mode of expression?

The oriental planet is not a magic measurement. It is an *interesting* one about which we do not know very much. And, there is a problem when Mercury or Venus is oriental: statistically, Mercury and Venus are always so close to the Sun; their occurrence as oriental seems biased; the potential significance seems to wane, especially with Mercury. However, with the other planets, there seem to be valid correspondences between symbolism and actual behavior.

With Pluto oriental, there is an interesting consideration to weigh: the individual is attracted to opportunities to gain stature through affiliation, especially with prominent people. There is the need to gain power and personal prominence through the work situation. If that opportunity is not present, *i.e.*, meeting celebrities, for example, feeling important by being with important others (or issues), this sense of style will be frustrated.

Merv Griffin is a perfect example of Pluto oriental. This performer became extremely wealthy and famous through other celebrities. He "collected" them for his talk shows and his genius acumen in business converted every opportunity to further prominence and profit. Newsman and panel host David Brinkley is another good example.

I have found Pluto oriental significant in the lifestyle of average people as well: they may be proud and fulfilled somehow to know local political figures, star athletes, key VIPs; some even collect memorabilia of the famous. In short, the need is to enhance status through affiliation. If the job provides this kind of fulfillment, it is ideal. If it does not, the person will work to that goal through job changes or in their social life.

When Neptune is oriental, there is a sense of searching for perfection in the pursuit of one's work. Dreams and visionary planning are important dimensions of the job hunt and work organization. There has to be a link between what is expected and what can actually be. Julie Andrews became famous for movie roles that fit her workstyle expression of Neptune oriental. Wilbur Wright, with Neptune oriental, pioneered flight; fantastic scientist/writer Immanuel Velikovsky as well; and Julia Child.

With Uranus oriental, we often see a style in the work situation that searches out anything that is adventurous, innovative, chancy, or experimental. Diversity and even danger appeal. The work situation can be an outlet for an intense nervous system. If this profile is not met on the job, the chances are high that the avocation, the hobby, and one's free time are caught up with fulfilling this press for excitement. El Cordobes, Jimmy Hoffa, Orville Wright (a perfect complement to Wilbur, see above), Lorne Greene, and Ronald Reagan all have Uranus oriental.

Saturn oriental symbolizes patience. There is an innate stick-to-itiveness, a mature perspective, and respect for the long haul; tolerance for the lone position. Ralph Nader and Martin Luther King are fine examples of the expression of Saturn oriental in their workstyles.

Jupiter oriental suggests taking the easy way within work situations. Getting things done quickly is fulfilling; it calls attention to one's mastery of the situation. John F. Kennedy, Richard Nixon, and the United States are good examples; so is Bob Hope with his "one-liners."

Because of its speed, Mars oriental carries with it a high frequency of manifestation. When in position, there is a strong sense of promotion, drum-beating; we see the person who can toot the horn in favor of the work situation. The sense of advertising is strong, promoting one's self or promoting something that is part of the job. Johnny Carson and Dinah Shore are clear examples of Mars oriental; also, P. T. Barnum, Lyndon Johnson, Evel Knievel, Liberace.

Betty's horoscope shows Mars oriental in the 12th House (buck-the-organization). Betty is a quiet lady, keeping much of her anxiety about relationships that goes back to great difficulties with her father (the Saturn retrograde phenomenon that is so strong here) inside and private. But in her new role as professional artist, she promotes herself to beat the band. She admits to a private Queen complex (the Leo Ascendant, the Sun trine with Uranus) and loves to see herself, on good days, "doing her thing" in terms of self-promotion. She has since called again about her new vista, saying, "Noel, I'm going to make it happen."

When Venus is oriental, the person needs a work function that can be personalized somehow. Evaluation of one's work then substitutes for evaluation of one's person, which might be hard to accept or believe. Often, Venus oriental suggests, as well, work with valuable things like jewelry, high fashion. It is a frequent signature in the horoscopes of movie stars whose screen image takes the place of their private persona, and of artists (Van Gogh, Picasso, Gauguin, Dali, Modigliani).

Mercury oriental is inconclusive. We should look in the direction of dotting "i"s and crossing "t"s, getting things right, respecting detail; perhaps the need to conform to clearly defined expectations and procedures.

When the Moon is oriental, rising just before the Sun, we get the suggestion of the "team coach," the teacher, the manager, perhaps even the prophet. The person needs to be in a position of telling lots of other people just what is going on or what they should do. With the Moon oriental, the person needs to preach, and the job situation ideally should give that opportunity. Frank Sinatra has the Moon oriental; so do Arthur Schlesinger, Dick Clark, and Norman Rockwell.

PEREGRINATION

This old astrological word "peregrination," comes from the Latin word for foreigner, *peregrinus*. The adjective connotes the tendency to wander. In astrology, a peregrine planet is a planet that does not make a major aspect (conjunction, sextile, square, trine, or opposition) with any other body in the horoscope. Astrological teachings suggest that the peregrine planet can appear to run away with the rest of the horoscope. For example, Jonathan Winters, a most creative comedian, sound-effects entertainer and fine arts painter, has Mercury in Sagittarius peregrine; his intensity of communication is remarkable and indefatigable.

While peregrination suggests that a planet is not tied in with the rest of the horoscope and may wander off to do its own thing to excess, and while there is evidence that this is indeed often manifested in people's lives, there is a major problem with the measurement: why has it evolved that "major aspects" are our guidelines? What if the planet in question is semi-square another planet, sesquiquadrate, semi-sextile or quincunx; what if the planet in question is making a clear aspect to the Midheaven or Ascendant or both? We do not know these answers yet, but a planet that is peregrine in the classical sense of being without "major" aspect does gain prominence in horoscopic analysis. It does stand out in behavior, within need profiles, within lifestyle, and certainly must be

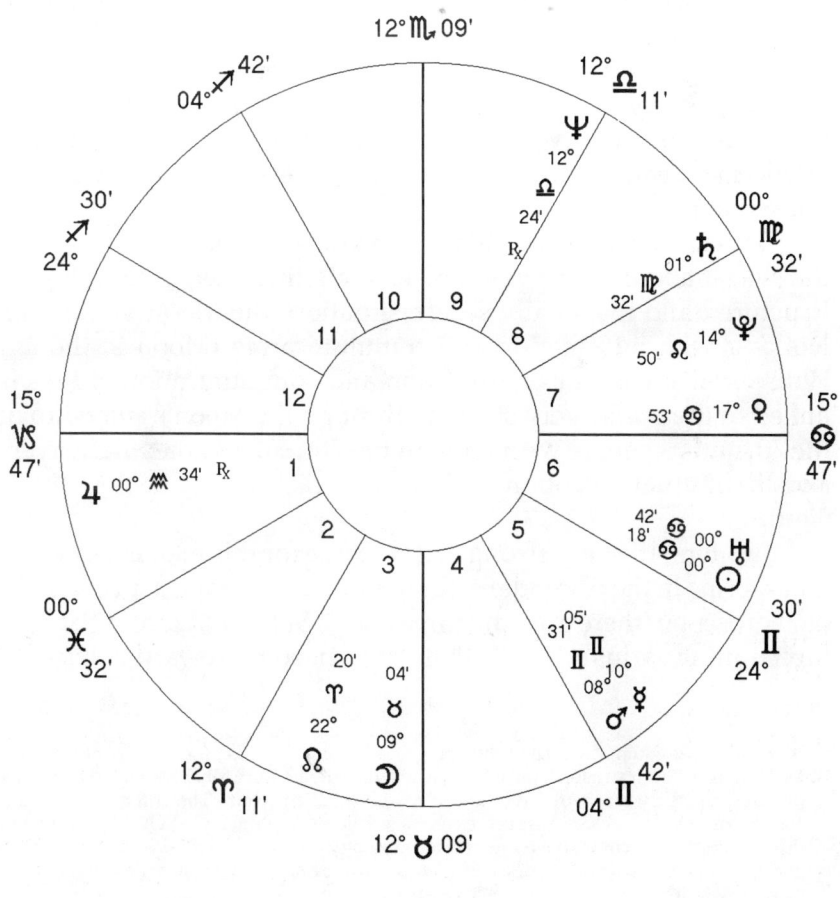

"Paul"

checked in terms of job selection. Curiously, most often, when the Sun is unaspected, there is not the runaway manifestation, but rather a sense of not being able to get "tuned in" properly to a life direction, vocationally speaking.*

The horoscope shown here belongs to a man who came to see me just before his 40th birthday. He is utterly charming and appears much younger than his years. He is filled with enthusiasm for life. Very quickly upon meeting him, you feel a personal charisma that is not at all threatening. He is gentle and gracious.

In terms of his horoscope, here is what we feel: his Jupiter in the 1st House blended with the settledness of the Capricorn Ascendant (with Saturn sesquiquadrate to the rising degree); the need for structure and reliability symbolized by the Moon in Taurus, and the intensified emotional security values of the Sun-Uranus conjunction in Cancer. Then immediately, through his enormous articulation skill, we gain corroboration of the emphatic Mars-Mercury conjunction in Gemini. Then, with his smile, he settles conversational paragraphs into neat, gentle packages, and we feel the swoon of Venus in Cancer square Neptune.

This is as it should be. Paul's horoscope radiates from him.

What about his profession? His reigning need is for a highly structured and maximally secure situation (the Moon in Taurus); working with information and communicating (Moon in the 3rd House). This need for organization and communication outlets is linked to the public very strongly through the Moon's rulership of the 7th and its square with Pluto in the 7th, ruler of the Midheaven; and the mutual reception with Venus (each planet in the other's Sign).

Jupiter—the very strong feel we have for this man in person— is peregrine in the Ascendant. Jupiter makes no major aspect within the horoscope (there are quincunxes with Sun-Uranus and Saturn). Jupiter in Aquarius suggests that Paul's need for reward in his life /

---

* A classic exception in the case of the peregrine Sun is Louis XIV, historically nicknamed the "Sun King" (not an astrological reference), who ruled France for 72 years. His birth was precisely timed by Morin de Villefranche, astrologer to the court. The Sun in Virgo in the 10th House made no classic aspect (except a sextile to Neptune, which had not yet been discovered; and, again we have a historoterminology problem). Louis was an overwhelming Virgo in all his characteristics, compounded by a runaway arrogance that reached the incredible (with a Leo Moon conjunct Venus, opposed by Saturn, squared by a rising Jupiter in Scorpio, and more). September 05, 1638; 11:11 a.m., LMT; Saint Germain; 002E09; 48N51 (Source: Gauquelin).

work is in humanitarian terms. This Jupiter will be extremely strong.

Mercury is powerful in its own Sign and through the conjunction with Mars. Undeniably, this registers communication skills, grandiloquence. Additionally, Mars rules the 3rd House of communication.

Over and over again, we see communication emphasized here. Astrologically, Paul's vocational profile says "humanitarian communicator in a big way, ideally highly-structured, out to the public at large." Paul is indeed a charismatic public speaker, very much in demand. He is constantly studying, writing, teaching. His grand structure—extremely secure—is the Catholic Church. Paul is a priest.

In my opinion, defining so clearly and, really, so quickly, that Paul needs to be a humanitarian communicator in service to the public through a highly structured and secure organization, astrology has been successful. If Paul had come to me for vocational guidance, this set of deductions would have been established conclusively early, and our discussion could then bring out other dimensions of Paul's personality that might reveal an important focus leading to the Church and priesthood.

THE DOMINATING MIDHEAVEN

Measurements to the Midheaven are uncannily reliable indicators of vocational choice. They focus our analyses sharply within our awareness of individual needs, the requirements of milieu and the expression of style.

"Stephen's" horoscope shows us an example of this special importance of the Midheaven. First, we see that his reigning need symbol, again the Moon in Taurus, suggests a grand need for security, structure, and stability. With the Moon in the 9th House, as we have seen, the probability is high that individuality loses significance to organization. There could be something very important here to do with education, ideas and programs of educational institutions; somehow teaching on the job.

Uranus is oriental (it would have been the last planet to have risen before the Sun on Stephen's birthday). Stephen is eager for adventure, innovation, experiments. This need conflicts with the stolidity and security needs of the Moon in Taurus, especially in its conjunctions with Jupiter and Saturn. Perhaps in the effort to resolve this conflict, the ego thrust gets lost; perhaps he gives in to which-ever structure receives him, in order to preserve and protect the status quo.

The Uranus factor is very important also, because of its close-ness to the Midheaven. Astrological teachings throughout this cen-tury have always postulated that a planet within, say, five degrees of the Midheaven is particularly strong, even if it is in the 9th House. (Gauquelin proved this statistically in his extraordinary research; see the introduction to this volume.) We can appreciate Uranus as conjunct this Midheaven.

The Uranian Midheaven receives a trine from Neptune in the Ascendant. Immediately, our analytical sensibilities must be aware of the arts, of aesthetics.*

We see that the Midheaven is ruled by Venus, another refer-ence to things artistic. In fact, Venus gains great importance by be-ing the dispositor of the Moon, Jupiter, Saturn, and Uranus, and by being in mutual reception with the Moon. Finally, Venus itself is *exactly semi-square the Midheaven*. Undeniably, something in the arts *must* speak within Stephen's work life.

Additionally, we see Mercury in Gemini, its own sign. Mercury becomes very, very important here. It rules the Ascendant and is the dispositor of Neptune.

As we saw in Paul's horoscope, the previous case example, the square between the Moon and Pluto suggests strong public pro-jection. It appears in Stephen's horoscope also. The rising Neptune supports this deduction by its rulership of the 7th House of the public.

The Gemini Sun is *peregrine*. It is searching for stabilization and high structure.

Let us review: Stephen needs structure for his well-being and for his work, to stabilize his nervous and highly alert mental dispo-sition (Sun and Mercury so prominent in Gemini); he is probably willing but not happy about giving up some individual ascendancy in order to protect his security; he is a born communicator, highly discriminating and exact (Mercury references); within any struc-

---

* Of the 26 performing artists presented in *Celebrity Horoscopes*, Prete and Gallo, Rising Sign Publishing Co., North Hollywood, CA, 1975, 92 percent showed Neptune dramati-cally active in their horoscope. Forty-two percent showed the Sun conjunct, square, or opposed Neptune. Seventy-seven percent showed Neptune configured with Sun, Moon, and/or Midheaven.

tural situation he innovates constantly, experiments, or wants to do so all the time; the influences of the arts and education are undeniably vitally important to him; and throughout all of these concerns, there is a strong force to public projection. The astrology says that Stephen should be a public performer or educator in the arts.

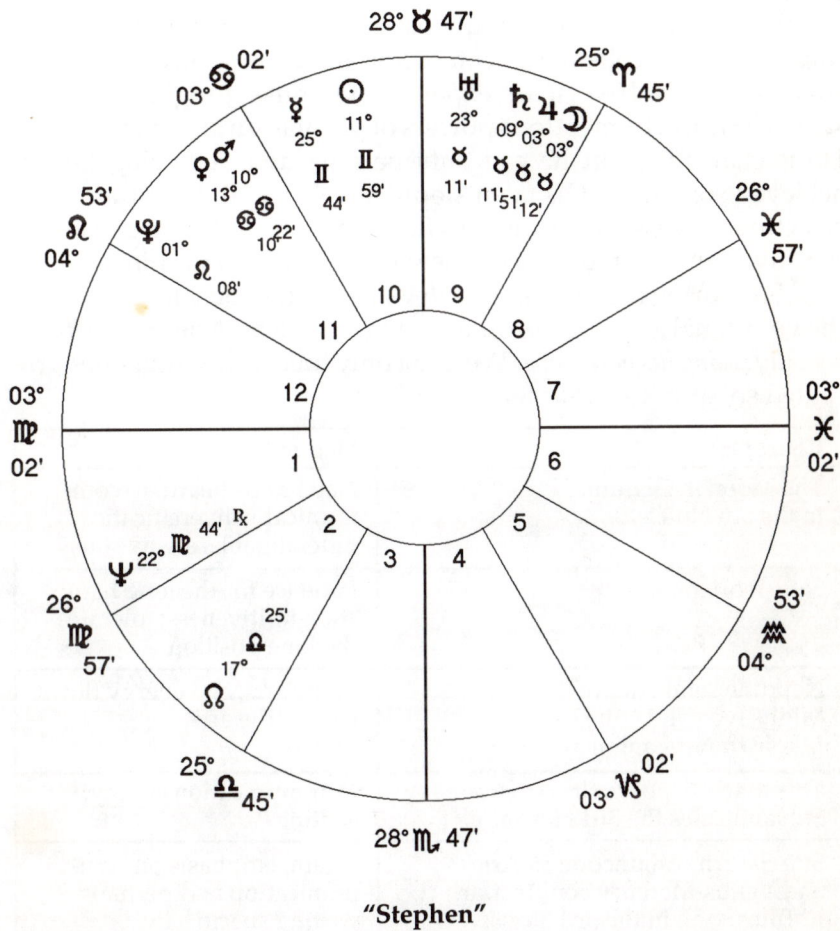

"Stephen"

Early in his adult years, Stephen studied graphic design as an artist. In music, he became an extremely talented pianist, cellist, and organist, and has taught the playing of those instruments. He studied conducting abroad (9th House references) and became a symphony orchestra conductor. Stephen works intensely and sometimes frantically to hold things together in his busy life, which often has had him at the helm of three different community orchestras, all at the same time, taking on enormously detailed and broad responsibilities. Stephen is *always* threatened by a breakdown of organization, the structure that could give him breathing time, so to speak. His individual career seems bogged down by peripheral organizational concerns.

He is always on the go, unable to find his perfect niche. He is unreservedly excellent as a conductor and community spokesperson for the arts. He teaches experimental music programs in local schools. He has tremendous powers of persuasion and story-telling. He is charming; but he can only be regarded as having underachieved somehow. His talents outdistance the all-important civic structures necessary for them to flourish. Stephen's Sun must take the adventurous step to find a new place in which to shine.

For our next case example, let's be courageous: let's establish the vocational astrology profile for a man with an Aries Sun *without actually seeing his horoscope!* We must only follow the guidelines presented so far in this chapter.

Chart Data	Deduction
The Moon in Gemini, in the 6th House.	Need to be heard, to communicate; diversification; indefatigable; always busy.
Saturn oriental.	Patience for the long haul; stick-to-itiveness; tolerates the lone position.
Neptune semi-square the Midheaven and trine to Mars-Uranus conjunction.	In the arts; ego energy flows well in the arts.
This Mars disposits the Aries Sun and rules the 3rd House.	Communication energy; writing?
Sun-Saturn conjunction in Aries and Venus-Mercury conjunction in Taurus, all in the 3rd House.	Again, emphasis on communication and perhaps writing specifically.
Venus in Taurus is square Pluto in the 7th; Pluto rules the Midheaven.	Again the arts; emotional intensity; public projection professionally.
Mercury opposes the Midheaven from the 3rd House and disposits Neptune in Virgo and the Moon in Gemini.	Conclusive: writing.

These seven simple observations unavoidably establish the vocational profile of a communicator, a writer in the arts, projected to the public through patient, hard work. The man is a very well-established composer, with some 400 compositions copyrighted; he waited some 30 years to become a conductor, and ascended quickly in that role as well.

As we see astrology at work establishing vocational profiles for people in terms of fulfilling their needs and gaining outlets for their lifestyles, we are uncovering the fact that the modern workplace is complicated with specialization and jobs that were not known 50 years ago. The most obvious example, of course, is computer technology. And within that field, we have programmers, analysts, operators, repairs, and sales.

Here in the "unseen horoscope," we came up with communication, probably writing, in the arts. From the prominent Mercury observation, we could wonder if this artist were also a singer. Indeed, he was a professional singer also; and a professional player of three instruments; and a teacher of music. This is successful astrology; zeroing in on the vocational target that *receives the individual* and helps with the fulfillment of needs. At that point, astrology then gives way to common-sense discussion of attitudes, education, age, financial concerns, and dreams.

PUTTING IT ALL TOGETHER

Look at the two horoscopes on the following pages. Please scan them along the study-guidelines we have shared together in this chapter; what job would best suit each of these women?

Chart A

Check the Moon: In Scorpio in the 8th: reformer, consultant; Moon is also oriental, suggesting a teacher-type.

Check the Midheaven: Sagittarius, ruled by Jupiter, another education dimension; Jupiter, the ruling planet, is in Cancer, disposited by the Moon; the Moon and Jupiter are about to be in trine aspect; Jupiter is intensified by Uranus, co-ruler of the Ascendant Aquarius intercepted).

Check the Ascendant: Capricorn, ruled by Saturn, introduces the sense of administration; Saturn is very strong in its conjunctions with Mercury, Venus, and the Moon. Mars is alone in the eastern hemisphere, in the Ascendant, and makes a very powerful opposition with Pluto in the 7th; Pluto rules the 9th, again education perhaps. We feel strong administrative energy out of the Ascendant.

There is little doubt about it; this woman is well suited for educational administration and/or teaching, leading, working with pedagogical reform. Indeed, her job is Kindergarten Administrator.

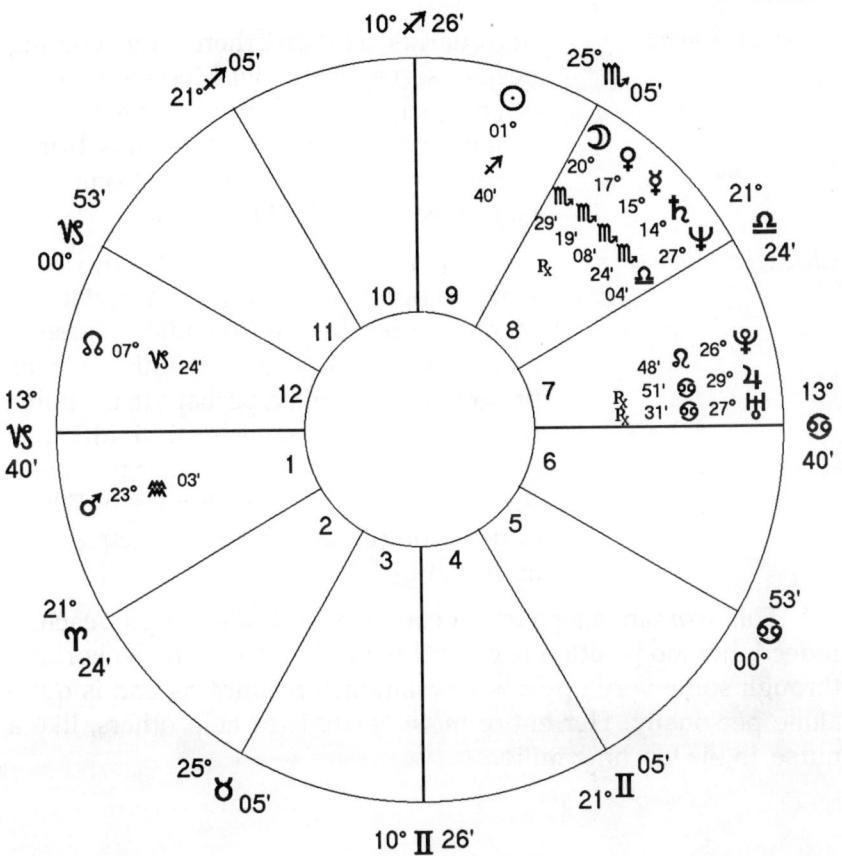

Female A

Chart B

Check the Moon:	In Aquarius in the 3rd: there is the reigning need to serve others; this Moon is also oriental, suggesting the coach or teacher; it is in mutual reception with Uranus, bringing even more attention to the strong 9th House (education) which it rules.
Check the Midheaven:	The Leo Midheaven is dominated by Pluto, which is opposed to the very important Moon; Pluto rules the Ascendant. These measurements very strongly link personal projection with career, perhaps to the point that the career *represents* the individual. (And this becomes an important point of surmise since Venus, which rules the 7th, is under strong aspect with Saturn retrograde in the 12th.)

This woman is also in education, as a Kindergarten Teacher. Indeed, her job position is everything to her, since she is working through some very oppressive relationship concerns and is quite alone personally. Her entire *raison d'etre* is to help others, like a nurse, in the teaching milieu.

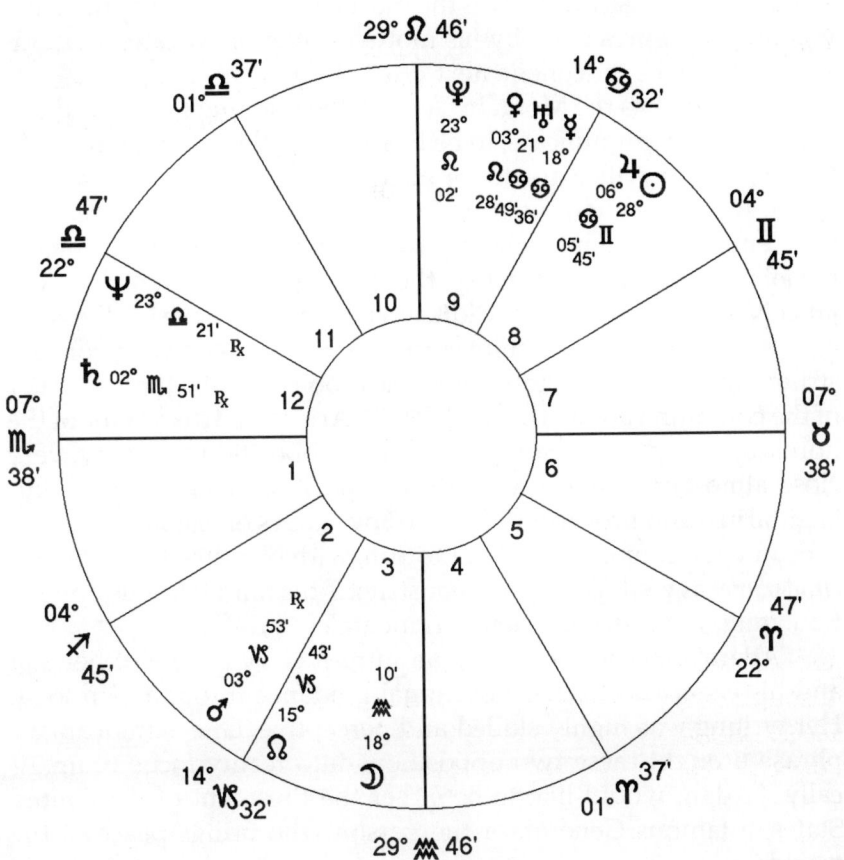

Female B

Our final case for study is the most recent case in my practice: a young man, represented by his mother, eager for vocational guidance as he plans for college next year.

"Adam" has the Moon in Gemini: the reigning need for diversification, to communicate, to be heard. With this Moon in the 12th House, Adam will want to be effective from behind the scenes, again, with consultant overtones. This deduction is reinforced by the Gemini Ascendant, echoing the communication dimensions of the job profile; and by Mercury, the Ascendant ruler, which is conjunct Neptune, ruler of the Midheaven, and square the Midheaven.

As an echo of the Gemini emphasis, we can see two major constructs dominating the horoscope: the Moon opposed the Sun, ruler of the communication 3rd, and Mars in Aries, final dispositor of the horoscope, opposed Uranus. Both these oppositions are very, very close, almost precise. The Moon-Sun opposition is cerebral (Gemini-Sagittarius) and probably "picks up" overtones of vision from Neptune in wide conjunction with the Sun, with Neptune being *the oriental planet* as well. The second construct is the Mars-Uranus opposition: militaristic, driving, temperamental.

Adam's mother wrote me an introductory profile of her son and his eagerness to find vocational guidance through astrology. Her writing was highly skilled and perceptive. One extraordinary phrase brought these two oppositions into reality focus dramatically: "Adam would like to be either the President of the United States, a famous General, or the person who brings peace to the world."

She continued: "He has also said that if he could join the foreign service today and be assured of doing something interesting, he would probably not bother going on to college, although he has always been an outstanding student."

This latter insight as well leaps from the horoscope: Uranus, receiving the opposition from Mars, rules the international/education 9th and disposits Jupiter in Aquarius in the 9th. In turn, this Jupiter is sextile Neptune ruler of the Midheaven.

This set of measurements tells us something highly reliable: when the ruler of the 9th House or a highlighted planet within that House is under strong developmental tension, the probability is very high that the education will be interrupted. Uranus fits this profile clearly, and the client, Adam, has basically corroborated that potential, *i.e.,* "probably not bother going on to college."

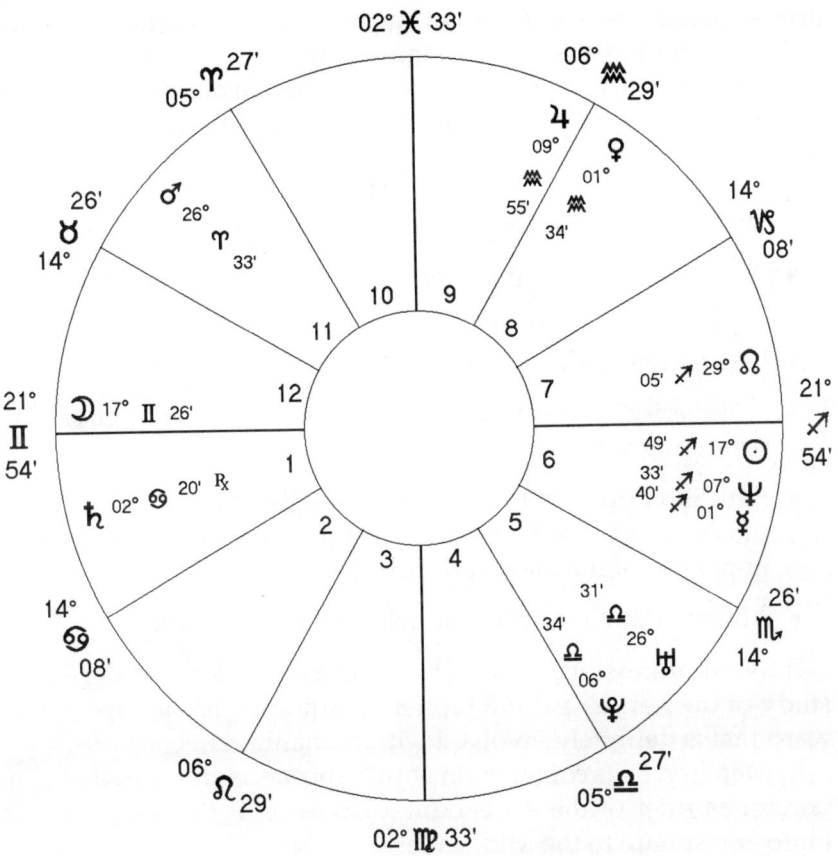

"Adam"

Immediately thereafter in her letter, Adam's mother continued, "He is considering several options, each of a very different nature, for continuing his education." Here is the Gemini vacillation, the indecision, the need for diversification, the difficulty assimilating the two major oppositions within the horoscope. A kind of duality emerges as the parts of the analysis come into understanding, and this duality is clearly a corroboration of the Pisces Midheaven, a double-bodied sign on the cusp of the 10th House, usually an indication of more than one profession or a profession doing double-duty.

Adam's Midheaven is trined almost exactly by an austere Saturn retrograde in the Ascendant and is squared dynamically by the idealized Mercury-Neptune conjunction.

In review, with client corroboration by the mother's letter and follow-up telephone discussion, we can feel sure of the following for Adam's job profile:

- Diversification need; communication need;

- A sense of vision and idealism always pressing behind the scenes;

- Internationalism and higher education very important;

- A "severity" of purpose throughout personal perspective (Saturn retrograde rising, square Pluto, ruler of the 6th);

- Education probably interrupted, possibly to discharge the explosiveness of the Mars-Uranus opposition, and then resumed in pursuit of the idealization drive;

- Always a duality operating within the job situation.

What profession fits this emerging astrological profile? In my study of the horoscope, the Jupiter in Aquarius has a hope for reward that is definitely involved with humanitarian concerns.

Mercury, in its conjunction with Neptune, is also extremely important as ruler of the Ascendant, dispositor of the Moon, sextile Pluto and square to the Midheaven.

A humanitarian communicator who wants to bring peace to the world or, at least, a refreshed idealism, and who will do so while, at the same time, bringing a political or reformation force to social issues. In great detail, I expanded this set of insights with Adam's mother. Their potential was strongly corroborated. The professional outlet of the activist ministry was discussed earnestly.

CONCLUSION

In modern society, our work tells a great deal about who we are as individuals. Diversification of the workplace allows for job specialization that in turn allows for more on-target need fulfillment for each worker. "Profession" as a descriptor has passed the word "job" as the goal of our vocational efforts. Our work must somehow profess, affirm, who we are.

What we do for a living is terribly important for our sense of personal fulfillment. Needs that are extremely individualistic must be accepted and rewarded somehow in the workplace, or frustration on the job will give rise to depression and the sense of insignificance. Dissatisfaction with the job then affects many other areas of life, especially marital relationships, relationships with our children, our self-esteem, our incomes and our dreams, our sexuality, and our thoughts of continuing education and self-development.

Yet not all jobs are professions, so to speak. In less defined work situations, the expression of self is more difficult to discover astrologically. The signatures for teacher and musician are ever so much clearer than the outlines that might lead us to identify housekeeper or mail carrier. I have clients who are very happy in the latter two "callings," if you will, but those choices are extremely difficult to corroborate as a work profile within their horoscope. In general, someone in management, the job label for so many, will find personal fulfillment in the job function in the firm and in the job focus of the firm.

In such cases, what we do see is that, within the work situation, certain needs are indeed being fulfilled in very special, personal ways: the housekeeper is finally glad to run the household the way her own home should have been run when she was growing up, *i.e.*, finishing up some "business" from difficult early years; the mail carrier is expressing strong leadership needs by busy involvement with labor union politics relating to the job.

The so-called more difficult or obscure job profiles really are job-profiles for which we do not yet have clear astrological outlines. For some jobs, we may never have a clear-cut profile in the horoscope. It is the astrologer's nature to *expect* such a profile; the books from older, more socially stratified times trained us to look for such configurations. But in our times now, the workplace and the astrology within it live and breathe differently. People have become persons. Signatures now tend to disappear, and identities come into focus.

The measurements covered in this chapter—the Moon, the oriental planet, peregrination, dispositorship, mutual reception, and aspects to the Midheaven—are everlasting astrological tools that can help us orientate ourselves to our clients in new humanistic sensitivity. Statistical sureness is not our goal; it can't be. Personal fulfillment is; and it must be.

Gina Ceaglio

Gina Ceaglio is a professional astrologer, counselor, teacher, writer, and lecturer with more than 25 years experience. She has been a leader in the movement away from event-oriented astrology to a psychologically aligned astrology of personal responsibility since 1970, when she established the Academy of Astrological Studies in San Diego to teach those principles. Gina enjoyed a close, inspirational friendship with the late Dane Rudhyar, whose philosophies influenced her greatly.

A dynamic speaker, Gina is in demand to lecture at seminars, symposia and conferences nationally and internationally. She has taught hundreds of students and has an extensive private counseling practice. Extremely active in the astrological community, she was coordinator of the United Astrology Congress (UAC) held in New Orleans, July 1989, and is again serving on the planning committee for UAC '92. Her company, Pegasus Tapes, distributes educational audio-cassettes on astrological, psychological, and mythological themes, by some of astrology's most renowned speakers.

Gina attended the University of Washington in Seattle and her background includes training in drama, public speaking, psychology and counseling. Before coming into astrology full time, she had successful careers in direct sales, business management, sales motivational training, and personnel management.

Money Patterns
in the Horoscope

Gina Ceaglio

"With Money a Dragon, Without Money a Worm"
—Old Chinese Proverb

"The Love of Money is the Mother of All Evil"
—Phocylides B.C. 540

Money, money, money ... it can cause a war, build an empire or buy a soul, but always it stirs deep emotions and spawns dichotomous attitudes. Ever since it replaced the barter system, mankind has argued over its virtues and vices. We worship or revile, adore or abhor, energetically pursue or spiritually reject money. Our slang pseudonyms are a testament to these divergent views. On the one hand, we deprecate money with expressions like "filthy lucre" and "pelf," or humanize it with negative emotions like "cold" or "hard" cash, yet somehow consider it divinely omnipotent with "the almighty dollar." We give it life-sustaining properties with words like "bread," "dough," "cabbage," and "lettuce," but disparage it in small amounts with "chicken-feed," "small potatoes," and "peanuts." When it brings joy, we gaily set it to music with "do-re-mi," but when it's an irritant, we call it "scratch."

Cultural attitudes toward wealth are cyclical, depending to a large degree upon the political, economic and religious climate of the times; but like it or not, a universal caste system of the haves and the have-nots has always prevailed. While the disparity fluctuates with changes in the economy, the line between them is clearly

65

drawn and one's opportunities and power are dictated by which side one is on.

Our country is very young. Our history of attitudes toward affluence is brief, compared to that historical profile in other nations. In the beginning, Colonial America struggled for economic stature independent from European investment and influence. Although the personal fortunes of the founding fathers seeded its birth, for the common man the Puritan ethic translated to economic survival as "a penny saved is a penny earned," and to the work ethic as "an honest day's work for an honest day's pay." The land of opportunity and refuge for the down-trodden attracted people from many cultures, among them artisans whose credo was pride in workmanship. This philosophy was passed down from generation to generation, until comparatively recent times.

Industrialists amassed fortunes by exploiting the working class and tapping the rich veins of a vigorous new country's virgin resources. Millionaires multiplied and their children and children's children adopted a snobbish reverence for "old money" and disdain for the *nouveau-riche*. The blue-blood, Social-Register groups, like royalty, were enviously admired, and entire sections of metropolitan newspapers were devoted to their activities.

Now, with the advent of high technology, robots and computers, old-fashioned factories and mills with assembly lines are being phased out, and the entrepreneur has become the hero-model for success. Except for a few Social-Register groups, the "idle rich" have gone out of fashion, and even silver-spoon recipients of inherited old money feel obliged to prove themselves by parlaying their inheritance through personal effort and enterprise.

Attitudes about money and work-ethics changed most radically in the 60s, the decade of flower-children, an unpopular war and anti-establishment movements. That time spawned a pseudo-spirituality in which money and worldly achievement were perceived as proof of ethical poverty. By the 70s, when the reality-crash of survival arose, most re-prioritized their values, rejoined the establishment and became high-achieving yuppies. This money-is-power philosophy, along with a national climate of great prosperity, translated into the quick-money, self-indulgent, me-first philosophy of the 80s. To children of these two decades, the savings account, work ethic of previous generations, is an alien concept; it often is the crux of a conspicuous generation-gap.

In the 90s, an increased sense of egalitarianism and dedication to noble causes is supplanting the drive to amass a fortune. Everyone took a peculiar pleasure, for instance, in Donald Trump's economic problems and the come-uppance of Leona Helmsley. Even Malcolm Forbes' extravagant birthday bash was viewed with a jaundiced eye. We have a growing sense of guilt about the homeless and may perceive the use of drugs and the rise in street crime as evidence of our past preoccupation with money. Today, a blatant display of wealth is considered not only vulgar, but dangerous.

MONEY-LOVE-ATTITUDES

The socio-economic and religious views of the times through which your clients have lived are certainly relevant, and have deeply colored their attitudes about money. However, the most compelling factors influencing their views are uniquely personal and can be found in their charts. The first grace for a counseling astrologer is to make sure personal biases do not taint your judgment of the client's chart. If we believe that seeking money and possessions is a crass or greedy endeavor, we can not be sympathetic or helpful to a client who relies on tangible results from work efforts for a feeling of self-worth. We must define our own attitudes about money before we attempt to define anyone else's.

Beyond its intrinsic value, money also represents other things. To all of us, and perhaps only on a subconscious level, *money is love*. There are two kinds of love which everyone experiences: unconditional and conditional. Unconditional love separates the deed from the person, and we are loved for *who* we are, not for what we *do*. Not only are we not obliged to do anything to get love; even if our behavior is unacceptable, we *are* loved.

Conditional love, on the other hand, is given only as a reward for constructive effort: we must *earn* it. It is love in exchange for performance (a child learns very early on, and in the most subtle ways, that the way to be loved is to do something good). For example, the parent who rejects the child instead of the deed by saying "You're a bad boy to spill your milk," gives a clear signal that love is contingent upon performance. When we say "I love you when you clean up your room," or if we only demonstrate affection in response to the child's achievements, we are placing a condition on love. In school, the higher our grades the more love-approval we receive, so the message is unmistakable: we must do good to get love.

In the adult world, a salary is monetary-love paid for effort on behalf of an employer. When we pay money to others for benefits received, we are giving them conditional love. The less unconditional love we receive, the more conditional love we will require to compensate and feel worthwhile. Those who feel they were not loved unconditionally as children can grow into love-starved, self-doubting adults who may compulsively seek to prove their worth by amassing wealth and high achievements. It is vitally important, then, for astrologers to understand the client's need-motivation behind whatever specific they are researching. While the Sun, Moon, Saturn, 4th and 10th House dynamics in a given chart may not refer directly to money patterns, we must determine the client's feelings of self-worth and how they derive from early environment and parental relationships.

There are as many attitudes toward money as there are people to hold them. To the realists of the world, money is power and a desire for control motivates them to accumulate assets. Religious fundamentalists could feel guilty about acquiring money if they subscribe to the admonition, "It is easier for a camel to go through the eye of a needle, than for a rich man to enter the Kingdom of God." Others will agree with John D. Rockefeller, who believed that the power to make money is a gift from God, or the anonymous sardonic wit who said, "I've been rich and I've been poor. Rich is better."

People will feel rich or poor according to the proportion between their desires and enjoyments. Often these feelings are not determined by the obvious reality of one's financial condition, but by one's early influences, self-image and personal philosophy. One client can feel wealthy with only modest means, barely sufficient to fulfill personal needs, while another feels poor with a storehouse full of money. It is often a hallmark of the love-deprived to pursue riches as compensation for their feelings of unworthiness, but find it is a bottomless well that no amount of money can fill.

In the past, most astrologers believed their clients should not be asked questions about themselves or their past because it was the astrologer's job to divine that information from the horoscopes. This old perception has changed radically. Today, the role of astrologer-as-counselor is vastly different from astrologer-as-fortune-teller of a few decades ago. If some clients object to being questioned about themselves, and a few who have not been to an astrologer before may do so, I explain that the more information I have about their life-experience, the better I can evaluate their current circumstance. To illustrate the point, I may say "Not to share yourself with me is like going to a doctor and asking him to guess where you hurt."

So, before speaking to money patterns in a horoscope, we should query our clients about their needs and attitudes about money and possessions in general to see if the interpretation we gleaned from the chart is in agreement with what they consciously believe. Also, we should ask them for their financial history, to determine which houses, planets and aspects may have been triggered by progressions and transits at those times. This allows us to check our accuracy, and to project with greater confidence into future cycles of activity.

ASTROLOGICAL METHOD

Tracking down money patterns in the horoscope is a fairly complex procedure, but if we go one step at a time and accumulate information bit-by-bit, we can flesh out many insights and possibilities. As in all astrological investigations, we will be concerned with specific houses, signs on cusps and their planetary rulers, planets in houses, planets in signs and aspects. Here is an operative outline of the methodology we will use:

(1) Locate the money houses. (2) Interpret the signs on the cusps. (3) Interpret planets in money houses and their aspects. (4) Determine which signs those planets rule and locate the houses with those signs on their cusps. (5) Locate the planetary rulers of cusp signs on money houses and note where those planets are posited by house, sign and aspects held. (6) Locate the natural zodiac's money planets and note where placed by house, sign and aspects held.

No one of these factors can ever stand alone. The process is cumulative, and each new component adds to, not replaces, what has gone before. All will be operative, and our biggest challenge is to synthesize them into a cohesive whole.

Step 1: Locating the Money Houses

We must decide where money comes from and then locate the house that defines it. Income earned through personal effort is represented by the 2nd House, and money inherited or derived from the efforts of someone else is represented by the 8th House. These are the primary money houses, but there are many more.

Any house that is 2nd from the one before it is the money house to its predecessor. The 11th House is income from career or profession and also a parent's money house (10th). The 5th House is income from real estate, lands or mining, and also a parent's money house (4th). The 12th House is money from friends or organizations (11th). The 4th House is money from siblings, activities relating to communications, teaching, advertising, community affairs and all types of intellectual commerce (3rd). The 6th House is money from talents, creative self-expression, gambling, speculation, children and sexual activity (5th).

The 7th House is money from services rendered, daily toil, health matters and employees (6th). The 8th House, as we already showed, is money from the mate, partner, joint ventures, cooperative endeavors, competitors, legal matters and other people's efforts (7th). The 10th House is money from religion, publishing, foreign exchange, import/export, professorships, sports, travel and adventure (9th). The 3rd House is income from parlaying one's own money and assets (2nd), and the 9th House is income from judicious use of one's inheritance or corporate interests (8th).

If a client asks about a specific way of making money, we will look at the money house describing that particular endeavor. For instance, if it is from real estate investment, we look at the 5th House for income from real estate and, of course, the 4th House for overall conditions governing the matter. If our client says telemarketing is the personal choice for making money, we will look at the 4th House for income from the 3rd, and the 3rd for overall conditions that govern telemarketing.

Step 2: Interpret the Signs on the Cusp

While the sign on the cusp of a house tells us much about the affairs of that house, it also offers information about the person's attitude and approach toward those matters. Gemini on the cusp of the 5th, for example, not only describes one's children as bright, versatile and talkative, but also indicates that one's attitude toward children is intellectual rather than emotional and one's approach is more as a buddy than a parent. Since it is our attitude toward anything that determines how we handle or manage it, house cusp signs on money houses are vitally important. Let's look at the 12 signs on the cusp of a money house to interpret what the person's attitude and approach is likely to be. Remember, this is a preliminary step only, not the final judgement. Much more information will come from where the ruler of the sign is placed and what planets are in the money house.

ARIES on the cusp suggests a strong desire for money and says that the person equates it with winning in competition with others, a personal trophy, so to speak. It means having more than one's peers so, rather than "keeping up with the Joneses," it means racing against and passing them. The person will want quick money, is likely to take risks, be daring in its pursuit and inclined to spend impulsively.

TAURUS on the cusp suggests that the person loves money, not for its intrinsic value, but for what it will buy to satisfy the senses and supply material pleasures. Money also represents love, so while it may be used hedonistically to gratify personal sensual needs and provide "the good life," it is also spent on beautiful gifts for others as evidence of their love. Some people may equate the amount of love another feels for them by the monetary value of the gifts they receive. The greater the stock of material supplies, the more securely loved these natives feel, so their motivation to make money will be proportionate to that need.

GEMINI on the cusp indicates the person gives a good deal of thought to making money, but regards it more as a medium of exchange than a static concept. Thought, knowledge, and communication are regarded as assets and resources rather than a stack of greenbacks. Possessing an extensive library, computers, telephonic and audio equipment, for example, will make the person feel richer than having a big bank account! Since money represents commerce between people in a constant state of flux, one's financial condition will continually shift between adequate and deficient.

CANCER on the cusp suggests that money is the person's emotional security. Gathering, collecting, nurturing and watching it grow is the modus operandi. Money is subconsciously viewed as one's progeny and therefore is protected with the same fierce devotion with which a mother guards her child. The less emotionally secure the person is, the greater the motivation to acquire assets. Plans for financial security will be patiently laid and carefully executed since building a reliable, deeply rooted and solid base of income assures this person of future well-being.

LEO on the cusp indicates that the native's ego and money are inextricably entwined. Money is regarded as life-giving and without it, one might even shrivel up and die. The greater the resources, the more important this person feels. Therefore, the motivation to accrue wealth is highly dynamic. Along with a robust, energetic effort to make money, there could be an open-handed, generous, "last-of-the-big-spenders" approach to spending it. These people often make a show of wealth in order to bolster their self-confidence and gain attention.

VIRGO on the cusp says the person is practical, analytical and realistic about money. Since it is regarded as tangible proof to others of work efficiently executed, being without money may become evidence of personal inadequacy. Much attention is given to keeping track of money, and every asset will be counted, recorded, carefully monitored and supervised. The checkbook is always balanced and tax records are assiduously kept. Since money is the result of diligent work-effort, expenditures will be paid out with equal regard and carefully metered.

LIBRA on the cusp means that money is viewed as necessary for social acceptance. Similar to Taurus, Libra on the cusp values money for the lovely things it can buy, but the purpose is less for personal gratification than it is to gain approval from others. Possessions are viewed as evidence of one's good taste and class in society, therefore the degree of motivation for making money hinges on the person's reliance on peers for feelings of self-worth. The compulsion today's teenagers feel to have expensive sports shoes, gold chains and the like is an example of this type of drive.

SCORPIO on the cusp describes natives who believe that money is power and the more one has, the greater the control. Since a small amount of power is in effect negligible, the drive is for big money and corporate interests. These people will be secretive about their financial affairs and probably have money stashed away that no one knows about. Depending on the entire dynamic, these clients could be obsessed with amassing assets and feel compelled to hide them for safe-keeping. They want to maintain complete control over their finances and it is unlikely that they would employ a money-manager.

SAGITTARIUS on the cusp says that the person is philosophical about money, perhaps even cavalier. The attitude is optimistic, expecting to be fortunate in money matters, and, unless there is astrological evidence to the contrary, that is usually the case. There is the feeling among such people that money will drop into their lap and that they need not be concerned with working hard for it. Again, depending on the entire chart, this either can be an unrealistic viewpoint or a reasonable expectation. There may be an easy-come, easy-go attitude and the money does go out as soon as it comes in.

CAPRICORN on the cusp means that these persons equate money and resources with their identity and value as individuals. They feel it is hard work to achieve financial security and the extent of their assets will dictate their degree of self-worth. If self-esteem is low, no amount of money can bolster it and no matter how much wealth they accrue, they still fear poverty. Their anxiety and worry levels are high, they will be shrewd and conservative in acquiring money and equally careful about how they spend it. To someone who is less anxious about money, they appear extremely frugal or tight.

AQUARIUS on the cusp says these people believe there are other things in life more important than money and that its value will be measured by its use rather than for itself alone. Their financial condition can fluctuate erratically because they experience alternating periods of reckless disregard and serious concern. Money will be spent to support progressive concepts and organizations, on humanitarian causes, new technology, inventions, or a friend in need.

PISCES on the cusp indicates an unrealistic, whimsical approach to money, and these people can be vague and inconsistent about what is required for economic survival. There is often a pervasive discontent with their financial condition, but a sense of victimization when necessity demands that they devote time and energy in pursuit of the dollar, *i.e.,* "If I didn't have to work nine to five in this pedestrian job, I could be creating beautiful visions that feed the soul." Money can almost dissolve in their hands and they may spend what resources they do have to help the disadvantaged and down-trodden.

As was stated before, these suggestions for money house cusp signs are a bare beginning, a place to start. Their meanings will take on new and sometimes conflicting overtones when we move on to steps three through six of our outline.

Refer now to Johnny Carson's chart on the next page. (The computations are "A" birth data from Lois Rodden's *American Book of Charts*.) Mr. Carson has hosted "The Tonight Show" on television for almost 30 years and is the highest paid talk-show host in history. Born on a farm in the Midwest where his father owned a hardware store, Carson has a traditional, middle-class background. At an early age he entertained his family and friends with magic tricks and later became a fairly accomplished amateur magician. His early television career included hosting game shows and starring in his own comedy show, "Carson's Cellar," which was aired locally in the Los Angeles area.

In 1962, at age 37, he got his big break as host of NBC's "Tonight Show" and has reigned as the king of late night television ever since. Recently, he announced his intention to retire in May 1992, after 30 fabulously successful years. Carson has shared his assets with three ex-wives in California's divorce courts and frequently remarks, semi-comically, of losing several residences in this manner. He has diversified financial interests, including a line of men's wear and a television company, Carson Productions, which produces his own show as well as the "David Letterman Show."

First, let's get a feel for Carson's overall dynamic before looking at specifics. With eight planets east, seven of which are in the personal-initiative sector, and Scorpio rising, he is extremely self-sufficient, wants sole control of his life, and operates primarily alone. This is not the chart of a team-player.

With Moon in Capricorn, conjunct Jupiter, opposed Pluto and square Mars, we get the picture of an emotionally insecure child who felt love must be earned. According to his perceptions, the mother placed a high value on performance, was undemonstrative, powerful and demanding. These early impressions of his mother could produce a subconscious hostility toward women and evoke power struggles, which contribute to his obvious difficulties in adult relationships.

With the Sun in the 12th House in Libra, sextile Neptune and semi-square Venus we can infer that the father was idealized but not readily available; and also did not supply the emotional warmth and love the child needed. With Saturn in the 1st House in Scorpio, conjunct Mercury, square Midheaven, trine Pluto, sextile Moon and Jupiter, we get the picture of a powerful, dedicated, high-achiever whose identity depends on personal accomplishment.

As to money patterns, let's begin our investigation with the 2nd House of personal income (step 1). We find Sagittarius on the cusp (step 2). Venus in Sagittarius is the only planet in the house; it is trine the Midheaven, sextile Mars, inconjunct Pluto and semi-sextile Saturn, Moon and Jupiter (step 3). Venus rules the 7th House, Taurus, and the 12th House, Libra (step 4).

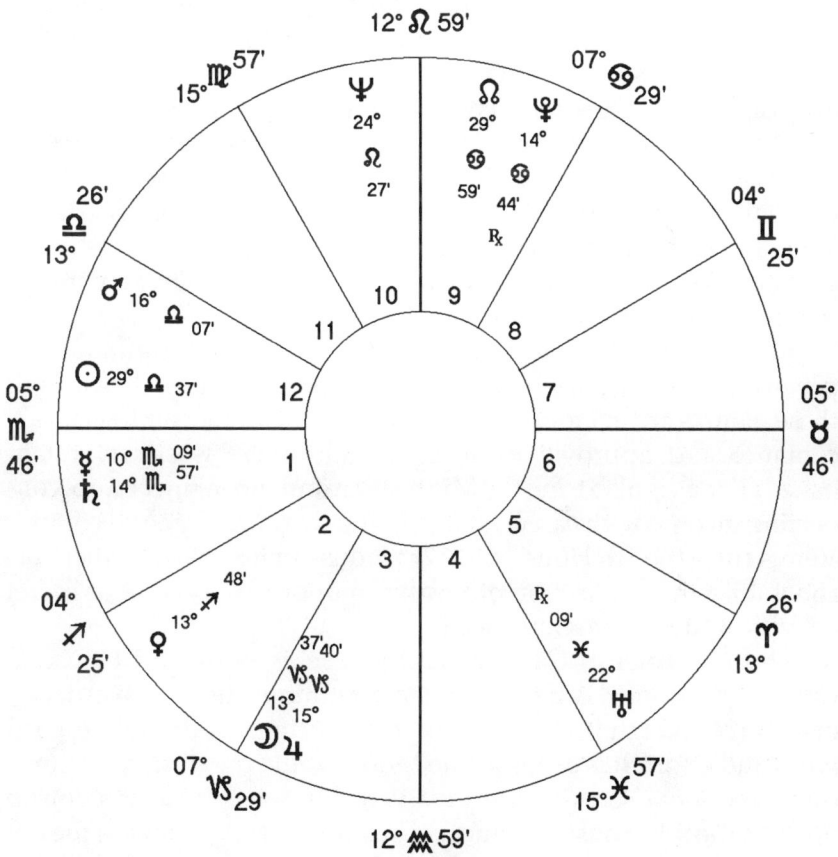

Johnny Carson
Oct. 23, 1925
07:15 a.m. CST
Corning, Iowa
94W44 40N59
Placidus Houses

The ruler of Sagittarius (Jupiter) is in the 3rd House, in Capricorn, conjunct Moon, square Mars, opposition Pluto, sextile Mercury and Saturn (step 5).

Money planets in the natural zodiac are Venus, as ruler of Taurus, and Pluto as ruler of Scorpio. In this chart Venus is in the 2nd House in Sagittarius, with aspects already noted above; Pluto is in the 9th House in Cancer, square Mars, trine Mercury and Saturn in addition to aspects already noted above (step 6).

That's a lot of information, and listing it all at once can make it appear confusing. However, the pattern gradually emerges when we carefully interpret each step as we go along. Sagittarius on the cusp of the 2nd House tells us that his attitude toward money is "upbeat." He expects to be fortunate, and accruing money is an adventurous game. Venus in the 2nd House says he loves money, that it gives him pleasure and reaffirms his good fortune. With its sextile to Mars and semi-square to the Sun, both in the 12th House, we know that he subconsciously equates wealth in a personal way with his ego and competitive drive.

Here is our first indication that Carson keeps his affairs very private and makes secret, behind-the-scenes money deals. Both these planets are in Libra, so the connection of money with social acceptance and approval from significant-others is clearly established. Venus is also trine the Midheaven and inconjunct Pluto, connecting income with career, status in the world, power and control. Venus rules the 7th House and 12th House in his chart, further corroborating the connection of wealth to approval, private or secret activity, and subconscious need.

Jupiter, ruler of Carson's 2nd House, is in the 3rd House in Capricorn. Money is derived from communications, advertising, commerce and intellectual exchange, requiring self-discipline, hard work and effort. It is conjunct the Moon, so the public and Carson's own emotional security are involved. Jupiter is in opposition to Pluto in the 9th House in Cancer. This says money *is* power, the desire for it is intense, and the drive is for vast amounts. It may come from publishing or world-wide communications and will be gathered, protected, and nurtured. The square to Mars in Libra in the 12th House underscores his strong desire and drive and adds an indication of one-on-one secret money deals.

This very strong drive will not be obvious to others because the T-Square is in Cadent Houses. However, those who are associated with Carson on an intimate level will be aware. Also, with the 3rd-9th House emphasis, siblings and in-laws may be drawn into the money-making process. We know, for example, that Carson's brother is a key player in his production company. The 9th House is also publishing, and Carson has written at least one book. Jupiter's sextile to Mercury-Saturn in Scorpio in the 1st House corroborate conclusively that money will come from a personal, long-term, disciplined effort to prove his self-worth in commercial, communication pursuits.

Now we get to the planets that are connected with money-making potential in *every* chart. As rulers of Taurus and Scorpio, the natural 2nd and 8th Houses, Venus and Pluto are always considered when we interpret a client's financial capabilities. Where these planets are found by house, sign, and aspects to other planets are reliable indicators of a source of income and the dynamics with which the client approaches those matters. Ties to Venus are favorable, but as Mayer Rothschild said 200 years ago, "It isn't enough for you to love money—it's also necessary that money should love you."

It would appear that money loves us in direct proportion to the energy we expend to attract it. In my experience with clients and charts of renowned individuals, I have found that Pluto is the mark of enormous wealth. Amassing money in the millions or billions appears to require the obsessive need symbolized by Pluto. Aspects to Pluto from money house rulers or the planets in money houses are such a frequent occurrence that one wonders if it may not be a *prerequisite* for multi-millionaires!

Of course, we all have Pluto in our chart, yet not everyone becomes a Croesus. Only when Pluto speaks directly to the money-making potential, and the rest of the chart corroborates that opinion, is the power directed toward great wealth. High-dynamic aspects like conjunctions, squares, oppositions and semi-squares, not only do not preclude our ability to make money, *they enhance it*. It is logical that the greater the energy, the greater the promise, so it validates the premise that our highest potential and unique genius lie in our so called "hard" aspects.

In search of the money planets in Johnny Carson's chart, we reiterate that Venus occupies a money house, holds a sextile to Mars and an inconjunct to Pluto. The 8th House ruler, Mercury, is trine Pluto. The 2nd House ruler, Jupiter, opposes Pluto and is one leg of the powerful T-Square with Mars. It is an energy that will be used in many ways besides making money. If this were an anonymous client and we did not know he already had made millions, we would point him in the direction of that potential and hope to facilitate his decision to use the energy positively.

Earlier in this discussion, I suggested that we need to confirm our interpretations by checking the progressions and transits that were effective when significant financial events occurred in the past. We know Carson was 37 years old when he was selected to host "The Tonight Show." Although he had had many successes and was earning a comfortable income before that time, this was his breakthrough to making really big money. It appears to have come suddenly, perhaps as an unexpected surprise and possibly, through the help of friends. Solar Arc Uranus opposed natal Sun, Solar Arc Saturn squared natal Uranus and Solar Arc Pluto was inconjunct Uranus.

Secondary Progressed Midheaven opposed Uranus, therefore the Nadir conjuncted Uranus, and Secondary Progressed Mars conjuncted natal Mercury. It certainly signified new creative freedom with natal Uranus in the 5th House, a complete change of career direction and residential move with the Uranus/Sun, Midheaven/Uranus and Saturn/Uranus emphasis. The Sun rules Carson's 10th House, Saturn and Uranus rule his 4th House and Saturn/Mercury are *in* his 1st House!

There is further corroboration of all this with transiting Saturn just entering his 4th House to begin the "emerge cycle" of new achievements, and with transiting Uranus and Pluto in his 10th House showing significant career changes. Transiting Jupiter was in his 5th House, conjunct Uranus, and transiting Neptune was in his 1st House conjunct Mercury!

In May of that auspicious year, transiting Mars opposed natal Mars and filled in the vacant leg of the Moon, Jupiter, Pluto, Mars T-Square. What a release of power! The scene was set and the action was forecast by two Solar Eclipses in 1962 that sandwiched Carson's Midheaven/Nadir axis exactly between them: one at 16 degrees Aquarius in February and the other at eight degrees Leo in July!

Let's move on to Howard Hughes chart, shown on the previous page. (This is "A" birth data from the ISAR Database and shows very interesting connections of money-houses to Pluto.) Mr. Hughes inherited $650,000 from his father and parlayed it to 2.5 billion dollars! The ruler of both his 2nd House of personal income and his 9th House of income from judicious use of inheritance is Venus. Venus is conjunct the Moon, ruler of his 11th House (income from career) and Mercury, ruler of both his Ascendant (personal effort) and 10th House (career). All three planets oppose Pluto in his 10th House.

Mr. Hughes' packed 4th House testifies to real estate interests and the ruler of his 5th (income from real estate), is Saturn, which is

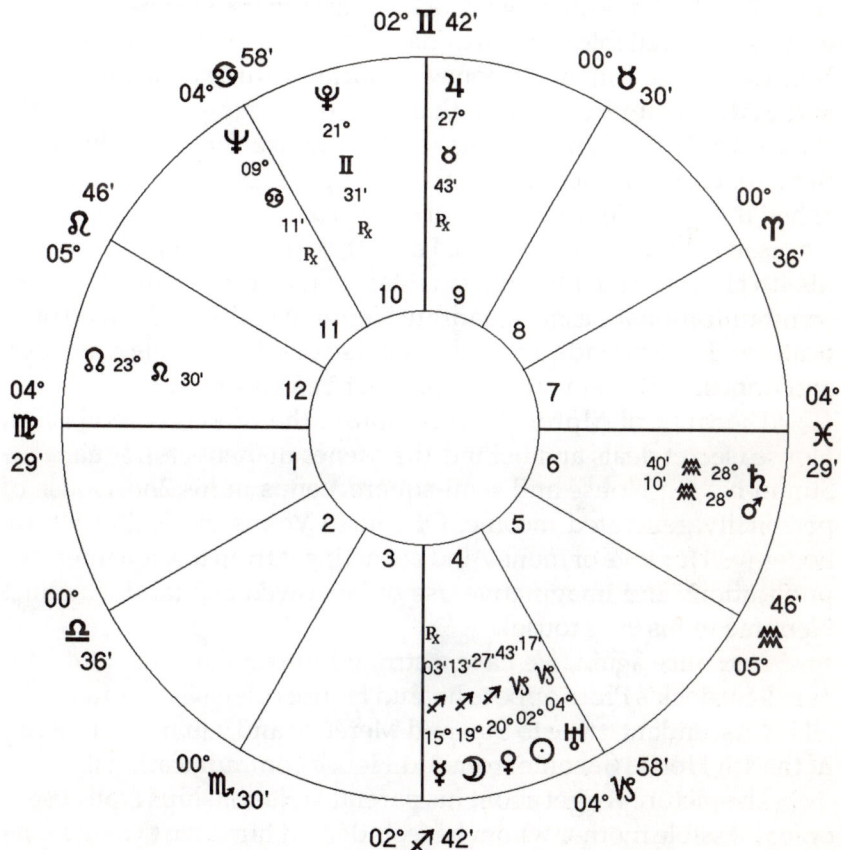

Howard Hughes
Dec. 24, 1905
10:12 p.m. CST
Houston, Texas
95W22 29N46
Placidus Houses

conjunct Mars, ruler of his 8th House. Both planets square Jupiter, sextile the Sun, and form a seven-degree wide trine to Pluto.

We have indications of a powerful, consuming parent through the Moon opposition with Pluto; and also, one parent playing both roles with Mercury, ruler of Hughes' 10th House placed in his 4th House. The compulsive need to find emotional security through acquiring wealth is indicated by the ruler of his 2nd House, Venus, tightly conjunct the Moon in the 4th House and opposed Pluto.

Now look at Rupert Murdock's chart (on the next page), based on the same reliable "A" birth data from the ISAR Database. Mr. Murdock is a self-made tycoon who started with a small newspaper and built an empire of more than 80 publications on three continents. An Australian who has taken America by storm, he has a thirst for corporate acquisitions or attempted take-overs, and established the Fox Television Network. The ruler of his 2nd House, Saturn, is in his 1st House (personal effort), sextile Sun and Mercury in his 4th House (land, mining, real estate and income from 3rd House communications), sesqui-quadrate Neptune in the 9th House (publications, foreign trade and judicious use of other people's money), and opposed Pluto in the 7th (cooperative ventures).

The ruler of Murdock's 8th House, the Moon, is in his 12th House (secret deals and behind-the-scenes maneuvers), square the Sun in his 4th House and semi-square Venus in his 2nd House of personally generated income. Of course Venus in his 2nd House bodes well for love of money and attracting it from foreign interests, publications and imaginative use of borrowed capital (inconjunct Neptune in his 9th House).

And once again, we have a strong Pluto connection. Not only does Murdock's Pluto oppose his 2nd House ruler, it is contra-parallel his Ascendant, trine to Sun and Mercury and square Uranus, all in the 4th House (income from 3rd House communications).

The picture we get about his parental relationships is an absent or inaccessible mother whom he feels denied him love (Moon in the 12th House, semi-square Venus) and one parent playing both roles, suggested by the ruler of the 10th placed in the 4th. The Sun square Moon and Saturn in opposition to Pluto speak to a powerful, consuming father-model and the existence of conflict between his male and female models. This could translate into an anima-animus discomfort in adulthood. Of course the Saturn opposition with Pluto alone describes an identity equated with money and power, per-

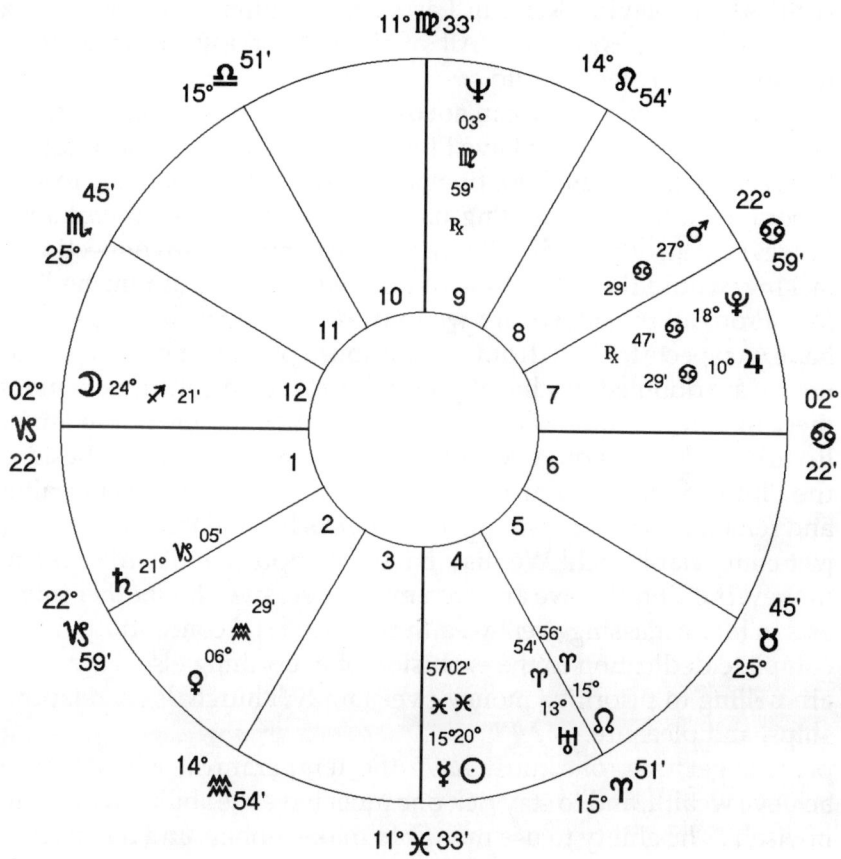

Rupert Murdock
Mar. 11, 1931
11:59 p.m. GST
Melbourne, Australia
144W58 37N45
Placidus Houses

haps to the point of cruelty or ruthlessness, and identifies a compulsive achiever.

Even when Luck is the Lady who delivers large sums of money, you will find Pluto in the pot. In Lois Rodden's *American Book of Charts*, there are five lucky people listed. All data is reliable, classified "A," and there are two males and three females. Each got lucky at different things—a radio show's random telephone call, a game show, playing Keno in Las Vegas, a lottery winner, and an Irish Sweepstakes winner. All of them have aspects from their money house ruler to Pluto.

Again, however, we can not draw the conclusion that a fortune will drop in our lap if we have Pluto aspects to money house rulers. Many other factors in these five person's charts would have to corroborate success at gambling or games of chance. One wonders, however, if all other indications are there but the Pluto connection is lacking, would the magnitude of their winnings be diminished?

From all the above, are we to draw the conclusion that if we have *no* aspects to Pluto from money house planets or cusp-sign rulers we are doomed to a life of poverty? Or, conversely, if our charts meet the Pluto requirement, are we guaranteed a life in the lap of luxury? Certainly not. As we have seen, many other factors besides the Pluto connection must converge to indicate enormous wealth, and remember, we are talking mega-bucks here, in the millions, not just comfortably rich! We may have a compulsive desire to make money, but find that we are even more obsessive about other interests in life. Amassing great wealth requires total concentration and complete dedication to the exclusion of everything else. Few of us are willing to prioritize money over family, church, love, relationships, and pleasure.

To get rich, one must have the temperament and drive to achieve wealth, and to stay rich one must have the ability to manage it wisely. The ability to use money to make money, and the insatiable appetite for more, are probably the most salient factors in creating large fortunes. Almost everyone has a windfall at some point in life: an inheritance, a legal settlement, an investment or real estate profit. How many of us would have opted for hard work to parlay a $650,000 inheritance as Howard Hughes did?

It is likely that, with more than half a million dollars, we would feel set for life, kick back and simply enjoy our good luck. Hugh Hefner started *Playboy Magazine* with a borrowed $600, and by the age of 40 was worth over one hundred million. Why didn't *he* stop at one million or twenty million or fifty million? Perhaps at some point, making money can become an addiction, separate from conscious intent, and have a life of its own. Certainly, if our self-indulgent desires continually increase at a greater rate than our income, we can never have enough.

Many of us may hunger for riches, but lack the personal talent, drive and ambition to make money ourselves, so we team up with someone who does. A good example is Marion Davies (birth data from Rodden's Profiles of Women), who was William Randolph Hearst's mistress for 37 years. She was 16 when they met, and he was 50, a 34-year difference in ages.

There are conflicting stories about her happiness in the relationship, some contending that he dominated her completely and that she was a virtual prisoner, with little joy or interests to occupy her time. Her chart seems to bear out the high emotional price she paid to live in luxury. The Sun-Moon conjunction in her 1st House is caught in the middle of a square between Saturn and Uranus in her 11th House and Venus in her 2nd House. The Saturn-Uranus conjunction in her 11th would place limitations on her freedom to enjoy friends and social life, and their square to her Venus translates to denial of love and pleasure. The Moon is also inconjunct Neptune in her 6th House, signifying constant adjustment to emotional loneliness and discontent.

Looking at Davies' money patterns, we see that Venus and Mercury are in her 2nd House, indicating a love of money and thought given to its acquisition. To discover where it will come from, we see that Mercury rules her 7th House of significant others and Venus rules both her 5th House of romance and her 10th House of status, career and a parent. The sign on the cusp of her 2nd House is Capricorn with Aquarius intercepted, so Saturn and Uranus in her 11th indicate that feelings of self-worth, freedom and survival play into her money needs and that there is fear of poverty. The Moon, ruler of her 8th House, the partner's money, is placed in her 1st House, trine Jupiter. Jupiter rules her Ascendant and is placed in her 8th House of the partner's money. Here we have a reciprocal interchange between her resources and a partner's resources.

Davies' chart exemplifies the wisdom of understanding the native's entire dynamic before making a judgement about their money potential. Both the "unloved child" and "fear of abandonment" syndromes are here with the 10th House ruler Venus, square Saturn and Uranus. Saturn and the Sun symbolize the male parent-model and one is conjunct and the other semi-square Uranus, indicating *separation* from that parent. The Moon is semi-square Saturn, Uranus and Venus, with the ruler of the 4th House, Mars, conjunct Pluto and square to Jupiter. So it is the same story of denial with the nurturing parent as well and both parent models exerted tremendous control.

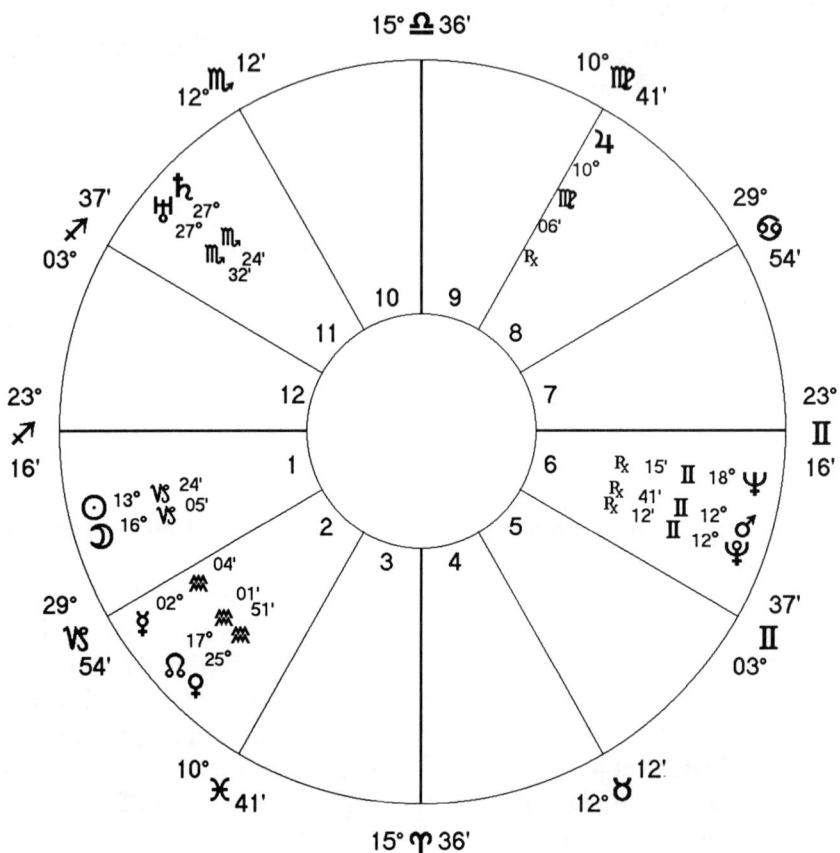

Marion Davies
Jan. 3, 1897
06:00 a.m. EST
Brooklyn, New York
73W58 40N40
Placidus Houses

This looks to me like the chart of a damaged child who replicated the pattern in adulthood. There is not enough energy from Pluto and Mars, in a Cadent House and holding only two aspects (one square to Jupiter and an inconjunct to the Sun and Moon), to motivate her on her own. Additionally, there is evidence that she may have been so wounded that she saw herself as a victim, searching for a savior. Neptune opposes her Ascendant and is inconjunct the Sun and Moon, which are already caught in a web of rejection.

Most clients come to an astrologer seeking insight and direction about the three significant areas of their lives. The first is relationships: love, marriage, family, and friends. The second is worldly success: job, career, and money. Third is health of mind, body, and spirit. We have concerned ourselves here with the second major interest a client brings to the counseling session and, although we have all heard that money will not buy happiness and that there are hundreds of unhappy millionaires, most of us would rather be rich and unhappy than poor and unhappy, if given a choice. In fact, it has been said that when it is a question of money, everybody is of the same religion.

We learn very early in life that money is power. Our parents threaten, reward, and control us with their pursestrings. Observe youngsters in the supermarket begging parents for goodies and see how clearly the message comes through that their pleasure depends on what money can buy. It is not coincidence that in astrology the 2nd House refers to both our value system and money. How quickly we learn its value when we go out and try to borrow some!

One thing is certain, though: there are few things in life about which we hold more passionate and widely divergent views than money. Even the world's finest minds have vehemently disagreed. Bacon contended that great riches have sold more men than they have bought, and Schopenhauer declared that money is human happiness in the abstract. Does it corrupt or liberate? Is it at the root of all evil, or manna from heaven? The truth may lie, not in money itself, but in the character of its possessor.

> *"Gold, like the sun, which melts wax and hardens clay, expands great souls and contracts bad hearts."*
> —Antoine de Rivaroli

Jayj Jacobs

Jayj Jacobs has had a full-service astrology practice in San Francisco since 1972, counseling businesses, couples, individuals, and politicians. He also designs and sells complete computer systems, primarily to astrologers. He became interested in astrology in 1964, at age 15, and his initial training was with his father, Don "Moby Dick" Jacobs, with whom he developed an innovative approach known as "Experience Astrology."

Jayj has co-led The Annual Prediction Seminar since 1971, with accuracy always better than 90 percent. He has lectured on a wide variety of subjects for AFA, AFAN, Aquarius Workshops, ISAR, NCGR, NORWAC, SWAC, UAC, and numerous local organizations in the U.S. and in Canada.

Jayj's articles have appeared in *Astrology Now, Aspects, Welcome to Planet Earth, The Sun-Sign Astrologer*, and others. He writes a monthly column—Star*Light—for *Smoking Singles Magazine*. Jayj has revised the series of 10 "Moby Dick's Matrix Charts," and distributes his father's works as well as his own, notably "The Experience Astrology System," The Transit Dial, and his Graph Kits.

Jayj is an AFAN co-founder, on the Steering Committee, and is Chair of AFAN's Legal Information Committee.

Career Cycles, Job Changes, and Rewards

Jayj Jacobs

Your clients will spend the rest of their lives somewhere they've never been before. It's uncharted territory full of job uncertainties, strange co-workers, potential disasters, or detours, and fleeting career opportunities. It's their future.

Without you they may wander through this ever-changing mystery wondering what tomorrow will bring, questioning when or if they will reach their goals and realize their dreams. You can guide them to be in the right place at the right time; to take effective action; and to wait for the propitious points in their career cycles to deploy strategies—all this by analyzing and interpreting their transits. When you predict accurately, your clients can create effectively.

Transits are real (physical, observable) planets moving through real space (against the background measurement reference of the Zodiac) in real (measured, chronological) time. They are interpretable as circumstances or conditions, experiences (both subjective and objective), and developmental processes. While they carry a deep symbology, they are not merely symbolic constructs. Transits are as real as a horoscope: they are the continuing motions and changing relationships of the planets related to the planetary positions and angular structures of the birth horoscope.

I strongly recommend that, in addition to noting transits through natal houses, astrologers notice, counsel, and predict from solar houses. Solar houses are equal, 30-degree houses measured from the Sun's exact position as the cusp of the 1st House. For example, in the Solar chart of a person whose Sun is 12 Aquarius 14, the 1st House would begin at 12 Aquarius 14, the 2nd House would begin at 12 Pisces 14, and each successive house would begin with the same degree and minute of each successive sign.

In our experience, transits through the solar houses have the same meanings—and the same weights or import—as transits through the natal houses. The natural, natal, and solar charts are the length, width, and depth of a person's life. Henceforth, when I mention a house I mean either the natal or the solar house, and when I refer to the natal chart I mean to include the solar dimension equally.

In this article, we are concentrating on vocational astrology, rather than on the total complex of life. Interpretations of house transits and transiting aspects are limited to those that may have a direct impact on occupation, productivity, success, and reward, or the lack thereof. Techniques to synthesize interpretations are also covered.

SYNERGY, SEQUENCE,
CONTRADICTION AND BALANCE

Every planet is transiting some house at every moment. During each house transit, it is *as if* the transiting planet is imparting its energy into that house. Whatever that planet *is* or represents, it is *doing* itself, *i.e.*, injecting its essential nature, into that house. During the period of the house transit, the client's experiences and circumstances are similar to what they would be *if the person had that planet in that position natally*, but the transits are active rather than reactive principles, and they are temporary, rather than permanent placements.

Transits move and change at the rapid pace of life; they are the dynamic process by which life unfolds. At the beginning of the section on each planet that follows, I present an explanation of the essential nature or inherent energy of each transiting planet before I apply it to specific houses or combine its basic principle with that of the natal planets. I also list the planet's rate of motion in degrees per year, month, and/or day, the length of time its transiting aspects are within orb, and the average time it spends in a house (unequal houses will vary from this average depending on their size, of course).

During the course of its passage through a house, a transiting planet will make some aspect to all (or most) of the planets in the natal chart. It will consistently "hit" the planets in a specific order. The cusp receives the first aspect, followed by an aspect to the planet at the next higher degree of any sign, in any house. The rest of the planets are aspected, in degree order, up to 30 degrees, then 0 degrees and beyond, until the cusp of the next house, where the cycle continues. The aspects will then repeat themselves—in what we call "Transit Comb" order—as that planet passes through the next house. The aspects will be different in strength and level of tension as the transiting planet makes major or minor aspects and hard or soft aspects, but the effect is different only in degree, not in kind. *The actual planets involved in the relationship are much more important in determining what occurs, than their angle of approach to each other.*

Difficulty with a transit is more a function of the natal chart—and other simultaneous transits—than it is a result of the particular aspect made. Which planets are involved is primary, which aspect is being formed, in most cases, is only a minor modifier. Constructing a "Transit Comb" by listing the planets and their positions in degree order will allow you to see more clearly the client's cycle of experience over time. Natal planets that are within 4 degrees of each other will be transited concurrently—to the extent that their period of being within orb overlaps. The closer they are, the more simultaneous transits to them will be. Every transiting indicator can express separately from other simultaneous transits, leading to the contradictions that occur in life. However, they might combine their energies in producing one complex set of concurrent circumstances. When one planet or aspect can indicate love or money, while another only indicates money, love is out-voted and the client gets more money.

Transits, being dynamic processes, require different standards and criteria than natal, horary, or static predictive techniques. I find that the most effective orb for transiting aspects is two degrees, whatever the aspect, whichever planets are involved. The effects of the aspect begin when the transit comes within two degrees of the natal planet. They last *the entire time* the planets are less than two degrees apart (even across house and sign cusps) and peak near (but not usually precisely on) the exact aspect. *With transits, I recommend using only the aspects that are multiples of 30 degrees.*

Each planet moves the life at its own pace, according to its Net and Gross motion. Net motion is a measure of forward progress through a sign or house, of degrees newly transited and the potential for new contacts. Gross motion includes degrees re-crossed due to retrograde and re-direct motion and shows repeating contacts.

Some houses (notably the 2nd, 6th, and 10th) are more important in financial, employment, and vocational-professional issues than others, for most people. However, certain careers and some individuals will emphasize other houses to the extent that any of the houses may be relevant for prediction of success, reward, and change.

I describe the effects of transiting planets, in the overview that follows, in rich causal language. I don't really mean a planet "does, makes, causes, creates, etc." Rather I intend the sense of "indicates, corresponds to, reflects." But, it would be a shame to waste the full palette of colorful causal words and phrases available, as well as awkward to write without them. This presentation is experiential, rather than clinical, psychological, or mythological. The use of contemporary idioms is deliberate, and I hope artful. The objective is to plant an image in your mind that will take root and blossom into a harvest of food for thought to nourish your ability to nurture your clients.

PLUTO
Catalyst to Commitment, Obsession, or Crisis

Due to its extremely elliptical orbit, Pluto varies in speed from less than one degree of net motion per year within Aries, Taurus, and Gemini to a maximum of 2.5 degrees within Libra, Scorpio, (its current sign transit), and Sagittarius. Its gross motion is currently about 4.5 degrees per year. Aspects from transiting Pluto will be in orb for about 18 months out of a two-year period. During that time most people will experience three exact hits, (two of which will not be separated by an out-of-orb period), but some planets will undergo a full five hits from Pluto.

Pluto's solar (and average natal) house transits currently consume life in 12-14 year bites. Pluto will usually cross the cusp of a house three (and perhaps five) times as it enters a house and again transit the trailing cusp 3-5 times as it leaves that house to enter the next. It often hits hardest in both the first sucker-punch and in the last-gasp knock-out blow. Since Pluto takes 248 years to circle the Sun, it will never transit all the natal houses in anyone's chart. But, since Pluto is in the middle of the fast half of its orbit, those born with Pluto in Leo—who live into their 80s—could experience the transits of Pluto through six houses and even get transiting Pluto opposite natal Pluto. By including solar houses, one could extend the number of Houses transited.

Pluto's essential nature is transformative and catalytic. It is disruptive and regenerative. It brings crisis and breakthrough. It means danger, perhaps death (of something), and potentially rebirth. Pluto is power. It dominates and it empowers. It represses and it reveals. Pluto is obsession, preoccupation, commitment, and purpose. Pluto is as two-faced as the stereotype of the exploitative con-man, as dangerously seductive as the cultural attache/secret agent of spy novel lore. Even in vocational astrology, Pluto can be sexual and may be metaphysical.

Pluto's house transits direct the play, set the stage, and *serve as a backdrop for shorter-term transits*. Clients may eventually get used to Pluto transits in the sense that they assume Pluto's influence to be a natural and permanent part of their life, as if it were a natal factor in their chart (*i.e.*, "been down so long it looks like up to me")—until Pluto *changes* houses and changes their personal world as it does. Pluto's impact often seems overwhelming and compelling.

As Pluto crosses into the 1st House, the aura of bad luck disperses, the sense of impending crisis dissipates. Clients develop a new sense of power, as if they had been purified by passing through the crucible. This feeling of rebirth is a prelude to a long period of new beginnings. The personality and the appearance will become more direct and committed. Increased obviousness of sexuality may manifest in excitement or in harassment hassles—in either direction. The awareness of personal power often manifests as daring to take on new career challenges or a new life-direction. It arises out of a new sense of self and out of a new recognition of the importance of purpose. Pluto commitments pay off, if they don't deteriorate into obsessions.

Pluto detonating in the 2nd House wipes out a person's value system, destroying it piece by piece, so that nothing has the same worth as before, and transforms it into something more personal and profound. Pluto changes the currency with which people measure their life. Along the way, finances fluctuate to extremes as does the importance of making, saving, and spending money, and being, doing, and having what financial resources allow. People with the potential make their fortunes during this transit.

Pluto driving through the 3rd House makes the demonstration

of intelligence and the mastery of factual data the most important factors in the life. People moved by this transit are driven to prove they are right, that they know, and that they can convince you. Curiosity becomes compulsive and the communication catalytic, or merely overpowering. Watch for some clients to leave business for academia, while others become better paid consultants.

Pluto marching through the 4th House brings forth a driving search for the dream home, as if God promised them a land, if they could only find it! A series of crises (deaths?) within the family can regenerate or alter the family commitment (or power structure), triggers a break away from it or an uprooting from the past. Release from the "family script" may reveal new possibilities for (career) commitment.

Pluto frolicking through the 5th House triggers a series of drastic changes in the patterns of pleasure, as the toys of a former age give way to the joys of the new (and then the next). Soul-driven creativity and romance call to the heart with a siren's song that cannot be denied. Occult avocations, dangerous recreations, and sexual interludes entice or impel the person to recreate the self's performance or display.

Pluto working its way through the 6th House produces profound changes in work habits, (demonstrated by compulsive activity), an alteration in attitude toward application (resulting in a commitment to excellence and expertise), and a craving for employment to fulfill the purpose of their existence (which can propel the client into jobs involving death and danger, prevention and protection, or re-birth and empowerment). Anywhere they land, they must make a difference. Breakdowns and disasters often are the force behind change: health crises cripple careers, companies collapse options, plants close, supervisors sexually harass, and coworkers conspire—all to get people back on their path.

Pluto moving into the 7th House sends clients in search of that special someone they are certain is somewhere on the other side of the sea of suitors that surrounds them. Destiny is the best man and Fate the maid of honor every time they feel compelled to marry! Lives entangle with spouses (and exes), business partners (and enemies), attorneys, organizations, and politics.

Pluto prowling the 8th House turns the client on to the joys of sex and excess, to the pure pleasure of pushing the envelope and breaking through, to the delight of dancing within an inch of death and the rapture of being reborn, to the serenity of power and the ecstasy of empowerment. Inherent natal rigidity may reverse this transit into repressiveness and anti-sexual fanaticism. Who needs position when they have the personal power to impact the population?

Pluto landing in the 9th House catapults the client into contemplation of the meaning and mechanism of life and sends them on a quest for knowledge and adventure. Life-altering studies may prepare them for satisfaction and/or success. Developing, integrating, and dispensing wisdom take precedence, leading to writing, lecturing, and counseling.

Pluto starting into the 10th House fuels the engine of ambition and propels people into striving for success, social acclaim, authority and the establishment of position, status and respect. Radical changes in attitude and ambition career people into career directions never imagined, long abandoned, or achingly longed for, to fulfill the demand of destiny's design. Natal planets here take on new levels—heights and depths—of meaning as Pluto's conjunctions purify and empower them. The career becomes all-absorbing, swallowing the life. The willingness to take great risks (and dangerous paths) leads to great reward (power, authority and influence), awful disappointments, and even excruciating disasters.

Pluto entering the 11th House launches the native's personal *Argo* in a quest for the golden dream, the life's shining aspiration and shimmering future. The crew of colleagues and friends metamorphosizes into monsters and mates. Some abandon ship and resign themselves to a little atoll. The client must create a new something to live for, once dreams are either fulfilled or abandoned.

Pluto cleaving the 12th House can carve the heart out of the chest (through defeats and disasters) or open it to a universe of unity, spiritual immensity, and "magical" power. A dedication to active service and effective contribution enrolls the cosmos in the client's hopes and makes miracles happen. Those who don't go with the flow are torn apart by the tide; those who do may know the "unknowable."

Aspects of Pluto

♇ — ☉ While in aspect to the Sun, Pluto grinds the identity into a fine powder and invites the winds of change and threatening circumstances to separate the wheat from the chaff. During harsh aspects, the client feels and fears that some essential kernel, the bran or the wheat germ, or something, is being blown away and lost. All Pluto-Sun aspects—the upper square and the quincunxes in particular—bring a new sense of power and a willingness to risk everything in meeting great challenges or serving high purposes. This can lead to great accomplishments and subsequent rewards or cataclysmic downfalls.

♇ – ☽   Pluto-Moon aspects profoundly affect the emotional condition and nature and the need-fulfillment structure of the client. When there is a preoccupation with family responsibilities or if emotional security is linked to financial security or accomplishment, it generates a churning urge to earn and own, and a commitment to satisfying those needs that, in turn, spawns the actions necessary to produce the desired results.

♇ – ☿   Internally, Pluto-Mercury aspects catalyze changes in the mental processes, the habitual patterns of thought, and the usual manner of apprehending and organizing information that manifest externally in more impactful communication, and occasionally in life-altering decisions or utterances. Circumstantially, hard Pluto-Mercury contacts can trigger the death of a commercial enterprise, especially for the self-employed or for independent contractors. The mental construct (the idea, decision, vision) that supports the business dies, like the branch that holds the treehouse. A new vision can erect a better edifice, one more securely nailed to reality.

♇ – ♀   Pluto-Venus aspects may express as changes in financial values as well as personal ones. Individuals who can regenerate a current value system or who can transform an outworn one into something appropriate for the emerging future may preclude the financial crisis in the offing. Most clients will have the breakdown before the breakthrough, lose nearly everything before gaining it back. The new sense of values (and a shift in the importance of money as a means) leads to a new orientation toward earning a living and often to a new livelihood.

♇ – ♂   A Pluto-driven Mars is relentless in the pursuit of aims, goals, ambitions, accomplishment, domination and revenge. Although the latter pair may surface only in hard aspects or aspects to a natally harsh Mars. Clients with transiting Pluto in aspect to natal Mars tolerate no opposition and will bulldoze or outrun competitors with a determined drive to win and a commitment to conquer. Clients feel unstoppable and are reluctant to apply the brakes to the energy within themselves. While there is a danger of foolhardy recklessness ("Damn the torpedoes, full speed ahead!") or rash vindictiveness ("Patience my ass, I'm gonna kill!"), if the energy can be constructively channeled there is nothing the client cannot surmount or accomplish. Look for Saturn contacts to gauge the ability to manage or stabilize this transit, and to Mars (or Uranus) to aggravate it.

♇ – ♃ Pluto-Jupiter uncorks the bottle to release the *jinn* within, or so it appears. The unprepared client may not know what to do with the sudden surplus of opportunity, and the cocky one may not take the time to consider which three wishes to make (beyond sex and money, of course). The right choices can make one's life permanently better in ways that involve profound change; grand possibilities become realities. A choice that merely burns the candle at both ends still makes a lovely light. Clients with this transiting aspect come with magic. They can create wisely, or carelessly, like the Sorcerer's Apprentice.

♇ – ♄ Pluto-Saturn aspects generate a serious commitment to success that manifests as a period of extreme overwork. The drive to accomplish becomes obsessive and clients may work themselves into an early grave and are worried that they are doing so. Frustration (from dealing with major obstacles) or resignation (from past failures) or fear (from a sense of inadequacy) may suck the client into a pool of depression and despair if the aspect is hard, if natal Saturn is harsh, or if transiting Saturn is making difficult contacts. Success, and the reputation may be destroyed, the position lost, and the career ended. Productivity protects the client from the downside of this transit.

The empowering option here within the workplace and career arena is to transform the burdensome senses of duty, obligation, and blame into a refined sense of responsibility: the power, right, and willingness to respond effectively. A powerful, purpose-driven, commitment to mastery can lead to great success, fame and fortune for a client in this sign.

♇ – ♅   Pluto-Uranus aspects explode the life into every direction. They uproot clients from their past, disrupt their present, and
isolate them from their current sense of the future. Habitual patterns
of living are blown away and life will never, ever, be the same again.
Self-determinism, independence, and volition erupt in importance,
while obstinacy and rebelliousness follow in their wake. A re-
newed, conscious commitment to freshly invented aspirations takes
control of the life. Even when neither transiting Pluto nor natal Uranus is in the 2nd, 6th, or 10th, the extreme restlessness and divine
dissatisfaction may drive clients into a new career. Their ornery attitude may force someone to fire them.

♇ – ♆   Pluto-Neptune is an age-related transiting contact for
people born with this natal aspect. It occurs currently at intervals of
approximately 12-16 years beginning with teen disillusionment
(Santa Claus, the Easter Bunny, and the Tooth Fairy go down in a
plane crash, and the music dies, along with the first love that was
supposed to be eternal). The dreams that die at 28-30 are often
blamed on the popularly recognized first Saturn return, but Pluto-
Neptune contacts are commonly the real culprit. This painful loss of
a vision often leads to abandoning the chosen career, the mate, or
the faith of one's parents. The fairy tales that people tell themselves,
or tell about themselves, no longer hold water, and the mist that
hides reality evaporates. "The truth will set ye free," but almost no
one seems to recognize the benefit of being fogless until the aspect
moves out of orb. A stiff dose of reality prevents many detours now
and disappointments later.

♇ – ♇   Pluto-Pluto, like all aspects of any transiting planet to itself, is age-related, but the ages vary by generation since Pluto
speeds up and slows down erratically. (Early Pluto-in-Cancer clients, now trined in their 80s, had the square in their 60s. Pluto in Leo
clients will get squared in their 30s and 40s and may live to be opposed by Pluto in their 80s. Virgo Pluto clients also get 30s-to-40s
squares). Pluto-Pluto stuffs the life full of crises, usually concen-
trated in Pluto's natal (and solar) house(s), or running from the tran-

sited house to the natal one. The crises lead to metamorphosis; yet while not every caterpillar becomes a butterfly, everyone feels "bent out of shape" under this transit. If this one doesn't "wipe out" or hobble clients, or their career, they will be reborn full of personal power, with an invigorated sense of purpose and a determined commitment to impact the world.

NEPTUNE
The Spirit of Inspiration, the Illusion of Deception

Neptune takes 168 years to orbit the Sun, so in 84 years it can transit six natal (and solar) houses. Its regular speed of 14 years per sign takes it through a house (on average) in the same time period and brings it back into aspect to each natal planet at regular 14-year intervals. Its two-degree per year rate of net motion makes its aspects last two years from start to finish, but the gross motion and annual retrograde period leave aspects in orb for only 18 months. Neptune will always hit each planet three times during its pass, and will only rarely make five hits to some of them.

Neptune operates over a wider range than most transiting planets. At its best, it is inspiration and illumination; at its worst it is paranoia, dissolution, and victimization. Most people experience it somewhere in the middle: uncertainty and confusion; gullibility and naivete; vagueness and fantasy, with some people elevating it to intuition, faith, and imagination. Neptune operates on the deepest currents of the consciousness, but as its waves reach the shores of awareness it may sweep away the unwary with high tides of fear and dangerous undertows of deceit. Those who tune in to the real Soul-music can swim with the dolphins and sing with the whales, bringing in bushels of fish to feed the multitudes. A rare few who play the music will teach others to fish. Only its elevated expression will have a material benefit, or a spiritual one for that matter.

Neptune transiting the 1st House softens the self-expression and makes a person mellow. It makes a person vulnerable to rumors, gossip, and false accusations. People with this transit become targets for projection, ungrounded assessments and, occasionally, character assassination. Clients need to explain themselves and make clear declarations about who they are and what they are about, especially in relation to their job or company.

Neptune flowing through the 2nd House may bring income from services and contributions, or inspiration and imagination. It's a good time to work in medicine, music, or metaphysics, if you can live with the economic uncertainty. Uncomplaining poverty in service of a good cause may improve your karmic account balance, but it won't do much for your credit rating (which decreases in importance). Clients should be cautioned to be wary of swindles and schemes during this pass (most notably during aspects to Venus, the Moon, or to 2nd and 5th House planets).

Neptune's emergence in the 3rd House suggests that heightened imagination and inspirational speech may be either aimless or truly motivational (and thereby profitable).

Neptune in the aimless wandering of the 4th House might move someone to the ideal environment with perfect work possibilities or send them drifting after a dream; a "Bali Hai" with neither toil nor timetables.

Neptune in the 5th House brings psychic or spiritual recreations which may become a profitable hobby. Inspired creativity may be sale-able. Faith and gullibility bring loss in speculative investments.

Neptune transiting the 6th House produces more creativity on the job since inspiration and intuition seem to flow into practical channels. Clients may psychically sense or naturally know what needs to be done and how to get it done. Jobs that require, draw on, and reward imagination or service are appropriate: film, video, theater, and the arts, graphics, design, and printing, music and medicine, etc. Many people will be uncertain (or totally at a loss) as to what to do. They and others will drift into and out of different jobs and fields; often taking employment simply because it was offered, or because someone needed them. Clients hope to contribute but may get hung out to dry. They need to be careful to avoid jobs involving deception, and be wary of deception about job security and conditions, wages and benefits, duties and responsibilities. Accessing the deeper wellsprings of intuition can raise a bucket of inspiration and insight into what work produces the satisfaction that comes from doing the right thing, from doing good works.

Neptune transiting the 7th House represents a danger of crooked or incompetent partners and contracts made with smoke and mirrors.

Neptune through the 8th House can present illusory loans or settlements and deception in inheritance.

Neptune in the 9th House dissolves fixed formulas for life and opens the client to acceptance and inspiration.

Neptune transiting the professional 10th House produces "careers" rather than merely jobs or employment, in fields of inspiring images: film, video and theater, the arts, music and dance, graphics, design and printing. Careers in medicine, the ministry, or metaphysics become attractive and available. People wish to "make a contribution" through their accomplishments, and often enter one of the helping professions or a service industry. Manufacturing and mercantile careers seem a waste, except when medicine or chemicals, or an oceanic or maritime element is present. Anything will do as long as the client considers it a contribution. Many people have difficulty finding a place for themselves and they wander from one career to another, looking for a calling. It's the inner voice that calls; those who listen inwardly get the message and can massage it into a medium for successful service.

Neptune wafting through the 11th House is will-o'-the-wisp wishes, disappearing friends. Alternately, it is supportive friends, aspirations for service.

Neptune transiting the 12th House melts reality with a psychic overload or turns on a shining inner light to guide the life.

Aspects of Neptune

♆ – ☉ Neptune-Sun aspects confuse the hell out of people! They forget who they are or who they said they were or were going to be. As the fixed identity dissolves, so does the resolve, and people become more impressionable, even gullible. As the aspect builds, the buzzing in the back of the brain (like a radio at low volume, off station) distracts the person from the now-here and takes them nowhere. Most jobs and many careers can survive this out-to-lunch period—if it isn't a long lunch. Tuning into the sub-conscious broadcast, turning up the psychic volume, getting the mystical message, allows people to manage or moderate the spacey impulses, stay on the planet, and *in the job*.

♆ – ☽ Neptune-Moon aspects open the flood-gates of the subconscious. If there are irrigation channels to direct the energy into fertile areas, the person won't feel inundated or washed away in wonder (or woe). Uncertainty, indefiniteness, vacuousness, forgetfulness and "Huh?" result otherwise. Some who are lost find themselves in the fog and return to reality "enlightened." Love of a spiritual nature is available, but that may only be the costume the con-artist wears to guide the gullible to the milking machine.

♆ – ☿ Neptune-Mercury aspects stimulate creativity, imagination, lies and deception. People paint verbal pictures with poetic speech and gloss over disturbing details, air-brushing reality. Inspired art, gripping graphics, precious prose, and moving orations may result. Those who kid themselves can be conned by others. Hard aspects to or from the 2nd House (or 5th) often indicate swindles.

♆ – ♀ A Neptune-Venus aspect makes a person more accepting, trusting and gullible. It does *not* make others more trustworthy, in spite of the client thinking so. Deceptions focus on love or money and frequently both: the pretense of one for the other. Alternately, employment and income from music, the arts, and cinema (but be wary of the casting couch) are possible.

♆ – ♂ Neptune-Mars aspects generate a charismatic glamour, a magical quality, a mystical element within the self-expression that turns the client into a Pied Piper or a prophet able to lead others, like children, from or to the promised land! Unfocused energy and activity may be dissipated or dispersed wildly. Fine tuning and focusing produce inspired action and effective service (without detrimental sacrifice).

♆ – ♃ Neptune-Jupiter aspects produce prophetic insight, crystal clarity, and complete understanding of a kind that may be applicable on the job and invaluable in business. Harsh contacts sometime produce deception involving books, education, or theater. Milder hits bring metaphysical studies at a profit.

♆ – ♄ Neptune-Saturn aspects may dissolve the ambition into a puddle of apathy and wash the career down the drain when these aspects are hard hits to harsh placements or tenuous positions in the natal horoscope. Illusions about authority and success lead to unrealistic careers and delusions of attainment. If natal Neptune is well-integrated, and natal Saturn is not too difficult, Neptune's transit of Saturn may bring the imagination down to earth, focusing and manifesting the vision, as a means of accomplishing goals. Inspiration about career choice and professional direction is possible, but should be carefully checked against the facts and kept in line with what can actually be created. Careers that draw on the high levels of Neptune manifest well at this time.

♆ – ♅ Neptune-Uranus contacts spark creativity and spatter it wildly, like water (or paint) dripping onto an exposed electrode. Realizable visions of the future alternate with fantastic fantasies of surrogate realities.

♆ – ♆ Neptune-Neptune aspects are age-related, returning at every multiple of 14 years of age. They bring a psychic sensitivity that reads the world with depth-radar and people with a motive-analyzing CATSCAN. Spiritual insights and enlightening experiences occur in response to smooth aspects. In harsh contacts, the signal-to-noise ratio distorts the message toward indecipherability or into purely internal, imaginary events.

♆ – ♇ Neptune-Pluto aspects bring disturbing dreams of or about, death, as subjective and subconscious fears; the flotsam and jetsam of the mind drift to the surface. The dream deaths may look physical and signal danger, or be psychic precursors to catalytic breakthroughs. The potential for insight into purpose may inspire a new commitment, and a new career.

URANUS
Individual Futures, Ideals, and Shocking Possibilities

Uranus makes a complete circuit of the Zodiac, and a chart, in 84 years, searing through a sign (or the average house) in seven years, re-aspecting natal planets (in Transit Comb order) with the seven-year itch for change. Most natal planets will get zapped three times during a period of contact that lasts from nine to eleven months out of a year and a half. Uranus moves eight degrees ahead, its five-month annual retrograde cancels half of that, which it regains on the re-direct, and a net motion of four degrees per year results.

Uranus is the shocking bolt of independence, idealism, and rebellion against the ordinary, the everyday, and the mediocre. Its house transits spark a period of experimentation in search of viable new possibilities, of an ideal for the individual or (just maybe) one for humanity. Its aspects shock natal planets into new, different, and better expressions, except when they produce startling, freakish, and bizarre occurrences.

Uranus disrupts, alters, invents or re-invents, shatters and scatters; it does the unexpected, when you least expect it to, or when you need it the most!

Uranus transiting the 1st House alters the self-expression away from the ordinary through the modern and the avant garde into the free-spirited fringes of eclectic eccentricity and individual aberration. Capricious choices and arbitrary decisions about dress, hair, and behavior may startle others out of their complacency or merely isolate the client in an individualist's world. The disruptive consequences of insistence ricochet from relationship to career, from residence to employment.

Uranus striking the 2nd House sends shock waves through the client's financial structure that reverberate through their value system. People reassess their resources and reconsider *what they are willing to do for money*. Money is made from culturally unusual sources or earned in personally atypical ways. Sudden financial windfalls may allow clients to capitalize a successful self-employment enterprise and earn a living on their own recognizance. Independence and ingeniousness are rewarded as income comes from inventions, innovations, and insight into the human condition. An obstinate refusal to follow the norm may ruin profits or make a fortune.

Uranus ricocheting through the 3rd House triggers writing brilliance and jobs in writing that start and stop suddenly; perhaps as a free-lance professional or an independent reporter. Incredible ideas translate into credits on the ledger (especially if Uranus returns to the 2nd House or other aspects add a financial focus to the flash).

Uranus transiting the 4th House: family feuds lead the client away to exotic destinations. A break from tradition may disclose previously unconsidered occupations.

Uranus transiting the 5th House: new pleasures, hobbies, and odd tinkerings may lead to or become new employment as the transit ends.

Uranus transits ignite the 6th House, firing people up to do unusual work, taking advantage of unique and remarkable skills or experience. Sometimes it's just being fed up that triggers the change: a rejection of being told what's what for the right to say what's so. Self-employment signals freedom here, counseling and consulting call for abdication from the corporation. Usually routine and regimentation are repugnant, but occasionally people have had enough of the sacrifices for self-sufficiency and want something completely different for themselves: regularity and security. Jobs start, stop, and step sideways as if Simon doesn't say "Simon says."

Uranus transits in the 7th House jolt relationships out of complacency as the (business?) contract is re-written for the individuals involved, or one finds strange and changeable partners and surprise endings.

Uranus plugging into the 8th House sends a surge of electricity through the pleasure centers, burning out old zones and activating new ones, triggering a taste for the strange and a willingness to try things on for size. There could be odd sources of capital and, rarely, unexpected inheritance.

Uranus transiting the 9th House digs a new reality, strip-mining the belief systems and excavating ancient or futuristic codes of individualism. An eclectic collection of fragments from a variety of philosophies is woven into a tapestry of personal truth.

Uranus, shaking up the 10th House, cracks the foundation of success, tumbling the conventional through strange, even bizarre, circumstances or provoking resistance to the insistence of conformity. New careers sprout through the cracks and clients reach for the stars. Some become rising stars themselves while others bet on the permanence of shooting ones. Remarkable recognition flip-flops with success missed by the skin-of-the-teeth, and unexpected breaks that go the client's way alternate with ones that take them away from the rewards. New careers and strange fields of endeavor beckon. Clients see the way to design their own career, own their own business, and do their own thing while winning votes of approval, shareholders, and customers.

Uranus moving through the 11th House swings the aspirations

in unusual directions, bringing odd hopes and aims to straight-arrows, and occasionally a standard path to oddballs. Surprises bring accomplishment to aspirations and "disappear" friends, who are replaced by strangers.

Uranus transiting the 12th House ignites a psychic revolution, extraordinary sensory perception, weird spiritual concepts, and different means of service. "Instant Karma" zaps clients who break their own code.

Aspects of Uranus

♅ – ☉   Uranus-Sun aspects peel back the layers of social conditioning, revealing the self initially intended and finally attained. Clients trade appropriateness for authenticity, conformity for independence, cooperativeness for obstinacy, and society's thing for their own.

♅ – ☽   Uranus-Moon aspects may eclipse emotional connections, reject dependency, and sever relationships as the emotional responses and needs change suddenly. Bondings are as quick and strong as "Crazy Glue."

♅ – ☿   Uranus-Mercury aspects accelerate the bio-computer's main processor and add a math chip or language card as the mind goes turbo. Altered opinions, off-the-wall ideas, and brilliant cognitions may result in inventions and new ventures. Harsh aspects are hard to direct or contain, and ideas get displaced; smooth ones bring media interest.

♅ – ♀   Uranus-Venus aspects generate a synergy between changing values and financial changes. People rebel against an old system and choose new sources of income. Old loves are traded for new ones, often from love at first sight!

♅ – ♂   Uranus-Mars aspects strike the chimes of freedom and call clients to "man the barricades," to fight City Hall...or City Corp.! There is surprising victory against all odds, if they don't try to do it all alone. Organizing, rabble-rousing, or cantankerous rebellion may lead to "You can't fire me; I quit!" Atypical behavior and change in style may initiate new job ventures.

⛢ – ♃ Uranus-Jupiter aspects deal the client four aces (or three and a wild card) or the luck to fill an inside straight. Other unexpected benefits surprise with prizes, odd possibilities, or inexplicable windfalls. Accidents and potential crises prove *beneficial* while prosperity or opportunity comes from unusual sources.

⛢ – ♄ Uranus-Saturn aspects insist on career changes: altered attitudes, different directions, brand new bailiwicks; new insights into distinctions between authority and responsibility, burden and duty, guilt, blame, and responsibility. Structures that hold the life together, or the client in place, break up to be rebuilt realistically.

⛢ – ⛢ Uranus-Uranus aspects itch where the client can't scratch without disrupting the life! Changes in aspirations or in the rate of change bring restlessness (and resentment), a re-ordering of priorities or rebellion; obstinate insistence on ideals, especially independence and self-determinism. Under these transits, clients can create a new future for themselves through following a vision of tomorrows.

⛢ – ♆ Uranus-Neptune aspects release the hopes and dreams from the confines of conventional reality. Mental adventures and speculations coincide with changes in belief away from the norm.

⛢ – ♇ Uranus-Pluto aspects ricochet clients through an intersection and around a corner into a new sense of purpose, a new direction for their life. Here is where two paths diverge, and people need to consciously choose a course to follow and a commitment of consequence (or face the consequences!). Harsh aspects throw people up against the wall to wake them up; smooth ones only turn everything upside down. The alert, who jump at the chance to be committed, only get nudged into action.

SATURN
Responsibility to Re-evaluate, Manifest, and Succeed

Saturn marches through the zodiac in 29.5 years. While it almost always spends two and one-half years in each sign, Solar house, or (the average) natal house, it will usually take three years to pass through that chart sector as retrogrades take it across either the leading or trailing cusp. Saturn arrives at a net yearly motion of 10 degrees by moving ahead 18 degrees and retrograding eight degrees (in 4.5 months) each year. Saturn re-applies itself to each natal planet about every three years (hitting one or three times). Single hits on a direct pass last about one month. But, Saturn is in orb to planets trapped in its retrograde triple-whammy for five or six full months—out of a period that will take 10 months to conclude.

Saturn periods feel like climbing uphill on tricky, twisted trails; exhilarating, if you're prepared and conditioned for them; a nerve-racking struggle ("watch your step, it's a long rocky way down") if you're not; or like slogging through the muddy bottom of a slimy swamp ("if the 'gators don't getcha' the sinkholes will"), if you're not effective or are running from responsibility. Its aspects restrain or restrict the expression of contacted planets which manifest excellently when they are managed responsibly, but are otherwise stifled.

Saturn's house transits insist on the re-evaluation of what is being done, and what has been done, to prepare for what will be done. Saturn often plays "take away" (it lessens), or delays to teach lessons of importance. Saturn typically manifests initially from its down-side (delay, lack, and struggle) when it first enters a house. Responsible re-evaluation and application raise its level of expression through management to success and (rarely) even mastery.

Saturn also moves through the quadrants of a horoscope in three interlaced cycles that are the measure of progress in the Survival Career, the Glory Career, and the Duty Career.

The Survival Career is the mundane, make a living, material management, application of responsibility which is undertaken to produce tangible results, security, and stability.

The Glory Career is the path of self-management in pursuit of a respectable goal that reflects self-improvement and worthiness in the magnifying mirror of personal and social approval, prestige, and position.

The Duty Career is a course of dedicated action and endeavor to establish or accomplish, requiring perseverance and endurance, all recognized as being necessary and one's own obligation, responsibility, even privilege or right.

The Saturn quadrants are measured from the Ascendant, the Sun, and Saturn itself, to lower (opening) square to each of them, from lower square to opposition, from there to upper (closing) square, and back to conjunction with the Ascendant, with the Sun, and with Saturn's position.

Saturn runs people through all three Career Cycles simultaneously: withdrawing, empowering, elevating, then leveling different careers, or different facets of the same career. As examples: astrology is often the Glory Career for people whose Survival Career is in business or commerce, and whose Duty Career is elsewhere, perhaps their family or volunteer work. An astrologer might have a Survival Career as a counselor, a Glory Career as a lecturer (or writer), and a Duty Career as a writer (or as an officer in an organization).

Glory and Duty Careers also produce income and tangible rewards (as the Survival Career also produces intangible benefits), and a great deal can be accomplished by judiciously shifting the emphasis of one's endeavors from a sliding career into a rising one. Catch the wave that is cresting and ride it for all it is worth, then change waves to continue advancing. Watch out for Peter Principle pitfalls (rising beyond the level of competence) and don't beat the dead horse that used to carry you in the direction you were going. Continued success depends on changing horses in mid-stream, at the right point in The Time Stream.

Which career matches each of these career types for a particular individual can only be determined by the client in careful consultation with the astrologer. But, as a guideline, the Survival career is found in the natal chart often through the 10th House (signs and planets, if any) and the house placements of the Sun and Saturn. The solar chart's Glory Career, for example, frequently reflects the Sun Sign, solar 10th House and Saturn's solar house position. Saturn, by sign, natal and solar house, and aspects can be the key to discovering the Duty Career. Pluto, where it is prominent, should also be examined, as well as the other modern descriptors of career selection and success.

Saturn's three cycles through the quadrants coincide and coexist with its transits through the individual Houses that comprise the quadrants and the whole.

The first transit quarter lands "heads you lose, tails they win" and begins obscurity in the world unless the client designs a strategic withdrawal into self-improvement through self examination, re-organization, and re-education. The time is ripe to shift emphasis to a rising Saturn cycle, if one is available.

Saturn transiting the 1st House begins with a mudpie in the face, raising doubts about appearance, image, and response from others. It forces people to withdraw or to get their act together. Verifying, and repairing or accepting, actual short-comings and dismissing erroneous assessments clear the desks for action. Practicality arises out of dissatisfaction, and maturity may result in a more professional presentation. Appropriate polish is profitable, while other tactics are developed to further job strategies.

Saturn over the cusp of the 2nd House overdraws a person's bank account and signals continuing financial trouble for most people. Cashflow slows to a day late and, if not a dollar short, then certainly to no spare change. New principles and practices, and sources seriously designed to prevent problems, may produce plenty, for some. *Restructure values to increase resources.*

Saturn moving through the 3rd House produces pessimism and slows down the mind enough to re-examine old decisions and to distill truth out of "common sense." Clients should study seriously to acquire a sound basis for future success. They need to learn about their field and about how to plow their way to the top of it.

Obscurity ends as Saturn reaches the lower square and "turns the corner": people recognize an even-money chance of "making it," and begin building recognition through diligent application and discipline.

Saturn entering the 4th House may force people out of their homes, into a smaller (restrictive) unit, or to their parents' home where issues of rules, duty and allegiance arise. Bring work home to get ahead, or start a home office to build a business. There is no way to go but up. Start fresh now!

Saturn transiting the 5th House takes the fun out of life as career concerns conflict with romance, people lose lovers and drop old recreations. Recess is a necessary nutrient for productivity; schedule some fun. Seriousness about an avocation may start the process of building it into an occupation.

Saturn working its way through the 6th House may make a person ill from stress or from long hours. Don't burn out; healthiness is next to business, as necessary for work as skill is. This is shoulder-to-the-grindstone time, accompanied by feeling overworked, underpaid and (as yet) unappreciated. Clients may hold down a (second) job while building up a career, or getting trained for one.

As Saturn turns into the third quarter, struggles begin to turn into triumphs. It's "heads you win, tails nobody loses." Clients can often see the attainable crest ahead of them, and yet be concerned about walking the path to it.

Saturn crossing into the 7th House makes the partner cross, and the relationship a cross to bear. Marriage (business partnership) and career conflicts force re-evaluation of both and may produce more integrity in agreements, and, sometimes, a solid partner(ship). Caution clients not to make promises that won't be kept; Saturn brings consequences.

Saturn's grinding through the 8th House may dry up sexual interest, energy and/or opportunity. The frustration may come from duty, be raised to self-control, and translated into work. There may be delayed inheritance or settlement, difficulties raising capital. Breakdowns are opportunities for breakthroughs in self-management and development of personal power.

Saturn's passage through the 9th House demands re-looking at basic concepts, contexts, and considered opinions. A more pragmatic philosophy develops and may lead to (or come from) education for advancement, if obligations don't interfere. There is dull, duty-oriented travel, which may bring attention, and even (practical) wisdom. Demonstrate judgment to achieve recognition and success.

Saturn's attainment of the upper square signals a peak at which time clients may build a base camp to provide security, stability, and shelter from the elements, making consolidation and later advancement possible. Otherwise, they may take one step beyond and fall off the landing. Prepare wisely for maintenance and coasting.

Saturn's entrance into the 10th House introduces clients to the center of attention and makes the career the near-total focus of their attention; absorbed by attainment, the pursuit of acknowledgment, the use of authority, and perhaps the display of status. Accelerated success may push people to reach for a bridge too far. Clients at this critical time should concentrate on dynamic consolidation, carefully building a permanent foundation. It's not how high you get, it's how long you stay at the top.

Saturn drops into the 11th House and people drop associates for proven friends, but may join professional societies for contacts. Dropping blue-sky aspirations, re-ordering priorities, putting hopes on the back burner, and intending to manifest goals allow people to get what they really want.

Saturn slides into the 12th House, not with a bang, but with a whimper. People get hurt where it hurts the most, personally and professionally, if they don't let their conscience be their guide. Dismissing—or succumbing to—the former deeply-buried doubts that surface now are dangerous; they need to be faced and dealt with. Being true to one's own code, in spite of others, provides the best protection, when it's a viable, current code. Those who haven't sought and found how to serve will suffer. Those who have will survive. Clients who learn the lesson before the test do best.

The cycle continues as Saturn re-enters the first quadrant.

Aspects of Saturn

♄ – ☉ Saturn-Sun aspects drag people into the murky world of their self-doubts, with low or no vitality, where options appear to be slim or none. A serious decision to proceed anyway ("just do it!"), leads to developing perseverance and practicality, responsibility and productivity. Remember, aspects to the Sun begin important passages as transiting Saturn changes Solar Houses, interpreting them also. The conjunction, both squares, and the opposition are turning points in the Glory Career, described earlier.

♄ – ☽ Saturn-Moon aspects are a cold front moving in on the emotions, stormy weather in relationships, and potential separations. They can indicate getting serious about what is needed and wanted, and clients being realistic enough to realize they can—and must—do something about it. Diligent doing is "Drano" for depression. As always, the degree of severity depends on the birth chart's components as well as which transiting aspect is being formed.

♄ – ☿ Saturn-Mercury aspects make people worry, whether or not there is anything worth worrying about. Harsh cynicism and hard words surface in the harsh transit contacts; pessimism and sarcasm under medium conditions; and practical, organized thinking in mild cases. Clients should take worry as a warning and prepare plans for the probabilities, *i.e.*, if problem #1 happens, insert plan "A"; if #2 then "B." People have problems so they can find solutions. If you have the solution it's "no problem" if the problem occurs. *Since the problem serves no purpose, it may not appear.*

♄ – ♀   Saturn-Venus aspects chill the affections (but they may feel like the slow boil of simmering resentment) and can freeze the financial pipeline. Establishing budget criteria, prioritizing purchases, and scheduling expenditures can soften the transit. Work done now, as well as necessary investments (tools, training, inventory, advertising) can pay big dividends *later*.

♄ – ♂   Saturn-Mars aspects drain your tank of energy and repossess your ability to do anything with what you've got in reserve. The "Blahs." An acute case of "I don' wanna" produces depression if clients succumb to it. The first step is the hardest, and people who manage to get started *can* produce. They may be tired afterwards (they'd also be tired from doing nothing) but at least they got something done!

♄ – ♃   Saturn-Jupiter aspects force-feed difficult decisions in what initially looks like a "can't win for losing" situation. There are conflicts between what duty demands and what principle prescribes, sometimes between the demands of success and the freedom to do as one pleases. Hard hits suspend people between the devil and the deep blue sea where the lesser of two evils matters most. The zen possibility is a way out: when faced with two unacceptable alternatives, one must select a third.

♄ – ♄   Saturn-Saturn aspects produce career anxiety, fear that the mountain can't be climbed before the sunset years. Struggling against obstacles and delays, going as fast as one can to stay in one place. Clients need to deliberate on career objectives and strategies. Career anxiety is a pain for gain or challenge-versus-ability conundrum. Redefining the nature of responsibility and the limit or extent of one's responsibilities—owning up to what can and cannot be done—will turn this trying time to the person's long-term advantage.

Saturn's conjunction, both squares, and its opposition to its natal position are turning points in the Duty Career, described earlier.

♄ – ♅ Saturn-Uranus aspects denigrate many aspirations, some of which are discarded; they delay others which can be dealt with later; and they draft the best of the winnowed wishes for manifestation, as re-examined preferences and priorities re-design the future. Ideals may be curtailed or refined because, as they are at the moment, they interfere with progress. Clients can hock their high hopes (even the heirlooms of their future) for more immediate gratification.

♄ – ♆ Saturn-Neptune aspects drain the color out of hope's rainbow and short-out circuits in the psychic radar. People do dumb things, like giving up, or they stand up just before the "it" hits the fan. Getting the imagination's image in clear focus and concentrating on manifesting previous hopes, dreams, and visions (rather than trying to dream new dreams) directs the vision to a safe landing in reality. Practical visions can guide clients to the payoff at the end of ambition's rainbow.

♄ – ♇ Saturn-Pluto aspects put life on trial. The course and direction of the client's life are accused of being invalid and the existence of a personal purpose is cross-examined. If the conclusion is negative (and the guilty client is hopeless), serious depression results. A course-correction based on a review of intentions and accomplishments, and a re-dedication to the life purpose (with a commitment to fulfill it) produces a period of constructive over-work and concomitant rewards.

JUPITER
Opportunity for Freedom, Enhancement, and Waste

Jupiter bounds around the zodiac at a-sign-a-year pace and stays one year in each solar (or average) natal house. Its house passage may be broken into two or even three time segments if Jupiter's annual retrogrades drag it across both cusps. The total time allotted for enhancing the affairs of each house is the same, but people sometimes get it all together, and at other times some extra assembly is required. Jupiter will usually contact every natal planet each year and will tap some of them three times. Its aspects normally last for about three weeks, but if they occur around the stations (as it slows while turning retrograde and direct) they can last for four months!

Jupiter is the "Great (but over-rated) Benefic," the Wizard of Oz of the zodiac who never gave the Tin Man (or another client) anything he didn't already have. Jupiter transits bring opportunity. Opportunity knocks. *Period*. And that's all it does. It doesn't open the door, come in after the client, and carry them to the land of milk and honey. Yet, Jupiter does offer the opportunity to elevate the level of manifestation of each house and to enhance the expression of each transited planet.

It is empowering to show clients that they have to do something to get (the best of) what Jupiter has to offer. When the wind blows, it will move the ship even if one is asleep; but if you want to get anywhere you have to raise and set the sails. Clients won't get the benefits available if they don't answer the knock on the door, respond to the ad, return the phone call, actually mail the letter, or trim the mizzen. Like Oz, Jupiter allows people to see what's so, to recognize that they do have what it takes, or that they can get it (with less effort or more payoff than they assumed). Jupiter introduces an honest optimism, a clearer perception and more complete understanding. Jupiter allows freedom *to*, freedom *within*, and freedom *from*. When clients take the chance and bet on themselves, Jupiter pays off with enough, more, and too much; with good, better, and wow!

Jupiter crossing into the 1st House brings an increase in confidence, self-expression, enthusiasm, and light-hearted playfulness. Enhancement follows the increase. Most people give themselves more permission to be themselves, and to do whatever they choose. They take center stage and show off their best qualities, along with some of the others. If this pleased-with-one's-self attitude doesn't get obnoxious, they get a more positive response and better feedback, winning the support of others, especially in jobs where enthusiasm pays off. If they can maintain a modicum of decorum, this is an excellent time to apply for a job position or request a promotion.

Jupiter passing through the 2nd House is when the client's ship can come in ... providing that they sent it out. Otherwise, one of the best opportunities for riches will pass in the night. Several excellent opportunities for new income sources appear during this transit. While it might be possible to take all of them and make most of them pay off, most people should be wisely selective. It's okay to say "no" to Jupiter, since it often presents enchanting opportunities that turn out to be wild goose chases, or temptations that distract from something with better potential. Clients should be advised to search for what they really want—this is no time to settle for second best. Ask for a raise, a transfer, a promotion, or open a business. This is a likely time for more money, but it is also one for *better* money; income from a better source, from what the client wants to be paid for being or doing, by whatever criteria they apply.

Jupiter moving through the 3rd House is prime time for enhancing education and communication skills. For many people, this will directly or indirectly enhance their job and income potential. It is a great time to take a position that involves teaching, sales, travel, or in these technological times, telecommunications or telemarketing, information networks and Bulletin Board Services.

Jupiter transiting the 4th House is a great time to move to a better location, which may mean to a city with a better job market or just a better neighborhood.

A 5th House transit of Jupiter is so much fun the client won't be much concerned with material matters. Jobs in entertainment may appear and the enhanced creativity that surfaces may be applicable to the job. But don't count on it happening that way without conscious intention and active direction.

Jupiter transiting the 6th House brings an increase in the amount of work that needs to be done, along with an increased ability to get the job done. Confucius really did say "He that would improve his work must first sharpen his tools." There is no better time to do both than with Jupiter in the 6th. While some improvement will occur spontaneously, clients who seek training or find a good coach will make the most of this transit. Clients can find great jobs, more compatible co-workers, a better work environment, or they may be able to create the same enhanced conditions in their present employment. Don't settle for work that doesn't work. Discover excellence.

Jupiter moving into the 7th House brings a more supportive mate or business partner, and better relationships, all around. Professionally, it is an excellent time to add a partner or to join a partnership. It is also a good time to buy out a partner, or leave one to set up a private practice (especially if Jupiter will return to the 6th).

Jupiter's 8th House transit, for most people, most of the time, expresses as increased sexual energy, opportunity, activity, variety, and pleasure. It also produces a greater understanding of sexuality, tolerance for preferences, and a release of inhibitions. While there are some professions that would benefit directly from this, most people will merely enjoy it (and perhaps translate being energized into being productive). A few times in life, at most, it may manifest as an inheritance, an insurance settlement, or a litigation victory which enriches and empowers the person to pursue or develop business interests. More often it indicates the infusion of outside capital (from loans, grants, shares, etc.), into the client's enterprise.

Jupiter transiting the 9th House ought to send clients to school, weekend workshops, the library, or bookstores to acquire the knowledge they will need to meet the career challenges and opportunities they discover when Jupiter enters the 10th.

Many people will travel (which may have career benefits), begin lecturing, teaching, lead workshops, or train others (which prepares the context or lays the groundwork for advancement or independence).

Jupiter in the 10th House is your clients' best opportunity for promotion, recognition, awards and honors. It may produce sincere acknowledgment and approval; it may put them in the spotlight or make them (semi-)famous. It produces the kind of popular positive acclaim that gets politicians elected (or appointed), and regular people promoted into better and better-paying positions.

However, it may promote without providing—without increasing their income or ability to accomplish. It's more likely to yield one-time awards and bonuses than raises. A 10th House transiting Jupiter is an excellent time for people to enter the field they *really* want to be in, to apply for the position they aspire to, to boldly go into business for themselves. Some people will take this transit and thumb their nose at the boss, family, and society; they quit their job to enjoy freedom from career and responsibility. Ask them if there is some way to have their freedom and eat their success, too. There is.

Jupiter in the 11th House is a time for expanding aspirations while dreams are coming true. What the client wanted to realize or enable out of being successful often materializes. New societies open to the client and better associations become available. These may lead to business leads, contacts, and contracts. Improved relationships with colleagues and within working groups are available.

Jupiter transits of the 12th House, with their other-worldly enhancement of spirituality and increase in psychic ability, may seem unrelated (or antithetical) to material success. However, surveys demonstrate that the most successful executives are also the most intuitive. Hunches pay off, gut feelings guide accurately, and extra senses support effective action (in the Boardroom, the clerical pool, the grease pit, or the assembly line). Nothing that appears to be bad will be as bad as it appears, and the client is "providentially protected" from disaster. Now, since every cloud has a silver lining, one should look for the payoff within every price, the benefit in every setback.

Aspects of Jupiter

♃ – ☉ Jupiter-Sun aspects are periods of personal growth, expanding confidence, and positive outlook. Confidence, vitality, creativity, and luck combine synergistically to enrich each other and the client. Schedule important meetings, proposals, and requests for this beneficial period. Use the opportunity or lose it; even a deck stacked in your favor is useless if you don't play your cards right.

♃ – ☽ Jupiter-Moon aspects are good for publicity and public response that the client will find satisfying. They open the heart and fill it with warm fuzzies (rose light, peace and love ...). If the Moon or Cancer connects to House 2, 6, or 10, the joy is related to events in that house.

♃ – ☿ Jupiter-Mercury enhances the willingness to communicate and the ability to do so effectively, with stylish virtuosity, to accomplish the intended result. This great aspect for interviews, meetings, presentations, phone calling, corresponding and writing reports or proposals can be ineffectively expressed if the client, instead of establishing context, and creating clarity, falls into the Jupiterian traps of ostentatious erudition, pompous pontification, overly clever construction, glittering generalities, long-winded loquaciousness, repetitive redundancies, and run-on sentences, of which this is a deliberate, illustrative, example(!). Jupiter-Mercury also signals good news about, for, or to the client.

♃ - ♀ Jupiter-Venus contacts bring love, money, generosity, and joy. It's joyful to lavish gifts on someone you care for deeply and completely, but financial over-confidence may leave the client spent when the transit passes. Since the aspect brings appreciation of the client it signals a good time to request a raise. A dollar saved is a dollar earned, so bargains abound and items planned for future purchase go on sale, instigating splurge-to-save behavior.

♃ - ♂ Jupiter-Mars aspects energize people, and infuse them with the kind of positive enthusiasm that others enjoy being enveloped in. It's a great time to sell a product, a service, an idea, but most of all a relationship with the person carrying the aspect. It's time to DO something to make money; action and expression are what are profitable.

♃ - ♃ Jupiter-Jupiter contacts in a major transitory aspect bring opportunities for triumph, and chances for victory or a good score in medium or minor aspects. You only have to enter to win, but the grand prize is reserved for people who set important events for this period and bet on a positive outcome. The sky may rain dimes to dollars if this is a major aspect, especially if it connects to or from the 2nd House (and/or the 5th, 8th or 10th).

♃ - ♄ Jupiter-Saturn aspects place the client in a dilemma, and force a difficult choice. The choice of a material blessing at a spiritual cost is unwelcome, but so is "happy but broke." The stronger thrust, for most people, is to overwork, and they usually take the career opportunities out of an expanded sense of practicality or ambition, or from thinking that those will eventually buy happiness.

♃ - ♅ Jupiter-Uranus aspects bring sudden, unexpected good luck that comes like a bolt out of the blue in hard aspects and like a rainbow in a clear sky in soft ones. Surprise! You've won a prize! It's frequently an unexpected financial windfall. Hopes people forgot they had turn into dreams that come true, if they can drop their dance card and swing with the "Prince of Serendip."

Jupiter-Uranus aspects often spark an interest in astrology or other oddities that turn out to be beneficial.

♃ - ♆ Jupiter-Neptune aspects add experiential depth to spiritual perceptions. Enhanced intuition may assist judgment, but the soul benefits more than the ambitions or the income, unless one of these planets (or Pisces) is in (or on) the 10th, 6th, or 2nd.

♃ - ♇ Jupiter-Pluto aspects can trigger big, beneficial changes and important breakthroughs in major aspects. In hard aspects, they may be disguised (as a confrontation or a challenge), but time and perspective prove their positive worth. You've got to get into the cocoon to get the butterfly out of the caterpillar. Minor aspects nudge people through doorways into a roomful of friendly strangers. People are cocky and adventurous, but bold enough to pull it off, if they can keep a clear head. The almost certain sexual "busyness" may lead to a lack of sleep, exhaustion and reckless commitments.

SUMMARY

Interpretation of the transits should support prediction for strategy as well as for understanding. Astrologers can stun and amaze clients by accurately describing what's developing in the inner world of their thoughts, moods, and experience as well as what's happening in the outer world of interactions, circumstances, and endeavors. The astrologer can also intrigue clients by referring to future opportunities, challenges, and pitfalls. Astrologers can serve clients best by discussing possibilities through which the clients can maximize the values available through the transits active at the time or fast approaching.

Client goals are always success and satisfaction, no matter how idiosyncratically they are defined and measured. Clients want to thrive, not merely survive, even when resignation has overtaken them. Many will come to you in times of crisis, on the cusp of catastrophe, or on the brink of depression. Remember that human beings are remarkably resourceful and exceptionally resilient. *People just don't get problems they can't solve*, providing they are willing to do what it takes to implement the solutions that are available to them. And, they can recover from *anything*, given time, attention, and intention.

Some few will come to you at the beginning of an open road, looking for an owner's manual for their vehicle, a map of the future, and a personalized guidebook to the best sights and resorts (jobs and careers) along their route. Real astrology can assist them with all of that.

People come to an astrologer for wisdom and counsel, for timing and for tools. We need to know as much about life itself as we know about astrology. Discover and learn what works in life and share it with your clients. Perhaps it's communication and enrollment, requests and promises, negotiation and acceptance, responsibility and resourcefulness, declarations and commitment, self-expression and courage, response and nurturence, vitality and centeredness, openness and wonder, independence and assistance. There are effective ways to operate with *each* of the planets and with *all* of the transits.

In working with transits, remember that outer planets are more important than inner ones; they determine the long-term directions of the life; their transiting aspects occur from within longer and usually more potent house transit periods. Planets transiting natal or solar houses are effective even when they are *not* making aspects. It only takes one transit to instigate a process. Each transit occurs in the "life space" created by previous transits—and the decisions made under them—and sets the stage for those transits that will follow.

Transits are effective while within a two-degree orb, both applying and separating, not merely at the exact hit. There are always several concurrent transiting aspects within orb. Any, or all of them, may operate separately and distinctly from the others. Any aspect or position may combine with a variety of others to trigger complex circumstances.

Interpretations suggested by multiple transits are the ones most likely to manifest. While transits may influence each other, none can totally block the effect of another. Contrary transits will be experienced as contradictions in life. Life is usually more hectic or more exciting the more transiting aspects there are within orb.

The clearest way to understand the combination of stellar influences—the ebb and flow of simultaneous and sequential transits—is to graph them. A picture really is worth a thousand words, and a "map" is always clearer than "directions."

To attain maximum value and achieve optimum results in the workplace (and in life) I suggest going with the transit flow, *actively*. Don't merely float downstream, *swim* with the current. Don't just sit on the horse, *ride* it—in the direction life's going. Use the reins of reason and intuition, knowledge and desire, intention and action to steer a course that results in the exciting and satisfying life you love to live.

How to Evaluate Personnel for Profit

Noel Tyl

Personnel selection has become a people-science of the first order in the corporate world. Psycho-sensitive technologies and testing procedures are focused on discovering individual aptitudes and matching those strengths with specific job demands. More often than ever before, astrology is one of the tools being used to evaluate personnel for profit.

The objective is not only to get a *good* worker, one who fits in with the immediate work force of others and will identify personally with the job function, but as well to get a worker who will be "happy" on the job. Personnel directors in employment agencies and in corporations know that a "happy" employee will be a good employee. Business knows it is good business to help the employee fulfill personal needs through the job.

From the employee's perspective, how often does one hear, "Well, I was earning good money, but I just wasn't happy?" From the corporate perspective, how frequently do we hear, "Well, so-and-so just didn't fit in?"

To be helpful to personnel executives, the astrologer must translate astrology into personnel terms. Many times in my own counseling experience to personnel executives I have been impressed with how easy it is to share the potentials of astrology as an evaluation tool *when my presentation did not mention any astrological jargon*, when as much as I possibly could, I zeroed in on personnel concepts. Any reference to "magic mumbo-jumbo" must give way to management method.

My presentation to management introduces what I call an AMA, an Astrological Management Analysis. Immediately with that title, I've got the concept of astrology stated and out of the way and, in the outlining of what services I will perform to help management, I begin to talk in operation terms of evaluating personnel dimensions that I know management is interested in (and which I have been able to derive from certain groups of astrological measurements). I'm talking corporate language.

For example, in outlining the AMA, I indicate two major areas of strategic content (note the executive, management-method verbiage): general character and the time-frame of change. The former deals with need profiles, general aptitudes, and core character concerns; the latter with reward cycles, developmental pressures, and individualized perspectives of growth. These two areas will help the employer to place the right person into the right job function: the job will get done most efficiently and economically, stimulating the employee's creativity and job identification for benefits to the firm, make economical the training investment, and allow predictability about longevity of service, which protects the employer's investment in the employee.

For example, it would be very, very strategically important for a corporation to recognize in someone that "practicality and emotionalism struggle for the center of the stage" (Sun in Capricorn and Moon in Cancer). The astrologer can define this character generalization further in individualized terms by noting aspects to the Sun and/or the Moon within the horoscope. Then, as we will see, many measurements grow tellingly out from the Sun-Moon polarity generalization (and there are 144 of them, remember) and gain individualized focus and balance, which can be translated into business insights by the astrologer.

The AMA report will be able to separate instantly the "take charge" person from the "behind the scenes person" (10th House Moon or 12th House Moon, respectively); isolate the employee who needs to be on display during the job function (Venus oriental, for example); spot the employee who needs urgently to "do his or her own thing" in a unique way (Moon in the 1st House, Aquarian emphasis, etc.); the employee who will display enormous patience (Saturn oriental, relationship with Mercury); the one who is a promoter (Mars oriental), the adventurer (Uranus oriental), the idealist

(Neptune oriental, Mercury-Venus conjunction, etc.). As the analysis grows, the focus of the characterological theme will take its place *within the job description*; the harmony or dissonance will become apparent to management who studies the individual in relation to the job profile.

Going further, the astrologer will be able to inspect how a person needs to think in order to behave most characteristically efficiently (Mercury, its sign and aspects); how a person needs to relate to others to be most socially comfortable (Venus, its sign and aspects); what kind of energy needs the person has in order to apply him or herself most effectively (Mars). Does the person scatter energies, focus on detail, take authority well? What kind of reward does the person need to feel fulfilled: does a pat on the back mean more than a raise?

Is the employee applicant or someone already on the job actually someone who will do best in personal terms "bucking the organization" (Mars in the 12th)? Management will understand just how tolerable this behavioral tendency will be on the job. Perhaps the energy need in such a case has the support of other strengths to qualify for a position of leadership, or perhaps the behavior pattern will be disruptive. At the very least, this kind of observation in the AMA can stimulate interview questions that will help job applicant/employee and management appreciate each other better.

With regard to the presentation of time structures in life, the outline of social cycles of development keyed to transiting Saturn's quadrature aspects to its natal position is always fascinating to management; it is undeniable (at 7, opening square, the child is out of the home, off to school; the adolescent crisis at 14, opposition; released into society at 21; changes in life direction and/or level 28-30, Saturn's return; shift of gears at 35; "second adolescence" at about 42, etc.). Understanding and credibility are then extended to other cycles that key reward times (Jupiter transits to Jupiter's natal position, the Sun, and the Moon) and grand developments involving the outer planets, their transits and Solar Arc development within the horoscope.

One of the key points of wisdom in presenting the AMA report plan to management is that rarely is the employee who is hired going to remain at that job or with that firm for eternity! More than ever before, employees move on, ever in search of greater fulfillment; *i.e.*, they respond to astrological concomitants of change much more reliably than ever before. Management needs to know that the astrologer/consultant is thinking in these terms too, to protect management's investment in the employee and acknowledging the employee's needs for a fulfilling job as well.

The AMA report must get "personal" often. Special concerns like health, emotional security, "chips on one's shoulder," wanderlust, major event involvement like marriage, divorce, or going into business for one's self; temperamental explosiveness, feelings of inferiority, "hidden agendas." These dimensions are subtle deductions from the horoscope, indeed, but with skill and experience, the astrologer/consultant to management can make suggestions about these dimensions with grace, fairness to the employee, and be helpful in the valuation process.

In all my experience with corporate management, I have tried always to work with the highest executive I could settle in with. Ideally, the president of the firm is the best target; then the Vice-President of Human Resources or Director of Personnel. I have never found the decision-maker who knew me as an astrologer, *i.e.*, social meeting, on an airplane, prestige referral, etc., unwilling to talk with me about how astrology can help management evaluate personnel. By definition, the highest executive echelon is the most open-minded; if the astrologer's presentation is dignified and confident, framed in business and human resources language, and not in any way imbalancing with technical jargon that the executive does not understand, the astrologer/consultant *will be heard*.

TRANSLATING MEASUREMENTS

When I do an AMA report on an employee or employee prospect, I describe the core character profile and general development time structure (perhaps 500 words) and then I give concise descriptions of 17 personnel evaluation items. Ideally, management solicits the birth time from the applicant/employee, explaining that astrological profiling is a technique that is being used in addition to others to help the corporation position the applicant/employee in the best way possible for the firm and for the applicant. Couched in this way, the applicant shares the birth data immediately or goes to get it from the birth certificate, county records bureau, etc. There is nothing to lose and everything to gain.

The corporation provides me with the employee's birth data, the date when the employee had been hired, often a copy of the employee's resume (which will state job objective, work history, dates of job changes), the employee's present job description, and, often, a polaroid photograph of the employee.

Case #1 is a male who had just been hired by the firm as Director of Franchise Relations, representing a major advancement in his young career. Cursory astrological measurements corroborated this clearly: transiting Jupiter was just finishing its conjunction with his 6th House Piscean Moon, squaring his Sagittarian Sun, and transiting Saturn was just finishing conjunction with Uranus at his Midheaven; transiting Pluto was just into his Ascendant and was squaring the 10th House Uranus.

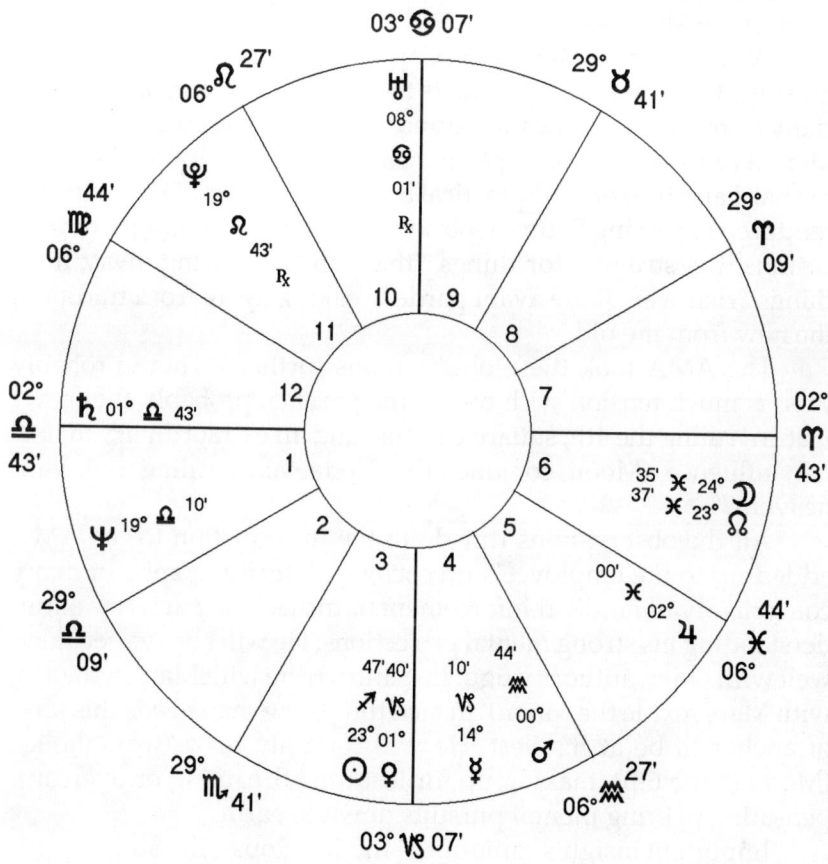

Case #1, Male

The AMA for this young executive began, "The major theme of this man's life development is philosophical. The mind gains enormous support from intuition. Dream and visionary planning are important resources within his work organization. The hope is for harmony between what is expected and what can be."

This major, initial observation issues from appreciation of the Sun-Moon blend, *i.e.*, Sagittarius and Pisces. These positions are the positions of the philosopher. Often, two different planes are at work in life experience: the actual and the idealized. This is reinforced by the occurrence of Neptune oriental, *i.e.*, rising just before the Sun, by Venus rulership of the cerebral 9th and the Ascendant, conjunct the Sun and opposed the Midheaven, also in square with the Moon, ruler of the Midheaven.

We can see that Mercury in Capricorn, *i.e.*, needing "to hear the grass grow" (Lewi), complements the visionary side strongly, especially with the intensification opposition with Uranus. But we see Mercury in square with Neptune rising. There is a flip-flop between the hard and the soft, the practical and the visionary. This, in turn is reinforced by rising Saturn (sobriety, maturity) and its square with Uranus, the struggle for things "that can be" tearing away from things "that were," the avant garde breaking away from tradition, the new from the old.

The AMA took these observations further: "There probably was/is much tension with one of the parents, probably the father (Saturn ruling the 4th, square Uranus) and an extraordinary maternal influence (Moon conjunct the Nodal axis, ruling the Midheaven)."

All the observations I made in the introduction to the AMA added up to the employee's precocious maturity in spite of many concerns about family reinforcement or the lack of it in terms of understanding his strong mental projections. He will always get along well with older, authority figures (Saturn trine with Mars in the 4th, with Mars sextile the Moon). In fact, the young man needs this kind of anchor to be at his best. He will certainly be a "workaholic" (Moon in the 6th), making up for lost time dreaming or overcompensating to bring mental pursuits down to earth.

Important insights came out of the 3rd House: the Sun in Sagittarius, Venus ruling the 9th; Pluto, ruling the 3rd, in sextile with the very important Neptune; Jupiter, co-ruler of the 3rd trine Uranus in the Midheaven, "the more travel connected with his job, the more pleasing it will be. He needs to be off on a jaunt unto himself, seeing to the short-haul urgency and coming back a winner. He needs to dream up a situation and see it come into reality. He is a sensitive planner."

The man's resume revealed very high grades in college, membership in college honorary societies, high office held in fraternity, and a marriage shortly after the present job assignment.

His hobbies were listed as "reading, travel, backpacking, sports," all corroborations of the Sagittarian, 3rd, 9th, and 5th House references.

His academic major and degree were in finance. This is certainly suggested by Venus rulership of the 2nd House, opposing the Midheaven, ruling the Ascendant, and in mutual reception and square with Saturn. In fact, it is the tie with Saturn that brings the entire character "down to earth," that gives the philosophical mental thrusts a practical anchor.

But the man had been hired as a Director of Franchise Operations, apparently following the trine line of Mars-Saturn, with Mars ruling the 7th. And then, his resume lists his job objective as a career in Finance/Banking, leading to top management responsibility.

There is confusion here. The man is young, extremely bright, thanks to his emotionally sensitive way of thinking and the sobriety of the Venus-Saturn ties. Into the future in two years, Solar Arc Midheaven would oppose natal Mars (27 degrees, *i.e.*, approximately 27 years) with transiting Saturn conjunct Pluto, and Mars-Jupiter transiting in opposition to the Sun. Additionally, the Secondary Progressed Moon would conjoin natal Jupiter. "In two years, he will be speculating further on new perspectives for his job involvement, projecting still newer dreams, specifically in July-August. Management should be sensitive to this, explore his need to be in finance management, and make provisions for promotion or adjustment of job status—or risk losing a fine, young executive to opportunities elsewhere."

Closing out the AMA were these 17 personnel evaluation items:

Leadership—   Very good [high Cardinal emphasis, *i.e.*, taking action; condition of the 7th House ruler, here Mars in Aquarius sextile the Moon and trine Saturn]; more subtle than overtly expressive [Ascendant ruler Venus in square and mutual reception with Saturn].

Consolidation of strengths—

Not especially well developed; the balance between intuition and practicality is not yet well formed.

Flexibility—

Quite good, acknowledging easily that he too needs leadership; high receptivity to any suggestion [The Piscean Moon, the Mars-Saturn trine; Mutable Sun, Venus and Moon].

Attention to Detail—

Extremely perceptive; he can hear the grass grow. When the thinking is down to earth, the attention to detail is beyond question [Mercury in Capricorn].

Innovation—

Probably extremely high [the visionary bent, the Uranian prominence].

Ambition—

Tactful administration of his strengths with the benefits of other people in mind [Saturn in Libra, mutual reception with Venus, and trine with Mars in Aquarius]. His administrative thrust must be graced with some significance greater than the routine in order for him to be pleased.

Reward Needs—

Opportunities hoped for must suit a private, unassuming, personal feeling or dream [Jupiter in Pisces sextile Venus, trine Uranus].

Pride—

Calm, sober, natural [Ascendant dimensions].

Intelligence—

Wins through intuition and perception [Sun-Moon cerebration; Neptune square with Mercury; although the Moon's speed on the birth date was average].

Cooperation—

Excellent, especially with older people or senior people in the corporate structure [Piscean Moon in the 6th, ruled by Neptune rising; Moon sextile with Mars].

Financial Management—

Very conservative [Venus, ruler of the 2nd, in square with Saturn] but not without the potential of impulsive, highly intuited "larks," *i.e.*, if the vision is clear, he can gamble [Venus in relation to Saturn yet, in opposition with Uranus].

Communication— Mature, deep, serious, a reasonable amount of enthusiasm [Venus condition; Pluto and the Sun].

Speculation— Based upon intuition and is very strong; he knows how to dream [5th House condition].

Employee Relationships— He "feels out" situations [6th House condition].

Intuition— Tremendous; vitally important.

Relationship with the Establishment— Fine, by temperament, but career progress is still unsettled; the man has a dream.

Limitations— Inexperience getting the intuiting plane to work easily with the routine reality plane.

Case #2, Male; no birth time; Governmental Executive born February 1, 1931

☉	☽	☿	♀	♂	♃	♄	♅	♆	♇	☊
11≈	20♋	17♑	24♐	5♌R	12♋R	17♑	12♈	5♍R	19♋R	17♈

Some organization must be brought to the noon–GMT ephemeris listings of the planets:

1. The Sun is in Aquarius opposed Mars retrograde, and the Moon is in Cancer with very fast diurnal speed (15°).

2. The Moon in its own sign probably conjoins with Jupiter and Pluto in a triple conjunction which, in turn, is opposed the exact conjunction of Mercury and Saturn in its own sign.

3. This powerful axis in Cardinal signs is squared by Uranus in Aries.

4. Saturn in Capricorn is the oriental planet, rising last before the Sun [see Chapter 2 in this volume].

5. And Venus in Sagittarius is peregrine, not making any classic aspect within the horoscope.

6. The Lunar Node is square the dominating Mercury-Saturn conjunction in Capricorn.

Our AMA about this man would proceed then, in management terms as follows, covering the astrological observations above in consecutive order.

1. This man has a very strong humanitarian, people-centered, innovative, adventurous energy that is chomping at the bit to be expressed. This energetic drive has extreme sensitivities attached to it: the need to respond emotionally is enormous, yet there is a check on the energy not to make waves. However, the merest hint of emotional recognition and security can ignite the loyalties and stir up action.

2. The emotional sensitivity is extremely intensified and may indeed be projected out to the world at large; it is probably too much, if you will, for the private sphere. Dramatizing emotions and humanitarian thrust in fact can *become* the ambition, the goal of life. Perception and strategy are inordinately well-developed.

3. The powerful Cardinal cluster—taking action to help others—is jolted constantly. There is a sense of reform here, a way to champion the new, the avant garde over the old and traditional.

4. There is enormous patience to see plans put into effect.

5. Ethics and ideals run away with the system and may even sometimes be frittered away in emotional enthusiasms that break out of usually more sober restraints.

6. A great deal of the impassioned sensitivity and emotional concern for the people at large stems from an extremely significant attachment and influence from his mother.

Leadership—	Extremely high.
Consolidation of Strengths—	Almost monomaniacal; break away from the old to establish a new practical security. Reform.
Flexibility—	Strategically accommodating, but is his own boss.
Attention to Detail—	Probably weak, since he is so emotionally convinced of the big picture.
Innovation—	Rampant.
Ambition—	All consuming. Somehow, this man needs to prove a personal point, fulfill his emotional security need over and over and over again. He feels he must make the world a better place to live in, not just for himself but for everyone!
Reward Needs—	His reward needs are seen in emotional terms. The noble view is personal fulfillment.
Pride—	Probably understated; with all the bravura this man can show on the job, the energy, the source of pride, is working through an inner filter before it explodes outside himself.
Intelligence—	Extremely fleet; needs to hear the grass grow.
Cooperation—	Probably only strategically cooperative, reliably so when his ideals are echoed and his ideas make impact.
Financial Management—	Inconclusive.
Communication—	Probably heavy, plodding in delivery, with ideals that fly sky-high; the emotional approach is his key.
Speculation—	Inconclusive.
Employee Relationships—	He is loyal if you share his views or are important to his success, but he is the boss.
Intuition—	Too practical for reliance on intuition.

Relationship with the Establishment—	Not good. The man is a reformer; he demands a new order.
Limitations—	Extreme vulnerability to emotional appeals; perhaps the ideals can get sidetracked for intermediate gratification before the real goals are reached.

This AMA would be helpful to anyone evaluating the executive performance of this government executive: Boris Yeltsin, at present in the summer of 1991, President of the Russian Federation.

The astrologer/consultant could take this astrological profile into the future quite easily: in late February, early March 1992, Yeltsin faces a tremendous challenge to everything he stands for, caught up in an explosive people's revolution throughout Russia. With transiting Mars-Saturn in conjunction square his Sun and, at the same time, transiting Uranus-Neptune exactly conjunct his natal Mercury-Saturn conjunction, Yeltsin will be pressed into action as never before in his life. If he is without a supportive government structure, he may be swamped by emotional demands; the reform at this time will be too big for one man to lead. His health may be jeopardized by the strain.

JOB CONFUSION

With practically every horoscope we do in our work, we match what we see in the horoscope with what we know the client does for a living. Finding the symbols brought to life to fit the vocational profile gives us a security to go on with the analysis. The horoscope starts to live in terms of confirmed reality.

Even if someone comes to us for out-and-out vocational guidance, there undoubtedly is past work experience which we try to corroborate through the person's horoscope—and indeed, there are cases when the work chosen is *not* corroborated by the horoscope, when we begin to feel that the client has been on the wrong track. This is perhaps job confusion, with two paths demanding attention at the same time.

Case #3 is such a case of job confusion. With the Sun in Virgo and the Moon in Capricorn, we can anticipate accuracy and devotion to a goal taking the young man to a successful administrative position. There is undoubtedly enormous self-assurance with Jupiter in Sagittarius ruling the self-worth 2nd and occupying it along

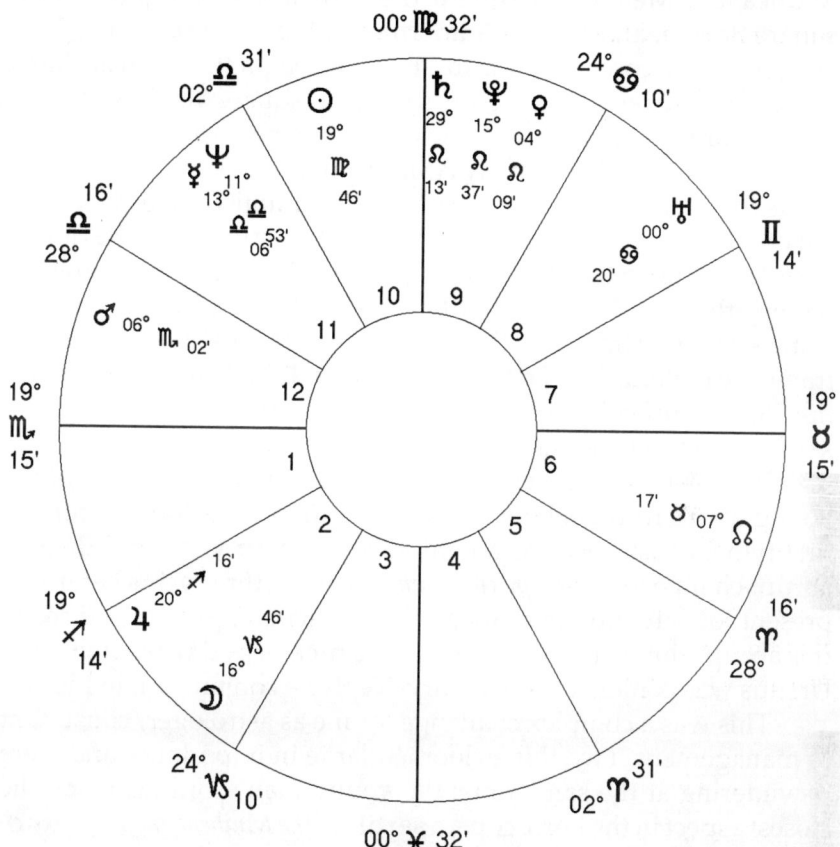

Case #3, Male

with the Moon; with Jupiter square the Sun, sextile Mercury, and trine Pluto, ruler of the Ascendant. In our vocational analysis, we could jump to conclusions here and start to think about finance, even international finance, what with the Moon ruling the 9th, with Pluto in the 9th, and with the extraordinarily important Saturn—peregrine and conjunct the Midheaven—lording over the entire horoscope just inside the 9th House.

But when we inspect the Midheaven carefully, checking its ruler, Mercury, we come up with a different train of thought: Mercury is conjunct Neptune, and this conjunction is semi-square the

Midheaven. Mercury is square the Moon, sextile Jupiter, semi-square Saturn, and sextile Pluto, ruler of the Ascendant. The Mercury-Neptune conjunction is in Libra. We begin to feel an aesthetic sense trying to be expressed. We see Venus square Mars. We start to feel uncomfortable with a financial management career.

This was the thrust of my AMA report on this young man: "He fights the need to adapt the artistic to the administrative, the imaginary to the real. On the one hand, he is so very sure that he has all the answers (Pluto in the 9th), so strong is his self-assured presentation; on the other hand, he repeatedly senses that something is missing, some aesthetic dimension that he can't quite frame as well as he can frame the material and factual dimensions. The result at this stage in his life is a difficulty finding focus for his capabilities. He doesn't know where to hang his hat."

I asked his employer for more information and I was sent the young man's résumé. I got the corroboration I was looking for: his first two jobs had been as a bank teller for four years and then an abrupt change to *motion picture cameraman* for three years before his present job situation in management. Fascinatingly, he had made this abrupt shift in career exactly in the time period when transiting Uranus was conjunct the Mercury-Neptune conjunction in Libra!

This was a complex challenge for me as astrologer/consultant to management. Two things loomed large in importance and were bewildering at the same time: the young man's Uranus made the closest aspect in the horoscope, a sextile *to the Midheaven*; and Saturn was simply overwhelming in Leo conjunct that Midheaven.

Both these planets, Uranus and Saturn, ruled the horoscope's 3rd House. Self-assured, dramatic, grandiloquent communication seemed indicated; promotion, publicity, image-creation, public relations and advertising; *not* routinized financial management.

The objective of the AMA then was to bring this quandry out into the air, to stimulate open, mutually supporting discussion between management and the very talented young man. In situations like this, astrology brings about a strategic moment of truth.

Another case introduces the concept of "level" to the concern about job confusion: a man has a prominent 9th House ruled by Mars. Mars is conjunct Venus in the 7th, and Venus rules the Taurus Midheaven. This suggests, of course, that 9th House affairs could very well be tied to the public somehow and certainly figure within the man's vocational direction.

In the 9th House, there is a conjunction of the Moon and Jupiter in Taurus, disposited by Venus, ruler of the Midheaven. This is even more emphasis of 9th House importance in the choice of profession. The man has an Aquarian Sun. All of these initial observations emphasize the 9th House, public service, losing one's self in some large concept (Moon in the 9th), the introduction of things legal, international, academic.

I asked the man if he had ever thought of studying law. Yes, he definitely had wanted to become a lawyer, but family difficulties and personal matters had kept him from this course. Instead, my client had become a *prison guard*. Further in the horoscope, his Pluto is in the 12th squaring the Midheaven. The 12th House is ruled by the Sun.

My client had adopted another level of what the horoscope was promising. It is rare that astrology can anticipate such a switch. The client is pressed by personal affairs, the environment does not cooperate with personal plans, if you will, and a new level is adopted. Just as astrology cannot tell gender, astrology cannot tell level. Astrology can tell *conditions* and therefrom support astute deductions, but level evades us.

Another example: there simply is no astrological signature for "president;" president of a corporation, a tiny business, or a country. The nature of the business, the conditions that will be personally fulfilling can usually be seen, *i.e.*, a major Gemini-Sagittarius emphasis and 3rd and 9th House references will certainly support the statement "I'm in the transportation business." But that this man is president of his own messenger service eludes astrology. We can corroborate that level and specificity, but we can rarely anticipate them.

A horoscope has the classic measurements of a performing artist: Libra Midheaven ruled by Venus, Venus in Pisces sextile Mars rising in Sagittarius. Neptune is in the 7th and is exactly square the Midheaven, ruling the 3rd ... this man was indeed a famous actor and celebrated communicator, but he also became president of the United States! Where do we see *that*?

The president of a corporation for whom I eventually did Astrological Management Analyses for one year submitted several horoscopes "blind" to me as an audition, to see if the AMA reports would be helpful, indeed, even accurate! One of them turned out to be his own. There was a Sun-Mercury-Jupiter conjunction in Aries trine Moon-Mars in Leo, which I described in the AMA as "intrepid individualism. Success is *expected* to fulfill the inner self-image." That the Moon-Mars conjunction was in the 12th House, with a Leo Ascendant, suggested that "this major characterological theme adjusts itself at two levels: one is a whole-hearted self-projection into experience with confidence that he will take over any situation, and the other is that there is more to experience in life that is private. He must be his own man, must buck the organization of things in order to create organization *his own way.*"

Certainly, as the analysis started to gather steam, I was describing a man of powerful drive, one who would not surprise anyone as head of his own business, president of some enterprise. While his horoscope showed this type of entrepreneurship, this strong self-projection—especially with the Moon-Mars conjunction opposed by Uranus in the 6th—the horoscope did *not* suggest the field he was in, a national chain of restaurants.

So, there is confusion in these cases as well, and this confusion—rather than showing astrology to be inadequate—merely reflects the complexity of personal choice and marketplace specialization that are standard in these times and in this society. Astrology is necessarily incomplete as we are all still learning, and yet it is out of dialogue and investigation of inclinations and needs that dynamic, rewarding synthesis does come, more often than not.

TIMEFRAMES

One of the most secure areas of astrological analysis has to do with major passages of time, the transition times that are so regularly repeated in the course of life that they have actually helped to mold our social structure. While these passages are obvious and thought to be "natural" (certainly not having anything to do with anything astrological!), they are ignored by Personnel Directors...or they are simply not known as a strategy that will help evaluate personnel sensitively and profitably.

The astrologer in the consultant role can put together a very simple table that captures, say Saturn transit probabilities (closing square at age 21, the return at 28-30, the shift of gears at 35), Jupiter returns and conjunctions with the Sun, and major contacts made by the outer planets *within a projected period of time* to help Personnel Directors appreciate the transitional stages of the applicants they are interviewing or the employees that are being evaluated.

For example, taking the period from June to December 1992 as an example timeframe, we know that transiting Saturn will be retrograding between 18 Aquarius and 14 Aquarius. This would be the closing square to natal Saturn positions for all those people born when Saturn was in 14–18 Taurus, in May–July 1970 and November 1970 through April 1971.

This position of transiting Saturn in 18–14 Aquarius would be the Saturn return position for those people born early in 1963.

Transiting Saturn will be conjoining the Sun of all people born *any year* between February 3 and February 9; opposed the Sun of those people born *any year* between August 6 and August 13.

These time periods, keyed not to astrology but to birthdates that will appear on résumés, can be explained concisely on the Table: the closing Saturn square, feeling a push to independence; the Saturn return, feeling the need to change direction and/or level in life, to get on with a whole new sense of job in terms of ambition and fulfillment; in conjunction with the Sun, a powerful time of assessing one's lot, making a commitment or making a change; opposed the Sun, feeling frustrated, put upon, dragged out, insignificant, etc.

The same plotting can be accomplished with transiting Uranus, Neptune, and Pluto relating to natal-Sun-birthdate-groupings. With Jupiter, it is very easy to alert the Personnel Director to reward cycles that can certainly reinforce any applicant's resume or employee's bid for advancement. Personnel experiencing these very important transits are the personnel who are changing jobs; they are the ones in the limelight!

The astrologer/consultant clearly can put together quite a package for personnel directors in employment agencies and corporations, without one word of astrology being recorded. In human terms and in business terms, the times *can* be captured to help employees and job applicants fulfill *their* needs through interaction with business firms; and, at the same time, help business firms care about these people's needs and evaluate personnel for mutual profit.

Anthony Louis

Anthony (Tony) Louis is a psychiatrist who has been studying astrology for the past 30 years. His articles on astrology have appeared in *American Astrology, The Horary Practitioner, Aspects Magazine, The Journal of the Astrological Society of Connecticut*, and Llewellyn's *Sun Sign Book, Astrological Calendar* and *Daily Planetary Guide*. His recent book, *Horary Astrology: The History and Practice of Astro-Divination* (Llewellyn Publications), has received wide critical acclaim. In addition to horary astrology, his astrological interests include Local Space, Electional and Vocational astrology. He participates with several local astrologers in a monthly study group, in Orange, Connecticut.

Tony has a private practice in psychiatry and serves as the Medical Director of a psychiatric day hospital. His interest in astrological symbolism is consonant with his study of dream theory and psychoanalytic depth psychology.

Void-of-Course Moon Strategies for Doing Business

Anthony Louis

What if there existed a simple yet effective method to increase your business productivity? What if a quick glance at a calendar could help you decide when to start major projects to avoid snafus? You probably wouldn't believe it, but read on before you reach any conclusions. Let's start with an example.

In the fall of 1989, a new restaurant specializing in gourmet pancakes opened a block from my office. For weeks, I observed workmen carefully preparing the space and getting ready for the opening day. Finally a sign appeared in the window: Grand Opening Tuesday 9:30 a.m. I checked to see what aspects were in effect for the Grand Opening. Noticing that the Moon was Void-of-Course that Tuesday morning, I debated whether or not to introduce myself to the owners and suggest that they postpone the start of their business to a more propitious time. I told my wife I was concerned about the possibility that the opening of the new establishment would amount to nothing.

Not knowing the restaurant owners and not wanting to meddle in other people's affairs, I decided to let matters run their course. I began to frequent the restaurant and enjoyed the excellent food. Over the first couple of months, the restaurant had a hard time keeping its staff. There were also problems with the plumbing which caused the establishment to close briefly for repairs. Within a year, the restaurant went out of business. I was not surprised because the opening of the restaurant had indeed occurred during a Void-of-Course Moon! I even felt a bit guilty for not having warned the management of the potential danger on opening day. If only they had postponed the opening, they might still be in business.

My observation confirmed the ancient wisdom that activities begun during a Void-of-Course Moon seldom work out as originally intended, if they work out at all. What is a Void-of-Course Moon and why should it make any difference in our lives? Let's review some basic definitions.

Because of its link with the human female menstrual cycle, the Moon's cycle and its influence on human affairs is part of the warp and woof of the history of our species. About every 28 days, the Moon completes its 360-degree passage around the earth, passing through each of the 12 signs of the zodiac. Each zodiacal sign spans 30 degrees. As the Moon travels from the beginning to the end of each sign, it makes certain angles or aspects to the Sun and to each of the eight planets (Mercury, Venus, Mars, Jupiter, Saturn, Uranus, Neptune, Pluto). In astrology, particular angular separations link the energies of the two planets involved in the aspect.

When the Void-of-Course Moon was discovered, astrologers only considered five aspects to be significant. The five so-called major or Ptolemaic aspects include the conjunction, sextile, square, trine, and opposition. Since Claudius Ptolemy first codified them in his famous four books on astrology in the 2nd century, these five aspects have been the backbone of the Western astrological tradition.

Ptolemy considered these five aspects major because the ratios formed between any of the major aspects and the 180 degree half-circle were the classical Greek ratios for musical harmony. In the 5th century B.C., Pythagoras and his followers discovered that if you simultaneously plucked two taut strings whose lengths formed certain whole number ratios, you got harmonious tones. In the horoscope wheel, certain signs are as distant from one another as the whole number ratios of the strings of musical instruments. Planets the same angular distance apart as harmoniously distant signs formed the so-called major aspects with one another. Thus the "music of the spheres" determined which astrological aspects were most significant.

At some point in its travels from one sign to another, the Moon enters a region of the zodiac where it makes no further major aspects to the Sun or any of the planets before entering the next sign. In this aspectless zone (twilight zone?) the Moon is considered Void-of-Course (devoid of aspects on its course). As Firmicus Maternus aptly described in his 4th century text, the Void-of-Course Moon is traveling in an "aspect vacuum." Although modern astrologers use many newer minor aspects, the definition of the Void-of-Course Moon has remained that the Void-of-Course Moon is one that makes no further major aspects (0, 60, 90, 120, 180 degrees) before leaving its sign.

Why should a Void-of-Course Moon matter in business affairs? Why should a Void-of-Course Moon, like a void check, buy you nothing? The answer lies in astrological symbolism. Each of the twelve signs of the zodiac represents a different realm of experience. The Moon is the speediest body that astrologers consider. It travels an average of 13 degrees 11 minutes of zodiac longitude per day, or passes through one sign of the zodiac every 2.3 days. Thus, at some point every two to three days, the Moon may pass through an aspectless zone where it makes no major connection with other planets. Because of its phase shifts and rapid motion, the Moon has come to symbolize all the ephemeral and fluctuating facets of human affairs. The Moon signifies the routine, humdrum, trivial matters that preoccupy us daily.

In her classic text on horary astrology, Barbara Watters suggested that the Moon represents function. When the Moon is active (involved in major aspects), there is much activity in the matter under astrological investigation. When the Moon is without major aspects, Void-of-Course as it were, there is little activity or function. The Void-of-Course Moon is just sailing along, not interacting with the other planets, until it enters the next sign of the zodiac. A Moon without connections symbolizes a matter likely to fizzle out because it is not, at its moment of inception, *an integral part of the general flow of the universe.*

Some modern astrologers pay the Void-of-Course Moon no mind; they regard it as an erroneous remnant of a past age of astrology. When I first learned of the Void-of-Course Moon, I too found it hard to believe that the Moon's failure to make a major aspect could much affect our lives. A skeptic by nature, I began to test this astrological hypothesis. I kept track of purchases made during Void-of-Course Moon periods. Frequently, but not always, I had to return such purchases because they were defective or inoperable. A tape recorder I bought would play tapes but would not record sound. Clothing I purchased under a Void-of-Course Moon would not fit properly. Toys requiring assembly had missing parts. Items advertised on sale would be out of stock or did not work as advertised. After many such experiences, I switched to making purchases only when the Moon was about to make major harmonious aspects. The results have been rewarding. I return many fewer items to the stores these days.

My experience with shopping during the Void-of-Course Moon prompted me to study its effect on my professional life. I am a psychiatrist with an office-based private practice as well as a hospital staff position. For a while, I kept track of patients whose initial visit fell on a Void-of-Course Moon. To my amazement, many of these patients did not even keep their first appointment. Often they would neither show up nor cancel, thus unproductively tying up an hour of my time. Those who did come for the first visit when the Moon was Void-of-Course frequently dropped out of treatment. Based on this survey, I stopped scheduling first visits during Void-of-Course Moon periods, and my no-show rate has dropped dramatically. Among patients who entered the hospital program during a Void-of-Course Moon, I noticed that many had complicated courses of treatment and prolonged lengths of stay.

OLD RULES AND NEW ONES

Astrologers have been attending to the Void-of-Course Moon for nearly two millennia. Firmicus Maternus wrote about it in 334 A.D., and Guido Bonnatus, the most notable horary and electional astrologer of the 13th century, regularly used the Void-of-Course Moon in advising his clients. In fact, Bonnatus was so renowned for his skill at predicting the future that Dante, in *The Divine Comedy*, placed him in hell with his head put on backwards for eternity as punishment for usurping a talent that should belong to God alone!

Bonnatus wrote that the Void-of-Course Moon "signifies an impediment to the thing in question; it will not come to a good end, but the querent shall be forced to desist with shame and loss." He added that projects started with a Void-of-Course Moon proceed with "much labor, sorrow, and trouble, unless the Lord of the Ascendant or significator of the thing shall be in very good condition, and then it may be hindered but not wholly frustrated." The only matters the Void-of-Course Moon was good for, according to Bonnatus, were "drinking, bathing, feasting, etc., and to use ointment for the taking away of hair, especially if she be in Scorpio."

Following Bonnatus, the famous 17th-century horary astrologer William Lilly paid close attention to the Void-of-Course Moon in his professional consultations. Lilly wrote, "all manner of matters go hardly on (except the principal significators be very strong) when the Moon is void of course; yet sometimes she performs if void of course, if in Taurus, Cancer, Sagittarius, or Pisces." Lilly here is quoting a rule laid down in Bonnatus' 13th-century text. The Moon rules Cancer and is exalted in Taurus, so it does well in these signs. Jupiter traditionally rules Sagittarius and Pisces, and the Moon does well under the auspices of the "greater benefic."

On the other hand, tradition tells us that the Void-of-Course Moon is especially debilitating when it is in Gemini, Scorpio, or Capricorn. The Moon is in its fall in Scorpio, which lies opposite Taurus where the Moon is exalted. Luna is in its detriment in Capricorn which lies opposite Cancer, which the Moon rules. Gemini is the sign preceding Cancer and thus the natural 12th House of confinement and undoing of the Moon. Gemini, sign of Jupiter's detriment, is opposite Sagittarius where the Moon benefits from the greater benefic.

Knowing these rules can sometimes give you lightning insight into a situation. Recently a friend of mine was going on a job interview. He asked me what astrological influences would be in effect during the interview. A quick glance at Llewellyn's *Daily Planetary Guide* told me that the Moon would be Void-of-Course in Capricorn at the scheduled time of his interview. Based on the Moon's Void status in Capricorn where the Moon is in its detriment, I told him his prospects did not look promising. He did not get the job.

Successful people seem intuitively able to tune into astrologically propitious times for action without even consulting a chart. They have some kind of knack for correct timing. On the other hand, some people pick the worst times to begin almost anything. I have a friend who is a single mother of two adorable children. Her husband left her on Father's Day (!) when the children were quite young. Since then, she has met many men but has been unable to settle into a new long-term relationship. She frequently calls me with horary questions about a new prospective partner. Invariably, at the time of her inquiry, the Moon is Void-of-Course and I have to tell her "nothing will come of the matter." Her highly stressed natal Moon in Pisces seems to give her a knack for picking unfortunate times.

The late Ivy M. Goldstein-Jacobson was one of the 20th century masters of horary astrology, the art of answering questions from a horoscope cast for the time of the inquiry. She assigned the keyword "nothing" to the Void-of-Course Moon: "a project or anything begun will be abandoned or reversed so that NOTHING is to come of it and the querent gives up his objective & eventually stops worrying about it." Goldstein-Jacobson felt that if the Void-of-Course Moon were to aspect the Part of Fortune, "there is NOTHING to worry about."

Other astrologers who address horary and electional issues have their own key words or phrases for the Void-of-Course Moon. Bruce Scofield considers the Void-of-Course Moon to imply a "lack of direction." The cerebral astrologer Marc Edmund Jones found that querents asking horary questions under a Void-of-Course Moon were "playing with life" or "toying with reality." C. C. Zain found in horary charts that "the matter is seldom brought to maturity." Astrologer Jim Maynard noted that we can feel "unconnected" or uncentered during Void-of-Course Moon periods. He advised doing spiritual rather than materialistic work during those times.

A major proponent of the influence of the Void-of-Course Moon in the 20th century is New York astrologer Al H. Morrison. More than 50 years ago, Morrison was struck by the late Barbara Watters' prediction that "Mayor LaGuardia's project of putting a map of Greenwich Village in tile on Village Square would not come to reality because it was being announced with the Moon void of course" (Al H. Morrison, personal communication). Since then, Morrison has championed the awareness of the Void-of-Course Moon in electional astrology.

Morrison has been tracking the influence of the Void-of-Course Moon for over half a century. He publishes an annual ephemeris of Void-of-Course Moon periods. Several years ago, Morrison attended a lecture by the late Walter J. Bruknus at the Astrologer's Guild of America about the charts of U.S. presidential nominations since 1900. Although Bruknus' focus was on astrological factors for political victory, Morrison noticed that *all the losing candidates declared their nominations under a Void-of-Course Moon.*

Most of the findings on the Void-of-Course Moon are anecdotal. Until I can personally review the primary sources and the horoscopes for the announcements of U.S. presidential candidacies since

1900, I remain skeptical of such sweeping and dramatic results. Perhaps some enterprising student of astrology will wade through the *New York Times* from the beginning of this century and publish these charts in a scientific study of the Void-of-Course Moon effect in U.S. politics. My hunch is that if we subjected the Void-of-Course Moon to scientific scrutiny, we would see a statistical effect similar to that found by Gauquelin in his study of planetary positions in nativities.

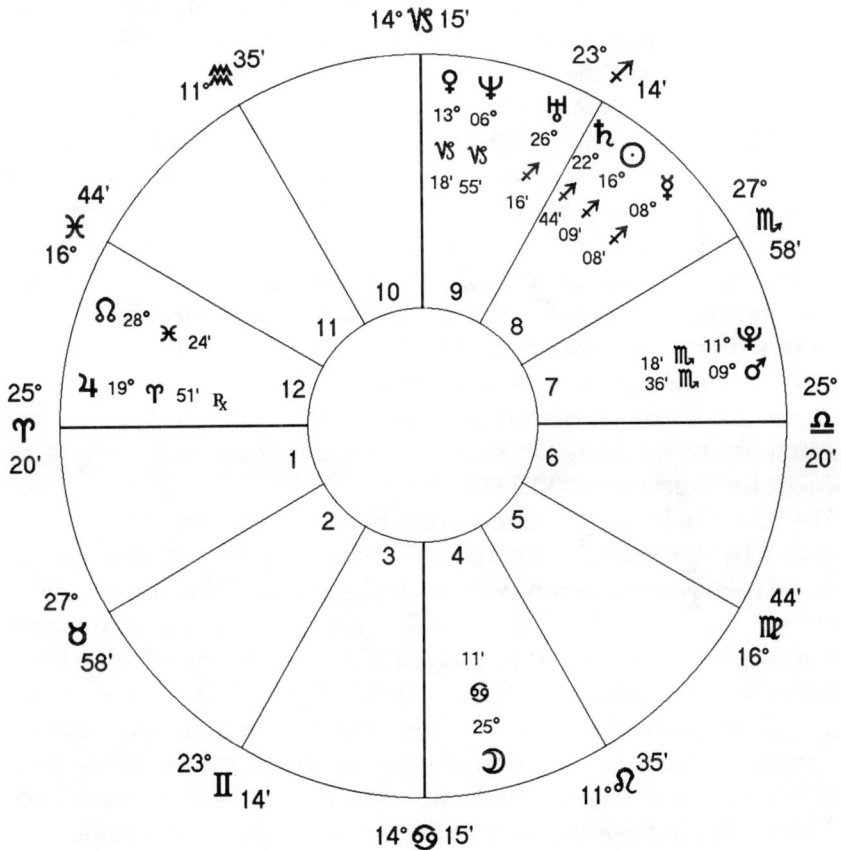

INF Treaty
Washington, DC
Dec. 8, 1987
2:02 p.m. EST
38N54 77W 2
Koch Houses

Interestingly, *both* George Bush and Michael Dukakis announced their candidacies under Void-of-Course Moons, making it impossible for astrologers to use this rule to predict who would win the election. Dukakis also has a Void-of-Course Moon in his natal chart. Astrologer Al H. Morrison feels that people born with a Void-of-Course Moon in their natal charts "suffer a subtle distortion or hindrance in their fluent expression or experience of emotions." As Morrison's delineation suggests, Dukakis was criticized during the presidential campaign for his sometimes icy lack of emotional expression. Morrison also feels that individuals like Dukakis adopt an excessively disciplined or career-oriented life to compensate for their difficulty with emotional expression.

The most notable politician to use electional astrology for successful decision making was Ronald Reagan. Guided by astrologer Joan Quigley, the president was careful, whenever possible, to launch projects and make announcements when the Moon was not Void-of-Course. According to the *New York Post*, "Quigley's charts, stars, horoscopes, cusps, planets, graphs, timetables and phone calls were running the whole Reagan White House." After the Judge Bork fiasco which occurred without astrological guidance, Reagan, on the advice of his astrologer, used a stop watch to time his announcement of Anthony Kennedy's nomination to the Supreme Court for precisely 11:32:25 on the morning of November 11, 1987. The result is history. Judge Kennedy was a shoo-in; he was confirmed by the Senate on February 3, 1988 by a vote of 97 to nothing!

There were occasions when astrologer Quigley could *not* avoid a Void-of-Course Moon. In early December, 1987, Gorbachev came to a summit meeting in Washington, D.C., to sign the Intermediate-range Nuclear Forces Treaty. The signing had to occur on December 8, 1987 while the Moon was Void-of-Course. To make the best of a compromised situation, Joan Quigley tried for a time of 1:48 p.m. EST, when Jupiter would be rising and Venus would be on the Midheaven, *i.e.*, in positions of prominence. Unfortunately Reagan and Gorbachev did not sign the treaty until 14 minutes later at 2:02 p.m. EST suggesting that matters governed by the treaty will not work out as intended.

The well-known contemporary astrologer Marion March has found positive uses for Void-of-Course Moon periods. In a recent lecture, she remarked, "the Void-of-Course Moon rarely brings the desired results in an electional chart, unless you are opting for a non-occurrence." She added that, for years, she has mailed her income tax during a Void-of-Course Moon, and the IRS has never subjected her to an audit. March's keyword is "non-occurrence."

Marion March suggests there *are* times when you would want to start something under a Void-of-Course Moon because you want nothing of significance to ensue. I know of one astrologer who advised a client to make a proposal to the board of directors of his company during a Void-of-Course Moon to ensure that the proposal would not be accepted. Presumably the astrological guidance was correct and the proposal was voted down.

I did my own simple test of March's theory. On Friday, July 12, 1991, at 8 a.m. EDT, I took my car for mandatory emissions testing during a Void-of-Course Moon. The car passed inspection without difficulty and "nothing came of the matter." My experience doesn't prove anything because the car probably would have passed at another time as well. If the car had failed emissions testing, an astrologer might have claimed the failure also as a Void-of-Course Moon effect because things "did not work out as planned." One of the problems with astrological prediction is that the same factor can have contradictory meanings which can be used to justify anything.

For example, some horary astrologers interpret questions about impending disasters, if asked under a Void-of-Course Moon, to mean there is "nothing to worry about" because "nothing will come of the matter." From this point of view you should rejoice if you doctor announces you have terminal cancer when the Moon is Void-of-Course because nothing significant will develop from the announcement. So much for the theory—I don't think I'd like to put this one to the test.

Several years ago I heard a lecture about electional astrology. I do not recall the name of the speaker, but she shared the following vignette. A woman consulted the astrologer because of marital difficulties. The client felt that she needed to kick her husband out of the house to teach him a lesson, but she did not want to dissolve the marriage. She wanted her husband to come back. The astrologer advised the woman to kick her husband out and threaten divorce during the next Void-of-Course Moon so that "nothing would come of the matter." Apparently the client followed her astrologer's advice, and everything worked out well.

Because activities on the material plane tend not to work out as planned during the Void-of-Course Moon, Al H. Morrison advised using these periods for "subjective, spiritual, non-material concerns." He feels they are good times to alter neurotic behavior by engaging in psychotherapy, meditation, or prayer. In his 50 years of investigation and observations, Morrison says he has confirmed much of the traditional wisdom about the Void-of-Course Moon. He has found that enterprises begun during a Void-of-Course Moon "fail after long and costly effort." Morrison also takes note of the aspects the Secondary Progressed Moon makes to natal planets. *When the progressed Moon goes Void-of-Course in relation to the natal planets*, Morrison predicts slumps in the political or business affairs of the native.

In addition, Morrison finds that minor aspects and parallels of declination do not "save" the Moon from being Void-of-Course. Aspects of any kind to the comet Chiron also do not "save" the Moon from its Void-of-Course status. In a review article in *The Mountain Astrologer*, Morrison summarized his years of findings on the Void-of-Course Moon as follows:

> "The common thread is the same as it was written in ancient times: that which is decided with the Moon void-of-course does not produce the expected results." He continues, "Actions taken while the Moon is void-of-course somehow always fail of their intended or planned results."

Lest you get the idea that all you need attend to when electing a propitious time for action is the Void-of-Course Moon, let me issue the following caveat. Life is complex. No single factor in astrology is all-encompassing or fully explanatory. The Void-of-Course Moon is useful to consider, but it does not tell the whole story. Other factors in the chart can outweigh or influence the meaning of the Void-of-Course Moon. Some projects begun under a Void-of-Course Moon do exceedingly well. In addition, some prominent astrologers regard the influence of the Void-of-Course Moon as overrated or irrelevant. The following case studies will help clarify these points.

THE BERMUDA TRIANGLE AND THE VOID-OF-COURSE MOON

Consider, for example, the fate of the legendary Lost Squadron that supposedly disappeared in the Bermuda Triangle. Fourteen crewmen aboard the five fully armed Avengers of Flight 19 left from Fort Lauderdale on December 5, 1945 at 2:10 p.m. EST under a Void-of-Course Moon, never to return. Realize that airplanes have been taking off for years during Void-of-Course Moon periods without suffering similar fates. The key to the astrological understanding of Flight 19 must lie elsewhere in the chart, that is, in the *interaction* between the Void-of-Course Moon and the other astrological factors.

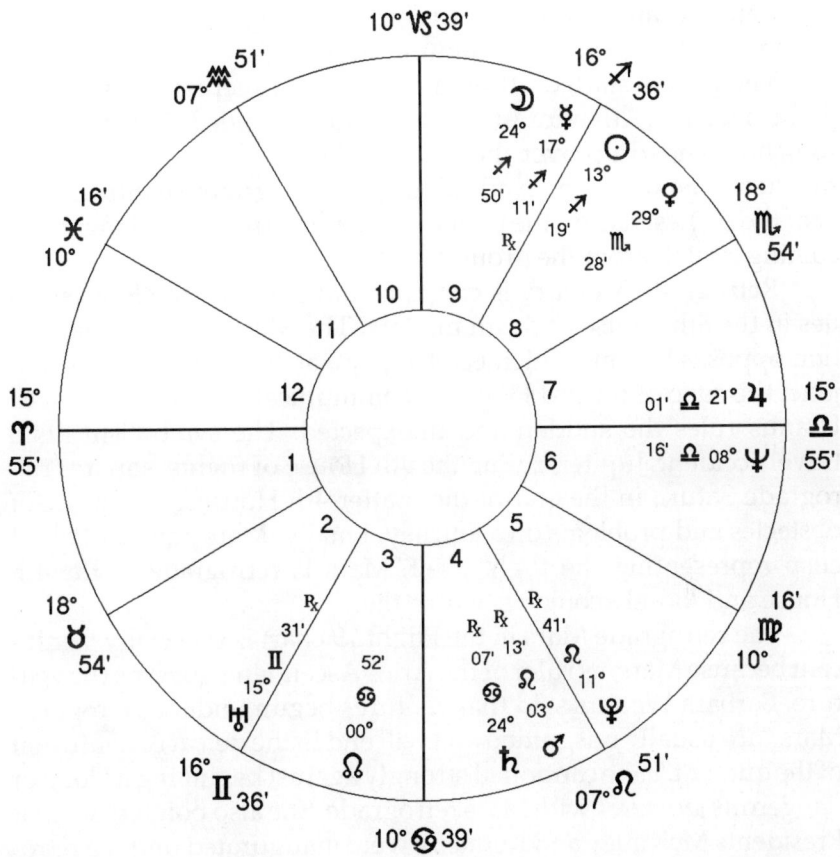

Flight 19
Fort Lauderdale, Florida
Dec. 5, 1945
2:10 p.m. EST
80W8 26N7
Koch Houses

No competent electional astrologer would have recommended that a flight take off at the time of this chart. First, the Moon at 24 Sagittarius 50 is Void-of-Course, suggesting that matters will not turn out as originally intended. The Moon has just completed a quincunx to Saturn which is retrograde in the end-of-the-matter 4th House, an ill omen. Mercury, a planet of travel and transportation, is retrograde in the 9th House of flights. Retrograde Mercury usually indicates mixups, confused directions, and problems with communication. This anticipation is reinforced by Mercury's sign Gemini on the 3rd House cusp of communication.

The planes started off with 5.5 hours of fuel for a three hour flight over the Atlantic. At 4:45 p.m. they radioed that they had somehow ended up over the Gulf of Mexico, a typical retrograde Mercury phenomenon. In addition, although ground control could hear the planes' radios, the pilots were having trouble picking up incoming signals from the ground.

Retrograde Mercury is conjunct and combust the Sun which lies in the 8th House of death matters. The Mercury/Sun conjunction opposes Uranus which is retrograde at 15 Gemini 31 and conjunct the cusp of the 3rd House of communication and local travel. Uranus rules the sudden and unexpected. The symbolism fits a travel accident. Jupiter, ruling the 9th House of flights, squares retrograde Saturn in the end-of-the-matter 4th House, a signature of obstacles and problems on a journey. Finally, Mars governs the 1st cusp representing the flight itself. Mars is retrograde in the 4th House and loosely conjoins Saturn there.

The retrograde Mars in the Flight 19 chart is especially significant because Mars, as ruler of the Aries Ascendant, governs the venture. Barbara Watters said that ventures begun under a retrograde Mars "are usually misguided and will end in the defeat or confusion of the querent." She cautioned strongly against beginning a "long or dangerous journey" with Mars retrograde. She also pointed out that Presidents McKinley and Kennedy were inaugurated under a retrograde Mars and were killed in office. President Lincoln was reelected in November, 1864, when Mars was retrograde, and he also was assassinated.

A widely accepted theory about what went wrong with Flight 19 is that the flight leader, Lt. Charles Taylor, got confused about his whereabouts. Confusion about locations is common when Mercury is retrograde. Prior to his recent transfer to Fort Lauderdale, Charles

Taylor had been stationed in Miami where he was used to flying over the Keys. Apparently some of the islands around Bermuda look very much like the Keys.

Under the influence of the Void-of-Course Moon combined with the retrograde Mercury, which ruled the 3rd House of communication and local environment, Taylor apparently misidentified the Bermuda islands as the Keys and falsely concluded that his compass was malfunctioning. Astrologically confirming the confusion that plagued the flight is Neptune, planet of foggy-headedness, powerfully placed in close conjunction with the Vertex. In fact, in the local space (horizon system) horoscope, Neptune dominates this event by its prominence.

There was another Neptunian facet of Flight 19. The wife of Captain Edward Powers, one of the pilots, awoke suddenly in the middle of the night feeling a sense of panic. At 2 a.m. on December 6, 1945, she called the base from her home in Mount Vernon, New York and was told her husband was not there. The next morning she heard on the news that her husband's squadron was missing.

RETROGRADE PLANETS AND ELECTIONAL ASTROLOGY

We see in the Flight 19 chart how retrograde planets, particularly a retrograde Ascendant ruler, like the Void-of-Course Moon, can alter the expected outcome of a venture. By way of review, a planet only appears to move retrograde with respect to the earth because of the earth's forward motion on its orbit and the planet's apparent backward motion relative to the earth. A planet's apparent retrograde motion is an optical illusion as occurs with two forward moving trains when passengers on the faster train are fooled into thinking the slower train is moving backward.

Electional astrologers advise that we should mirror the action of the retrograde planet for best results. If the planet governing the matter at hand is traveling in apparent backward motion, the time is right for going back over things, for reviewing, tying up loose ends, being introspective and inwardly directed. It is not the time to begin a new project or move forward regarding matters related to the retrograde planet. Below are some suggestions for each planet's retrograde periods. Because Mercury, Venus, and Mars are the personal planets, their retrograde periods will have the most individually felt significance. Remember that no single astrological factor tells the whole story. If you must act during a retrograde period, there are usually times that minimize the potential negative effect of the retrograde planet, or even take advantage of it.

Mercury Retrograde

Mercury turns retrograde three or four times each year for periods of about three weeks. If Mercury, Gemini, or Virgo is prominent in your natal chart, you are more likely to feel the influence of the Mercury retrograde periods. Mercury is the ruler of communication, writing, mail, thought, travel, transportation, commerce, detailed work, and manual dexterity. Mercury rules the signs Gemini and Virgo which are connected with communications, speech, transit, automobiles, computers, illness, and detailed work.

During times of Mercury's apparently backward movement, you can expect confusion, mix-ups, misunderstandings, errors, omissions, overlooked details, inattention, and forgetfulness in the areas Mercury governs. A lack of information can impair your decision-making. Scheduled arrivals or departures may be late. Messages may be lost or delayed. Your car, computer, or compass may malfunction. Minor injuries to the hands or fingers are common. People may forget to keep appointments or may wait for each other at mutually misunderstood times or places. Ideas conceived under a retrograde Mercury may seem full of promise only to appear flawed when Mercury turns direct.

It is wise not to start important new projects under a retrograde Mercury. You also need to be cautious if you must sign contracts, make important trips, buy expensive items, or send important messages during Mercury's retrograde periods. Read any fine print carefully because mistakes and misunderstandings are likely. Think of the fate of Flight 19 whenever Mercury turns backward in the sky.

Do not, however, simply stay in bed for the three weeks Mercury remains retrograde. It is an excellent time to do things described by many verbs beginning with "re": revisit, revise, review, repair, reinvent, replace, repeal, relearn, reflect, remodel, readjust, reply, relive, relish, remain, renew, repay, repent, report, repose, repossess, reprieve, rerun, rescind, return, research, reserve, retreat, restore, retire, retrace, retract, retrench, return, reunite, revere, reverse, revamp, revive, reword, reward, and rewrite. The idea is to mirror, to mimic the action of Mercury in the sky by returning or going back over something.

Venus Retrograde

Venus is astrology's ruler of love, beauty, luxury, social affairs, and the fine arts. She rules the signs Taurus and Libra which are associated with valuables, money, contracts, agreements, treaties, partnerships, relationships, reconciliations, legal disputes, and justice. Barbara Watters writes that when Venus goes retrograde, "large social affairs go badly, attempts to raise money are disappointing, and attempts to conciliate others come to nothing." It is unwise to enter into contractual agreements under a retrograde Venus. Even treaties between nations do not fare well under these circumstances. This is not a good time to buy luxury items or make financial investments. Relationships entered into now will not live up to expectations.

On the other hand, Venus retrograde periods are excellent times for inner reflection on what you value or find beautiful. Visit a museum, enjoy the classics of literature or art, meditate on the beauties of nature, renew a relationship, review what your spouse or partner means to you, or take a spiritual retreat to reconsider on your value system.

Mars Retrograde

Mars represents the aggressive and passionately sexual side of human nature. Mars rules the signs Aries and Scorpio associated with the body, the head, leadership, assertiveness, initiation of action, impulse, drive, sex, death, penetration, transformation, and joint finances.

Barbara Watters regarded retrograde Mars as an especially nasty influence in an electional chart. She went so far as to write that "nothing is accomplished by activity under a retrograde Mars." Such an extreme position is not warranted by experience; however, it *is* wise to use caution when Mars is retrograde. We saw earlier the devastating effect of retrograde Mars as the Ascendant ruler in the flight of the lost squadron.

People are often impatient, tense, irritable, impulsive, passive-aggressive, or contentious during the retrograde periods of Mars. Mechanical devices purchased at such times are prone to accident or breakdown. Sexual activity may have deleterious consequences. Lawsuits and disputes begun under a retrograde Mars tend to go against the initiator. The perpetrator of an aggressive act often has it backfire. Travel may be dangerous, and any new venture may be marred by conflict or animosity.

Jupiter and Saturn Retrograde
Jupiter and Saturn retrogrades are felt much less personally than those of Mercury, Venus, and Mars. The effect of either of these planets turning retrograde will be seen mostly in society at large. People may be unrealistically optimistic when Jupiter has apparent backward motion. When Saturn is retrograde, there is a general atmosphere of frustration, hesitation, and delay. If Jupiter or Saturn are prominent in the natal chart, the retrograde periods of these planets will have a more personal effect. You should avoid beginning a new venture when a sign ruled by retrograde Jupiter or retrograde Saturn is on the Ascendant or rules the cusp describing the nature of the project.

Uranus, Neptune, and Pluto Retrograde
The retrogradation of Uranus, Neptune, and Pluto are the least personal of all. These three outer generational planets affect the global transpersonal conditions of society. If one of these planets is retrograde, it is best to avoid starting a new project when the sign ruled by the retrograde planet is on the Ascendant or rules the house of the matter at hand. The next chart example for the Stonewall uprising illustrates this point.

Retrograde Planets and the Gay Liberation Movement
Historians date the beginning of the Gay Liberation movement to the midnight raid by six of New York's finest on a seedy gay bar called the Stonewall Inn. Such raids were common in Greenwich Village in the 60s. Under the socially sanctioned pretext of checking for IDs, police would harass the drag queens, leather boys, transvestites, and other gays who frequented such establishments.

But the night of Friday, June 27, 1969, was somehow different. Judy Garland, an icon of the gay community, had just died and many of those in the crowd had filed past her coffin earlier in the day. As the police emerged from the Stonewall Inn with their catch for the day, the onlooking crowd began to fight back against years of gay-bashing by hurling beer cans, bottles, and other objects at the police. Reinforcements had to be called in. For the next two nights skirmishes broke out between the New York police and groups of gays in Greenwich Village. The Gay Liberation movement had begun, and Stonewall became its symbol. One gay group labeled the Stonewall incident "the hairpin drop heard around the world."

The accompanying chart is cast for midnight, Friday, June 27, 1969 (0 a.m. EDT Saturday, June 28, 1969). The precise time is not known for certain, but this chart works fairly well by transit and progression for timing events in the Gay Liberation movement. The Moon was not Void-of-Course for the Stonewall raid, but two significant planets were retrograde.

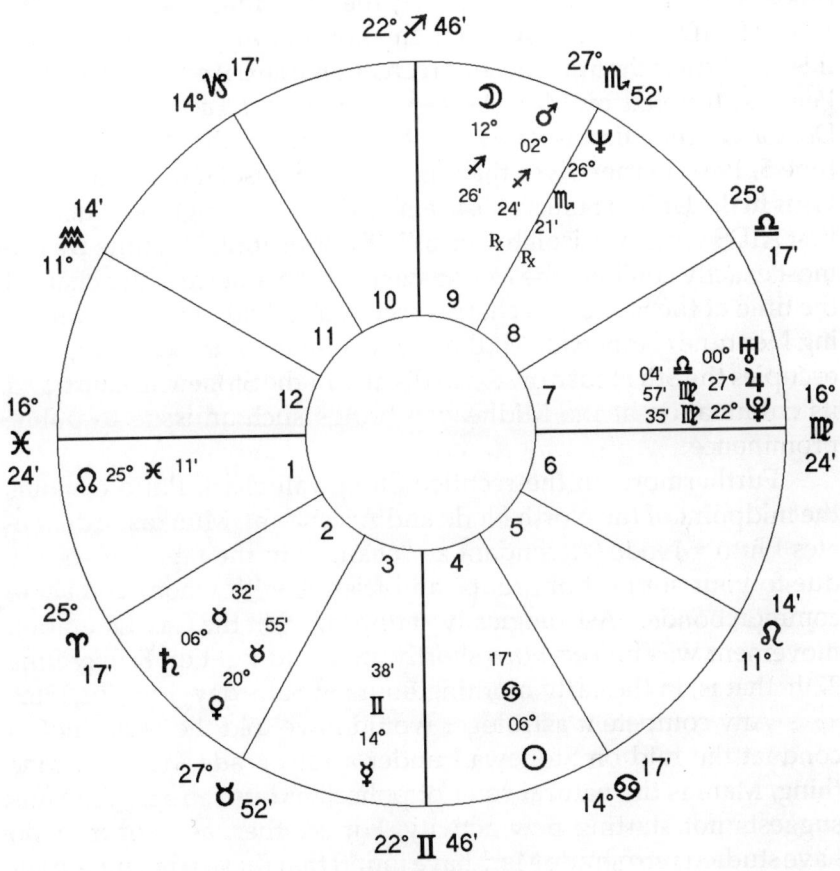

Stonewall
New York, New York
June 28, 1969
00:00 a.m. EDT
73W57 40N45
Koch Houses

Pisces, the sign of secrets and clandestine affairs, ascends as fits an unexpected police raid and the beginning of a movement which allowed gays to come out of the closet. Pisces' ruler, Neptune, is retrograde in the 8th House of sex and death matters in Scorpio, the sign of sex and death, no doubt presaging the AIDS epidemic. The closest aspect in the chart is a square to the Midheaven from Pluto, a planet closely associated with sexually transmitted diseases and epidemics.

The progressed Moon of this chart came around to oppose Ascendant ruler Neptune occupying the 8th House when the first cases of AIDS were diagnosed in this country in 1981. The Moon in this chart rules the 5th House of recreational sex. According to Marc Penfield (quoted by Mark Lerner in his *Planet Earth Magazine*), a Doctor Gottlieb first isolated the AIDS virus on the West Coast on June 5, 1981. Lerner gives the time of the first isolation of the AIDS virus in the United States as 5:46 a.m. PDT in Los Angeles. When the first AIDS virus was isolated on 6/5/81, transiting Neptune was almost exactly conjunct the Midheaven of the Stonewall raid chart. If the time of the Stonewall chart is rectified to 12:04 a.m., the transiting Neptune/Stonewall Midheaven conjunction is exact. Neptune occupies the 8th House of sexual disease in the Stonewall chart, and its culmination at the Midheaven brings such an issue to public prominence.

Furthermore, in the rectified Stonewall chart, Pluto conjoins the midpoint of the North Node and Ascendant. Munkasey delineates Pluto = Node/Ascendant as "changes in the fabric of society due to your support of groups and friends with whom you share common bonds." Astrologically, it appears that the Gay Liberation movement was indeed born shortly after midnight on Friday June 27th, that is, in the early morning hours of Saturday, June 28, 1969.

Any competent astrologer would have told the police not to conduct the raid on Stonewall under a retrograde Mars. For one thing, Mars is the natural ruler of police, and its retrograde status suggests not starting new activity. For another, astrologers who have studied retrograde Mars have found that those who initiate aggression with Mars retrograde usually suffer in turn as a result. As Barbara Watters remarked about aggressive situations under a retrograde Mars, "however remote and impossible victory may seem to be for the defenders, it will be theirs." The gays who defended themselves at Stonewall achieved the victory. Finally, Mars has always been a symbol for the male sexual energy. It is fitting that Mars is retrograde, traveling opposite it usual direction, in a chart so important to the Gay Liberation Movement.

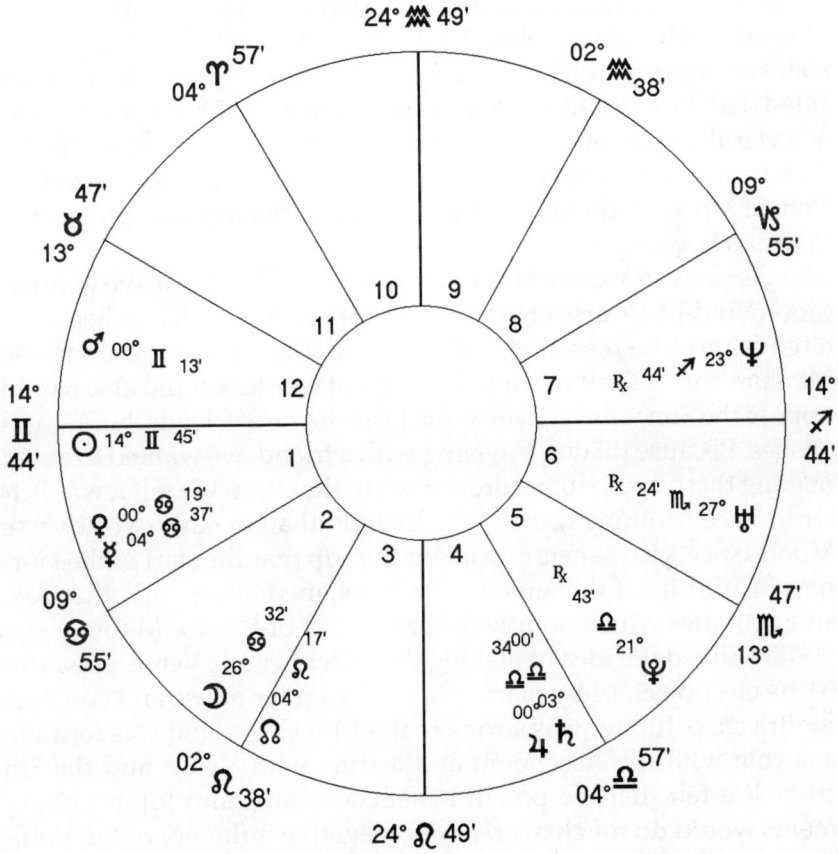

AIDS Virus First Isolated
Los Angeles, California
June 5, 1981
5:46 a.m. PDT
118W15 34N04
Koch Houses

A BUSINESS TRIP UNDER A VOID-OF-COURSE MOON

My friend Jill planned to travel to Jamaica for a three week combined business trip and vacation. She had enrolled to study yoga and other New Age topics, and had planned to give readings and teach an astrology course to cover her expenses. Jill had sent a course description to the woman organizing the trip.

Due to circumstances beyond her control, she could only leave home for the trip during a narrow period around 8 p.m. on the evening of Wednesday, February 27, 1991. Jill called me to consult about an electional chart for the best time to depart. Together we decided that the time she left her house and irrevocably began the journey was the time for which to cast the chart. The problem we immediately faced was whether she should leave during a Void-of-Course Moon. Although I normally use Koch cusps, Jill prefers the Placidus house system.

As you can see from the chart, we opted for Jill to leave with the Moon Void-of-Course at the very end of Leo rather than when it entered Virgo. We reasoned that, in Virgo, the Moon would oppose Mercury ruling the 9th House of long distance travel and also would oppose the Sun which governs the 11th House of friends, hopes, and wishes. Because Jill was traveling with a friend, we wanted to avoid making these oppositions prominent in the chart. We felt it was better to have "nothing come of the matter" than to have two adverse Moon aspects to planets crucial for the trip mar the start of the journey. In addition, Jill planned to do Yoga, mediation, and other passive activities which flourish under a Void-of-Course Moon.

We liked the idea of making the lesser benefic Venus powerful in the election chart by placing it in an angular house and conjunct the 7th cusp. Jupiter was strong in the 10th House and was forming a sextile with the Ascendant and a trine with Venus and the 7th cusp. We felt that the potent beneficial Venus and Jupiter placements would do much to offset any negative influence of the Void-of-Course Moon. In this chart, Saturn rules the end-of-the-matter 4th House with Capricorn on the cusp. Fourth House ruler Saturn is applying to a trine of the Ascendant, another favorable feature in an electional chart.

The result of Jill leaving at the time we selected paralleled the symbolism of this chart. Jill decided to extend her trip by two weeks to stay a total of five weeks. (Note Saturn, planet of delays and

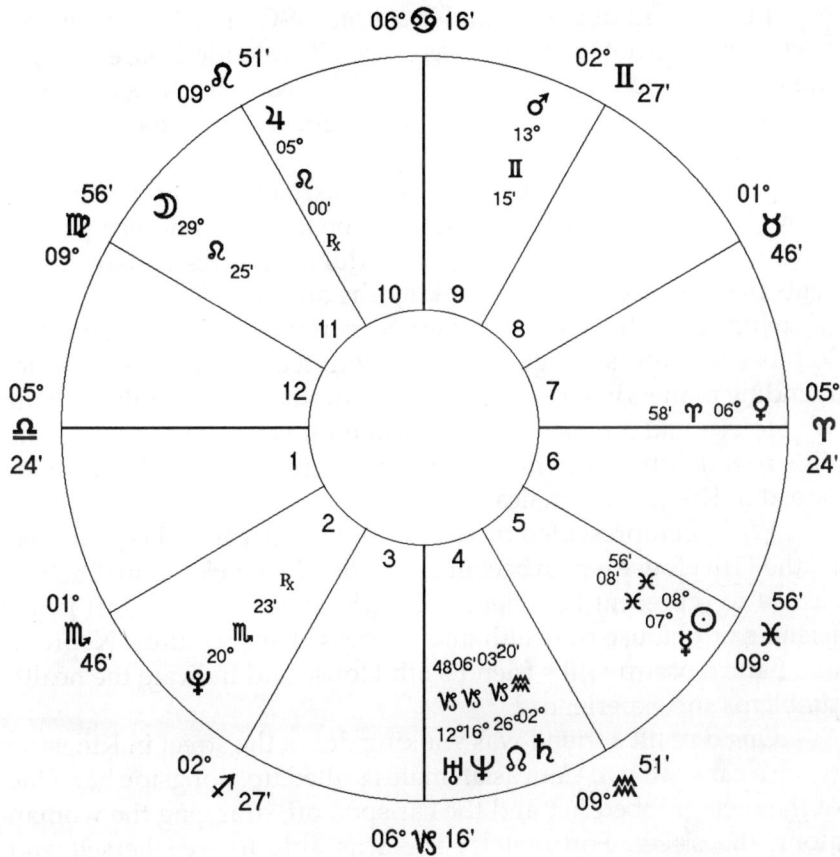

Jill's Trip
Feb. 27, 1991
7:50 p.m. EST
73W01 41N19
Placidus Houses

drawn-out matters, ruling the end-of-the-matter 4th cusp.) Be-
causeSaturn trines the Ascendant, the delay was a pleasant one.
With Jupiter sextile the Ascendant, Jill did not have to pay extra to
extend her plane flight. On the way home, the airport attendant first
told her to pay an extra $200 fare, but he decided to let her board the

plane with her original ticket and no extra fee.

Because Jill departed under a Void-of-Course Moon, she expected matters not to work out as originally intended. Sure enough, the woman who organized the trip neglected to list Jill's astrology course in the brochure and Jill never got to teach the astrology course as she had planned!

Jill was worried about having Uranus, Neptune, and Saturn occupy the angular 4th House. In electional charts angular planets have the most power. Among other things, the Ascendant represents the querent, the person asking the question, in this case—Jill. With Jupiter sextile the Ascendant, Saturn trine the Ascendant, and Venus strong on an angle, Jill was protected against the three demanding planets in the 4th House. Jill's mother, also signified by the 4th House, had a miserable time while Jill was away. In addition, Jill's friend suffered gynecological problems and was almost kidnaped in Kingston, Jamaica.

With Jill represented by the Ascendant, her friend is governed by the 11th House which becomes her friend's 1st House in the chart turned to represent her friend. The 4th House of Jill's chart is her friend's 6th House of health and distress. Thus, Uranus, Neptune and Saturn occupy Jill's friend's 6th House and indicate the health problems she experienced.

One day Jill's friend was walking down the street in Kingston when a car with two Caucasian males pulled up alongside her. One of the men grabbed her and the car sped off, dragging the woman along the street. Fortunately, she was able to free herself and escaped with some severe abrasions to her legs. She had come to Jamaica to do therapeutic massage, but her arm was injured in the car incident and she was unable to fulfill the purpose of her journey. Because Leo is on the cusp of the 11th House of friends, the Sun governs Jill's friend in this chart. Mercury conjoins the Sun in Pisces, natural ruler of the 12th House. In this chart Mercury rules Virgo on the cusp of the 12th House of kidnaping and secret enemies.

AN EMPIRICAL STUDY OF THE VOID-OF-COURSE MOON

Noel Tyl called my home on Wednesday, June 5, 1991, while the Moon was in Pisces and about to sextile Neptune and trine Pluto. When I arrived home at 6:30 that evening, I found his message on my answering machine. At 6:40 p.m. the Moon trined Pluto and went Void-of-Course. Not knowing why he called, I phoned him back after dinner about 9:15 p.m. EDT under the Void-of-Course Moon. I had considered waiting until the Moon entered Aries the next day, but I recalled Lilly's dictum that the Void-of-Course Moon can perform in Pisces, a sign traditionally ruled by Jupiter. Besides, I was curious about the call and didn't want to wait a day to find out what he wanted.

Tyl was calling to invite me to write this chapter for the upcoming Llewellyn volume on vocational astrology. Because of my expertise in horary astrology, he felt I would be a natural to write about the Void-of-Course Moon in the workplace. Tyl also urged me to study the effect of the Void-of-Course Moon by presenting a list of Void-of-Course Moon times to a business like a car dealership and asking them to track its effects for a month.

I called Noel back on Tuesday morning June 11, 1991, to agree to do the chapter when the Moon was in Gemini (writing) and was about to sextile Mars and Jupiter and conjoin Mercury later in the day. These aspects were especially favorable for a writing project. Because the Moon was Void-of-Course, though in Pisces, at the time of Noel's initial proposal, I expected that matters would not work out exactly as planned.

I could not get a car dealership to agree to the experiment. I did, however, convince two people, the manager of a popular radio station in Connecticut and a stockbroker in Maryland, to track the influence of the Void-of-Course Moon in their business dealings during a four week period in June and July, 1991. They both warned me that their workplaces were hectic and they could not guarantee to record every occurrence. I might have to settle for impressionistic data.

For my own part, I did a retrospective review of the six months from January to June, 1991 at the psychiatric day-hospital where I work. Part of my job is to interview all patients who apply for treatment to determine whether they are appropriate for our program. A day-hospital provides the same kind of care as an inpatient psychiatric hospital. The difference is that the patients go home at night and thus avoid the considerable cost of an inpatient stay.

During the six months under review, we had 72 admissions. Of the 72, 12 had their initial intake with me while the Moon was Void-of-Course. Of the 12 Void-of-Course patients, two dropped out of the program after a few days and one had the longest stay (more than four months) of any patient we had ever treated. The remaining nine Void-of-Course patients had rather typical treatments in the day hospital.

I also looked at patients who made intake appointments which they did not keep and did not call to cancel. We have many more intakes than we have admissions. In the six months being studied, there were a total of seven patients who simply did not show up when scheduled for an intake. Two of these "no-shows" (29 percent of this small sample) occurred when the Moon was Void-of-Course. Although the Moon was not Void-of-Course on February 28, 1991, one person did not show for an appointment just minutes before a Full Moon on that day. My day-hospital survey is of a rather small sample. The results suggest that the Void-of-Course Moon sometimes functions as described in the literature but not invariably so.

Now let's turn to the radio station and the stockbroker to see how they made out. As you recall, I gave the radio station manager in Connecticut and a stockbroker in Maryland a one month listing of Void-of-Course Moon periods that occurred during business hours. I asked each of them to track business activity during the Void-of-Course Moon times.

The stockbroker began his observations toward the end of June, 1991. The first Void-of-Course Moon he encountered occurred from 1:24 p.m. EDT on Tuesday, June 25, until 12:59 p.m. EDT on Wednesday, June 26. Beginning around 2 p.m. on Tuesday, June 25 and lasting all morning on June 26, telephone problems plagued his phone lines. The stockbroker was unable to call outside his immediate phone district and his business was adversely affected for almost the entire Void-of-Course Moon period!

Not only was the Moon Void-of-Course until 12:59 p.m. EDT on Wednesday, June 26, but Mercury (communications) opposed Neptune (confusion) at 12:03 p.m. EDT. One would *expect* communications problems during a Mercury/Neptune opposition. As an article in the *New York Times* explained, "a computer malfunction disrupted local telephone service for more than six hours today [June 26, 1991] for millions of customers in the capital as well as Maryland, Virginia and parts of West Virginia." The article neglected to mention the telephone problems the stockbroker had experienced the previous afternoon.

The next Void-of-Course Moon period this stockbroker had agreed to track occurred on Friday, June 28, of the same week. I called him early Friday afternoon to ask what observations he had made. His secretary said he had already left for the day. When I spoke to him the following week, he explained that he was so impressed by the foul-ups that occurred during my first "prediction" that he decided not to conduct any business during the Friday Void-of-Course Moon time. (This sort of reaction explains why true scientists do double-blind experiments.) One stock he purchased did not do as well as he had expected. The remaining Void-of-Course Moon periods appeared to have little effect on his business. However, some of the decisions he made during Void-of-Course Moon periods will take months or years to come to fruition and are beyond the time span of this study.

The radio station also reported mixed effects of the Void-of-Course Moon. The station manager's assistant, who happens to be an astrologer, was given the task of tracking the Void-of-Course Moon. Despite the fact that she had been hired during a Void-of-Course Moon, she did excellent work and even received a letter of commendation from the station owner while this study was underway. She set out to keep track of projects or contracts initiated when the Moon was Void-of-Course.

The first project she reported was a proposal to have a "Commuter's Day" as a promotional gimmick for the radio station. The idea received the go-ahead from the management and was scheduled for Labor Day. Because I completed this article in July, I cannot provide follow-up on the outcome of this proposal.

The second activity she tracked was a potentially lucrative contract to do radio advertising for a local popular restaurant. The contract was signed during a Void-of-Course Moon. Initially everything appeared to proceed smoothly. The ad copy department, working with the salespersons and the sponsor, came up with a creative advertisement for the business. Everyone was pleased with the effort, and new revenue, sorely needed in the current economic recession, was flowing into the station. It appeared that the Void-of-Course Moon was having no effect. At the last minute, however, the disk jockey misunderstood the timing of the advertisement and did not air the ad on several days which the restaurant owner regarded as crucial to his business. The station, of course, extended the advertisement to make up for the lost days; but, because of the mix-up, the restaurant decided not to renew its contract.

The station manager's assistant also noted that a meeting

scheduled for a Void-of-Course Moon period did not work out as planned. The purpose of the meeting was to edit a show. The producer simply did not show up, and the work could not go on as intended. On another occasion during a Void-of-Course Moon, a local television station called her to solicit a story about the astrological influences of the State of Connecticut's inability to pass a state budget. She was prepared to discuss the topic, but the television station never followed up on its initial invitation and nothing came of the matter. In one final instance, her boss asked her while the Moon was Void-of-Course to work collaboratively on a project with another employee. When she approached the other employee, she was told that the project was already well under way and no help was needed.

What can we conclude from this less than scientific research?

Noel Tyl and I agreed on this research project under a Void-of-Course Moon. As you can see, the project did not proceed as originally planned. The stockbroker was quite impressed by the first Void-of-Course Moon period he tracked and its negative effects on his business. His first experience of watching the Void-of-Course Moon affected the way he conducted his business afterward. Nonetheless, he made transactions during other Void-of-Course Moon times without apparent adverse consequences. At the radio station, the Void-of-Course Moon had some noticeable effects but the manager's assistant could not keep track of every idea, contract, or project begun under a Void-of-Course Moon. Although several events at the radio station did fit the traditional meaning of the Void-of-Course Moon, other projects begun under a Void-of-Course Moon seemed to proceed without a hitch.

SUMMARY

Where does that leave us? It appears that the Void-of-Course Moon, when considered as an isolated chart factor, sometimes works as described in the literature. At the same time, other astrological factors can mute or override the Void-of-Course effect. It should not surprise us that life is complex and there are no easy answers. The wisest course for the astrologer is to consider the whole chart, to weigh and synthesize all the astrological factors, before electing a best time to act.

Because of space limitations, I cannot go into detail about the fine points of electional astrology, but I will review some basic principles. Unless the chart is strong, avoid making major decisions when the Moon is Void-of-Course unless you are opting for a non-occurrence. It helps to have the Ascendant sign symbolize the situation. For example, the beginning of a research venture might do well with Scorpio rising. The planet ruling the Ascendant should apply to a harmonious aspect (conjunction, sextile or trine) with the planet which rules the cusp of the house in question. At the same time, the Ascendant ruler and the planetary signifiers of the matter should be free of stress, especially from strong aspects with Mars and Saturn. The principal significators should also not be retrograde. Conjunctions to Venus, Jupiter, or the Moon's North Node are helpful. Unless one of these planets or points symbolizes the situation, conjunctions to Mars, Saturn, Uranus, Neptune, Pluto or the Moon's South Node are usually detrimental in some way.

The Moon is very important in electional astrology and its condition should be carefully considered. New projects should mirror the action of the Moon. It is best to start a new venture during the waxing Moon between its New Moon phase and its Full Moon phase. The Moon is traditionally debilitated when close to the Sun. The New Moon is actually a Sun/Moon conjunction. Most electional astrologers advise waiting 12 to 24 hours after the New Moon to begin a project so the Moon has time to come out from under the sunbeams. If you want to keep something hidden, do it close to the New Moon when the Moon is obscured by the Sun.

In electional astrology, only applying aspects are important *because they show what is going to happen*. The closer the aspect is to perfection, the more potent it is. Separating aspects show what has already transpired. It is most helpful if the Moon and the primary significators are applying to close harmonious aspects with one another or with Venus and Jupiter. Favorable aspects to the relevant house cusps or to the Ascendant or Midheaven can also be beneficial.

The Cadent Houses (3, 6, 9, 12) of electional charts are the weakest. If you have a chart with a difficult aspect, try to place the stressfully involved planets in Cadent Houses but not too close to the angles (Ascendant/Descendant, Midheaven/I.C.) because planets conjunct the angles are powerful. You should "bury" malefic planets in the Cadent Houses if possible. At the same time, keep the "demanding" planets out of the angular houses unless they rule the matter at hand. For example, Mars rules machinery and a project involving machines might do well with Mars prominent in the electional chart. Emphasize positive aspects and beneficial planets by placing them in angular houses or conjunct the Ascendant/Descendant or Midheaven/I.C. axes.

And remember, in a pinch, try not to start an important project when the Moon is Void-of-Course. If unable to study the entire chart, why risk having the matter not work out as intended?

BIBLIOGRAPHY

Andrews, Edmund L. "Computer Failure Disrupts Phones for 6 Hours in Washington Area," *The New York Times*, National Section, Thursday, June 27, 1991, page A27.

Cozzi, Steve. *Local Space Astrology*. St. Paul, MN: Llewellyn Publications, 1988.

Dorotheus Sidonius. *Carmen Astrologicum*, translated by David Pingree, BSB B.B. Leipzig: Teubner Verlagsgesellshaft, 1976.

Goldstein-Jacobson, Ivy M. *Simplified Horary Astrology*. Alhambra, CA: Frank Severy Publishing, 1960.

Jones, Marc Edmund. *Problem Solving by Horary Astrology*. Philadelphia: David McKay Publishers, 1946.

Lerner, Mark. "AIDS: 10 Years Later," *Welcome to Planet Earth Magazine*, pages 3 & 34, Vol. 11, No.1, Cancer, 1991.

Louis, Anthony. *Horary Astrology: The History and Practice of Astro-Divination*. St. Paul, MN: Llewellyn Publications, 1991.

March, Marion. *Electional Astrology*. Encino, CA: Astro Analytics Audio Tapes, 1990.

Maternus, Firmicus. *The Mathesis of Firmicus Maternus*, translated by Jean Rhys Bram. Park Ridge, NJ: Noyes Press, 1975.

Morrison, Al H. "Ephemeris of the Void of Course Moon." Al H. Morrison, Box 75 Old Chelsea Station, New York, 1991.

Morrison, Al H. "Notes on the Void-of-Course Moon," *The Mountain Astrologer*, August/September 1989.

Morrison, Al H., personal correspondence, June 14, 1991. (My thanks to Mr. Morrison for his permission to quote his published works on the Void-of-Course Moon.)

Munkasey, Michael. *Midpoints: Unleashing the Power of the Planets*. San Diego: ACS, 1991.

Parsons, Pamela. "Mercury Retrograde," *Welcome to Planet Earth Magazine*, Vol. 10 No. 12. Gemini 1991.

Quigley, Joan. *What Does Joan Say?* New York: Pinnacle Books, 1990.

Scofield, Bruce, "Financial Planning for 1991," *Llewellyn's 1991 Astrological Calendar*, page 47. St. Paul, MN: Llewellyn Publications, 1991.

Scofield, Bruce. *The Timing of Events: Electional Astrology*. Orleands, MA: Astrolabe, 1985.

"Stonewall," *Newsweek Magazine*, pages 56-57, July 3, 1989.

"The Sea Yields Its Lost Squadron," *People Magazine*, June 3, 1991.

Watters, Barbara. *Horary Astrology and the Judgment of Events*. Washington, DC: Valhalla Paperbacks, 1973.

Zain, C. C. *Horary Astrology*. Los Angeles: The Church of Light, 1931.

Henry Weingarten

Henry Weingarten, founder of the New York School of Astrology and director of the New York Astrology Center, has been a professional astrologer for more than 25 years. He is a past director of the National Astrological Society, is currently a member of the AFAN Steering Committee, and is the Managing Director of The Astrologers Fund, Inc. which uses astrology as the primary analysis tool to manage investment funds.

Henry is internationally known as the author, editor, and publisher of many astrological publications. Formerly editor of The Aquarian Agent and Astrology (1976-1981) magazines, he is the author of *The Study of Astrology*, *A Modern Introduction to Astrology*, *Principles of Synastry*, and his forthcoming *Principles of Rectification*.

Henry is a member of AAAI, AACD, AFAN, ATP, IAKE, and IIF and continues to lecture at astrological conferences around the world, appearing frequently on television and radio talk shows. He is also a professional microcomputer systems designer and has taught computer science at NYU and the New School in New York. In addition to writing and financial astrology, his primary interest is the application of artificial intelligence to the study of astrology; specifically, the development of the expert astrological computer programs MERCURY, RECTIFY & GALAXY.

Vocational Signatures for Astrologers

Henry Weingarten

Common to the ancient Babylonians, Chaldeans, Chinese, Egyptians, and Hindus was the preeminent stature of the astrologer-priest. The astrologer's role in subsequent civilizations has varied from positions of honor and prestige to those of mere tolerance and ridicule, and even to heretical criminality!

Today, according to the Department of Labor, astrology is the ninth best profession in the United States.[1] With the growing new age awareness in Western society, astrologers are once again finding their work in demand. Since 1965–1969, the number of clients seeking astrological counsel has increased dramatically. Correspondingly, the demand for trained astrologers has increased as well. Today a career in astrology can be a creative opportunity for individuals to make a significant contribution to society.

Astrological advice is most often sought on the two great issues of personal life: LOVE and WORK. This article is designed to assist students in addressing the fundamental issues of choosing a vocation, that which *Webster's New 20th Century Dictionary* defines as "The function or career toward which one believes himself to be called."

The two perennial focal points of natal astrology, love and work, require astrologers to have knowledge other than that of

---

1. The 1989 U.S. government study, as reported in the January, 1990 AFAN Newsletter, used six criteria for rankings: salary, stress, work environment, outlook, security and physical demands. Interestingly enough, astronomers were listed as number 20!

169

"pure" astrology. It is my assumption that all serious students will read a few basic textbooks on *vocational guidance* itself in order to obtain the requisite minimum level of understanding of the issues.

It is well known that most people are unhappy with their work life. Why? Whose "original dream" or destiny are they following? Their parents', society's, or their own horoscope? Clearly, as astrologers, we know that it is only by following the dharma of one's horoscope that one will be fulfilled in this lifetime.

The question of "What is the best job for me" is to a large extent a question of values, as much as a question of astrology. Astrological counselors must work through their client's value set in addition to their own. It is also strategically important to appreciate that the choice of one's ideal vocation, especially in the 21st century, includes JOB CREATION, as well as an integrated and realistic plan to implement the personally expressive idea.

The following 12 points are benchmark considerations to be considered as we improve our skills with vocational guidance.

Point 1:   Vocational Choice is an Expression of Self;
Better Self Knowledge Implies Better Choice.

One's horoscope helps determine various issues of employment, including the selection of a working environment, *e.g.,* large corporation, institutional setting, small business, independent contractor, self-employment.

We must determine whether the vocational problem being presented in a consultation is a central or a symptomatic one; and *why* isn't the client able to solve the problem? We must remember that the ultimate goal is client growth, as well as a solution to the immediate problem.

Point 2:   One Life/One Job is a Dated Concept.

Modern Vocational Guidance does not involve one "correct" lifelong choice of the "right job," but rather a process of continuous changing and choosing. The average young person can then expect that occupational training will *not* last a lifetime and may be assured that the occupations will undergo marked changes in the course of the work-life.

Point 3: Multiple Vocational Choices are Inherent Astrological Possibilities.

Vocational guidance should answer the question: "What do you want to be when you grow up?" However, we postulate that *not one but multiple choices* are possible. Astrological counseling should help the client match personal requirements with job requirements. These should include the *client's* value system, educational and work-environmental considerations.

If the client is blocked regarding value selection, then asking two questions may prove helpful:

How would you spend your time if you had only six months to live?

You have just won the lottery! What would you do initially, and how would you spend your time one year from now?

A selection of critical values and what is truly important to the client thus becomes self-evident.

Point 4: Aim High: Plan and Execute Vocational Decisions as if This Were your One and Only Lifetime on Planet Earth.

The Midheaven, the primary astrological significator of vocation, is the *highest* point a planet reaches in its daily rotation. The Midheaven is our prime key for vocational decisions.

Point 5: Apply Vocational Guidance Theory to Astrological Knowledge, not Vice Versa.

Standard vocational guidance theory and practice, beginning with the pioneering Holland and Roe schemas on down, are *not* based on an objective and natural typology of human nature, *i.e.*, astrology. Like most psychological theories, they are based on the inventor's individual horoscope; they are not as rich, complete, or encompassing as the full spectrum of astrological theory.

Point 6: Selection Process is Important, but so is Rejection.

Our work is really comprised of a two-step process: first, to find *appropriate* vocational areas; second, to eliminate other areas.

It is just as valuable in the evaluation process to eliminate possibilities that are potential psychic-energy drains as it is to make selections. The selection process should be carried out by initially making a list of the major elements of the natal horoscope. Then match these factors to the nature of the work process involved in each potential vocational selection. The lowest number of matches should be eliminated as only partial or alternative solutions that would produce dissatisfying results.

Point 7: Classical Rulerships are Dated.

Suffice it to say, vocational guidance formerly was relatively easy; society's economic and social structure was far simpler, with a more limited number and variety of professions. Everyone usually went into the father's profession (note the connection among the Midheaven, career, and father).

Many occupations of today were not even predicted a scant 20 years ago, and it has been postulated that most of the jobs of the future are not known today. Even those occupations with the same titles today as yesterday do not call for identical training and skills.

Point 8: The House Group 2-6-10 is a Dodo!

The vocational selection process should be based on the *whole* chart, utilizing *all* its assets in vocational guidance. Work is a primary source of life satisfaction. Vocational success and satisfaction are affected by and have an effect upon success and satisfaction in other life areas. Since it is the whole person who is involved in vocational decisions, we must look at the entire chart when studying vocational processes.

Point 9: "Textbook" Cases that are Easy to Evaluate Almost Never Seek Advice!

It is true that outstanding charts must be studied as examples of basic principles to be tested and as a means of comparison. However, real life practice is seldom so simple. We must assess the client's interests, abilities, temperament and values, which are rarely clear-cut. Otherwise they would probably not be seeking advice in the first place!

Point 10: Timing is (Almost) Everything.

Choosing the best time to initiate an activity, be it the optimum time to interview for a job, re-enter the work force, or make a career shift, obviously requires skilled electional astrology input. We note how most new businesses go under in the first year. It is important here to check the electional elements of the owner's and principals' charts.

Point 11: Career Crisis=Opportunity.

A holistic view of astrology builds on previous experience rather than rejecting it. The well-known Chinese character for "crisis" is made up of two pictograms: "danger" and "opportunity." Forced retirements, being fired, or laid off are not necessarily "bad," any more than keeping a job you hate is "good." This is the time to re-evaluate old patterns. Ask questions.

Point 12: Know How to Counsel the Next Step.

There is an old Chinese saying: "The longest journey begins with the first step." An astrological client needs help taking the next step; it is not sufficient to tell someone that the horoscope suggests he would be a good fireman or doctor. Trained vocational counselors are expected to help not only in making an occupational choice but in assisting with career preparation and finding a job opening. This requires a basic knowledge of economic cycles, vocational trends, and training opportunities. *At the very least, astrologers should possess a good vocational counselor referral list.*

Vocational guidance consists of five steps: Analysis of the Individual; Occupational Information; Career Counseling; Placement Assistance; and Ongoing Guidance in Building a Career. How many astrological counselors go beyond step 1?

REASONS FOR WORK

Throughout history, the reasons for work have varied. Many early attitudes, especially those of the ruling classes, viewed work as a curse and as drudgery. Others such as the Puritans valued work as a means of salvation. Those spiritually inclined understand work as dharma, and dharma yoga is a means to enlightenment as long as one is not too attached to the fruits of one's labors.

Astrologically, we can look at job motivations as reflected primarily through these planetary principles:

Sun	Recognition
Moon	Being Needed
Mercury	Intellectual Stimulation
Venus	Companionship
Mars	Competition

Jupiter	Money
Saturn	Security
Uranus	Creativity
Neptune	Idealism
Pluto	Power
Nodes	Group Membership

Then we may recognize that many classical vocational schemes have obvious astrological correspondences. For example:

SCIENTIFIC: Uranus
An Interest in Knowing the Why and How of Things.

LITERARY: Mercury
Interest in the Use of Words and the Manipulation of Verbal Symbols.

SYSTEMATIC: Saturn
Keeping Records, Organizing Information, Computing.

CONTACT: Nodes
Meeting or Dealing with People in Connection with One's Business or Profession.

Similarly, an aptitude listing such as mechanical (Mars), computational (Saturn), artistic (Venus) has an obvious profile of astrological rulerships. Yet, while some of Dr. Michel Gauquelin's pioneering research work on vocation[2] did find "textbook answers," as Mars for sport champions and Saturn for scientists; other careers, such as acting, were ruled by Jupiter rather than by Neptune; or writing, by the Moon and not Mercury.

Often, one goes astrologically crazy in believing patterns exist where they do not. For example, one may assume that the basic three vocational strength-areas of data, things, and people naturally correspond to the astrological triplicities (Cardinal, Fixed, and Mutable, respectively). Yet, surely Virgo works better with data, and Libra with people. Just as we are taught to quickly associate firemen with Mars, or artists with Venus, Uranus has in recent tradition been the attributed ruler of astrologers. How valid is this?

In order to discuss the astrological rulerships of astrologers, we need to review the concept of rulerships in general. Even before

---

1. Gauquelin, Michel. *Cosmic Influences on Human Behavior.*

Gauquelin's work[3] indicated that planets do not rule professions so much as the temperamental types that are typical and appropriate to various occupations, we have had, early in the 20th century, such writers as Van Klockler saying: "There is really no such thing as a Saturn vocation, Mars vocation, etc. Of course, Mars plays a role in such professions as butchers, doctors, or soldiers, but always as a part of a larger configuration, and this configuration is the important thing. Besides, we know that a Mars component is important or even necessary in other vocational areas as well. Traditional astrology has little to say about this."[4]

SOME IMPORTANT WORDS ON RULERSHIPS[5]

It cannot be too highly emphasized that astrology signifies the symbolism and meaning of behavior and situations, and *not literal events*, so that we find astrological "rulerships" are constantly changing. As an example, what is the rulership for lotteries? All the old textbooks answer Jupiter-Pluto; however, modern observation finds Jupiter-Uranus to be the case—because rulerships change.

Formerly, lotteries like the Irish Sweepstakes were conducted so that a ticket was bought several months before the drawing date, hence the winning combination was signified by Jupiter-Pluto, *i.e.*, money developed in time. Lotteries today are organized differently. In the New York state "instant winner" Bingo-lottery, the ticket buyer discovers immediately whether he or she is the winner, simply by rubbing the ticket. Here, the winning combinations are signified by Jupiter-Uranus: instant money or windfalls.

What is the rulership of airplanes? Almost all the old textbooks answer Uranus, while many modern works add Neptune. This is not merely a situation of the old books being wrong, and the new right. Consider the nature of flying *before* WWII. It was a new, exciting and often dangerous activity, drawing strong Uranian personalities as does the Space Program today. Of course the need for change into "new" and "different" Uranian environments also continues to play a role.

In modern times, however, airplanes and aviation have become commonplace and flying an extremely safe and secure activ-

---

3. Gauquelin, Francoise. *Psychology of the Planets.*
4. Von Klockler, H. *Astrology & Vocational Aptitude.*
5. From the author's forthcoming: *Study of Astrology Book II.*

ity, statistically even more so than driving a car. Thus the natural symbolism of Neptune ("to get high") can function more purely.

Define Function

We must first carefully define activity or personality traits by their function; specifically with vocation, we study the nature of the daily activity, and the nature of the skills and talents required.

Then we are able to discern the appropriate astrological symbolism, remembering always *to test* our hypothesis by clinical observation. Consider the rulership of translators: naturally we turn to Mercury-Jupiter for good language skills. Often Neptune (or the Moon) is prominent, since such people have "an ear" for language. Keep in mind that Neptune is very sensitive and chameleon-like, taking on the color of its surroundings, hence the ability to pick up accents.

But suppose we were doing a study of translators at the United Nations. Would we also find a strong Uranus to the extent that they were engaged in *simultaneous* translating? However, in the translation of a scholarly book, wouldn't we be more apt to find a prominent Saturn, due to the need for precision in technical translation? Neptune would be appropriate for literary translators.

A Clue—When we aren't able to figure out a rulership due to lack of surety of the symbolism involved, it is often helpful *to define the rulership of its polarity function*. For example, if we are uncertain of the rulership of democracy but realize the rulership of royalty to be Jupiter, we may hypothesize that Saturn as polarity pair to Jupiter to be the correct answer. If we had suggested the Sun, symbolizing autocracy or dictatorship, then the polarity pair, the correct response for co-rulership, would have been the Moon.

Astrologically, what is the difference between being a chauffeur and a cab driver? (Think about this a moment before reading further.) Obviously both have a mercurial element, sharing transportation, but the cab driver is transporting the public, thus the co-rulership of the Moon. If we are thinking of a long-distance bus driver, he should not only have Mercury and Moon strong, but also Jupiter for the longer distances involved.

Body Analogy

Planetary influences do not work in isolation. This is a very important point to remember when we read a chart. Although in our early studies we need to isolate and analyze specific sections of the chart, this is not how an individual works.

An analogy to the physical body may be helpful here: while the functions of the liver, heart, kidneys, lungs, etc., may be studied separately, the functioning of each organ both directly and indirectly affects each of the functions of the other organs.[6] Similarly, rather than viewing the planets as separate elements in the chart, we should instead emphasize seeing *relationships and patterns* in the horoscope.

WHAT PROFESSIONAL ASTROLOGERS BELIEVE

An informal phone survey to more than 25 leading professional astrologers in the United States and the United Kingdom produced three basic responses to the following three questions. Naturally every respondent replied "yes" to the third question.

1. What are the astrological indicators of an astrologer?

2. Is your answer based on observation, and if so, how many charts have been taken into account?

3. Are these configurations present in your own chart?

Astrological View #1
The first group generally consisted of astrologers who had viewed fewer than 100 professional astrologers' charts. They provide a relatively standard variation on the theme: Uranus Rules Astrologers.

"All have strong Uranus."

"Strong Uranus, or strong aspects to Uranus and to the 10th House."

"Strong Saturn/Uranus; Uranus connection with the Midheaven."

"Strong 1) Uranus and 2) Mercury."

"Strong Uranus/Neptune and strong Chiron."

A special subset of this group had viewed a much larger number of horoscopes of astrologers and the "rules" became more com-

---

6. Until recently, the false assumptions of western medicine to treat each organ separately gave devastating results of course. Today there is a healthy trend toward holistic astrology.

plicated. Here are two examples:

"Strong 1) Uranus and 2) Jupiter, especially Sun/Jupiter; Moon/Jupiter combinations."

"5th Harmonic linking of Saturn, Uranus, Sun, Midheaven + Uranus and Neptune to the Midheaven plus classical Witte (Uranian Astrology) formulas."

Astrological View #2

The second group consisted of astrologers who had studied the greater number of astrologers' horoscopes. They believed "there is no such animal as the horoscope of an astrologer *per se*," although this group as a whole believes "there are certain astrological configurations that are helpful in forming an opinion as to whether one could/should earn a living as an astrologer."

A composite quote for this group would be: "There are many different types of astrologers. Some are counseling/practitioners, while others pursue the discipline for their own self-guidance. Some are Financial astrologers, other specialize in Political, Horary, etc. *Therefore it is not possible to point out one simple set of configurations that would define ASTROLOGER.*"

Below are three specific examples of this view, given by prominent astrologers.

"There are many kinds of astrologers as well as many different approaches to the subject. I don't believe one becomes an astrologer because of some configuration of Uranus or Neptune or a combination of the two. Since there are many different kinds of astrologers, just as there are various medical practitioners, astrological configurations will vary. One must look at both the heliocentric chart and, as well, at the geocentric in order to discover what Dharma the general life paths will take. An astrologer should be good at analysis as well as at interpretation, especially connecting the various elements together. My study of astrology above all else is learning to understand my own chart. I learn to understand what is specific and unique to me, and what is average."

—Michael Erlewine

"There is no specific profile of planets, aspects, or house placements, but rather, a dynamic accentuation of behavioral resources like analytical skill, communications facility, relationship poise, education, a sense of caring, even healing, showmanship and a sense of drama. These resources emerge, respectively, from situations of Uranus and Mercury, the 3rd House, the 7th House and the 9th, the sign Cancer and the Moon's placement, Leo and the Sun. Then, of course, the rest of the horoscope speaks about *what kind* of astrologer one can be, what style, what specialities, etc. Indeed, this profile could show *any kind* of counselor, and I am at a loss to specify 'astrologer.' This specification is accomplished by the person and not by a set of measurements."

—Noel Tyl

"There are so many different kinds of astrologers! In my observation of many hundreds (700+?) of charts of students and practitioners, I have certainly not found any common denominators. There seem to be both Uranus and Neptune types. Angular Jupiter seems common (Playing God?). Degree areas that I see as strongly suggestive of a likely interest and affinity with astrology are 27 Leo/Aquarius and sometimes 27 Taurus/Scorpio though less common, and 18 Gemini/Sagittarius. 22 Cancer/Capricorn seems related to forecasting.

"I associate Mercury-Uranus and Mercury-Neptune aspects with progressive and metaphysical pursuits generally. Certainly Mercury/Uranus seems essential for the more technical astrologer. Uranus and Apollo (Witte) are certainly common with the Midheaven or Sun in my experience."

—Charles Harvey

Before I present astrological view #3, I would like to comment on the lack of substantial research in this matter. Like almost all astrological opinions extant, few, if any, are backed by real scientific study, and unfortunately little more is supported by clinical observation. Historically, the best research into the horoscopes of astrologers comes from England; the best known study undertaken by Charles Carter. His pioneering work showed a much greater than chance correlation with planets in 26 Aquarius/Leo, which today has become known as the "astrologer's degrees."

More recently, England's Michael Harding completed a study of 284 astrologers from Great Britain, the United States and the Netherlands, which was reported at the 1989 AA Research Conference. The four major findings were:

1. The prevalence of 18° Mutable; particularly Jupiter in Gemini and Sagittarius.
2. Most frequent signs: Midheaven-Sagittarius; Sun-Aquarius; Moon-Sagittarius.
3. The most frequent planetary combination: Moon-Jupiter.
4. Moon = Saturn/Uranus 13.6 percent; 13.2 percent had Sun = Mercury/Saturn.

Astrological View #3

The third view, which I endorse, is that, in addition to the interest in astrology as expressed through Uranus and Neptune configurations (especially to the Midheaven, if professional), one just allow for other factors. Specifically, these include self-promotion required for self-employment, as well as the communication and empathy skills needed in counseling. That is to say, a well-designed research study should be prepared to explore finding variations for 1) Astrological interest, 2) Astrological skills, and 3) Professional Astrological skills.

THE ASTROLOGICAL PROFESSION: YESTERDAY, TODAY, AND TOMORROW

Clearly, as the profession of astrologer changes, so will the nature of the people drawn into the field and therefore the astrological profiles for astrologers. It is important to distinguish strongly between those who entered the field before 1965 and those *after*. In 1965, there occurred the great conjunction of Uranus (Astrology) and Pluto (Rebirth).[7] There was a clear distinction among astrological students. Those in the field before 1965 came largely from theosophical and other metaphysical belief systems; thus a very large Neptunian population. Those entering *after* 1965 were relatively mainstream counter-culture and somewhat more "scientifically oriented"—although one would be hard-pressed to make a case that the practice of astrology is even mildly scientific, given the largely untested belief system espoused by its devotees and practitioners!

Before 1970, practically no "professional" astrologers made their living from counseling clients. Indeed, when I began my study

---

7. Since 1965, Astrology has had two waves of great popularity correspondent with the Jupiter-Uranus conjunctions of 1969 and 1983. Note also the upcoming 1997 configuration.

of astrology in the early 1960s, no such role models existed. All the great contemporary astrologers were writers; they were devoted amateurs who supported their astrology habit from other fields. Today it is quite different; when any professionally trained, technically qualified astrologer can make a good living.

Training and Education

Contemporary astrologers are mainly self-starters, as were those 19th century country doctors who at that time were often self-taught, but today must graduate from an accredited medical school. Today, we have four types of astrological training:

The self-taught. As the Director of the New York School of Astrology, I feel these to be among the least qualified, especially since astrology today is still largely an oral tradition with less than one-third of the extant known knowledge codified.

Those who have apprenticed. They are of a higher caliber than the self-taught, but are still limited and lacking in exposure, which results in too narrow a perspective.

Private-school graduates. My preference, as this is a performance-based method of learning astrology.

Academic college. Not yet an option for learning astrology, but may well become one in the next century.

Finally, we arrive at the question of the nature of astrological practice itself, and the specialities contained therein. Not all police officers are Mars-ruled (some don't have guns and shoot); in a like manner, astrological teachers, researchers, and practitioners do not all share the same traits, *i.e.,* horoscopes.

It is well known that excellent technical skills alone do not guarantee business success. Many different types of skills are necessary to cultivate a profitable astrological practice. Astrologers today do not have the option, like social workers for example, to work for government or industry except as outside contractors. In our case, skills and attributes such as risk-taking, communication, and knowledge of marketing become essential for business success.

What Does One Need to Know to Become an Astrologer?

The study of astrology is a lifelong, if not multi-life, process. At the very least, one must have a working knowledge of the branches of Natal and Predictive Astrology, Synastry, and Vocational Guidance in order to address the most frequent, and basic, client issues.

To practice specialities such as Astro-Economics, Medical Astrology, and, of course, Vocational Guidance, in-depth knowledge of these disciplines is also required. Finally, the study of the human psyche, developmental processes, therapeutic modalities and basic counseling skills are needed to communicate astrological insights in a helpful, healing manner.

What are Our Career Prospects?

Most new astrologers begin work independently on a part-time basis until they enlarge their clientele sufficiently through personal recommendation. While group practice or institutional settings are relatively rare, an increasing number work as the staff astrologer in New Age centers, in the special services division of health clinics and spas, or by referral with psychotherapy centers. Teaching in various adult education forums is a further option. As the public becomes better educated about the benefits of astrological counseling, we believe the job opportunities will continue to expand as astrologers serve an ever-growing segment of the population.

The success of a private practice is not a mystery. It is based on a combination of sound business principles and professional competencies, which students must learn. In addition, graduates are able to benefit from having already established a beginning practice during their clinical internship, as well as belonging to a referral network of new age professionals, a continuing source of future clients.

The most important point to keep in mind is that as the nature of the profession changes, *so do its practitioners*. Let me repeat the interesting parallel which lies in the history of the medical profession: the 19th century doctor was required to practice, without medical school, certainly differing enormously from a 20th century doctor. As the life and therefore the horoscope of a street-walker is not the same as that of a costly call girl, so too should we expect to note differences among the horoscopes of the gypsy-type astrologer, the six-month, self-taught, self-proclaimed professional, and today's graduate who has completed studies in the newly emerging worldwide professional astrological institutes.

Further dramatic changes will take place as astrology becomes part of mainstream culture, as it is in India, for example, where astrology is an acceptable profession. The vast majority of today's astrologers are the result of a career change. While some astrologers began in their teens and chose astrology as a first career, either because of belonging to an astrological lineage or as a past life prompting, this is a relatively rare phenomenon. How often do school children say they want to be astrologers when they grow up? After all, it is not well-known, even in the astrological community that astrology is the ninth best profession in the United States! Further, mainstream vocational counselors are no more likely to recommend astrology as a career choice than they would be to urge an average New York City child toward a job as a forest ranger, or a hippy pacifist to a life in the military!

Not only does the issue of professional versus non-professional need addressing, but we must also deal with the semi-professional class of astrologers. Many professionals choose to do astrology "plus." This choice is often made because many of the colorful types attracted to astrology would be bored with just one profession, even one so infinitely interesting and encompassing as astrology, with its broadest definition being "The study of the universe and everything in it."[9] Also, amateurs who do view astrology as a sacred science may not have the ability, or choose not to, to develop the requisite business skills needed for self-employment as a professional astrologer.

My vision of the 21st century astrologer-practitioner is one who, rooted in the original sacred Neptunian wisdom, is armed with Uranian technology and insights. Accordingly, I see the 1993 conjunctions of Uranus (Astrology) and Neptune (Spirituality) as a potentially important milestone in the transformation of our field.

In the *Dictionary of Occupational Titles, Vol. II*, issued by the United States Department of Labor, occupations are listed according to five categories: Training Time, Aptitudes, Interests, Temperament, and Physical Demands. Let's look forward to the day when the Labor Department adds a sixth category: ASTROLOGICAL RULERSHIPS!

---

9. Its more formal definition being: A mathematical psychology based on astronomy.

Bob Mulligan

Bob Mulligan holds two degrees, a Bachelor of Arts and Master of Arts in Philosophy, from Roosevelt University in Chicago. He started his career in astrology while in graduate school. In 1974, Bob founded his business, Astrology Information, and has been a full time professional astrologer since then.

Bob operates a correspondence school with a four-year program in training called "The Mastery Of Astrology," and has written astrological software for computers, including a comprehensive chart interpretation program called INDRA.

Bob travels continuously and has clients and students around the world. He operates a regular local astrology practice in *eight* cities in the United States. He has written and lectured extensively, and wrote a regular astrology column between 1981 and 1989.

Since 1989, Bob has been involved in the formation of NCGR/PROSIG, an organization for professional astrologers, of which he is currently President. Bob's professional affiliations include the National Council for Geocosmic Research (NCGR), Assocation for Astrological Networking (AFAN), and the Astrological Association of Great Britain.

Bob is a resident of Naples, Florida, where he lives with his wife, Kathryn, and seven-year-old daughter, Juliana. Bob travels frequently to India, as a follower of Meher Baba since 1970.

How to Fulfill Your OWN Career as a Professional Astrologer

Bob Mulligan

A fulfilling career means you are personally happy and look forward to your work each day; you earn enough money to meet responsibilities in the material world; and you feel successful while contributing something of value to your field. In this sense, I have been successful as an astrologer. Further, I have worked professionally with many other astrologers to help them make their careers more rewarding. I have trained professional astrologers with my classes, correspondence school, and a series of testing and consulting sessions; and for years, I have donated many hours every month to the organization for professional astrology, PROSIG. The ideas presented here are a consolidation of exactly what has worked in terms of practical results.

The five-step process that I want to share comes from years of talking to professional astrologers and comparing notes with astrologers all over the world. The five stages are: *Preparation, Apprenticeship, Getting Started, Building Your Practice, Sharing Your Knowledge*. Each is very important in its own right. Before embarking on a career in astrology, you can use these steps as an indispensable road map. If you, as an astrologer, have difficulty in your career, the problem can be traced, diagnosed, and treated by carefully examining how you approached and dealt with each of these five benchmark points. These demarcations are five prominent aspects or facets of one continuous process. Each step affects and profoundly colors the other four significantly.

After the description of this process, there will be a discussion on money and the astrologer's place in society. These two additional topics are necessary in order to have a rounded picture of how an astrologer achieves a personal sense of success in career. For our purposes here, I define an astrologer as someone who uses some standard astrological techniques to talk to clients about their lives. The astrologer is paid to do this, to read charts. Further, the money so earned forms the majority of personal income. If you don't fit these criteria, you will have a different set of considerations powering your career decisions. This puts you clearly on a different career path and the comments here will be less significant, and maybe even tangential.

PREPARATION

First of all, is this what you want to do?

Most astrologers remember the moment when their relationship with astrology began. We have charts for practically everything and, if you are lucky enough to remember the exact moment that a professional astrologer told you that you would become an astrologer, you can set up your personal "Astrological Conception Chart." Regardless of whether or not you can remember the exact time and day, this moment is quite important in your life. This was astrology reaching out and *selecting* you, an important rite of initiation. Just as the moment of birth foretells for you the history of the soul in this incarnation, how and when you enter astrology (just as how and when anything begins) will tell you how you will perform as an astrologer. The moment an established astrologer predicts you can or will become an astrologer, your "Astrological Conception Chart" is put in motion.

This basic acceptance is necessary for you to feel at home in astrology and among astrologers. If this hasn't happened, *i.e.,* if you have not heard or felt the "calling," seek out an established astrologer's professional opinion. *Can* you make it as a professional astrologer?

If you really want to be an astrologer (or already are an astrologer) and this "recognition" hasn't happened for you, the "swim upstream" to become a successful astrologer can be "against the current" of collective astrological thought. You may not make it because you will unconsciously feel that all other astrologers are wrong. You may end up sentencing yourself to be yet another isolated critic on astrology's sidelines, unaccepted by your peers, unable to build a practice and eventually proving everyone else right, *i.e.*, you can't make it as an astrologer. Like Excaliber knighting King Arthur, astrology selects and initiates its own, regardless of the personalities in your environment.

If you can't get an established astrologer to say your chart indicates that you will become an astrologer, you are probably having some inner resistance to this career move. This will be shown in your chart. This pattern of resistance is manifesting through your environment when you aren't able to "hook up" with someone who will affirm your desire to be an astrologer.

Since astrology is the study of the structure of the universe considered as time, astrology can be a faithful ally in every line of work. Many of my corporate clients have gone on to be fine "astrologers" (or users of astrology) from behind the scenes, using it to plan personnel work, dividend and investment strategies, changes in organizational structure, and hundreds of daily decisions, without talking to anyone about their charts. The same is true for stock brokers using astrology, medical personnel, historians, psychologists, social workers, teachers, police, and on and on. Actually, even most astrologers would be surprised at the number of people in our society who use astrology as a tool while being in a different career.

Ask yourself this vital question: "Is this what I want to do with my life?" Do you want to interact with clients over specific concerns that come up in their daily lives? This is to say, you love astrology, *but* do you love people? Just like being a dentist, counselor, or social worker, a career in astrology means a lifetime of working with people. Be certain that you really find other peoples' lives interesting enough to be involved with them all the time, that you receive some deep satisfaction in helping others. If you love astrology but aren't that crazy about people, consider using your astrological interest for a different type of career other than astrology.

Next, it is important for you to evaluate how astrologers earn a living. What is it that astrologers do for money? We talk to people about their lives. We give information; we render opinions. Astrologers have an insatiable curiosity about people and life and the universe and everything. Without this burning desire to know, forget trying to earn a living as an astrologer. I guarantee, you won't make it without this. Further, you had better love talking to people about their lives. If you don't enjoy helping people with issues in their lives, then forget this line of work. But if you love astrology, love knowledge in general, and love people and their lives, then perhaps this is a line of work for you.

Finally, to make it as an astrologer you need to be able to be self-employed. This requires incredible self-discipline. Most people who try to be self-employed end up going back to work for someone else. This part of personal appraisal is critical. There are a few jobs available to people who can't be self-employed and yet still want to be doing astrology. Most of these people are part-time astrologers and full-time something else.

In the Western world today, there are a number of part-time astrology positions in entertainment: doing cocktail parties, reading charts in restaurants, working on a 900 telephone line, etc. This has not been an interest of mine, and the whole approach tends to give a bad image of astrology to society. Still, this lighthearted, fun orientation can be a legitimate outlet for honest practice in the field. While the astrologers who take this approach tend to "dead end" in their careers, one should examine its potentials.[1]

Sometimes, people involved in astrology who can't or don't want to be self-employed end up working for other astrologers or an astrology company. These jobs usually boil down to occupations *around* astrology, like working for a chart service company or being an assistant to an astrologer or an office manager. I have had several assistants work for me in the last 18 years, and sometimes it was a natural transition point for a person deciding to get into the field. All of these people earn very good incomes today, except one who has chosen not to work. If you are not sure about your motivation or discipline, this type of position can work out nicely for you while you are deciding on whether to go forward into astrology or to use your astrological insight in a different way.

Next, We Have To Consider Education.

After years of conferring with successful professional astrologers all over the world, one common property emerged in everyone's conversation as to how they got to the position of feeling successful in their work: EDUCATION. Education seems to be important on three distinct levels: your own continuous process of *personal education, teaching students,* and *educating your clients.*

Because astrology is a path of knowledge, becoming an astrologer means being committed to a life of self-education. You will never reach a point of being finished with education. There will always be more to do. The more formal education you have, the better your chances are of succeeding in the profession. This is so important that, although I teach a four-year correspondence school in astrology, having a college degree is necessary in order to graduate. You will find that astrology doesn't happen in a vacuum and that knowledge of many other things is necessary in order for you to be of any real use in the world with your astrological knowledge.

High levels of mental determination and education are essential in order to become a professional astrologer. Study with everyone that you can. Take any local classes that you are able to take. Consider relocating to study with someone whose work you admire. Just as people grow up and go away to school, you may go away to astrology school. I have gone far and wide to get an astrological education, and it has always been worth the investment. I might add that the travel and study were always a great financial sacrifice, but *dealing with limits organizes your priorities*. Getting a good astrological education should be a top priority if you are going to be fulfilled as an astrologer.

Being an astrologer is very important to our society; yet, how much time and money do we spend preparing to practice? Doctors go to medical school. Lawyers go to law school. Astrologers should go to astrology school! You need a B.A. degree to get into law school or medical school. Astrology school should be four years in length and require at least a four-year college degree as a prerequisite. Doctors and lawyers spend more than $100,000 on education. How many astrologers spend this much on education?

As a profession, our first real coming-of-age will be to have a comprehensive, well-organized educational procedure. We need a place where people can get a real astrological education. I had eight years of college, finishing an M.A. in philosophy and an assortment of astrology classes when I entered astrology in 1974. I was ill-prepared, poorly trained, and I knew it at the time. I was like an airline pilot getting training on the job by reading manuals and then attempting to fly a plane. For all of my ridiculousness, I was still more prepared and educationally fortified than most people entering the field!

The best way to get training right now is to take correspondence courses, attend local classes and private instruction under an astrologer you respect. Have your own chart done by at least ten different astrologers so that you can become familiar with what astrologers do. Take a series of astrology exams. There are many correspondence schools. (See Appendix).

Local classes take place everywhere privately, through metaphysical and New Age type book stores. Adult education and university extension classes are successfully taught by some astrologers.[2] There are some well-meaning (mostly ideas at this stage of the game) "Schools" in New York, Seattle, San Diego, London, etc. In the future, each of these places and others will be able to implement actual comprehensive four-year curricula. At least some of your study should be directly under the supervision of a professional astrologer who earns a decent income and whose work you respect.

Your education needs exposure to a number of astrologers' work. This does two things; first, it helps you know yourself better through the use of the therapeutic modality you will actively encourage others (your clients) to use—you can tell your clients firsthand that astrology has value; second, this procedure gives you great exposure to several different styles and approaches so you will have more structural knowledge for what the field can become and what others are doing with the astrological tools.

It is important to take examinations, either self-administered, from a school, or from NCGR (The National Council For Geocosmic Research), whichever is most convenient. This will build self-confidence. The examination process should include some consulting with another astrologer who comments on and critiques your interchange with clients.

APPRENTICESHIP

After your education is secure enough to start a practice, find someone under whom you can apprentice. I did not have this opportunity, so I worked on my own for six months, seeing five clients a day *at no charge*, in order to gather experience and to see whether or not I could handle the load of work and the pace of life to practice astrology as my life-work; this is one way of getting practical experience. It was, however, hard, time-consuming, and mistake-ridden. It is much better to have an astrologer whom you trust sit in on your readings and give you some supervision and comments; I had been in the field for years before I had this opportunity. Supervision is so important, and students today need this in their learning process.

A less formal apprenticeship is possible by getting permission from your clients to make a copy of the tapes from your sessions and share them with another astrologer who can provide supervision for you. This type of work is so valuable: I monitor sessions of all my advanced and professional-level students to help them avoid costly mistakes; to help them find a consulting style that is appropriate to the way they wish to practice, to their personal resources and talents.

GETTING STARTED

Elect a chart for turning professional. It is important that you chose this chart yourself. Since you will be working for yourself, this self-initiation, this rite of passage, is very important symbolically. It will help you to understand and believe in the integrity of your work.

When you start, make sure that you have your business procedures down cold; getting them right from the start will save a lot of grief later as you and your practice grow:

1. Know how to take and schedule appointments;

2. Get every client's name, address, and telephone number recorded on a data base;

3. Know how to refuse work that you are not prepared for (the client's needs are out of your range of expertise);

4. Have a quick way of screening and placing clients to determine the beginning level of your consulting work;

5. Devise a rapid and reliable way to have the materials that you need, including the client's chart, ephemeris, graphic ephemeris, dials or whatever you use (either from your own computer and/or a chart service) up and ready, neat and organized, for efficient operation;

6. Have your office workspace neat, comforting, and comfortable;

7. And, finally, make sure all the equipment and tools of the trade are in order and working.[3]

Setting Your Rates

Before you can charge clients for your work, you have to set rates for your services. How you set your rates is determined by what you feel your work is worth to others. If lots of people come to see you and pay you your fee, you were correct as to your worth. If no one comes to see you, or just a few do, you have set your rates too low or too high. At least we know that your fees were not set appropriately.

I recommend that you do not use a sliding scale. A few astrologers use a sliding scale and make a very good living, but most astrologers who use a sliding scale have poor practices because they have an inaccurate picture of their self-worth. Not everyone on the planet is supposed to be able to afford your work. To believe so is to have feelings of inferiority and a messianic complex simultaneously. At any rate, your inaccurate self-picturing will make it difficult to earn a living in astrology.

Rather than adjusting your rate to meet a client's financial needs, better see if you can heal your client's pocketbook through your work. If money is their chief concern, then concentrate on helping them get more of it and handle it better. It is good to do work for free once in a while, to donate a certain amount of your time to volunteering your professional services. It is a sane principle and will possibly help others become familiar with good astrology and see the good that astrologers can do.

One way to set your rates is to ask your teacher to set them for you, initially. Alternately, you can ask the people whose charts you have been doing for free or those whom you have been seeing under instruction of your teacher, how much your work would be worth to them. Take an average of the numbers given to you and let it be your rate. You can always adjust it later.

Some people can't afford your work. Fine. There are plenty of people who can, and they need you as much as you need them. Don't let the people whom you can't help use up your time so that it is unavailable to those whom you can help.

Make your policies having to do with money very clear to your clients. Do you take postdated checks? *Don't!* Will you take partial payments? *Don't do it!* Will you do trades? *Don't,* they are insulting and unnecessary. It is better to just give your work away. Do you want deposits in advance? I don't, but some astrologers have found this to be helpful in making sure that the client will show up. I deal with this through my *no-cancellation policy* and taking new clients only by referral. This ensures that time and money won't be issues between me and my clients.[4] It also saves the extra accounting hassle of having to record money twice for one appointment.

Setting your rates, getting your time/money equation correct for your talent and your preferred way of working, is very important. Until you know your own stride, keep your astrological reading light, short, and cheap. This will allow you to present an honest, sincere, and positive picture of yourself and your work. *Further, you become affordable to a large client base.* Charge $30 for 15-minute readings and you become an instant success. Everyone can afford you, and you can do 20 appointments a day! This requires some real work with the issue of boundaries and time, but this is one fast way to success. I have seen some astrologers do this and succeed. This is one winning formula.

Those of you who need more time than a 15-minute session can try working in 30-minute or 45-minute or one-hour segments. You will need to charge enough for your work so that you will be able to survive, of course. Remember, however, if you have an interactive consulting style requiring sessions to last one or two hours, your practice will build more slowly. Your work will cost more because it requires more time and, by the nature of interactive dialogue, it will require more commitment from the client. It's very important that you have a clear picture in mind as to *what you want to achieve with your client* and *how you want to achieve it.* There is a pitfall here. Don't forsake astrology and become a psychotherapist, thereby ignoring your best tools. This has been a mistake taken by some modern astrologers. (See "Astrologers and Psychologists are Different."[5])

Legality

Astrology is not legal everywhere, locally or internationally. In the United States, it is of different legal status in each state. The astrology organization AFAN (Association for Astrological Networking) publishes a Legal Aid Kit for astrologers, as well as a media package, which can be very helpful in making your young practice secure in the face of any local legal problem.

So it is good to know exactly where you stand legally before you start practicing. Find out from other astrologers who practice in your area what their perspective and experiences are about. Many anti-astrology laws are very antiquated and unenforced; many are unconstitutional and actually unenforceable. Talk to others about this issue and stay in contact with other astrologers. We astrologers often represent a different point of view than the one expressed in the rest of the community, and it is helpful, when the time is right, to let everyone know what astrology is and what it isn't. Often we are lumped together with people who are *not* part of the community and who aren't really involved in trying to improve life on the planet.

Equipment

Today's astrologers need certain equipment to have a cost-effective practice. As a minimum, you should have a tape-recorder, computer, printer, answering machine, telephone, and maybe a fax machine. The financial sensibility of owning equipment as opposed to just renting, or using a service with the equipment, is a twofold proposition: accounting and time.

For accounting, there are simple formulas as to how long it will take you to amortize the cost of a piece of equipment and how much income is lost if you do not own the equipment. Renting or using a service may be helpful if you are not in frequent need of the equipment.

It takes time to learn how to use a new piece of software or a new computer. It may be very difficult for you to factor the time of learning a new system into your procedures. Talk to other owners of the same system to appraise how long it will take to learn reasonable proficiency. Even answering machines, tape-recorders, fax machines, and printers require some hours of learning to know the machine well enough to use correctly. Buying equipment without factoring in the learning time is a mistake people frequently make. If, for example, you see something on sale but won't have time to work with it for several months, you are better off generally to wait until you *do* have the time; *then* look for a sale. Prices on all electronic equipment tend to go down in time. The longer you wait, the better deal you will get.[6]

Investment

When you develop a Business Plan be sure to include time and money each year for your continuing education. Your knowledge is what produces income in astrology. Your mind is your most valuable equipment, it is your factory, your means of production. Your knowledge base is not a static fixed asset. What you know goes down in effectiveness if you are not making some conscious effort to improve it on a daily basis.

Continuing education is required in every major profession and service occupation. Be willing to allot time and money for this process. The investment that you make in your own education before and during the practice of astrology is such an important investment that all other investments are insignificant in terms of time and money. Most successful astrologers will invest thousands of dollars in their initial education and several thousand more annually. Very few of us will ever invest this much in equipment or other factors.

Finding Your Spot

You must make some type of investment in real estate. After all, you will have to see clients somewhere. You have four options: your home, your clients' home or office, your office, another public or private space.

Of course, it is most important that your space be private. I was asked to do readings in a bookstore one time while traveling, and the proprietor of the store wanted me to see clients in a public space. This wasn't good for the type of work that I do, and it presented astrology to the public in such a casual way that people easily could get the feeling, "If you don't take this stuff very seriously then why should I?" This is wrong. Astrology is too powerful to be played with. An entertainment-oriented, exhibitionist astrologer can inflict much damage during a client-reading in a casual setting. The most professional rule I can offer is never to look at a person's chart casually or make offhanded comments. You will certainly damage your credibility as an astrologer, but more importantly, you may do some real damage to the other person.

So, see people in a place that guarantees privacy. An office is nice, but you may want to operate out of your home if you have a room that is private and comfortable enough for both you and your client.[7] This is one way to avoid making a frivolous investment.

I work under all four circumstances: I have a home office, an office away from home in an office building, I have used other people's homes and offices, and I use classrooms, hotel rooms, and even the park. An office in my home is my favorite because I have everything that I need at my fingertips and the environment can be decorated and organized to meet my moods easily.[8]

In an office building, it is easy for your clients to picture you in the "I'm doing business" mode. In the home, it can become too casual if you do not go to lengths to keep it professional.

A personal informal survey I've made of astrologers through the years has shown that astrologers who earn the least and those who earn the most (more than $100,000 a year) practice astrology from their home. It may be that the astrologers who have little experience are forced to work from their home and the astrologers who are very well-paid do so out of choice and close identification with their work.

Surely, in the future, astrologers will work in an office with other astrologers where there will be lots of shared resources, equipment, staff, space, journals, etc., just as doctors and lawyers work in clinics and firms. Astrologers will have some kind of collective enterprises that will benefit everyone.

BUILDING YOUR PRACTICE

The All-important Client Base

Treat every client with your full attention and patience. It will take a while to build a practice by word of mouth, but it is the only way to plant the roots of your work deeply enough so that you will *always* have plenty of work. You must be the best listener you can be. The first five years of practice will be slow for most people, but as your work improves in quality you will get a higher and higher return rate of old clients.

Before I see clients for the first time, I send them "General Notes For My Clients" (See Appendix). It is good to put into print for your clients *exactly what you do and what you do not do*. This is very important because it screens out people who will only be troublesome. Further, this practice gives you some reasonable assurance that your time in session will be productive. Also, it leads the mindset of your new clients toward your work in a manner that enables you to assist them in realizing their goals. Don't let your time be wasted, repeating many times over the phone your policies and details of your practice. Put the information into print and give it to people.

Look for ways to make sure the people coming to see you are on the same wavelength as you are. If a person has unrealistic expectations about themselves, life, or you, know this in advance. It will make your life simpler. If potential clients expect you magically to change their life, let them know that it can change, only they must ultimately do the changing. Your job is to give advice and help them create a realistic and comprehensive vision of their future.

In order to grow in understanding, be sure that you have a fail-safe system to get feedback from your clients and do case histories every so often. I do case histories with my clients after they have seen me for a number of sessions and are committed to our work together. After our third session, the work starts taking on a new dimension. At this point, I do a case history matching and timing events to their chart. Some astrologers do this before they see a person for the first time. I find it helpful to wait until clients have *committed* to working on themselves in our relationship before I devote this kind of time and energy to their life.

Be very certain about what you do do and what you do not do. Don't ever say to a potential client, "Astrology can't do what you ask." Who can speak for all of astrology or even all astrologers? What you *can* honestly say to a client or potential client is "I can do that," or "I don't do what you are asking; please see so and so, or try someone else." This is honest and to the point. All you do need to know on this topic is what you can do and, further, what you *like* to do. Have a referral list for sending people to astrologers and non-astrologers who specialize in other areas.

When you are working, work. When you stop working, stop. This means, when clients meet you on the street, don't talk to them about their chart or, for that matter, anything professional. This is a very important way to set boundaries that will allow your client to respect your work, plus help *you* maintain a psychological balance and perspective on your own life.

Everyone who sees you should see you again at least once a year, just for an update, which means that *every new client will be a growth in your practice*. Obviously, after about five years of practice, you will have more clients than you can possibly serve. You will end up referring most of the new people who call you to other astrologers. At this stage of your practice, you will start to specialize quite a bit, even if you, like me, are in a general type of practice, meaning that you do a bit of everything.

There are four *specialty practices* on which you can build a practice: horary astrology, relocational astrology, medical astrology, and financial astrology. Each of these specialties has its own career path, but both horary and relocational astrology are pretty straightforward and astrology-intensive without requiring special training in other fields. Medical and financial astrology are specialties that require extensive training in things non-astrological, *e.g.,* health and finance.[9]

If your memory is not excellent, you should take notes on every client and session, during the consultation or shortly thereafter. Written notes help you build an inner bridge to the person whose life you have become involved with and facilitate your work with this person in the future.

Set up an annotated data base with the client's address and birth information in your computer. This allows you to determine when you last saw the person and review what you talked about. You can use the information to mail the client a birthday card as a reminder that it is time to see you again. I personally write a note to each client within a month of seeing them. This lets them know I'm thinking about them. It reminds them of the things we talked about. Further, it helps me to organize my own thinking about our session together.

While in the process of working with your clients and building a client base, *you will make at least one very bad mistake*. This is an in-itiation rite-of-passage. It has been confessed to me so many times by other astrologers that I realize it is an archetypal principle of the practice! Even the very good astrologers pull back, sometimes for quite a while, when they make a big mistake. The great astrologers however, push through the mistakes; the gravity of their error ac-knowledged (to understand is to heal), and they proceed.[10] As I have said many times in my professional classes, show me an as-trologer who has never hurt anyone, and I will show you an astrolo-ger who has also never helped anyone. *We make mistakes and other people suffer.* But hopefully, we also grow. And through our growth we become better astrologers. Better astrologers are going to make a better planet.

Advertising

The best advertising is word of mouth. One satisfied client tells another. Take the time to write notes to your clients and keep them informed about your intention and what you see for them. This can be just a simple reminder as to what you last talked about, what they might do now, and when they should see you again.

Kathleen Burt has some thoughts on how she built her practice by writing thank-you notes. This is a novel approach and it boils down to learning how to acknowledge those people who are helping you build your practice.[11]

About 80 percent of my clients set up appointments again *while they are with me*. If they don't do this they can't usually get on my schedule and I am a schedule-driven person, *i.e.,* if it isn't on my schedule, it doesn't exist. Further I have a n*o-cancellation policy*. Anyone who misses an appointment with me pays me for the time and apologizes. If someone does this twice, that someone is an ex-client because I can't allow anyone to steal my time. It is too valuable to waste. As an astrologer, the management of your time is important because it is ultimately the commodity for which your clients are paying.

Some astrologers have a listing in the telephone Yellow Pages and advertise on television or radio or in magazines. I have not done this because I feel that it is unnecessary and tends to present a less-than-professional image of astrology. If you have doubt about going it alone without advertising, read *How to Start, Maintain, and Expand an Astrological Practice*, Section 5, "To Advertise Or Not To Advertise," by Barb Gessler, an astrologer in the Chicago area, who wrote this section of the booklet which outlines the pros and cons of advertising and how to go about it. This booklet is given out to every new member of PROSIG (The Organization of Professional Astrology).

Money spent on display ads can be a real waste. On the other hand, high-quality brochures that you can put *directly into people's hands* who have expressed a genuine interest in your work are *always* worth the money. The brochure should tell exactly what you do and how much you charge for doing so. (By all means, avoid flowery, overstated, inflammatory, and technical language.) This brochure can be a tremendous aid in helping establish a solid client base. A local copy shop or printer will help you achieve a visual image that conveys how you feel about yourself and your practice.

Having a publicist and a media consultant is also helpful, but unnecessary. If you choose to use such specialists, be sure that they are very "in tune" with your work, that they understand it, *and* support it philosophically. The second thing to do is to sit down with your accountant or business planner and make sure, very sure that the extra cost of having these people on board is worth it at the bottom line. It is best that you don't hire clients to do this, and never, never trade your service for theirs. I promise you that it will not work out for you or them as a business deal. Trades breed poverty-consciousness and cloud your vision of what you are doing and what you are worth, what the universe will give you and what you need. If you want someone's service, get the best people for the job and pay them real money. You are worth it and so are they; otherwise, why do it at all? Always make cost-effective business decisions when you are talking about business. This sounds very trite, but I mention it because most of us astrologers have deficient skills when it comes to making these kinds of business decisions.

Whenever you print up fliers for a workshop or for the newspaper, make sure that you save a copy of it in an advertising file. The art work and wording can save you a lot of time and expense if you want to have a starting point for doing the same workshop later. Further, this can be a great source of ideas and a helpful way to let sponsoring astrology groups know how to promote you when you are asked to speak for them. It is also very helpful to have good black-and-white photographs that can be used for publicity. This can be important when you are talking with anyone who can help you with your advertising.

Your advertising file should contain everything that you have done for the public. If you decide to run advertisements in the newspaper, phone book, etc. (which I have been advising against right along), then do be sure to keep notes about how much you spent on the ad, where it appeared, and what kind of a response you got. This allows your advertising dollar to be self-correcting over a period of several years. You may find some ad sellers who try to "educate" you as to the value of name-recognition type of advertising and the residual effect on your business over a long period of time. This actually doesn't work for astrologers. It does work for Coca Cola, Macy's, and other businesses selling a product by name recognition. It doesn't work for astrologers, period!

Many astrologers have their own radio or television shows. Some of these shows can even be useful in terms of creating a better image of what astrology is about in our society. But beware, these shows are usually not a way to build a local or even national client base. At least, this has been the experience of astrologers so far.

In one sense, everything you do with your life is advertising—either positively or negatively—for astrology in general, and for your practice in particular. In this vein, I might mention that normal business practices often bring new clients. The importance of making tapes of your sessions with clients can scarcely be overesti-mated. So many new clients through the years have come to me *be-cause they listened to a tape I made for another client*. Further, many times clients have returned to see me because they were listening to an old tape and it perked their curiosity.

The Importance of Teaching

I taught my first astrology class in 1974, right after I started my practice. It was a great boon at three levels. First, it was a source of clients since every student became a client at some later date; sec-ond, it was a way of directing my own study of astrology to a deeper level; and third, it gave me a gathering point-of-focus for clients who have an interest in learning astrology.

Every astrologer with whom I have ever discussed this has told me that *teaching was an important form of advertising* for them. It got their name out before the public and created interest in their work. The continued source of income comes from new people coming into the classes every semester and those people becoming clients.

I have personally counseled a large number of professional as-trologers and helped them improve their practices. The number one complaint that astrologers have when their career is floundering is that they aren't seeing enough people to earn a living. (Once in a while, the astrologer is actually seeing enough people, but is just not charging enough for the astrological service. This leads the astrolo-ger back to working on issues of self-esteem.)

Teaching astrology not only expands your client base but al-lows you to continue your own study at a deeper level. If you have to explain something to others so they understand it—and make it interesting enough that it holds their attention—you will have to study the material at a level deep enough so you really understand it. This not only helps you build your practice through expertise, ex-pand your understanding and clarify for yourself what it is that you do, but it also helps bring real astrology before the general public, something for which you can feel justifiably proud.

Recently, I was chairing a panel of professional astrologers on the issue of giving consultations to clients. People in attendance were practicing professionals as well. I asked the question, "What other kinds of knowledge do you think are essential besides astro-logical techniques for anyone making a living as a consulting as-trologer?" Almost everyone in attendance wanted to say something! People suggested four years of college in humanities, business skills, computer skills, knowledge of advertising, scientific knowledge, history, psychology, philosophy; the list went on and on. Every practicing astrologer seemed in complete agreement that astrology requires the study of many things. To study real astrology is to study the whole universe and its inherent structure in time and space. To do astrology is to commit to the project that knowledge makes us better. After all, our very job implies that people's lives will somehow be better through receiving information from us. In the words of Plato, "The Good is to Know."

Writing's Place

There are astrologers who have attracted some of their clients by becoming popular through their writing. Writing articles for magazines will not attract a client base for you; but if you have written an astrology book, and it becomes widely circulated, it may attract some clients in your direction. Still, to write a best selling book may be income for you immediately, but it cannot be relied upon to attract a long-term, meaningful, and income-producing clientele.

Most astrology books on the market are very poor. Most good professional astrologers are so busy that they don't have writing time. Most astrologers who have written books in order to build a practice have suffered the hard lessons of putting the cart before the horse. *Build a successful practice first,* then share your proven insights, techniques, and perspective with others. This is an operational principle that astrologers have to import from other professions.

If you are a good, natural writer by temperament, you may supplement your income in astrology if you were to write an article every month for a paying astrology magazine, but you will probably not get the amount of money for your time that you would seeing clients. Let's say you write an article in two days and are paid $250 for it. This is certainly not as much income as you could receive for the time seeing clients. It may be OK one day a month, but it will not take you over the hump of having to see clients most of the time in your workday, and, oddly enough, it will not attract new clients, even if you are writing for a local newspaper.

Still, writing always helps astrologers to sort out and clarify their thinking. Writing is part of any educational process. Instead of writing term papers, astrologers write articles. Since you are taking the time to write anyway, you might as well share your thoughts in print, and get paid for it.

Other People as Employees

Since my beginning days in the practice of astrology, I have always had people working for me. I paid them money to do so, and could not have had a practice without such assistance. Still, as I became more successful and started to pay higher salaries to employees, two things became very clear: first, the type of people in those jobs totally determined whether I was going to do well or not, and their income had to rise or fall as mine did; second, whenever these factors were ignored, I lost money. When these issues were correctly addressed I made money.

Be very sure if you need more people in your business and make very sure that the people you are hiring are making a very positive step in their career pathway. If these people are deeply committed to your work but still aren't growing in their personal and professional lives (instead, are just looking for a place to retreat from the world for a while), you are in big trouble if you hire them.

Attaching peoples' wages to your income can be done by percentages (best) and bonuses (next best). The way salaries are set is to examine the needs of everyone all around the business. If people working for you are in need or are dissatisfied with their work or disappointed in their personal life, *your business will suffer*. I have discovered that hiring people who are growing personally is very important. Everyone's job should change and grow today in our modern culture. There comes a time when employees will need to move on. Make sure that you thoroughly understand *their* job. I had a person working for me on a computer I purchased for them. I paid for their instruction on special computer software. I didn't learn the system myself. When they left quite suddenly, I was left in bad shape. It took two years to straighten out my client files!

SHARING YOUR KNOWLEDGE

What it Means to be a Professional

In the process of giving to other astrologers, your insights and understandings of astrology, your own work moves to a higher level and a new dimension.

Treat other astrologers with respect. To the best of your ability, put aside political, economic, sociological, and public differences and *do something for astrology*. Be courteous and friendly and don't put your colleagues on a pedestal even if they are very famous. This can stand in your way of learning from them, or of them learning from you.

I had been doing astrology for about a year when I met Dane Rudhyar and Marc Edmund Jones for the first time. I had some professional questions for them, some technical issues that had been brewing in my mind from having read their books. I approached Rudhyar when I saw him at a reception and asked him some rather direct questions. Rudhyar answered me directly and clearly. I met M. E. Jones after one of his classes. I hadn't understood something that he had lectured on and I hadn't understood some of his points on the same subject when I read his books. We talked for a while. I didn't understand his answer right away even though he was polite enough to keep explaining. He was a very nice person. My point here is that it never occurred to me not to ask them the questions on my mind. Why? Because it was and is every astrologer's responsibility *to build a better astrology*. In this realm, who we are as people doesn't matter; only that the discipline, the field of astrology, gets better. We have a duty to share our insights with others and to purify and clarify our own understanding.

The Importance of Networking and Organization

Joining an astrology organization can be a way of contributing to the growth and development of astrology. NCGR is the organization that has the most comprehensive materials for astrological education and research; ISAR is an organization of internationally known astrologers doing research; AFAN has the best information for astrologers on dealing with the media and with the legal issues surrounding astrology; PROSIG is the organization for professional astrology. Belonging to these organizations can be an important way of staying in touch with other astrologers and perpetuating the field in general, which will in turn help your practice. (See Appendix for further information).

MONEY: SOME STRAIGHT TALK

The need for money leads astrologers to charge their clients for their services. Although it is possible to earn a good living through astrology, I have never met a good astrologer who practiced astrology "for the money" in it. Generally speaking, the best astrologers could make more more money quickly and with less effort by using astrology as an edge in other fields, like the stock market or gambling, or sales, etc.

Still, it is important to address the issue of money. Today astrologers charge anywhere from $35 to $500 for their work. Most appointment times are one to two hours. If you charge $100 per session and see 100 clients a month, you can work five days a week—have weekends off—seeing five clients a day. This lets you earn $100,000 a year and take two months off every year. I call this a regular middle-class income, allowing you a regular middle-class life style. Just as for any other professional.

There are very good astrologers who, because of *other* choices they have made, earn much less than this. There are good astrologers who work harder and charge more who earn a lot more than this. I want you to see that becoming an astrologer is not necessarily a life of poverty and great restriction. But further, it is not a life of easy money. Astrologers are paid well, and they work much harder than most people.

In the 70s, many of my most talented students did not manage to make the transition from astrology as a hobby to astrology as a career. Earning a living as an astrologer is always tension-producing, especially for people with high security needs. If someone studying with me wants to be an astrologer, the preliminary questions I ask are: Can you be self-employed? Can you live with the insecurity of a fluctuating income? Can you be focused enough to put your own life out of your mind while you are concentrating on being an astrologer for someone else?

Developing a business plan does not have to be complicated, but it is essential to ensure success as an astrologer. If you don't have a vision of where you are going and how you are going to get there, it shouldn't surprise you if you don't get anywhere or don't recognize where you are when you have arrived. If you don't have a plan for your own life why should anyone pay you to help you plan theirs?

A business plan is simple. There are two parts, one philosophical and the other technical: "What is it that you want?"; "How do you plan to get what you want?" The philosophic question should be answered first. What DO you want to see in your life? What is it that you want to accomplish? Remember, as astrologers we can answer this question if we wish, for any life, including our own, becomes open through the chart. You can lay out the events and circumstances for a whole life, from cradle to grave, using a birth chart. You will make mistakes on your own chart just as you will with other people's charts, but there will be a learning, a growth in the process. Astrology is a path of mental growth. Here, as on so many other issues in astrology, getting another astrologer's opinion is invaluable.

After you have established your philosophic framework (as to what you should, or want to, or will, achieve in your life) focus on the *technical* dimension of your Business Plan. To do this, first figure out your expenses for a month and for a year. Project your income for a year. Refer to your chart. You will have ups and downs as any business does. Plan for the down point in the year. Next, break your income down into categories based on how you will earn your money.

Plan time correctly. Plan time for business meetings with accountants, agents, office managers, anyone and everyone who is an integral part of your business.[12]

It is important for you to manage your time as well as your money. Astrology is the study of time and astrologers need to live up to a higher standard than most people in terms of handling their time. Save time every day for yourself alone. Time spent alone is necessary in order to assimilate what you are learning. Make time to write clients in some fashion every day. Make time to study a bit each day. (Astrology is my yoga. I do it as a discipline every morning when I get up. I think through the signs, houses, planets, and aspects. As a way to keep limber and in shape with their instrument and discipline, pianists practice scales.)

And finally, make sure that you understand the tax laws and have your taxes paid. It is hard enough working in the field of astrology without having money issues with the government. Some astrologers don't record all of their income and don't report it honestly to the government. I have yet to find one astrologer living this way who does well and feels fulfilled in the practice of astrology. I always encourage people living outside the law to get right with the government. The profession of astrology can only be built on the shoulders of astrologers who act with integrity. Be honest.

THE ASTROLOGER'S PLACE IN SOCIETY

Why should society treat us with respect if we astrologers don't treat each other with respect? It is a sociological fact that a suppressed group tends to turn inward and repress itself. Members of the astrological community have unconsciously adopted society's intellectual prejudices against astrology; while at the same time, we members of the astrological community have consciously believed in our own individual goodness. Consequently, we have tended to undermine each other's effort and improvement of the field through narrow criticism. This has prevented us from working very closely together. We have been slow to outgrow this negative quality, but education and honest and continuous reappraisal of our enterprise will raise our standard.

As we get better at what we do, our craft will reshape society. What will happen to the insurance system when no one will buy it except people who really need it? What will happen to the stock market when investments are made by everyone based on clear and natural motions of cycles in nature? The material basis of fear and greed can be eliminated from our culture through right understanding. This will be the dawning of a new age. Think what role we as astrologers will play in this culture. We have now, and will have in the future, the place we deserve in society. The raising of social consciousness comes though the raising of individual consciousness, thus we build a better astrology and a better world.

APPENDIX A

The following material is a sample of the advance information I send to people who ask about working with me. These are thoughts I want clients to see before I work with them the first time.

General Information for My Clients

Read the following information carefully. These general notes describe feelings, attitudes, and policies of our work together. Share your thoughts with me as I revise this material from time to time.

The Goal of the Work

It is totally understandable and valid to seek advice from an astrologer in order to gather more information about your current situation. The better informed you are, the more likely you are to be happy with the decisions you make. Astrology always gives you more than you are asking for, so it is important to keep a few things in mind as you embark on this pathway.

First, astrology is a therapy, and as such it will alter your perceptions of yourself and of life. Astrology as a frame of reference always presents us with more information than we were requesting. Astrology reveals everything about you that can be known. As a consequence of this vastness of information before us, I may see things in your chart and your life that you are not aware of and are not asking me about. It is my duty to tell you things that I honestly feel will help you, even if you are not interested or curious. Inversely, I may overlook or miss certain things that you feel are critical in your life. If you inform me of your interests and concerns before our session I do my best to address these issues. I am as "client directed" as possible.

Having your chart done for the first time can be quite a surprising experience. When you ask me to look at your chart you are asking me for my interpretation of the facts of your life. You may not agree with my insights or opinions. I have a different picture of you than you have of yourself and that is why we are together. Our differences of perception should be a great resource to you through which your perspective on life can change.

Second, my conscious aim is to augment the growth elements and instructional ingredients in the system of astrology during our initial session together. Our time together should assist you in placing the concerns and specific issues of this period of your life into a larger context. Receiving this new information will require some self-stretching. Consequently, you may feel overwhelmed by information in your initial appointment. This is not unusual.

Getting help from astrology is not a passive act of gathering information. Regardless of whether or not the information you receive matches or even exceeds your expectations ... IT WILL CHANGE YOU ... and you will respond in some manner to this change.

OUR POLICIES

As a courtesy to you and as an aid to your memory I tape our sessions together and give you the tape. This is so you can go back and review the material. I do my best to make the highest quality tape possible, but take note, I can't guarantee the quality of the tape.

If anything goes wrong with the tape, which happens rarely, you are left with this as an inconvenience. You are welcome to make your own tape if you wish.

Because I put such energy and time into the sessions of the people that I work with and because my time and my professional life is so valuable to me, I ask you to not set up an appointment if there is any doubt in your mind as to whether you can keep it or not. I ask you to not cancel an appointment once you have set it up. If you do I will understand that it was necessary. However, you will still owe me whatever my fee was for that appointment.

If you know you may be running into a scheduling problem, call my agent or Kathryn in Florida and see if a scheduling adjustment is possible. Although you and I are friends, we have a professional relationship and I cannot be there for you if you do not respect this simple request on my part. I will do the very best that I can to be there for you.

You may have curiosity about other people in your life and wish me to take a look at their chart. The answer is no. Even if the person is not a client of mine I consider it a violation of confidence for me to give you information out of their chart. You can however have a chart comparison done with this person, or, you can get an Indra Report done for them. By the same token, you should know that I will not discuss your chart with anyone else but you.

One aspect of astrology is forecasting. My approach to prediction is to involve you in dialogue over your own future. Regardless of our discussion or what I think about your life, I want you to act from your own intuitions. While astrology is the perfect science, I've never met an astrologer who understood it perfectly. While I have a professional opinion over the events in your life, an opinion is less than knowledge. A weatherman has an opinion about the weather just as I have an opinion about your life.

Ongoing Use of Astrology Information

After our initial session, our work together will revolve around specific issues that we agree on as pertinent to your life pattern. We can set up a program of self-development that includes regular sessions. I see some of my clients monthly or bimonthly to discuss current issues and situations in their lives. This is an opportunity to get further insight into your process of self development.

I consult with some of my clients over the phone to do regular (up to two hours) or short (up to one hour) sessions. It is necessary to book these appointments through Kathryn. For regular telephone appointments I phone you. For short appointments you phone me. Sometimes it is advantageous to do a lot of work at once. We may have a double appointment lasting four hours, we may do a day of work or several days of work.

We will always hit a place in our dialogue where an issue becomes stuck. This happens regardless of how earnest you are and how much you try. We all have barriers. When you reach a place of not being able to move forward, we switch from dialogue to a different therapeutic modality. This may include body work, psychic healing, some work with artistic skills and your imagination, or past life regression. I may ask you to consider letting me refer you to another type of therapist for this stage of our work.

Being in therapy with me will always require some homework. Desire to work on yourself is necessary in order to make real progress. Your correspondence keeps me current with the happenings in your life.

The fee for our work together is $150 per session. Most appointments last for up to two hours. Sometimes we are working in blocks of time where we are together for two or more sessions at one time. My fee is $75 per hour of extra time. Short sessions which are for any length of time up to one hour are $75. If your appointment is scheduled for the telephone, it is your responsibility to insure that I have received your check before our appointment time. Otherwise, please understand, your appointment is automatically rescheduled.

APPENDIX B

Some Important Organizations

These organizations are all helpful in their own way to the professional astrologer. They all have their role to play in helping astrology improve as a discipline.

ISAR (International Society for Astrological Research)
P.O. Box 38613
Los Angeles, CA 90038

NCGR (National Council for Geocosmic Research)
Margie Herskovitz, Membership Secretary
5826 Greenspring Ave.
Baltimore, MD 21209
   They have a very comprehensive education program as-
sembled by a consensus of 50 astrologers.

PROSIG (Organization for Professional Astrology)
P.O. Box 9237
Naples, FL 33941
   This organization keeps on top of every aspect of practicing
astrology as a life's work. They have a quarterly newsletter:
"The Career Astrologer," and a hotline, an active membership,
an annual conference, and new ideas emerging continuously
for professional astrologers.

AFAN (Association for Astrological Networking)
8306 Wilshire Blvd., Suite 537
Beverly Hills, CA 90211
   AFAN has an interesting newsletter and distributes a Media
Kit and a Legal Aid Kit to its membership. The organization
sponsors ongoing activity in these areas.

Astrological Association of Great Britain
396 Caledonian Rd.
London, N1 1DN, ENGLAND

Some Important Correspondence Schools
   Learning astrology through the mail has picked up popularity
in the last ten years. The caliber of the material offered has improved
dramatically during this same period.

Astrology—The Cosmic Pattern
Correspondence Courses on Tape by Joanne Wickenburg
Write: Search
P.O. Box 75362, Northgate Station
Seattle, WA 98125

Correspondence Course in Horary Astrology by Gilbert Navarro
112 Palmetto Dr.
Edgewood, MD 21040-3520

or

Mary E. Shea
14185 Day Farm Rd.
Glenelg, MD. 21737

Faculty of Astrological Studies
Hook Cottage
Vines Cross
Heathfield
Sussex, England TN219EN

The Meonen School-Correspondence Course in Horary Astrology
Maurice McCann
73b Dresden Rd.
London N19 3BJ ENGLAND

Qualifying Horary Diploma Course
O. Barclay, QHP
Mongeham Lodge Cottage, Great Mongeham
Deal, Kent CT14 OHD, ENGLAND

The Mastery of Astrology
PO Box 9237
Naples, Florida, 33941
    A four year correspondence school leading
to professional practice.

Astrologisch—Psychologisches Institut
Louise und Bruno Huber
Postfach 614, CH - 8134
Adliswil, Zurich, Switzerland.
    The Huber School, an international school based in Switzer-
land, has special emphasis on Alice Bailey Esoteric Astrology
and Assagioli-based psychology. Instruction is offered in German or English.

Some Important Books
    There are many astrology books available, but, very few books
available on practicing astrology as a profession. The material that
I'm familiar with is listed here. More helpful books will be coming
out over the next few years.

Arroyo, Stephen. *The Practice and Profession of Astrology: Rebuilding
    Our Lost Connections With the Cosmos.* Reno, Nevada: CRCS Pub-
    lications, 1984.

Larson, Peggy & Chris Rogers. *The Complete Guide to Establishing a Professional Astrological Practice.* San Diego: ACS Publishers.

McEvers, Joan., ed. *Astrological Counseling, the Path to Self-Actualization.* Vol. VI in Llewellyn's New World Astrology Series. St. Paul, MN: Llewellyn Publications, 1990.

Mulligan, Bob, ed. *How To Start, Maintain, and Expand an Astrological Practice.* Naples: PROSIG, 1991.

Pottenger, Maritha. *Healing With The Horoscope.* San Diego: Astro Computing Services, 1982.

Rudhyar, Dane. *The Practice of Astrology.* Baltimore: Penguin Books Inc., 1968.

END NOTES

1. A good article representative of this approach is *NCGR Member-letter*, Vol. VIII, No. 6, "How to Make Astrology Pay from A-Z." By AdZe MiXXe.

2. See "Our Chicago Conference" by Chris McRae in *The Career Astrologer*. Vol 2, No. 1. for an outline of how to get a job teaching astrology at your local College or University.

3. There is a very detailed checklist in the first section of *How to Start, Maintain, and Expand an Astrological Practice*. This section was written by Monica Dimino, a Boston Astrologer.

4. "Between Astrologers and Clients," an ongoing column concerned with these issues in *The Career Astrologer*.

5. Article by Jacob Schwartz in *The Career Astrologer*, Vol. 2, No. 2, pp. 8-9.

6. A complete and detailed discussion of these issues are contained in the ongoing column called "Technology for Astrologers," in *The Career Astrologer*.

7. The "extra bedroom" profession. "Report on an Informal Survey" by Monica Dimino. *The Career Astrologer*, Vol. 2., No.1, p. 5.

8. Where your work place is located will control certain aspects of your career. A good book to read is *Healing with the Horoscope*, by Maritha Pottenger, which has pertinent material on this point.

9. There are dozens of other specialty practices in astrology, but making a living from them is not a viable career path now (*e.g.*, astrometeorology, mundane astrology, etc.); doubtless this will change.

10. See "Between Astrologers and Their Clients," an ongoing column in *The Career Astrologer*.

11. "Building a Practice with Thank You Notes," *The Career Astrologer*, Vol.1, August 1990. pp. 5-6, by Kathleen Burt.

12. There are many books and workshops on time management. If you have any difficulty in this area, address it immediately or this can be your "Achilles' heel."

Appendix

Vocational Guidance by Astrology

Charles E. Luntz

This volume, *How to Use Vocational Astrology for Success in the Workplace*, gives you the newest look at Vocational Astrology, evolved from the traditional grounding that was put in textbook form 50 years ago by Charles E. Luntz in his celebrated book, *Vocational Guidance by Astrology*. A second edition was published in 1962. Now, for the most thorough overview of the development of Vocation Astrology, from then to the present day, review the Luntz classic here in the Appendix.

Charles E. Luntz

Charles E. Luntz led an active life on many levels. For years a successful business executive in the advertising-sales field, his energetic business life was balanced by vigorous participation in occult areas: member and officeholder in the Theosophical Society of St. Louis since the 1920s; founder of Charles E. Luntz Publications in 1956; author of innumerable articles, many of which appeared in his own monthly periodical the *Ancient Wisdom*; lecturer, and other public relations activities on behalf of astrology and theosophy. *Vocational Guidance by Astrology* combines his lifelong experience in the practical business world, his understanding of the dynamics of human relations, career motivations, individual desires for creative and appropriate vocations, and his understanding of astrology. He is one of the few astrologers who has tackled this difficult yet vitally important area of human activity.

Vocational Guidance
by Astrology

Charles E. Luntz

LLEWELLYN PUBLICATIONS
St. Paul, Minnesota, 55164-0383, U.S.A.

ISBN 0–87542-448-1 (cloth)
ISBN 0-87542-435-X (paper)

Copyright © 1962 by Charles E. Luntz

Revised Edition 1962
Reprinted 1969
Reprinted 1971
Reprinted 1973
Reprinted 1978
Reprinted 1992

Publisher: Llewellyn Publications, St. Paul, MN

CONTENTS

PREFACE TO THE SECOND EDITION

Vocational guidance by astrology made its debut just 20 years ago and apparently filled a long felt need as it has been out of print for many years. A constant succession of orders for the book both from the public and from the trade have continued to come in and as the original publishers had merged with a British firm in the meantime, no reprint was feasible.

The present publishers commissioned the author to revise the work, bringing it up to date in the light of researches and discoveries in the astrological field during the past two decades. This has been done and a chapter added on the vocational influence of Pluto, the most recently discovered planet, also three additional horoscopes and their elucidations—Khrushchev's, Lyndon Johnson's and Nelson Rockefeller's.

Forecasts made in the 1942 edition which have since come to pass are indicated by asterisks and a footnote. They are valuable as evidence that the horoscope, properly interpreted, is in very fact a guide to the trend of one's destiny. It does not, however, "tell fortunes." The natal chart assuredly shows in what fields the greatest possibility of good fortune resides. It does not insure that the native (subject of the horoscope) will cultivate these fields or go anywhere near them. He has free will. He can do exactly the things the horoscope indicates are disadvantageous for him. Or he can follow this God-given guide to success and well-being.

But he must do his part. The horoscope will point the way, but it will not do the work for him. As an example, a native might possess an excellent fifth house (a department of the horoscope), showing good influences for investments such as stocks and bonds. At a certain period these influences might be stirred into action. If he used ordinary prudence in making his selections during this period taking into account the factors any careful investor would consider and not buying blindly, his chances of profit would be good. But if he did all these things when his current influences on investments were adverse, he would still be likely to lose or at least wind up with a profitless transaction.

This is neither theory nor imagination but is based on the author's lengthy experience, both in making his own investments and advising others. Similarly, while a good tenth house and its affiliates (Saturn and Capricorn) show high possibilities of business or professional success, this will not come without the personal efforts of the native, nor without proper training for the type of occupation the horoscope shows he is qualified to engage in.

Here again, the training should begin at the right astrological time (for him—it might be the wrong time for someone else). Always it is the individual's own horoscope that must be the guide, not the day-by-day aspects of the Sun, Moon and planets to each other. These, when favorable do help somewhat, and when unfavorable mitigate a little against the horoscopic influences. But the horoscope is a personal not a generalized thing and must be so treated.

If the present work is employed with these fundamentals borne in mind, it should be of the utmost help in choosing a suitable career and in timing the steps to be taken to implement it.

CHAPTER I

ITS NEED

One of the weakest features of our civilization is the haphazard fashion in which our young people are permitted to select what they hope will be their life's work. Worse still, it may be selected for them, in which case the chance that the ideal choice may be made is even more remote. The schools and colleges, the instructors, the parents, the youngsters themselves, do their best to make a wise selection. Sometimes they succeed. Far more often they miserably fail.

It is comparatively rare to meet a man (or woman) who is perfectly happy in his chosen vocation. The test comes 10, 20, 30 years later, perhaps. If he is among the multitude of parents who declare, "I don't want my son to follow my profession," it may be taken for granted that even though he may deny it, in some manner or other that profession is uncongenial to him. This may bring a challenge from the successful. "I am a doctor," a physician may say. "I have made a satisfactory competence. I have achieved some recognition in my field. I enjoy my work. But I don't want my son to follow in my footsteps. My time is never my own. The hours are completely irregular. I may have to turn out in the middle of the night after an exhausting day and drive five miles because Mrs. Brown's baby has colic. Half the time I don't get paid." And so on and on—all perfectly true. Let Junior get into something easier. But the doctor who talks like that is obviously far from satisfied with his own profession, even though he has contrived to be reasonably successful in it. If he were satisfied, there is no other profession in which he would desire his son to be, unless, of course, the latter had obvious talents in another direction or none at all in this. And even then his father would see with lingering regret the boy preparing to follow some alien line of endeavor.

Because the man who is wholly and completely successful in his work is the man to whom no other vocation appears possible. He is so wrapped up in it—he loves it so unreservedly—that it would seem a sort of blasphemy to him to stress its inconveniences and use them as an excuse for the son or daughter to pass it by. If he is a medical professional, he may tell the youth, "Yes, the hours are long and irregular, you work like a dog and when you think you are done for the night you may have to start all over again. Your patients often may not pay you. All these things and many more you will have to contend with. But," he would conclude in a tremendous burst of enthusiasm, "it's the only profession in the world, and those things are trifling inconveniences that don't matter. I can't imagine myself in anything else. And I shall be the happiest person alive if you decide to follow in my footsteps."

There speaks the truly successful man, and if his horoscope were expertly examined it would be found that as a physician he was "a natural." He would be the "one in a thousand" who somehow had contrived to discover his niche and fill it. To him his profession is his life, and he glories in it. And for the doctor, one may substitute lawyer, business man, engineer, artist, writer, politician, teacher, contractor, scientist, social service worker or any other of a hundred or a thousand vocations open to civilized man.

What makes the "successful man," and what accounts for the myriads of failures?

Disregarding the conclusions of the vocational specialists, some of which undoubtedly have merit, we return the unequivocal answer, which does not necessarily conflict with these conclusions, that success is found where the obvious trends of the natal horoscope have been followed; failure, where they have been disregarded.

We must, of course, avoid over-simplification of the problem. A man of strong will-power, fixed determination and perseverance, may achieve moderate success in a vocation for which his horoscope shows him to be unfitted. But the horoscope also shows the preponderance of fixed signs and other indicators that mark the will that did it. To what heights, however, might this will not have carried him had he followed the lines of his natural aptitude as laid down in the natal chart? Swimming against the current is good exercise but slow progress. Enough natural obstacles are usually provided to the attainment of success that we need not go out of our way to seek artificial ones.

Here it may be pointed out that if the popular conception that man's future is cut and dried by his horoscope were true, vocational guidance by astrology would be impossible. But planetary and sidereal "influences," so called, merely chart the course. They do not force anyone to follow it. They declare in language plain to the astrologer, what any given person should do, for greater success and happiness. They by no means proclaim that he will do it. He may choose the opposite course. Fatalistic astrology, with all its will-weakening implications, disputes this but has never successfully disproved it. Man does have free will. The horoscope may urge—and for our own benefit. It does not dictate.

And a natural aptitude is also an urge. An Edison *must* invent. A Ford must manufacture. A George Bernard Shaw must write. A Kreisler must play. Can anyone imagine those named following vocations other than the ones in which they have reached such eminence? Their horoscopes indicate the measure of success each has attained and the lines along which each has marched to his goal. In each horoscope doubtless are to be found warning signs barring the way to success in many other fields which these men, so fortunate in their own, might have followed. Some of them, perhaps, they did follow for a time—finding themselves in blind alleys from which they were able to retreat. The life of almost every famous man contains early episodes of disappointment and failure due to the wrong choice of a life-work. Sometimes it is, or seems to be, a forced choice. Inwardly the deep-seated urge is present to do something, anything, rather than the unpalatable drudgery which circumstances seem to have compelled. Somehow opportunity presents itself, is seized, made fullest use of, and the "lucky" man finds himself doing the one great thing he loves and are best fitted for. But how many "career" tales have this happy ending? Statistics tell us the sad story of the few, the infinitesimally few, who reach the top "where there is always room." They tell us of the few more who wind up somewhere near the top, and of the small percentage of near-successes who land within range of the upper brackets. Immediately below them come a sprinkling of the good second-raters, then more, many more, third-raters, and we need not trouble to classify the fourth to the sixth-raters who constitute the rest of the population. They are the millions who go through life thwarted. Ether they "haven't quite made it," or they have not come within a thousand miles of making it. They may be comfortably off or in poverty; well-known in their circle or obscure. That has little to do with it. Success may sometimes be a matter of money—and sometimes it may not be. Success may sometimes mean the limelight—and sometimes it may mean the cloister. These things are not its gauge or measure. True success is synonymous with happiness. Are you happy? Have you no regrets? Can you look about you in your work and say, "I can want nothing better at which to labor than this," and mean it? Has it given you, whether your income be large or small, enough to satisfy your tastes and those of your family, to provide for your future and theirs, and to gratify your desire (if it may be thus crudely expressed) to "amount to something."

If you can answer all these questions with a quick affirmative, you are one of the successes and we need not tell you that you should be happy. You are happy.

But if the very questions bring a hollow laugh—if you have to answer no to all of them or to any of them, then in some particular you have fallen short. If you are too young to have reached the consummation stage—if you are still struggling, still trying to find yourself, then does it seem you are on the way to an affirmative answer to all these questions? Young or old, if you are in the right line of work, you should be happy in it and have no regrets because you are not engaged in something else. And if you are still in the sacrifice-making stage which nearly all have to go through on their way up, they should be happy sacrifices, sacrifices you are glad to make because you can see forward in your mind's eye to a day when they will no longer be necessary. Meantime you are in your beloved work, whatever it may be, and the temporary self-denials are part of a price you do not begrudge paying because it is part of what goes with the job.

To those, and unfortunately their name is legion, whose work is hateful monotony, who look at it as something to keep body and soul together and nothing besides, it may see incredible that one may regard labor in that light. Yet in the natal horoscope of each there is indicated just that kind of vocation for him. There is something he (or she) can do which will not seem like work but like play, so absolutely fitted are they to do that particular thing to perfection. And the tragedy is that most of these unsuccessful, resentful, baffled millions will (until selecting vocations by the horoscope is the law of the land) go through their entire lives without finding themselves.

Round pegs in square holes—square pegs in round holes; physicians who should have been lawyers and lawyers who should be designing houses, and failures in business who never should have entered business but who belong in one of the professions! The stupendous need for some absolutely certain way of determining natural aptitudes and linking up those aptitudes with their money-making possibilities (for people must live) surely need not be stressed.

It is of little use to ask the child, before his training begins, what he would like to be. He knows less about it than his parents, and he probably knows nothing. His answers may range from a street-car conductor to a fireman—or maybe he would like to be a meter reader. It is hazardous to assume, because he "likes to draw," that he has the makings of an artist or architect. Nearly all children like to draw. It may be meaningful or entirely meaningless. He may play with soldiers a great deal, too, yet grow up to be a pacifist. His natural inclinations may have no opportunity to show themselves. Mozart might never have been a musician if his parents had been too poor to buy a piano or its 1eighth-century forerunner, the harpsichord.

True, genius plus will surmounts the most staggering obstacles to manifest itself, but this work is not written wholly for geniuses. In every normal human being (and most of us are normal at base) there exists the capacity for doing some one thing (occasionally more than one) better than most of the others in our circle can do it. We can shine somewhere—excel in something or other. School and college may or may not bring it out. We may get switched onto another track—a false track—and waste years or a lifetime imagining we are good at something in which we are only mediocre. Opportunity may arise for us to swing into the very thing the horoscope cries out that we were meant to do. If the natal chart indicators are at all strong the opportunity is almost certain to arise. We may miss it entirely for want of recognition. We may be urged, begged, to make a change which would start us on the highroad to the success we crave. Yet doubt, fear, disinclination to make a move may keep us chained to a profession or business for which the horoscope shows we have poor aptitude and no likelihood of anything above mediocre returns.

There is, of course, another side to the question: the possibility of our being attracted to a vocation which will provide much inner satisfaction but meager financial recompense. The horoscope shows that, too. Then it is up to us to make the choice. To some, monetary returns are a matter of indifference if they are in the work they love. Good and well, but isn't it wise to know ahead of time that the compensation is likely to be wholly spiritual? And there may be and probably is something else in the horoscope which will supply both.

Conversely, the natal chart may offer highly lucrative possibilities along lines in which the inner satisfactions will be nil. If the subject of the horoscope, or "native" as astrologers term him, regards the financial factor as all-important, he may select this rather than a "second-choice" which might be full of interest but from which the pecuniary gain would be less. That, too, is strictly up to him. It is not the province of this work to preach to anybody what they should or should not do, so far as their freedom of choice is concerned. The astrological facts will be presented, the astrological consequences of this, that, or the other course pointed out. The native may apply them as he will, to his own case.

This introductory chapter set out to show that a need existed for some trustworthy guide to the selection of a life-work. It has attempted to show that conventional methods, valuable though they may be, are at best "hit-or-miss." It is more than probable that the really shrewd appraisers of human aptitudes are those who, while perhaps crediting their success to other methods, secretly rely on astrology. It is pretty well conceded that it is used extensively in Hollywood in casting important parts. The writer, who for 20 years has hired and trained a sales personnel of many hundreds has, for more than half that time, relied on the aid furnished by a knowledge of astrology.

To the unfortunate folk who, not having the slightest familiarity with the subject, insist that it is all imagination, all he can say is that, if this be so, it seems to work just as well as the real thing. But it is not imagination. Astrology is one of the grandest and most perfect of sciences. In the forthcoming chapters its enormous possibilities as an aid to choosing the right vocation will be clearly set forth.

CHAPTER II

ITS PRINCIPLES

The basic principles of vocational astrology, like those of astrology as a whole, are simple. Their ramifications, however, may become exceedingly complex. Yet when understood they are not unduly hard to apply to individual cases. It cannot be too often stressed, however, that *all*—not some but *all*—of the numerous factors in the natal chart must each be carefully studied, or correct judgment is impossible.

Right there is the weakness of the cheap vocational analysis cheerfully offered by incompetents, who haphazardly glance at two or three of these many configurations and positions (if they do that much) and then presume to pass on the business or professional talents of the native. It cannot be done that way with any hope of success. Nature has not made the natal horoscope too easy to read. Nature requires, in this branch of research as in all others, painstaking digging out of the facts—and then the exercise of careful thought and judgment as to what those facts mean.

Fortunately the modern astrologer falls heir to the vast body of knowledge accumulated over centuries and millennia which is embraced in the so-called traditional astrology. And in the main this traditional astrology is very sound. Some fanciful accretions doubtless have fastened themselves on the proven teachings as they came down the years. Sometimes these were the product of sensationalists eager for self-advertising by propounding something new, regardless of its truth. Occasionally they may be traced to sincere masters of the science working with insufficient knowledge. Thus Kepler, a very great astrologer, invented the minor aspects (in which this writer has not the slightest belief) to account for phenomena he could not otherwise explain. Kepler did not know of the existence of Uranus, Neptune, or Pluto. He was handicapped by trying to account for conditions which in all probability the presence of these planets would amply explain. He formulated the so-called minor aspects, and there are enough of these constantly available to "explain" virtually anything.

Kepler meant well, but his "minor aspects" clutter up the horoscope with misleading junk which is not only valueless (at least in

230 / How to Use Vocational Astrology for Success in the Workplace

the writer's opinion) but positively harmful. Students who have always regarded these aspects as sacrosanct because they appear in well-known ephemerides and aspectarians, may be shocked by this conclusion, but they may be assured it was arrived at only after many years of experimentation. It is shared by a number of well-known astrologers; Cheney, one of the best of a couple of generations ago, was outspoken in his denunciation of them. They will not be taken into account in this book.

The more one practices and studies the magnificent art of astrological delineation, the greater respect one develops for the wisdom of the fathers who have handed it down to us. This does not minimize the value of the immense labor of moderns like Leo, Sepharial, Carter and others, who in truly scientific spirit have experimented, classified and analyzed a constant succession of horoscopes, charting down what appeared to be new facts, but always working within the great traditional principles which have never and will never be disproved. It is along these lines that research will be most productive. The attempts to discredit basic facts, accepted for ages by astrologers of all schools and nations, may result in some temporary publicity for the individual who tries it, but the ancients, whose labors built up this knowledge, are not likely to turn any handsprings in their graves because of it. Traditional astrology is too well-based and well-established. And it is on the principles of traditional astrology applied in the modern manner but with full deterence to its undoubted truth, that the suggestions made in this book are based.

In setting forth these principles, the "reasons" behind them will be omitted. This is intended as a practical work of reference for students as well as professionals, and, in fact, for individuals who would not claim to be either, but who have sufficient elementary knowledge of astrology to be able to set up and progress a horoscope and who desire a clear set of reliable rules formulated which, if they are followed, will yield the information they seek. There are sound reasons, exoteric and esoteric, why the midheaven has rule over the occupation, why the Sun governs influence and authority, why the sixth house relates to employment. Others have set forth these reasons. Here they will be taken for granted.

Neither will the perennial question of whether the planets "indicate" or "influence" the things they stand for be considered. The writer has his own opinion as to this and has stated it at length in other works, but it would be out of place here. The terms "indicate" and "influence" will be used impartially and interchangeably. The stars and planets certainly act as though they radiate "influences," whether they actually do or not. They also act as "indicators" of conditions, circumstances, qualities or their lack and all the rest of the great horoscopic bill-of-fare. The theory behind it all does not affect the application of the undoubted facts.

And so the principles may now be stated and will be quite readily grasped by all to whom the reading of a horoscope is reasonably familiar.[1]

Factors to examine in determining vocational possibilities are these:

1. Planets[2] (if any) in the tenth house. A planet nearest the Midheaven normally takes precedence over those further away, though this general rule is subject to a number of modifications which will be explained in the proper place.

2. A planet in the ninth house but within 5° of the tenth has a tenth as well as a ninth house influence and should be treated as if in the tenth. A planet in the eleventh house but within 5° of the tenth also has a tenth house sway but this is weaker than if in the tenth or ninth. Examine the sign on the cusp, its ruler, the sign and house in which the ruler is found.

3. Next look for any planet exactly aspecting the Midheaven. If none, then the planet or planets configured with it by platic (inexact) aspect, if within five degrees of orb.

4. If Saturn has not already appeared in one of the above categories, viz., in or within 5° of the tenth, ruling the tenth cuspal sign or aspecting the M.C., he should next be considered, as he is normal planetary ruler of the tenth. Examine the sign he is in.

5. If Capricorn has not similarly appeared, this sign is now up for consideration together with planets occupying it. Capricorn is the normal tenth house sign.

6. This exhausts tenth house factors. We must then look to the sixth house and its affiliates. The sixth house governs employment, whereas the tenth is concerned with the nature of the occupation. In the horoscope of an employee the sixth represents the employers. If and when he becomes an employer it then has reference to his em-

---

1. See Appendix A for explanation of symbols.
2. Sun and Moon (luminaries) are included as planets to avoid repetition.

ployees. "A good servant makes a good master" (or "A bad servant makes a bad master") is literally true astrologically. The same factors largely (but not wholly) govern both. Take planets in the sixth (or in the fifth or seventh if within 5° orb of sixth) in the same way as described in Rule 1.

7. Take sign on cusp of sixth as in Rule 2. However, planets aspecting the cusp of sixth as in Rule 3 have no influence and are disregarded.

8. If Mercury has not appeared in applying any of the foregoing Rules, he is next in line for consideration, as normal ruler of the sixth. Follow Rule 4, substituting Mercury for Saturn.

9. The sign Virgo normally governs employment just as Capricorn rules occupation. Follow Rule 5 substituting Virgo for Capricorn.

10. There are no more factors peculiar to employment. Next on the agenda is the second house which has to do solely with money, gain, profit, and loss. Good configurations between the second, tenth and sixth are excellent for the things ruled by the planets or signs concerned. Follow Rule 1, substituting second house for tenth.

11. Follow Rule 2 similarly. Rule 3 is ignored as in the case of the sixth house.

12. If Venus has not yet appeared she should now be taken as normal ruler of the second. Follow Rule 4, substituting Venus for Saturn.

13. Follow Rule 5, substituting Taurus (normal second house sign) for Capricorn.

14. Now carefully note down all aspects between planets concerned with tenth, sixth, and second houses; also between planets in Capricorn, Virgo, and Taurus; finally between Saturn, Mercury, and Venus.

15. Examine the planet rising closest to the Ascendant.

16. Finally take the best planet in the horoscope, if this has not appeared in the foregoing. The question of what constitutes the "best" planet will be exhaustively analyzed in the chapter dealing with this feature exclusively. In general, however, it is the planet most strongly placed by sign, house, and elevation, with fewest adverse and greatest number of favorable aspects.

These 16 rules constitute the principles to be applied to determining (a) the ideal vocation of the native from the standpoint of natural aptitude, (b) the occupations which offer greatest possibilities of financial return; not necessarily the same as (a).

But another problem immediately confronts us. Should the native be content to remain in the employ of others or should he aim at becoming the head of his own business or profession? It is quite certain that in many cases the horoscope is such that it points to greater success in a well-paid executive position than could possibly be attained as sole owner of a commercial or professional enterprise. Yet there are those who are happiest as "their own boss," with a small income rather than working for someone else for a much larger one. Additional rules for determining this must now be formulated.

17. Examine the Constitutional groupings of the planets (Cardinal, Fixed, Common). For greatest success in one's own enterprise, there should be a preponderance of the planets and angles in Cardinal signs.

18. How many planets are Accidentally Dignified (in first, fourth, seventh, or tenth houses)?

19. For high executive positions in the employ of others but not calling for "ultimate" decisions there should be a preponderance of planets in Fixed signs. Examine.

20. In connection with Rule 19, for best results, Succedent houses (second, fifth, eighth, eleventh) should be well occupied. How many planets are succedently placed?

Finally we come to the question of Partnership. Many a deficient vocational horoscope can be redeemed by selection of a partner who supplies the deficiencies, even though himself lacking in other qualities possessed by the native. Partnership possibilities are to be analyzed as follows:

21. Planets in the seventh house. Follow Rule 1.

22. Sign on cusp of seventh. Follow Rule 2. Disregard Rule 3 in relation to seventh.

23. Venus rules seventh, through the latter's normal sign, Libra. As Venus has been analyzed already by reason of its rulership of the second house sign, Taurus, its position, aspects, etc., already taken should be noted again for seventh house consideration.

24. Follow Rule 5, substituting Libra for Capricorn.

25. For accurate appraisal of the harmony and success of any given partnership, the individual natal horoscopes of the prospective partners should be compared. The technique is set forth in the chapter devoted to "Partners."

When all of these rules have been conscientiously applied, the

Vocation, Employment and Partnership possibilities of the horoscope will have been as completely explored as our present astrological knowledge permits, subject to some amplification which need not be embodied in additional rules but which will round out the information arrived at by their application.

Thus the Ascendant, the Sun sign, and to a lesser degree the Moon sign, show certain aptitudes and success possibilities inherent in the sign. They are subordinate, however, to the distinctively vocational factors embraced by the formulated rules. Also any particularly strong house or sign may have a minor bearing on the analysis, even though in no way linked up with the exclusive occupational or money-making factors.

These are important, because, in very weak vocational charts, the astrologer may be driven to fall back upon these ordinarily subordinate indicators as a last resort.

There remains the question of the best periods in which to undertake to put into effect the recommendations arrived at by the vocational analysis. When is "exactly the right time" to apply for that position, launch that business, open that store? The progressed or "directed" horoscope furnishes the answer.

Each of the above rules, its application, examples taken from actual horoscopes, and its various modifications will be treated in the chapters which follow.

It will be seen that vocational guidance by astrology cannot be tackled in the lighthearted fashion in which it is often undertaken. It is a serious business, requiring much time and concentration for reliable and effective conclusions to be reached.

Yet after all it is worth the time and effort involved, if there is thereby obtained positive knowledge of this line of endeavor which is most likely to lead the individual to success and happiness.

CHAPTER III

OCCUPATION RULERSHIPS: PLANETS

Before we can proceed to apply the principles laid down in Chapter I, it is necessary to have a clear picture of the planetary and sign rulerships of the myriad occupations open to people. In astrology we always proceed from the general to the particular. We ascertain the principle and reason from that to its many individual applications. The assignment of any given department of life to a specific planet is never arbitrary. There is always a sound underlying reason. And millennia of observation (except in the case of the three planets, Uranus, Neptune, and Pluto, discovered within the past two centuries) have borne out the rulership assigned in all cases. In fact, the observation came first—the theory later.

Thus Jupiter governs all things into which the element of abundance enters. Being the great benefic, it bestows abundance of good in all departments, physical, mental, spiritual. It rules prosperity on that account, but it also rules religion, which makes for "the more abundant life." Yet in affliction it still runs true to form. It may give adiposity—abundance of flesh. Its diseases are those of too abundant eating and drinking: gout, liver and blood ailments, abscesses (swellings), boils, carbuncles, biliousness and the like.

Jupiter itself is the largest (most abundant) object in the Solar System except the Sun, which rules "greatness" in other ways. There is always a connection, not fanciful or far-fetched but extending down into the very heart of being, between the planet or luminary, the things it rules and their relationship to each other. This should be remembered, otherwise a mere superficial recitation of "Things ruled by the planets" may lead the novice to believe that they are just a hodge-podge catalogue of arbitrary groupings without rhyme or reason. Nothing could be further from the truth.

With this understood, we may proceed to classify the various occupations according to their planetary and sign rulerships. The student will need often to refer to these classifications in interpreting his own vocational indicators in the natal chart. For convenience an appendix* is furnished giving the planetary ruler of each occupa-

---

* Appendix C.

tion in alphabetical order.

It is of course impossible to cover every conceivable line of endeavor followed by the two billion human beings who populate the earth. Of some of these the writer and the reader may never even have heard. It should not be difficult, however, by reference to the underlying basis of each rulership to arrive at the planet, sign and house concerned with any vocational not expressly mentioned.

A business or profession is likely to involve more than its main planetary ruler. Thus the element of "trading," ruled by Mercury may frequently have to be taken into account where buying or selling enters into the picture. Even an artist may need to sell his pictures after painting them. This is not invariable however. It is conceivable that supreme excellence in some profession may be exploited commercially by another individual who has trading talent, though this is wholly absent in the one whose work is thus marketed.

In the case of occupations with multiple rulership, all planets, etc., must be considered. Life insurance has to do with death (Scorpio, eighth house, Pluto, Mars). It also is involved with risk or speculation, at least so far as the single insured individual is concerned. (Leo, fifth house, Sun). And the contract of insurance brings in still other elements (Gemini, third house, Mercury). These are entirely apart from the principles common to all vocational selection, as set forth in Chapter I. There are still the occupational house, employment house and money house to consider, with the planets and signs that govern them. Also the first house with its peculiar dominance over the energies of the native, and the eleventh with its foreshadowing of the likely sources from which fulfillment of the native's ambitions will come, cannot be ignored. The Part-of-Fortune, too, contributes its moiety to the completed picture.

From all of which it may be gathered that anyone who feels that he can set a pointer to his birth month and drop a penny into a weighing machine, then by reading what is printed on the reverse side of the weight card that drops out determine his occupation, is the victim of acute self-deception.

Planetary vocations follow:*

SUN — ☉

Keynotes: Authority, Rule, Command, Power, Importance, Dignity, Government, Gold.

Vocations: Bankers, Presidents, Foremen, Department Heads, Stock-Exchange Workers, Stock Speculators, Investment Bankers, Occupations Involving Children, Jewelers, Workers in Gold, Heart Specialists, Workers in Amber, Impresarios, Entertainment Directors, Gin Manufacturers (Sun rules the Juniper), Lion Tamers, Spotlight Operators, Orange Growers, Park Keepers, Playground Directors, Theater Owners and Managers, Walnut Growers.

MOON — ☽

Keynotes: Change, Women, Liquids, Real Estate, The Public, The Secondary, The Temporal.

Vocations: Traveling Men, Sailors, Nurses, Fishermen, Liquor Dealers, Laundry Proprietors and Workers, Cabbage and Cauliflower Growers, Chicken Fanciers, Cheese Manufacturers, Bath House Proprietors, Bakers, Boat Owners, Brewery Workers, Brewers, Dairy Farmers, Dairies, Household Help (Female), Poultry Raisers, Chinaware and Glassware Manufacturers, Melon Growers, Midwives, Milkmen, Mushroom Growers, Obstetricians, Plastic Artists, Restaurant Proprietors and Workers, Tavern and Taproom Owners and Helpers, Waiters and Waitresses, Watchmen.

MERCURY — ☿

Keynotes: The Mind, Mentality, Memory, Transportation, Documents, Writing, Teaching, Intellect.

Vocations: Clerks, Accountants, Bookkeepers, Writers, Teachers, Lecturers, Orators, Secretaries, Mail Carriers, Bus Drivers, Train Conductors, Architects, Authors, Acoustic Experts, Beekeepers, Bookbinders, Actuaries, Correspondents, Typists, Interpreters, Recorders of Deeds, Diplomats, Dietitians, Errand Boys, File Clerks, Retail Grocers, Governesses, Handwriting Experts, Information Clerks, Jugglers, Reporters, Messengers, Merchandise

* Where a vocation appears under more than one planet, all govern it.

Managers, Buyers, Salesmen, Nerve Specialists, Paper Manufacturers, Editors, Notaries Public, Stenographers, Storekeepers, Stationers, Printers, Publishers, Doctors, Healers, Radio Announcers, Telephone Operators.

VENUS — ♀

Keynotes: Love, Beauty, Art, Young Women and Girls, Music, The Fine Arts, Adornment, Money.

Vocations: Artists, Musicians, Singers, Actors, Toilet Accessory Makers, Cosmeticians, Beauty Parlor Operators, Florists, Women's Apparel Manufacturers and Dealers, Dressmakers, Milliners, Tailors, Confectioners, Maids, Candy Manufacturers, Dry Goods Stores, Entertainers, Furniture Manufacturers and Dealers, Hotel Keepers and Workers, Bee Keepers, Landscape Gardeners, Interior Decorators, Social Secretaries, Throat Specialists, Perfume Manufacturers, Peach Growers, Society Editor, Amusement Concessionaries, Art Museum Curators, House Painters and Paperhangers, Photographers, Engravers, Illustrators, Cashiers, Tellers, Capitalists, Pursers, Money Lenders.

MARS — ♂

Keynotes: Fires, Quarrels, Energy, Metals, Initiative, Effort, Pain, Weapons.

Vocations: Soldiers, Army Officers, Pugilists, Assayers, Surgeons, Gun Makers, Butchers, Iron and Steel Workers, Dentists, Barbers, Armament Makers and Workers, Metal Workers, Carpenters, Executives, Firemen, Policemen, Guards, Hardware Manufacturers and Dealers, Implement Makers, Locksmiths, Lumberjacks, Mechanics, Machinists, Stock Raisers, Wrestlers, Occupations connected with things made by fire.

JUPITER — ♃

Keynotes: Abundance, Spirituality, Religion, Prosperity, Affluence, Wealth, Law, Publications, Voyages or Long Journeys.

Vocations: Lawyers, Clergymen, Editors, Publishers, Advertising Agents, Ad-Writers, Judges, Woolen Merchants, Wholesale Grocers, Aldermen, Appraisers, Bond Salesmen, Cashiers, Capitalists, Doctors (of Divinity, Literature, Law or Philosophy), Pursers, Financiers, Jockeys, Horse Trainers, Racing Stable Owners and Workers, Law-Court Attaches, Writers for Publication, Sporting Goods Manufacturers and Dealers, Guides, Whale Hunters, Chiropodists, Shoe Manufacturers and Dealers, Shoe Workers.

SATURN — ♄

Keynotes: Hardships, Delays, Obstacles, Difficulties, Misfortunes, Poverty, Hard Labor, Tradition, The Well-Established, The Practical, Real Estate, The Old, The Conservative.

Vocations: Miners, Real Estate Dealers, Farmers, Cemetery Lot Salesmen, Excavators, Builders, Contractors, Bricklayers, Gardeners, Tanners, Dealers in Hides, Leather Goods Manufacturers and Dealers, Coal and Ice Dealers, Watch and Clock Makers and Repairers, Laborers, Tombstone Makers, Undertakers, Efficiency Experts, Priests, Monks, Nuns, Sextons, Timekeepers, Farm Hands, Grain Dealers, Plumbers, Night Workers, Night Watchmen, Workers Underground.

URANUS — ♅

Keynotes: The New, The Unusual, The Surprising, Sudden Happenings, Inventions, Advanced Thought.

Vocations: Scientists, Inventors, Astrologers, Occultists, Faith Healers, Chiropractors, Clairvoyants, Aviators, Automobile Racers, Automobile Manufacturers and Dealers, Automobile and Airplane Mechanics, Electricians, Radio Manufacturers and Dealers. Radio Announcers, Moving Picture Producers, Movie Theater Owners, Garage Proprietors, Research Workers, Social Service Workers, Telephone Operators, Lighting Specialists, Psychotherapists, Nerve Specialists, Motormen, Metaphysicians, X-Ray Workers, Electrical Appliance Manufacturers and Dealers, Instrument Manufacturers and Dealers, Telegraphers, Lecturers, Engineers.

NEPTUNE — ♆

Keynotes: The Mysterious, The Subtle, The Obscure, The Secret, The Sea, Imagination.

Vocations: Poets, Mind Readers, Musicians, Occult Writers, Pharmacists, Chemists, Naval Officers, Oil Workers, Oil Well Operators, Filling Station Owners, Fish Markets, Anaesthetists, Distillers, Beach Life Guards, Astrologers, Detectives, Private Investigators.

PLUTO — ♇

Keynotes: Death, Great Catastrophes, Dictators, General Calamities, World Wars, The Completely New, The Entirely Exclusive.

Vocations: It is hazardous at present to use Pluto as a significator of occupation. His comparatively recent discovery, combined with the obscure nature of the planet, make it advisable to ignore him in vocational selection, except in connection with death and things appertaining to it. Thus he undoubtedly governs Undertakers, Embalmers, Cemetery Associations, Life Insurance Salesmen and other workers, and all occupations connected in any way with the end of life. It is probable that very outstanding success, such as makes the native a world figure, may be due to ability to express Pluto's good aspects. Apparently very few can do this fully, though all appear to be affected by his bad ones.

NOTE: See additional information regarding Pluto in Appendix D.

CHAPTER IV

OCCUPATION RULERSHIPS: SIGNS

Planets take precedence of signs in respect to occupation, as indeed they do in all departments of life. It is well-known that any planet in a house dominates the house, the sign on the cusp being secondary. This law is modified only in the case of the Ascendant. The rising sign marks the native more powerfully (especially as to personal appearance) than any planet in the first house unless such planet be within 5° of the Ascendant, in which case the latter will dominate. This applies even if the planet is at the end of the twelfth house, within 5° orb of the Ascendant.

If no planet is in a house, the sign on the cusp of the house must be examined and considered in conjunction with the planet which rules this sign. In the case of occupation the tenth house sign itself is of considerable moment and it may be possible to arrive at a satisfactory occupation even though the planetary ruler of the sign is afflicted, providing the Midheaven is well aspected.

It would not be true to say that a sign rules all the things governed by its ruling planet. Taurus, for example, is ruled by Venus but has no dominance whatever over some of the things Venus governs. It also possesses characteristics of its own, quite foreign to Venus. Thus the latter rules elegance, grace, delicacy, foppishness, all of which are alien to the sturdy, matter-of-fact Taurus, but which are found in full measure in Libra, the other sign over which Venus rules. The bulldog nature of Taurus and its fighting qualities when once aroused are the very antithesis of the peace-loving characteristics of Venus, itself the planet of peace.

Venus, however, rules money and so does Taurus. Yet Libra has nothing to do with money, and while Taurus people usually possess a certain money sense and are shrewd in handling finances, the native of Libra is frequently very impractical in this regard. Libra rules artists, whose improvidence is often marked. These statements, of course, are generalizations only. A Taurus native with a poor financial horoscope otherwise could quite easily live a life of want, while a Libra subject with the opposite type of natal chart might end up an international banker. The principle to bear in mind is that each planet has its own characteristics, part of which may be the same as those of the sign or signs it governs but some of which are its own exclusive property.

Some signs follow the qualities of their ruling planets to a much greater degree than others. Thus Sun possesses almost all the characteristics of its single sign, Leo. On the Ascendant it injects both the qualities and something of the appearance of the true Leo. The extent to which it swamps out the rising sign depends upon the strength of the latter. Common signs yield right of way very easily to a powerful planet such as Sun or Uranus; cardinal signs less easily; fixed signs are most resistant of all. Scorpio rising remains Scorpio as a rule, in spite of the impact of an ascending planet, and the latter plays second string.

A good example of the almost complete superseding of a common sign by a planet on the Ascendant is the horoscope of Franklin D. Roosevelt. Here Uranus is within 2.5° of the Virgo Ascendant; Sun is in Aquarius, as also Mercury and Venus. The fact of Sun being in the sign of Uranus, ascending planet, gives dominance to the latter which causes it almost completely to nullify the mutable Virgo. Mr. Roosevelt emerges a full-blooded Aquarian with Virgo feebly represented in certain little tricks of manner and perhaps a greater willingness to consult with others than the typical Uranian Ascendant (very dictatorial) ordinarily confers.

The occupational factors need not, however, be read in the same way as the personal characteristics indicated by the Ascendant. A planet on the Ascendant necessarily makes the native a blend of the ascending sign and the planet. One or other may be subordinate or they may be about equal in strength, but there they are and the native has to make the best of them. He may decide to cultivate the qualities of his rising sign and to suppress or mitigate those of his ascending planet, or *vice-versa*. He cannot, however, erase either from his nature.

In the case of a sign or planet concerned with occupation, he has considerable freedom of choice. If the planet is good, he may follow an occupation ruled by the planet and ignore completely the cuspal sign. Or he may try to find a vocation which is governed by both. As a matter of fact, the more of his good planets that are directly or indirectly concerned in the rulership of the occupation he chooses, the better.

Occupations ruled by the signs are given below. To avoid needless repetition, reference is made to the occupational rulerships of the planets where there is duplication of things governed by both the sign and by its ruler.

ARIES — ♈

Keynote: Leadership.

Vocations: Any occupation ruled by Mars which permits of advancement and promotion. Those with poor chance of advancement should be avoided. Those occupations of Mars calling for exceptional patience are not for the impatient Aries unless a good quota of fixed signs are prominent in the chart, or the patient Capricorn or Virgo very strong. Examples of Martian occupations coming under these categories and therefore to be avoided where Aries is the vocational factor are these: Assayers, Surgeons, Dentists, Carpenters, Lumberjacks, Mechanics. But Scorpio, also ruled by Mars, has the necessary patience to tackle these non-Arian occupations. Aries, ruling the head, may also denote occupations not governed by Mars, as Hat and Cap Makers or Dealers, Hairdressers or Beauty Parlor Operators. But in the last-named occupations Venus would also have to be strong. Of itself Aries is by no means ideal for these professions.

TAURUS — ♉

Keynote: Doggedness.

Vocations: Those occupations of Venus having to do with money, as Cashiers, Bank Tellers, Capitalists, Pursers, Money Lenders; also Throat Specialists (if regular medical significators strong). Taurus makes a good Boxer, Soldier or Policeman because of his fighting qualities and his unwillingness to concede defeat. He is excellent as Treasurer of a business or other organization. In these cases Taurus might be the rising sign or Sun Sign, with some other sign or planet more directly concerned with the occupation.

GEMINI — ♊

Keynote: Versatility.

Vocations: Any ruled by Mercury not requiring too much detail and especially those having to do with transportation. Gemini cannot stomach drudgery to the same extent as Mercury's other sign, Virgo. Thus normally Virgo makes better office help than Gemini but the latter is the better salesman. Gemini is more curious about *things* and Virgo about *people*. Gemini is inherently much the better speaker and superficially the better writer, but Virgo will be the more thorough in both cases. Virgo's facts are more likely to be right than those of Gemini.

Many of Mercury's occupations are common to both Gemini and Virgo. *Eliminate* from the former: Teachers, Bee Keepers, Dietitians, File Clerks, Retail Grocers, Governesses, Nerve Specialists, Storekeepers, Doctors, Healers. These are peculiar to Virgo, the normal sixth house sign, governing small animals, health and healing, food, and the more humdrum side of Mercury's activities.

CANCER — ♋

Keynote: Domesticity.
Vocations: Those of the Moon insofar as they have to do with the Cancer keynote. Thus Nursing would obviously be a Cancer occupation, but a Traveling Salesman, Fisherman or Tavern Owner would hardly come under that designation.

Of itself Cancer is greatly concerned with real estate and home ownership, though for best results Saturn should also be strong. Home appliances, house-furnishings and the like are within its guardianship.

LEO — ♌

Keynote: Greatness.
Vocations: Same as the Sun with no exceptions. This may be due to the immense importance of the Sun in the horoscope as in the Solar System. It apparently dominates its only sign, leaving nothing independent for the sign to govern.

VIRGO — ♍

Keynote: Detail.
Vocations: Everything ruled by Mercury, not exclusive to Gemini, *q.v.* Has especial relationship to service, healing, pets and all mental work involving much detail.

LIBRA — ♎

Keynote: Balance.
Vocations: All those of Venus not having to do specifically with fi-

nance. Vocations it has to do with independently of Venus are Judges (ruled by Jupiter but coming also under Libra because of the "balanced judgment" of the sign), Diplomats (for same reason), Lawyers—especially Trial Lawyers, owing to Libra's rulership of opposition. Paradoxical as it may seem, Venus being the planet of peace, its sign Libra actually rules war, it being the normal sign of the seventh house which governs public enemies. In this respect Libra is probably the most inconsistent of the twelve signs.

SCORPIO — ♏

Keynote: Strength.

Vocations: All occupations ruled by Mars and Pluto except things made by fire, the peculiar property of the fiery sign Aries. Is strong in occupations requiring great patience—where Aries is weak. Very specially concerned with all occupations having to do with death or things of the dead.

SAGITTARIUS — ♐

Keynote: Publicity.

Vocations: Occupations of Jupiter concerned with publicity. *Eliminate* these as peculiar to Jupiter or to Jupiter's second sign, Pisces: Woolen Merchants, Wholesale Grocers, Aldermen, Appraisers, Bond Salesmen, Cashiers, Capitalists, Pursers, Financiers, Whale Hunters, Chiropodists, Shoe Manufacturers and Dealers, Shoe Workers.

CAPRICORN — ♑

Keynote: Hard Work.

Vocations: Occupations of Saturn except Priests, Monks, Nuns, Plumbers, which come under sign rulership of Pisces. To Saturn's list of occupations may be added those for which Capricorn gives peculiar ability. Capricorn is the occupational sign itself. It is the sign of business as such and the distinctive mark of the business man. Capricorn excels in those executive positions requiring patience as Virgo excels similarly in subordinate posts calling for the same quality.

AQUARIUS — ≈

Keynote: The Up-To-Date.
Vocations: As Uranus. No exceptions. Also positions which require a friendly personality and skill in meeting the public. Aquarius rules friends.

PISCES —)(

Keynote: Solitude
Vocations: All vocations of Neptune without exception, and those of Jupiter having to do with the feet. Also occupations of solitude as Monks, Nuns, Prison Guards, Wardens; and those connected with large institutions such as Hospitals, Sanitariums, Museums, Libraries, etc. Clubs, Organizations, Secret Societies come under Pisces' rulership, and any occupation connected with these is indicated by Pisces as a vocational sign. If Venus is strong Pisces often is concerned with musical talent in some direction.

It should always be remembered that the foregoing list, as also the list in Chapter III, is not in itself sufficient as an occupational guide but is only one of the several factors to be taken into account. Without analyzing all of these the occupational adviser will inevitably come to grief. Over-simplification of the problem will lead to nothing but disappointment, but if one has the patience to consider all factors and painstakingly weigh their respective claims one against the other, conclusions of great and lasting value may be drawn which, if followed, should guide the native to the one best vocation for which he is fitted.

CHAPTER V

PLANETS IN THE TENTH HOUSE

Astrological instructors are familiar with the student who, on learning to set up his horoscope, makes the agonizing discovery that some of his houses contain no planets. He quickly leaps to the conclusion that those departments of life must be blanks for him—that if the second house is empty he will have no money, if the sixth no employment, if the seventh no marriage partner and so on. By this logic, if the fourth and tenth are void of planets he should also have no father and mother, and if the eighth he should never die.

Fortunately Nature does not operate in that way. It is quite true that houses containing planets likely to bulk more largely in the life than houses containing none. The horoscope is such a complex affair, however, that this can by no means be laid down as a general rule. The planet governing the sign on the cusp of an empty house may be so strongly placed by sign, house and elevation and have so many close aspects or positions to other planets, that it projects the house into a position of more importance than some of the full ones.

Therefore, while we first consider planets in the tenth house as the major significators of occupation (as often they are), the student should by no means conclude that if no planets are there this is detrimental to the occupational possibilities.

Thus George Bernard Shaw, who certainly has an occupation, and one in which he has made a very great success, has no planets at all in his tenth house, (29° Capricorn on cusp) though three (Sun from 4° Leo, Mars from 27.5° Libra and Uranus from 24.5° Taurus) aspect the Midheaven. Lord Kitchener, one of England's famous Commanders-in-Chief, who pursued with high distinction the occupation of soldier all his life, has nothing in the tenth (8° Capricorn on cusp). Nor are there any planets in aspect to the Midheaven. But Mars, the military planet, is in exact trine to the Ascendant (from 22° 47′ Leo to 22° Aries). Mars is also close trine Moon, which is in 25° 43′ Sagittarius. It is likewise trine Saturn in 19° 41′ Aries. It is in light trine Uranus in 29° 38′ Aries. Pluto is in 29° 30′ Aries and in similar trine to Mars. And Aries, of course, is the sign ruled by Mars. One does not need to have planets in the tenth house to indicate a successful military career, when this kind of Martian set-up exists. And so with any other occupation. Absence of tenth house planets is in no way significant, but their presence calls for first examination where the occupation is concerned.

It also seems to be true that in the natal charts of very outstanding people, the tenth house is likely to be occupied by at least one planet. Thus Adolph Hitler has Saturn there alone. Yet his success (up to this writing [1942]) is certainly not due to Saturn, which has a square, 4° out of orb, to both Mars and Venus, the former being reinforced by a parallel. Saturn's only good aspect is a very light sextile (7° out) to Uranus. Hitler, however, is the most successful (financially) writer in the world. His book, *Mein Kampf*, required reading for every Nazi, has sold millions of copies. The astrological answer is so easy, the most elementary student can perceive it at once. In the third house (writings) in Capricorn (intercepted), the tenth house sign, are the Moon and Jupiter. The Moon has six favorable and no unfavorable aspects and parallels, Jupiter has three favorable, no unfavorable aspects and parallels, and Jupiter rules publications and rules Sagittarius, the sign of publications, which is on the cusp of the third. Mercury, which rules writings, governs the ninth house (publishing), which has Gemini (sign of writings) on the cusp. Cancer is intercepted in the ninth, and the Moon which rules Cancer is in the third. The North Node, very beneficent, is in the ninth, and while the South Node is therefore necessarily in the third, the former governs the sale of the work which is successful beyond the dreams of avarice, while the latter merely indicates that there is something odd or peculiar about the nature of Hitler's written work. Which probably most unbiased or unintimidated people would certainly not deny.

Above is one of the most perfect examples possible of a man who followed the directions of his natal chart in every particular, so far as writing and publishing were concerned, and who reaped a harvest so bountiful as to be almost beyond belief. It is common knowledge that Hitler has long believed in and scrupulously followed the science of astrology.

Other famous personages with occupied tenth houses are Franklin D. Roosevelt, who has Mars and the Moon there, both unafflicted; Mussolini, with Uranus in close sextile Venus and exact trine Neptune; Lloyd George, Moon (in eleventh but within 3° orb of tenth) sextile Jupiter exact, sextile Sun (2° out) trine Mars (7° out) and with the South Node in tenth.

It may be of interest to note here that nations have horoscopes and famous nations reflect their horoscopes (or *vice-versa* if one prefers). In the natal chart of England (Coronation of William the Conqueror, High Noon A.D. 1066), the Sun is right on Midheaven in 9° 48′ Capricorn. It has five good aspects or positions—no bad ones. Mercury in 16° 20′ Capricorn is in tenth, with four good aspects or positions. Venus in the eleventh also has a tenth house influence, being less than 2° away, and has an almost exact sextile the Moon—no adverse aspects. The Midheaven itself has four good aspects, no bad ones.

Therefore while absence of planets in the tenth is in no way adverse to the occupational possibilities, their presence does make for distinction and, if the planets in question have more good than bad and are not adversely placed by sign (in detriment or fall) they are a desirable factor.

Consider then the planet in the tenth house. If more than one, take that one nearest the Midheaven. A planet in the ninth house within 5° of the tenth exercises a more powerful influence than one actually in the tenth but more than 5° away from the cusp. If two planets both hold the same degree in the tenth, give preference to the one better placed by sign. A planet in exaltation, for instance, over one not so distinguished—or a planet neutral by sign rather than one in detriment. An example may be given from Hitler's chart, though in this case it does not concern the occupational house. Venus and Mars are both in 17° Taurus in the seventh house, his house of war.

But Venus is essentially dignified and Mars in detriment in Taurus. Both are square Saturn in the tenth. Venus is the planet of peace, Mars of war. Peace had her dangers for Hitler but these, because of the fine sign-placement of Venus, were comparatively small. War is infinitely more dangerous to him because of Mars' evil sign position.

Planets in the same degree should therefore be analyzed with reference to their potentialities for good or evil. In the event of a tie the vote should go to a benefic as against a malefic because of its inherent power for good, apart from the things it signifies. It is impossible to anticipate every condition in a horoscope but the foregoing hints should be comprehensive enough to enable the practitioner or student to reach a decision in any similar situation.

Having decided upon the dominant tenth house planet, observe its aspects. Take every aspect (and position), not forgetting the parallels which so many astrologers slight, but which are of great importance. Ignore minor aspects and regard only the trines, sextiles, oppositions, squares, conjunctions and parallels. If the planet as more bad aspects than good, eliminate and proceed to the next selection. If it has a slight preponderance of good over bad (say 4 to 3), list it as a possibility. If it is exalted or in dignity, this in itself is as good as one or two additional favorable aspects. If it is in detriment or fall, better rule it out unless the proportionate good over bad is very marked—say 6 to 3 or some similar percentage.

Assuming you find a tenth house planet good enough to be considered, your next step is to determine if it has any kind of a hook-up with the second house (money). This may consist of a good aspect to Venus (normal second house ruler), or to any planet in the second house or to the ruler of the sign on the second house cusp, also to any planet in Taurus, the money sign. If none of these aspects are present, better leave that planet out of consideration if you wish to make money out of your occupation. A good aspect of the planet from Jupiter or the Sun may be some kind of a substitute for a direct monetary connection, but for lucrative results it is much better to have the money planet, house or sign directly concerned. Rather take a second-string planet with such direct hook-up than your first choice, if only a Jupiter or Sun aspect. You can return to the latter if you must, should the other selections prove to be lacking.

Assuming you have found a satisfactory tenth house planet with second house connections, another consideration may enter. Are you contemplating obtaining employment or launching into business for yourself? In the former case you must consider also if there is any connection between the tenth and sixth (employment). If you can also find aspects from the sixth to the second (money), you are indeed fortunate, but while this is highly desirable it is not absolutely essential if a tenth-sixth aspect exists.

Sixth house factors may be any or all of the following: A good aspect from the planet in the tenth to a planet in the sixth or to Mercury or to the ruler of the sixth house cusp, or to any planet in the sign Virgo. (Mercury is normal ruler and Virgo normal sign of the sixth house.)

The reader may logically inquire if a sixth-second house aspect would not be equally good for employment, disregarding the occupational tenth. The answer is yes, if "just a job" is the requirement.

Unless the tenth is included in the setup, however, the employment is likely to remain only that, with no advancement or recognition and with little or no hope of it ever leading to the native acquiring a business or profession of his own.

We are now ready to examine the things governed by our first-choice planet as set forth in Chapter III, but before doing so let us note the planet with which our selection is in closest good aspect. If it is in the second, so much the better. It will narrow down our choice of the many things our chosen planet rules. If we can find an occupation ruled by both planets, that is ideal.

Examples will be given in the next chapter.

CHAPTER VI

IDEAL OCCUPATIONAL FACTORS

Let us take our top-ranking occupational planet and, to begin with, assume that the most ideal set of aspects exists to it, as in rare horoscopes may be the case. Once in a blue moon an astrologer comes across such a horoscope. Most of the time, even in the charts of the very successful, while the setup may be quite good, it is far from ideal.

Also ideal astrological layouts must be backed up by the energy of the native himself. Otherwise he will be one of those who, having every opportunity placed in his way, made a mess of things. Of course a weak horoscope in other directions would then be indicated. Many successful people have only Grade B vocational factors in the very occupations in which they have climbed to the top. In that case, however, the planetary placements, groupings by constitution and other vital indicators are such that the immense drive necessary to succeed in the face of difficulties, is astrologically present. Even then these individuals are usually in the best field the horoscope indicates for them.

Consider, for instance, the occupational factors of John D. Rockefeller, Sr. (shown in Chapter XIX), the business genius who started the immense oil industry of the United States. The ideal planet in the tenth house for him would have been Neptune which rules oil well operators, or at least Uranus which rules the new (and therefore, in those days, held co-rulership with Neptune over oil). The Moon, which governs liquids of any kind, is secondarily concerned. But none of these planets appears in the tenth house or the second. In the tenth are Mars (in his detriment, Libra) and Jupiter. In the second no planet appears but Sagittarius is the sign on the cusp and Jupiter (ruler of Sagittarius) is therefore planetary ruler of the second. Ruler of the money house in the vocational house is almost as good as being in aspect to a planet in the house, and remembering that the keynotes of Jupiter are *Abundance, Prosperity, Affluence, Wealth* (among other things) we see that we are at once on the track of the astrological reason for the Rockefeller millions.

While Jupiter rules prosperity, however, he has nothing to do directly with oil. Yet he has a close hookup with Neptune who does rule it—an almost exact trine, the best aspect in the horoscope. Neptune is in the third house (the mind), making Mr. Rockefeller "oil minded." It is in Aquarius, sign of Uranus, the other oil ruler—a very significant placement. We do therefore have our second house involvement in oil even though it is a trifle roundabout, due to the trine of the second house ruler to Neptune. We also note that Jupiter has a light trine to the Moon, which is in the partnership house (seventh). Rockefeller benefited through partners, but he was always the driving force behind them. Neptune is also trine the Moon, somewhat closer. Pluto, a very potent planet in making millionaires if other configurations favor, is also trine Neptune from the fifth house (speculation—which the sinking of oil wells certainly is).

For good measure the secondary planet is the tenth, Mars, which we decided to ignore, is trine Neptune too. It is also in almost exact sextile Saturn (business planet). Jupiter is sextile Saturn as well.

We may take note likewise of the Sun's sextile the Midheaven. The Sun rules influence from those of higher station and such influence was exercised early in Rockefeller's career to his great benefit.

Turning to the other side of the picture we found that afflictions of the direct occupational significators are few and insignificant. The worst is a square of the Moon to Uranus, exact within 2°. There is a very light opposition of Uranus to the Midheaven. Outside of these only Saturn square Venus offers any real obstacle. Rockefeller had difficulties in plenty to encounter. Not the least were the Government prosecutions of Standard Oil, involving his companies in litigation extending over many years. Taurus is on the cusp of his seventh house which therefore is ruled by Venus. This planet normally governs the seventh house in any case and therefore is undisputed ruler of this house of litigation in Rockefeller's chart. Saturn, governing everything of a long-drawn-out nature, clearly indicates the type of legal difficulties by which he would be harassed. Yet so overwhelming are the favorable aspects that the damage done to him either mentally, physically or financially was entirely negligible.

This horoscope has been used as an example because it belongs to the most successful industrialist of the last century, to a man long since retired and now dead, and whose career may therefore be viewed in proper perspective.

Certainly the four good aspects, no bad ones to Neptune and its close connection with the second and tenth houses, even though not quite direct, paint a perfect picture of a successful oil magnate. There are other supporting features we have not even touched upon such as Uranus in Neptune's sign, Pisces, while Neptune is in Uranus' sign, Aquarius; the benefic North Node conjunct Uranus (though the South Node is in the tenth, accounting for the severe criticism and attacks to which Rockefeller was subjected for his business methods; also indicating that those business methods were not altogether of sweetness and light).

Mr. Rockefeller, of course, had the tremendous drive of his Scorpio Ascendant coupled with the extreme tenacity of his Cancer Sun. It may be asserted that no one could have made those Neptunian aspects pay greater dividends than did he. With a weak Ascendant and Sun sign, the bad aspects might have left him a mere mediocrity. It took power to accomplish what he did, in spite of the favoring occupational factors—and he had what it took.

With this digression we may proceed to analyze our tenth house and second house planetary aspects. Assuming something that rarely occurs—the ideal—let us suppose that Jupiter in his own sign, Sagittarius (essentially dignified) is in the tenth, trine Venus essentially dignified in her own house, Taurus. An intercepted sign would be necessary for such an aspect but this is an occurrence of great frequency in these latitudes. Such a set of positions and aspects is so extraordinarily good (and rare) that, given a first-class supporting horoscope, the native would be likely to make a success of almost any business or profession he tackled. However we must get down to cases.

Referring to occupations governed by Jupiter (Chapter III), we find we have a choice of between 30 or 40. Venus gives us as many or more. Our question is, "Have these two planets any vocations in common?" If so we have narrowed our choice, at least in the first instance, to some business or profession, smiled on by both. We must bear in mind that Jupiter is in Sagittarius, not its other sign of Pisces and that therefore the Piscean occupations are not to be considered. See Chapter IV for these. Also that Venus is in Taurus, not Libra. Its money rulership therefore is paramount rather than its artistic side. What then does Jupiter govern, most akin to money? The list offers us the choice of several things; Appraisers, Bond Salesmen, Cashiers, Capitalists, Pursers, Financiers. The Venusian list gives us Cashiers, Tellers, Capitalists, Pursers, Money Lenders. Three of these appear in both lists: Cashiers, Capitalists, Pursers.

Now obviously unless a boy leaving school or college is a scion of a very wealthy family, he cannot exactly select "Capitalist" as an occupation. If he is the son of a J. P. Morgan partner that may be a possible career, but to less favored mortals, a more modest ambition, at least at the outset, is indicated. The interpretation must be made with common sense, but if Venus and Jupiter are unafflicted (no or very few bad aspects as compared with their good ones), and there are no strong afflictions to planets in Taurus (money sign) or in the second (money) house, the course is quite clear.

Put that youngster, boy or girl, into some occupation where he or she will have the handling of money and then let him find himself. He may start as a humble assistant in the cashier's cage and, if he measures up to the quite reasonable possibilities of his natal chart, wind up as Treasurer of the Company. Ultimately he may really turn out to be a financier, capitalist or investment banker. But start him off in something which will give play to his inborn money instinct. Nature will take its course if he cooperates.

It must be borne in mind that the primary objective is not merely to place the native in some calling which is ruled by a good planet in the tenth (if such there be). The number of vocations each planet governs is very large and may differ widely from each other. Consider for instance the difference in temperament required by a policeman and a barber. Yet both are ruled by Mars. Clergymen and whale hunters are seemingly two professions with nothing in common (if we may leave Jonah out of it). Jupiter, however, rules the life-work of both. What could be less poetic than a fish market? Neptune governs poets and also fish markets.

It is not one planet alone, no matter how excellent may be its sign position and aspects, which gives the clue to the native's vocational abilities, but the nature of the planet or planets with which it is in closest aspect—their sign positions, house positions and aspects. And for financial success, the second house, when connected with the first in some manner by aspect or position of planets in both or planets ruling both, is of first importance.

We considered above an example of tenth-second planets having so much in common that it was an easy task to decide on the calling which would provide the greatest opportunities for success. Other harmonious combinations with similar possibilities may now be listed.

Sun—Mars: Because the Sun rules Authority and Mars Executives, such a tenth-second combination points strongly to the training of the native for a governing position, rather than that of a subordinate. This would be particularly the case if cardinal signs were in the majority.

Mercury—Uranus: An ideal occupation would be a Radio Announcer which both planets jointly.

Venus—Saturn: The former rules Art—the latter Building. A tenth-second combination obviously points to architecture as an indicated profession.

Uranus—Neptune: Both planets have rulership over the Occult. An occupation touching any phase of this is immediately up for consideration where these two planets connect from tenth to second in good aspect.

These few examples will perhaps convey an idea of the principle involved in tenth-second house occupational selection. Which particular planet is in the tenth and which in the second may or may not be a matter of consequence. It depends upon the house for which the planet has the greatest affinity. Thus in the Venus—Saturn example given above, it would obviously be a better setup if Venus were in the second, Saturn in the tenth. Venus is normal ruler of the second due to its government of Taurus, the sign previously identified with the second house. Similarly, Saturn, ruler of Capricorn, regular tenth house sign, is well posited therein. Neither is antagonistic to the house of the other. Saturn has no special affinity nor repulsion to Taurus, nor has Venus to Capricorn. The connection would still be worth consideration if Saturn were in the second and Venus in the tenth, but it would not possess the outstanding possibilities of Venus in second, Saturn in tenth.

Astrological analysis is largely a matter of common sense. Nature has made her occupational signposts very clear and has laid down precise laws by which they may be deciphered. Given a planet in the tenth and one in the second in good aspect to each other, and both planets exercising rulership over the same occupation or profession, and a first choice clearly presents itself. Complications, such as more than one planet in either house, can be resolved by eliminating the weaker planets and concentrating on the strongest. If it be remembered that fall and detriment are weakest, exaltation and dignity strength, that planets in the houses of their signs or exaltations are strong, opposite them weak; if it be held in mind that the nearer a planet is to the cusp, the more dominance it exercises, and finally that a planet which is the ruler of the Ascendant or Sun Sign is stronger than one which has no such rulership, it should not be difficult to apply the foregoing rules.

Seldom, however, is the horoscope such that the ideal calling can be arrived at with such beautiful ease. Only one natal chart in a very great number is likely to have tenth-second significators so clean-cut that the hunt for occupational factors may stop right there. Often one or both houses are empty, or, when occupied, the planets concerned appear to have nothing whatever in common. What are we to do then?

CHAPTER VII

TENTH-SECOND PLANETS
HAVING NO COMMON RULERSHIPS

The law governing planets in good aspect to each other from the tenth to second houses and both ruling some similar vocation, is so clear it can hardly be misconstrued. Suppose, however, we find that the two planets concerned appear to have nothing in common, what is the next procedure? The difficulty is more in seeming than in reality, for as Nature, in the physical world, brings together the most unlikely elements and by combining them produces new substances having qualities possessed separately by neither, so do differing planets in the horoscope act upon each other similarly when in good aspect.

We saw, in the last chapter, how a Venus—Saturn configuration would behave to produce a talent for architecture. Saturn of itself is no artist. It is inherently very unbeautiful. It is the planet of privation and its forms are stunted and cramped. Yet Saturn takes immense pains. It is the hardest working of all the planets and by far the most patient. It "can wait and not be tired by waiting." "Its outlines," says Sepharial, "are hard and clear-cut." Certainly it possesses qualities of great value to the artist.

Venus has little or nothing in common with the labor of putting up a building. Venus is graceful, elegant, averse to soiled hands, coarse manners, loud talk, manual toil—all of which are much in evidence in the building trades. Yet buildings should be artistic as well as utilitarian. The "four walls and a door" of Saturn without any influence of Venus, may evolve into the divine beauty of the Taj Mahal, the Rheims Cathedral or the Capitol at Washington, when Venus adds its mellowing touch. It is significant that Saturn, great malefic as he is, is exalted in Libra, artistic sign of Venus, the lesser benefic. Yet Venus finds her exaltation in a sign of Neptune and Jupiter.

We should not therefore too confidently decide that any two planets are so remote from each other in nature that they have nothing in common or that their blending may not produce valuable talent for some occupation. At first sight Venus and Saturn appear to be as opposite as any two planets in the Solar System. Yet we have seen how they may work together for good. And the fact that Venus is exalted in Saturn's sign gives us a lead as to how we may first track down the significance of blended planets.

By taking a planet harmonious enough with another in essence to find exaltation in the other's sign, it is unlikely that we can deduce suitable occupations from the blend if we apply common sense methods. Let us see.

Sun is exalted in Aries, sign of Mars. We noted in the last chapter the affinity of these two planets for each other.

Moon is exalted in Taurus, money sign of Venus. A tenth-second hookup between the two would be better with Moon in the second rather than in the tenth. The latter house is normally ruled by Capricorn, in which sign Moon is in Detriment.

Venus is not evilly affected here, however, while Moon in the second house of its exaltation sign, is excellent.

Now Moon rules women and Venus young women and girls. The two planets, therefore, shed exactly the right combination of influences on any of the several occupations listed under Venus, which primarily concern women. Without covering them exhaustively, as the reader can readily do this for himself, a few typical callings may be cited: Toilet Accessory Makers, Cosmeticians, Beauty Parlor Operators, Women's Apparel Manufacturers and Dealers, Dressmakers, Milliners, Perfume Manufacturers.

Mercury is exalted in Aquarius, sign of Uranus. A combination of the two formed one of the examples in the last chapter. Any ultramodern method of transportation would be indicated by this blend as Aviation, the Automobile Industry, Radio (which transports sound through space), Telephone and Telegraph (which transport speech or information.

Venus is exalted in Pisces, sign of Neptune and Jupiter. Music, which is one of the fine arts ruled by Venus generally, is definitely under dominion of Neptune. Occupations connected with the Manufacture or Sale of Women's Shoes are under the combined rule of Venus and Jupiter.

Mars is exalted in Capricorn, sign of Saturn. Both planets are malefics but also rule certain callings. They are likely to be of the strenuous kind because of the sturdy nature of these two planets. We do not find any occupation mentioned in both lists but Saturn has obvious affinity for some of the industries listed under Mars and *vice-versa*. Thus Contractors, ruled by Saturn, have much to do with

Carpenters, a Mars craft, and a favorable configuration of the two by tenth-second house would be an excellent indication of success in that line.

Jupiter is exalted in Cancer, sign of Moon. There is no direct joint rulership of any occupation, but Jupiter in Cancer in the second trine Moon in tenth is one of the finest signs of general financial success to be found in a horoscope. Given a good supporting chart and the native would have to play his cards very badly indeed to make a financial or occupational failure of his life. Nature has started him out with a deck heavily stacked in his favor. Any occupation either of Jupiter or Moon may be followed with good assurance of success.

Saturn is exalted in Libra, sign of Venus. This blend was also used as an example in the last chapter. Saturn and Venus also make a powerful combination for the conservation of money. It usually is made the "hard" way (by working for it), but is tenaciously clung to after being amassed. This is a good aspect for the financial officer of a business or other organization.

Uranus is exalted in Virgo, sign of Pluto and Mars. Crematoriums would fall to the rulership of a connection between Uranus and Pluto or Uranus and Mars. As between the two latter any occupation connected with very modern machinery would be indicated. Pluto would be concerned with all recently perfected instruments of death: Tanks, Bombers, Munitions generally. Slaughter on a large scale would be his specialty, while Mars would be likely to rule the more retail methods of killing. All rulerships assigned to Pluto are more or less surmise, due to the relatively short time which has been available for observation of his effects.

It is remarkable, however, and a tribute to the exactness of astrology as a science, how closely astrologers, working independently of each other, agree as to the nature of this newly discovered planet.

Neptune, as yet, has been assigned no exaltation. Several have been suggested—Leo for one, on the ground that it is not the exaltation sign of any other planet. No planet is exalted in Virgo, Gemini, or Sagittarius, though the North and South Nodes are said to be exalted respectively in the two last named. Some astrologers consider Virgo as exaltation sign of Mercury. However, Mercury is essentially dignified in Virgo and it is difficult to see how a planet can be exalted and essentially dignified in the same sign. The author's opinion is decidedly that Mercury is exalted in Aquarius. He inclines to the belief that Neptune's exaltation sign is Cancer, even though Jupiter is also exalted there. Neptune in good aspect to the Moon makes a nice combination. The two have in common. Certainly a tenth-second hookup between the two would have excellent possibilities along occupational lines.

Note that one of the Keynotes of Moon is Liquids, and that Neptune governs occupations having to do with oil. An obvious choice of occupations would be suggested by the two in good aspect.

Pluto's exaltation is also at present a mystery and not even a guess can be hazarded.

As may be seen, it is not difficult to decide on occupations suitable to the nature of two planets in good aspect from tenth to second even though they rule nothing in common, providing they are harmonious to each other. When one of the planets is exalted in the other planet's sign, such harmony is to be inferred.

Suppose, however, that the reverse is the case and one planet is in its fall in the sign ruled by the other, what then?

We may eliminate Sun and Venus (Sun in fall in Venus sign Libra) as no tenth-second aspect could be made between them—Venus never gets that far away from the Sun.

For the same reason we need not consider Sun and Mercury (Mercury in fall in Sun sign Leo) or Mercury and Venus (Venus in fall in Mercury sign Virgo).

But Moon is often trine Mars from tenth to second or *vice-versa*. And Moon is in fall in Mars sign, Scorpio. Also Mars is exalted in Moon's detriment, Capricorn. There would seem, therefore, on the face of it to be considerable antipathy between these two. Yet Moon in good aspect to Mars from any point in the chart is known to improve the vitality and give courage, enterprise, an adventurous spirit and much capability.

In many respects these two significators are opposites. Thus Mars rules Fire, Moon Liquids; Mars governs Soldiers, Moon Sailors; Mars Executives, Moon Household Help; and similar opposed occupations.

In such a case (Mars trine Moon—tenth to second) we have to consider the attributes of one of the planets—the type of influence it radiates—rather than the occupations it governs, and select the occupations governed by the other planet with which its qualities seem best to blend.

It is obviously better to have Mars in tenth (the normal house of Capricorn) than in second (normal house of Taurus) and to have Moon in second than in tenth. While the houses cannot exactly be said to influence the planets to the same degree as the signs, yet a house, the normal sign of which is the exaltation or dignity of a planet, is certainly better for that planet than one whose normal sign represents its fall or detriment. However, we have to take the planets, signs and houses as they come, whatever planet happens to be in the tenth, whether well or ill placed, is ordinarily a stronger significator of the occupation than one in the second.

We should therefore consider as representative of the calling the tenth house planet, and, if no occupation common to both it and the planet in the second which it aspects favorably exists, then study the type of influence the second house planet radiates and see how this seems to affect the varioud occupations of the other planet.

Thus Mars (from tenth) trine Moon (in second) poses the question, What Martian occupations are most responsive to lunar vibrations? Examine the keynotes of Moon. These are: Change, Women, Liquids, Real Estate, The Public, The Secondary, The Temporal.

Almost every Martian vocation perhaps has a little something to do with one or other of the above, but there is nothing outstandingly akin in any of them. Thus a soldier might experience frequent changes of location, or he might not. There is no real hook-up. An Army Officer might be in a department of the Government having to do with the leasing or renting of ground for army maneuvers, barracks and the like, but this is not an occupation which can well be *selected*. It might quite easily fall to the lot of a military officer having Moon in second trine Mars in tenth but Moon's influence on Mars is not very discernible in military affairs. Policemen, who come in contact with the public to a much greater extent than soldiers, are far more responsive to this keynote of Moon than the latter.

Barbers, likewise are dependent on public contacts for success, but in their case Venus, which rules personal grooming, should be strong. In a soldier's horoscope this is not so necessary. It is true he must be smart and neat in appearance, but if Venus has not given him these qualities naturally, his top sergeant will do it for him.

No attempt is here made to apply all of Moon's keynotes to all Martian occupations. The above examples are intended only as a guide. Once the principle is grasped it can be readily adapted to whatever planetary, sign and house positions may exist.

It may be here stated that such grasping of principles and the ability to apply them is the true mark of the competent astrologer. The student or practitioner who relies on "catalogues" listing the meaning of aspects, sign and house positions etc., does not clearly understand the basic fundamentals of the science. He will be in a perpetual quandary because of "conflicts" between one aspect or position and another or several others. He is likely to find the horoscope apparently blowing hot and cold at the same time.

It is necessary that there be such lists, and exceptionally fine, painstaking work of this nature has been done by a variety of Astrological experts. Interpretation, however, is based on principles, not lists. The lists have merely grown out of the principles.

In the case of Moon (and also of Sun and of the ruler of the horoscope) it is not so necessary as with other planets to trace a definite type of influence harmonious to the other planet with which it is in aspect. Moon of itself is ruler of the personality and if it appears in second trine a planet in tenth it is a good indicator of success for any occupation of the other planet, even though none of its keynotes can readily be applied to such occupation. If one or more of them can be applied so much the better.

Uranus trine Venus is a very good example of two planets, one of which is in fall in the other's sign. The fall of Uranus is ruled by Taurus, ruled by Venus. It is better for Venus to be in the second and Uranus in tenth as second's normal sign is Taurus. We do find occupations which, while not ruled by both, fit in surprisingly well with both. Thus Venus rules Music, Uranus Radio. Venus rules Actors, Uranus Moving Pictures. But note these pertain to the Libra side of Venus, in which sign Uranus is not badly placed, rather than to Taurus, the money side. Very satisfactory occupational guidance is given by the Uranus-Venus combination including, in addition to the above, Photographers, Airplane Designers (Airplane plus Art), Spotlight Operators (Lighting Specialists plus Theater) and many others not specifically listed but which can be deduced from the inherent nature of the two planets concerned.

For ready reference the affinity or aversion of the planets for each other is indicated in the following table:

⊙ and ☽:   Neutral.

{ ⊙ and ♂:   Sun exalted in Mar's dignity, Aries.
  FRIENDLY

⊙ and ♃:   Neutral.

{ ⊙ and ♄:   Sun exalted in Saturn's fall, Aries.
  UNFRIENDLY   Saturn in detriment in Sun's dignity, Leo.

{ ⊙ and ♅:   Sun in detriment in Uranus' dignity, Aquarius.
  UNFRIENDLY   Uranus in detriment in Sun's dignity, Leo.

⊙ and ♆:   Neutral (Neptune's exaltation and fall unknown).

⊙ and ♇:   Neutral. (Pluto's exaltation and fall unknown).

The "Unfriendliness" of the planets so labeled to each other is not to be taken too literally. In good aspect such planets will work for wholly favorable ends. The descriptions are comparative only and to aid in determining, where several second-tenth aspects are present, which are the most favorable. As the above table shows, if other things are equal, the following should be the order of preference:

1. Sun-Mars: Friendly.
2. Sun-Moon; Sun-Jupiter; Sun-Neptune; Sun-Pluto: Neutral.
3. Sun-Saturn; Sun-Uranus: Unfriendly.

———————

☽ and ☿:   Neutral.

{ ☽ and ♀:   Moon in exaltation in Venus' dignity, Taurus.
  FRIENDLY

{ ☽ and ♂:   Moon in detriment in Mars' exaltation, Capricorn.
  UNFRIENDLY   Mars in detriment in Moon's dignity, Taurus.

{ ☽ and ♃:   Jupiter exalted in Moon's dignity, Cancer.
  FRIENDLY

{ ☽ and ♄:   Moon in detriment in Saturn's dignity, Capricorn.
  UNFRIENDLY   Saturn in detriment in Moon's dignity, Cancer.

{ ☽ and ♅:   Uranus exalted in Moon's fall, Scorpio.
  UNFRIENDLY   Moon exalted in Uranus' fall, Taurus.

☽ and ♆:   Neutral.

{ ☽ and ♇:   Moon in fall in Pluto's dignity, Scorpio.
  UNFRIENDLY   Pluto in fall in Moon's exaltation, Taurus.

Order of preference:

1. Moon-Venus; Moon-Jupiter: Friendly.
2. Moon-Mercury; Moon-Neptune: Neutral.
3. Moon-Mars; Moon-Saturn; Moon-Uranus; Moon-Pluto: Unfriendly.

☿ and ♂:   Neutral.

{ ☿ and ♃:   Mercury in dignity in Jupiter's detriment, Virgo.
UNFRIENDLY   Jupiter in dignity in Mercury's detriment, Sagittarius

{ ☿ and ♄:   Mercury exalted in Saturn's dignity, Aquarius.
FRIENDLY

{ ☿ and ♅:   Mercury exalted in Uranus' dignity, Aquarius.
FRIENDLY

{ ☿ and ♆:   Mercury in detriment in Neptune's dignity, Pisces.
UNFRIENDLY   Neptune in detriment in Mercury's dignity, Virgo.

☿ and ♇:   Neutral.

Order of preference:

1. Mercury-Saturn; Mercury-Uranus: Friendly.
2. Mercury-Mars; Mercury-Pluto: Neutral.
3. Mercury-Jupiter; Mercury-Neptune: Unfriendly.

{ ♀ and ♂:   Venus in dignity in Mars' detriment, Taurus.
UNFRIENDLY   Venus in detriment in Mars' dignity, Aries.

{ ♀ and ♃:   Venus exalted in Jupiter's dignity, Pisces.
FRIENDLY

{ ♀ and ♄:   Saturn exalted in Venus' dignity, Libra.
FRIENDLY

{ ♀ and ♅:   Venus in detriment in Uranus' exaltation, Scorpio.
UNFRIENDLY   Uranus in fall in Venus' dignity, Taurus.

{ ♀ and ♆:   Venus exalted in Neptune's dignity, Pisces.
FRIENDLY

{ ♀ and ♇:   Venus in dignity in Pluto's detriment, Taurus.
UNFRIENDLY   Venus in detriment in Pluto's dignity, Scorpio.

Order of preference:

1. Venus-Jupiter; Venus-Saturn; Venus-Neptune: Friendly.
2. Venus-Mars; Venus-Uranus; Venus-Pluto: Unfriendly.

{ ♂ and ♃:   Mars in fall in Jupiter's exaltation, Cancer.
UNFRIENDLY   Jupiter in fall in Mars' exaltation, Capricorn.

{ ♂ and ♄:   Mars exalted in Saturn's dignity, Capricorn.
NEUTRAL   Saturn in fall in Mars' dignity, Aries.

(These two malefics are the only pair of planets both Friendly and Unfriendly to each other. May be considered as Neutral on account of this offset.)

{♂ and ♅:   Mars in dignity in Uranus' exaltation, Scorpio
FRIENDLY

♂ and ♆:   Neutral.

{♂ and ♇:   Mars in dignity in Pluto's dignity, Scorpio.
FRIENDLY

Order of Preference:

1. Mars-Uranus; Mars-Pluto: Friendly.
2. Mars-Saturn; Mars-Neptune: Neutral.
3. Mars-Jupiter: Unfriendly.

{♃ and ♄:   Jupiter exalted in Saturn's detriment, Cancer.
UNFRIENDLY   Saturn in dignity in Jupiter's fall, Capricorn.

♃ and ♅:   Neutral.

{♃ and ♆:   Jupiter in dignity in Neptune's dignity, Pisces.
FRIENDLY

♃ and ♇:   Neutral

Order of preference:

1. Jupiter-Neptune: Friendly.
2. Jupiter-Uranus; Jupiter-Pluto: Neutral.
3. Jupiter-Saturn: Unfriendly.

{♄ and ♅:   Saturn in dignity in Uranus' dignity, Aquarius
FRIENDLY

♄ and ♆:   Neutral.

♄ and ♇:   Neutral.

Order of preference:

1. Saturn-Uranus: Friendly.
2. Saturn-Neptune; Saturn-Pluto: Neutral.

♅ and ♆:   Neutral.

{♅ and ♇:   Uranus exalted in Pluto's dignity, Scorpio.
FRIENDLY

Order of preference:

1. Uranus-Pluto: Friendly.
2. Uranus-Neptune: Neutral.

Neptune and Pluto: Neutral.
Order of Preference: None

For instant use a summary of the foregoing is given below:
Symbols: F=Friendly; U=Unfriendly; N= Neutral; O=Omitted (as making no major aspects).

	☉	☽	☿	♀	♂	♃	♄	♅	♆	♇
☉		N	O	O	F	N	U	U	N	N
☽	N		N	F	U	F	U	U	N	U
☿	O	N		O	N	U	F	F	U	N
♀	O	F	O		U	F	F	U	F	U
♂	F	U	N	U		U	N	F	N	F
♃	N	F	U	F	U		U	N	F	N
♄	U	U	F	F	N	U		F	N	N
♅	U	U	F	U	F	N	F		N	F
♆	N	N	U	F	N	F	N	N		N
♇	N	U	N	U	F	N	N	F	N	

CHAPTER VIII

THE "BEST" PLANET

Occasionally it happens that all occupational factors are so inferior that the astrologer is almost ready to throw up his hands in despair of finding any planet, sign or house which offers reasonable hope of vocational success. Wherever he turns it is the same story. If planets are in the tenth, second or sixth they are so badly afflicted, so weakly placed by sign, they rather indicate failure than success.

A similar state of affairs prevails in relation to the business (Capricorn), money (Taurus), and employment (Virgo) signs. If planets are found therein they appear to be worthless. The planetary rulers of these departments, Saturn, Venus, and Mercury respectively, likewise offer not the least encouragement.

In other words it seems that entry into the business or professional world is barred by a planetary and sidereal chorus chanting "He shall not pass."

This assumes, of course, a well-nigh impossible state of affairs. Almost always some one planet, sign or house at least, which has more good aspects than bad, more strength than weakness, is present. Our task then is comparatively easy. We merely follow that particular indicator to the exclusion of others and select what seems to be the most logical calling or callings, based on its placement by house or sign or by its best aspects with other planets.

We are here considering, however, an extreme case. All indicators even remotely concerned with occupation have to be rejected. What are we to do then? Must we advise the unfortunate native that there is nothing left for him to do but go on relief? Must we tell him, "There is no place for you in industry, the professions or the arts. You are just an occupational misfit?"

Any astrologer who so misused his knowledge certainly should be read out of his honorable calling. There are no "impossible" situations in the horoscope. There is always a way out if one will painstakingly seek for it and not jump to the conclusion that none exists.

The way out in the case of the "hopeless" occupational chart we are theoretically analyzing is *to select the best planet, even though it has not a single occupational connection.* It may be in a house and sign apparently far removed from the three main departments which normally govern this field (tenth-second-sixth). No matter—take it anyway. Then look for some indirect connection and almost always one will be found. Thus the "best" planet may be in the seventh house or the sign Libra. Good enough! Then partnership is indicated as the way out of the *impasse*. If in the first, the native's own efforts will have to supply the missing astrological factors—as indeed they will, no matter where the planet is. Particularly, however, is this indicated by a first house position.

In the third the mind will play the greatest part. The native will have to plan and scheme to overcome the undoubted difficulties before him. The fourth brings the home into some kind of relationship with the occupation, if a planet in the fourth or ruling the fourth is to be the guiding occupational star. Perhaps the work or profession, whatever it is, can best be carried on at home or possibly it has to do with house-to-house work of some kind. The fifth, of course, is likely to bring children into the picture—doubtless a line selling or catering to children or where children play a part. Teaching children might be the solution, but not unless the horoscope has abundance of planets or angles in fixed signs, bestowing the required patience.

The eighth gives a clue to the fact that a silent partner investing money with the native may give him his great chance (eighth rules the partner's money). In the ninth the "best" planet would seem to recommend going abroad or at least a long distance from the birthplace for success. The advertising and publishing fields are likewise a possibility. The eleventh points to friends as the avenue from which help in the upward climb may come, while the twelfth inevitably suggests institutional aid of some nature.

Of necessity these suggestions are very sketchy. A 20-volume work would hardly suffice to list the infinite number of possibilities which the millions of possible horoscopic combinations hold in the occupational line as elsewhere. The native must use his knowledge of the inherent nature of the planets, signs and houses as given in this work or which he has learned elsewhere, to arrive by a process of analysis and elimination at the most suitable avenue to success. No set of examples can possibly be exhaustive.

It need not be disguised that in the case of a lone planet, selected because it is "the best of a bad lot," the fight for a competence is likely to be hard and prolonged. Success for the native will be no "pushover." But by following his star and supplying the missing elements out of his own strenuous endeavors, he may in the hilly journey develop a character far stronger and more worthwhile than a native with the "ideal" occupational set-up.

We still have to deal with the rare case of a horoscope which has no planets free from affliction or with a preponderance of good aspects over bad. Or with the even rarer instance of a chart where every planet has only adverse configurations—no favoring ones anywhere. The latter case is next to impossible. In such event it is doubtful if the native would have survived infancy. Theoretically, however, there is a bare possibility of such occurrence, and as this work aims at astrologically recognizing every type of vocational problem which could confront anyone, it takes cognizance of even the remotest problem which might present itself. Nothing is more annoying than to consult a book purporting to offer comprehensive advice in a specialized field only to find that your particular diffi-culty seems to have completely escaped the attention of the author, as he entirely ignores it.

The answer to the question, "What shall I do if I have no unaf-flicted planet?" is "Take the least afflicted." If several seem to tie for that distinction, then take the one best placed by sign. A planet in exaltation is obviously stronger for good than a planet in detriment or fall or even neutrally placed. In this writer's opinion (not shared by all astrologers) exaltation is slightly better than essential dignity, and fall slightly worse than detriment. If no planets are dignified or exalted, then give preference to one neutrally placed as against oth-ers in detriment or fall. If such distinctions do not exist then consider the house. While a planet in the normal house of the sign in which it is exalted or dignified is by no means as strong as if in the sign itself, it is still a little stronger than if in a neutral house. Thus Sun is well placed in the first or fifth (Aries and Leo houses) and not so well placed in the seventh or eleventh (Libra and Aquarius houses). Mercury is nicely posited in the third, sixth or eleventh (Gemini, Virgo, Aquarius) and adversely so in the ninth, twelfth or fifth. Mer-cury's disability in the twelfth is more pronounced than elsewhere, probably because of the opposition to the employment and health house.

Yet always there must be some planet a little less badly af-flicted than the rest, even in the worst of nativities. And that planet is in a sign and a house and these themselves furnish the clue to the occupation which offers the greatest possibilities for success. Here is a note of hopefulness for the native who "never had a chance" because of his terrifically afflicted horoscope. Nature gives everyone a chance if she allows them to enter the world at all. There is always a way out. It is the tragedy of our educational system that it devotes endless attention to preparing youth for the battle of life and ignores the one sure guide furnished by the natal chart.

Some succeed in finding their ideal calling (sometimes after years of misfit labor) without knowing that astrology could have placed them in their proper niche at the very outset. Others drop into the grave after unhappy lives spent in occupations Nature never intended for them. A few, with exceptional horoscopes, are attracted to their right sphere with little effort on their own part. An infinitesimal percentage, by sheer willpower, make good in the "wrong" vocation and never know the difference. But how much more they might have accomplished, successful as they are, had they followed the natural occupational lines their natal charts indicated.

CHAPTER IX

EMPLOYER OR EMPLOYEE?

Some natives can only be happy and fulfill their manifest destiny if they are at the head of their own enterprise. Others almost shudder with horror at the bare idea. The responsibility appalls them. Here again it is a matter of the horoscope.

To determine leadership qualities is almost elementary. A preponderance or otherwise of planets or angles in cardinal signs shows at a glance if this is present or subordinate. Planets in cardinal signs indicate a leadership which goes deeper than that shown by cardinal signs on the angles. The latter is more showy but less effective. If fixed sign planets and angles are below average, the need of a partner is indicated to supply the deficiency. The partner should be strong in this direction. However, if the partnership house is bad, the native might work the situation out through the agency of a competent manager long on fixed signs.

Without cardinal signs a native may still be successful in his own business or profession if fixed signs are powerful. He will do best in that case by delegating the figurehead leadership to someone else, preferably someone strong in the cardinal region, while he remains the power behind the throne. This role is frequently assumed by Scorpio and Leo—less often by Aquarius and Taurus.

Thus Mussolini, who has permitted Victor Emanuel to remain titular head of the Italian Kingdom and is said even to show the latter every mark of deference and respect, actually rules Italy, with the King a mere figurehead. Mussolini has Sun in Leo with Scorpio rising. Moon is in a common sign, Gemini.

On the other hand nobody rules in Germany except Hitler (as this is written). The fuehrer of the Third Reich has a cardinal sign, Libra, rising; Moon is also cardinal in Capricorn, while Sun is fixed in Taurus. Hitler has the horoscope of a born leader—4 planets, 2 angles cardinal; 4 planets, 2 angles fixed; only 2 planets common. It is no endorsement of his character or policies to point this out.

Mussolini, strange as it may seem, does not have the horoscope of a leader. He has only two planets and no angles in cardinal signs and neither of these planets are his rulers. His fixed signs are above the average, with 3 planets (including his ruler Sun, and Mercury the mind planet), also 2 angles, one of them his Ascendant. Common signs, however, are over-emphasized with 5 planets and 2 angles. The abject failure, at least up to the middle of January, 1941 when this is written, of his campaigns against both Britain and Greece which he is said to have planned himself, bear out the horoscopic evidence of lack of true leadership. Against poor weak Ethiopia he could prevail by sheer numbers and superior equipment. Confronted by the determined Greeks and British with as good and better than anything he could produce, his deficiency in resource was quickly betrayed. There have been few military failures in modern history so pronounced as that of the boastful Il Duce, whose title has turned out to be a pitiful misnomer.*

Common sign natives are not barred from the professions or from small "one-man" enterprises. They are obviously unsuited, however, for handling masses of employees. The common sign nativity often makes a most likable person who gets along well with everyone. Such an individual, however, does not possess the "drive" necessary to get the work out of his help. He is unfitted to assume great responsibilities, unequal to making important decisions, and lacks organizing ability. He may be excellent in carrying out details delegated to him by others, but if he in turn must redelegate some of the work to third parties and make himself responsible for their faithful performance, he is likely to be found wanting.

The common sign native is not likely to grieve himself about this state of affairs. Because common signs are preponderant in his chart he has little desire to "boss people about." His ambitions, while they may include wealth and position, do not embrace any desire for the domination of others.

As there are 14 constitutional factors in the natal chart (10 planets, 4 angles) and 3 divisions by constitution (cardinal, fixed, common), the average for each constitution must be 4.67 factors. Thus 4 would be somewhat below and 5 slightly above the average. This is a somewhat misleading method of gauging the relative strength of a constitution, however. There are several other considerations to be taken into account. Thus if only 4 factors were present in a given constitution, if one of these was Sun, the importance of this luminary is such that he may be reckoned as the equivalent of at least two other planets. The Ascendant is the most important of angles and

---

* Since this was written, Mussolini appears to have fallen under the domination of Hitler.

may likewise be accounted as equal to two planets. Moon is worth, by rule-of-thumb, perhaps one and one-half—in a female horoscope almost as much as Sun. The ruler of the Ascendant or Sun-sign, or any planet exactly on or nearly on the Ascendant should equal in value almost two others. Mercury, which rules the mind, is worth more than ordinary planets.

We thus see that Mussolini's fixed constitution with Sun (which is also his principal ruler) there and his Ascendant there, besides Mercury, is much stronger than the mere slight numerical preponderance would convey. Yet his two subordinate rulers, Mars and Pluto, are both in common signs, while the cardinal quadruplicity contains only the obscure Jupiter and Venus. Yet Jupiter is exalted in Cancer which gives it rather more than average significance but still leaves the leadership signs wholly undistinguished.

The fact that Mussolini, a very great world figure, has an inferior leadership horoscope yet holds in the hollow of his hand the destinies of millions of people, many of them with much superior leadership horoscopes to his own, should not be misunderstood.

The natal horoscope is always a relative thing.

Certain substitutes for a preponderance of cardinal signs may supply leadership qualities to some extent, providing planets or angles in the cardinal group are not wholly lacking. Thus many planets in angular houses ("Accidentally Dignified," is the terminology for planets so placed) will give a certain love of the limelight which will tend to thrust the native forward. Of themselves, however, accidentally dignified planets are by no means the equivalent in leadership of cardinal signs. They do, however, bring opportunities for the assumption of responsibility into the life, and with two or three reasonably strong planets cardinal, the native may still enjoy a certain prominence in his circle. Accidentally dignified planets minus cardinal signs may bring the opportunities but the native is little likely to avail himself of them.

A strong planet on the Ascendant (Sun, Uranus, Saturn or Mars) may be taken as of about equal strength to one in a cardinal sign—perhaps rather stronger. But it should be within 5° of orb of the rising degree. It is just as strong in the twelfth as in the first, providing it is within 5° of the Ascendant. President Franklin D. Roosevelt has Uranus in the first house within about 3° of the Ascendant. He is short on cardinal signs, having only 1 planet (the Moon) posited therein. He is tremendously long on fixed signs, no fewer than 7 planets being in this constitution. No one can deny that Mr. Roosevelt is a man of iron will, yet his leadership is rather unobtrusive and he is said to listen intently to advice before making up his mind. This example is cited without its being intended either to commend or condemn Mr. Roosevelt's politics. Your overwhelmingly cardinal leader seldom consults anyone but relies wholly on his own judgment. If the horoscope is otherwise good he may rise to great heights by this self-complacency. If on the afflicted side, however, it will certainly bring him to grief.

Never hesitate to follow the indications of the cardinal-fixed-common groupings in determining whether to play a lone hand, to strive for achievement within the framework of some large organization or to embark on the struggle for topflight recognition as a leader and director of others. A letter receive recently by the author from a lady in California whose son (personally unknown to him) he advised by all means to get into business for himself rather than remain in the employ of others, well illustrates the good that can be done by this method. It reads:

"I especially want to thank you for something. Some time ago you advised us, through my son's horoscope, he would be more successful as owner of his own business than as an employee. At the time could not see our way clear, but worked on it. A year ago succeed, and he finds himself so much happier that my heart is filled with gratitude to you. Thanks a million. Long life to you and much success."

NOTE: The references to Hitler, Mussolini, and Franklin Roosevelt have been left in as, although these three personages have long since vanished from the scene, their careers and personalities are so well known that they still serve as appropriate examples.

CHAPTER X

PARTNERS

While it is a traditional rule in astrology that natives of opposite signs are well adapted to each other matrimonially, this is by no means the case with a business or professional partnership. Those with opposite signs rising or Sun in opposing signs are not unlikely to be mutually antipathetic. However the harmony or otherwise of the two horoscopes concerned is the deciding factor.

Partnership should not be undertaken unless a preponderance of seventh house factors in the natal horoscope are good. There should be a clear preponderance, not merely a surplusage of one or two factors on the favorable side. Count the favorable and unfavorable aspects, the exaltations, dignities, detriments and falls, counting the two former favorable and the two latter unfavorable. This is as good a rule of thumb as any, and rule of thumb will suffice here because only one question is to be decided: Is partnership desirable or undesirable? Rules 21, 22, 23 and 24 in Chapter II should be followed to ascertain the factors involved.

If the answer is negative the native should dismiss the idea of partnership. But as this may be more easily said than done, due to conditions not within his control, suggestions will be given for mitigating a bad partnership horoscope by at least taking advantage of as many astrological offsets as possible.

The most important is the finding of a partner with a horoscope harmonious to the native's own. Uncanny as it may seem, this is far more likely to be found by a native with a good partnership horoscope than with a poor one. Some mysterious principle of attraction seems to draw the right co-worker to the possessor of a first class set of seventh house factors, and the wrong one to a native with a poor partnership rating. Under very favorable directions (progressions, etc.) the latter may, however, discover a partner as nearly suited to his own personality as the best factors in his horoscope permit. In any case partnership should be entered into under directions which favor it.

It is true there is an old astrological adage to the effect that one cannot get more out of the horoscopic bag than there is in it. In other words that the possibilities are always conditioned by the natal chart, no matter how good the current directions may be. Under wholly good directions, however, the best of the natal aspects of a similar nature are galvanized into activity, while those of a contrary type are held in abeyance. It is therefore possible to "defeat" an adverse seventh house, if it is not too bad, under good influences by direction, providing there is some leverage natally on the good side for the directional influences to take hold of.

It is assumed that the reader knows how to direct (or progress, as it is sometimes rather inaccurately termed) a horoscope. It must be insisted, however, that to take one type of direction and ignore all the rest as is sometimes done, is worse than useless as an entirely wrong picture may be drawn. In his own work the author takes the following current influences, lists them all under Favorable and Unfavorable heads and then casts a balance sheet:

1. Progressed Sun.
2. Progressed Moon.
3. Progressed Midheaven.
4. Progressed Ascendant.
5. Sun by 7-year cycle. (Sun moving from its natal place at the rate of one sign every 7 years or 4-2/7° per year. Figure from birthdate.)
6. Solar Eclipse. (Taking all aspects made by the Eclipse to positions in the natal chart within an orb of 5°. Conjunctions are usually bad unless both Sun and Moon are in natal good aspect to the conjoined planets.) A Solar Eclipse, in the author's opinion, has influence until the next Solar Eclipse and is strongest about half-way.
7. Transits of the major planets, Pluto, Neptune, Uranus, Saturn and Jupiter.
8. Transits by parallel of the major planets. (Orb of only 1° each way).

Except where otherwise noted an orb of 1-1/5° either way should be allowed. All directions are to natal positions only.

There are other types of direction but the above are most important.

In considering the net effect on the question of partnership of the prevailing aspects especial attention should be paid to:

(a) Aspects to natal planets in the seventh house. If to more than one, that planet nearest the cusp is the most important.

(b) Aspects to the planet ruling the sign on the cusp or of the seventh.

(c) Aspects to Venus, normal seventh house ruler.

(d) Aspects to planet ruling any sign intercepted in seventh.

Preference over all of the above should be given to any progressed or transiting planet or eclipse actually falling in the seventh house itself, especially if within 5° of the cusp. Such planet, if in conjunction with a natal seventh house planet, would be of extraordinary significance.

In estimating the power of the current directions take those involving seventh house factors as listed above, into principal account. Those not directly concerned should not be wholly ignored, but are cooperative only. If a majority of all partnership factors are favorable at a given time, even though numerically more bad directions than good are prevailing, partnership might still be undertaken. It is better, of course, in any enterprise, to select a time when there is a heavy general preponderance of good directions over bad. Lengthy periods sometimes elapse, however, when this does not occur. Often it is not possible to avoid certain kinds of specialized activity because the current influences are unfavorable to it. In that case there is always a minor cycle within the major cycle, even on a given day, when the "local" or temporary aspects are such as to mitigate the adverse nature of the prevailing major influences. Such periods are determined by *transits* of Sun, Moon, Asc. and MC. (Mars, Venus and Mercury may also be considered but are minor in effect and if the first four mentioned are favorable may be ignored.)

The technique of mitigation of unfavorable major directions seems to have been used with telling effect by Hitler in calculating the best periods for initiation of his various political and warlike moves. There is, of course, a limit to the possibility of a native neutralizing a bad natal or progressed horoscope by this means, but a long series of at least secondary successes may be obtained by taking advantage of the fleeting few moments which are constantly presenting themselves as "ideal" for the start of some given undertaking. The baffling ability of the Nazi fuehrer to outmaneuver his opponents in the early stages of the way is (astrologically) to be laid to his skillful manipulation of the daily aspects to his own horoscope. Yet when thwarted by the stubborn British who, unconscious of the astrological verities involved, of course, refused to let him take the initiative at the time and place he desired, his ever menacing background of major bad aspects asserted itself and he found himself held in check. At this writing the ultimate outcome is in doubt. It would not be, in the opinion of this writer, if the British knew and used astrology as their formidable opponent knows and uses it.

In comparing the horoscopes of the two prospective partners, certain harmonies (or the reverse) are of supreme importance. Everything else is subordinate, though where these major factors are not present, the matter has to be decided by such other comparisons as exist.

The "Number One" indications of a successful business association are:

(1) Sun in one natal chart in place of Moon in the other.

(2) Jupiter in one conjunct Sun, Moon, Asc. or MC, in the other.

(3) Jupiter in one conjunct any planet in seventh or ruling seventh in the other.

(4) Venus in one conjunct the points listed in (2) and (3).

In horoscope comparisons, aspects from a planet in one chart to a planet or point in the other are not nearly so important as the conjunctions.

Conjunctions and aspects should be exact within 1° either way. Regular natal orbs of planets do not apply in comparison horoscopes.

Principal inharmonious comparisons are;

(a) Saturn or Mars in one chart on any important point in the other, as Sun, Moon, Ascendant, Midheaven, ruler, or ruler of seventh.

(b) Saturn or Mars on any planet in seventh or tenth.

If only minor comparisons, good or bad, can be made, indications of any striking success is not great. There may be reasonable harmony but this is obviously not the prime motive behind a business partnership. Only in a natal chart brilliantly favorable to partnership, should a joint venture be undertaken with one whose comparisons are indifferent.

Many promising business projects come to grief because the wrong people (astrologically speaking) are associated in them. The simple method of comparing horoscopes which can be exhaustively done in an hour or two, may save years of incompatibility or downright antagonism between two people Nature never intended should enter into a business partnership with each other. The technique is not beyond the capability of even a beginner, providing he knows how to set up a chart accurately and observes care in making his comparisons. It is very much worth while, where partnership is contemplated.

The actual moment at which a partnership is entered into is the completion of the signing of papers. If the partnership is informal, without any written agreement, then the exact moment one or the other of the partners opens the door of the new establishment for business. If the business is already a going concern, then the moment the new partner enters the premises to take up his duties. Intent is everything in astrology as in law. Whenever the intent to consummate the partnership is definitely indicated by both parties, that is the moment the relationship has been entered into.

CHAPTER XI

THE RIGHT TIME TO START

The Wisdom that "mightily and sweetly ordereth all things" seems insistent upon the observance of its natural laws regarding time. We ignore them at our peril. The ancient scriptural writer enunciated this great truth in succinct language (Ecclesiastes III: 1-8):

"To every thing there is a season, and a time to every purpose under the heaven: A time to be born, and a time to die; a time to plant and a time to pluck up that which is planted; a time to kill and a time to heal; a time to break down and a time to build up ... a time to get and a time to lose; a time to keep and a time to cast away."

He might have added: "A time to go into business and a time to refrain from going into business; a time to look for a position and a time not to look."

In the last chapter (Partners) the technique of judging by the current directions the advisability or otherwise of selecting a partner at any particular period was given. The same technique differently applied governs the most desirable time to go into business, to hang up one's shingle in a profession or to apply for a position.

The most promising directions for the latter are the following:

(1) Good aspects to any planet in the sixth house.

(2) Same to the ruler of the sixth.

(3) Same to Mercury, normal ruler of the sixth.

(4) Same to planets in the second, to ruler of the second or to Venus, normal ruler of the second.

(5) General good aspects, which are cooperative only, especially those affecting the ruler or rulers of the type of occupation selected.

For the start of a business or profession:

(1) Good aspects to any planet in the tenth house.

(2) Good aspects to the Midheaven.

(3) Good aspects to the ruler of Midheaven.

(4) Same to Saturn, normal tenth house ruler.

(5) Same to planets in the second, to ruler of the second or to Venus, normal ruler of the second.

(6) General good aspects, especially to the planets ruling occupation selected.

Note: Progressions of the MC are particularly potent.

As with partnership, so intent governs the actual start of a business enterprise. Any symbolical act, as the opening of the doors of a store for business, marks the start of the project. But the act must not be far-fetched, merely to take advantage of a favorable time. The influences fasten themselves on an actual not a hypothetical birth, whether of an infant child or an infant business. The moment the child starts to lead a life independent of its mother is the moment of birth. Usually, but not always, this is the instant of the severing of the umbilical cord. The author knows of a case where the child was born with the cord wrapped around its throat, apparently strangled. It took half-an-hour to start breathing. The natal horoscope for the moment of delivery bore no relation to the appearance or disposition of the native—was in fact an astrological impossibility as applied to him. A horoscope set for the exact moment breathing started represented this native perfectly. The case is known to be authentic, details being furnished by the child's father, a prominent physician, who was present and assisted in starting the breathing.

Similarly, the moment the business or professional venture is launched is its birthtime, and the aspects then prevailing, as applied to the chart of the native concerned, marks the influences which govern. A secondary horoscope—that of the business or profession itself—may be set up in the same way as a regular birth horoscope of an individual. A good deal of information regarding the ups and downs of the venture as such may be gleaned in this way, but the important thing to consider is the relationship of the native's directions, prevailing at that exact moment, to his own natal horoscope.

By way of guidance in determining the birth moment of a new enterprise a few suggestions may be given. Reference was made above to symbolical acts. Thus the driving of a golden spike into the final connecting rail used to mark the completion of a railroad. The last hammer tap by the celebrity officiating at the ceremony would signal the birth of that particular line. Any final words spoken in the dedicating of the building would be of similar import with preference given to the actual statement, "I dedicate this building to . . ."

A young lawyer or doctor taking his seat at his desk for the first time, with intent to start practicing, would mark the commencement of his career, rather than the mere opening of his doors.

Alan Leo considers that the sale of the first number of a new periodical is the birth moment of the publication, and because of the eminence of this authority his view is entitled to respect.

In opening a store, however, where business hours are fixed, there seems no doubt that the exact start of the first business day would mark the birth moment. Thus if the store opened at 9 a.m., the fact that the first customer did not appear until 9:15 would be irrelevant; 9 a.m. would be the birthtime.

The exact moment of the filing of incorporation papers as recorded by the State, marks the official birth of a Corporation as such. This is of great importance in selecting investments. The subject is foreign to the purpose of the present work but it may be said in passing that the astrological harmonies or disharmonies exist, not only between the horoscopes of individuals but between the horoscopes of corporate entities and individuals. If the malefic Saturn appears in the Corporation chart in the same degree as, for instance, Sun, Moon or Venus in the investor's natal horoscope, in the absence of powerful offsets from Jupiter or other planets it is unlikely that the latter will realize much profit from his investment. This, however, is a different branch of astrology and cannot be dealt with here.

If a prospective employee can somehow obtain at least the birthdate of his employer-to-be, and compare planetary positions in his own and the employer's chart, as closely as may be without the birthtime, this has considerable value. The technique of comparison is as outlined in Chapter X (Partners), with certain modifications. Partners are presumably business equals but as between employer and employee a different relationship exists. Thus Sun in former's chart in opposition or square to Venus in the latter's would have a tendency to overawe the employee and prevent him from obtaining full recompense for his work (Sun = authority; Venus = money). Sun conjunct, or parallel, Venus would be favorable but employer's Mars over employee's ruler would denote oppression and irritability from the former.

The most valuable horoscope for comparison is that of the immediate superior with whom the employee will mostly come in contact. This will give day-to-day relationships, always very important for peace of mind and early advancement. The natal chart of the owner of the business or of the Corporation is, however, the long range factor for success or failure, astrologically speaking.

Needless to say, no cross aspects however favorable will take the place of hard and intelligent work, loyalty, and the right kind of ambition. The native must do his part, but his work may be rendered much easier and his path to promotion greatly smoothed if the comparative horoscopes are harmonious.

Should they be adverse he can still win his way through, but at the price of expending considerable unnecessary energy which could be better employed in other ways.

CHAPTER XII

THE TIME TO APPLY FOR A POSITION

It can hardly have escaped the notice of an ordinarily observant person that business interviews sometimes proceed with amazing smoothness, each party thereto saying and doing just the right thing to help matters along to a satisfactory conclusion. At other times the interview may go very well for one of the parties, not so well for the others. Still again it may go badly for all and break up with nothing accomplished.

Astrologers claim that the underlying reasons for these outcomes are the planetary and sidereal influences prevailing *at the beginning* of the interview. The influences referred to are those prevailing in relation to the natal horoscope of the individual initiating the interview. Current transits of Sun, Moon and planets to each other, so beloved of the daily newspaper horoscopes, are a factor so minor they need hardly be taken into account at all. It is quite true that if the daily aspects are mainly harmonious they will contribute a modicum of help to the native's own harmonious aspects. But the former may be quite adverse—even definitely antagonistic to the enterprise in hand—and if they are in favorable positions to key points in the native's own chart, he can still register entirely satisfactory results from his efforts.

It is easily demonstrable, for instance, that on a day declared to be "excellent to apply for a position," thousands will apply for positions and be turned down. It is a great deal more trouble to apply current transits to each individual's own horoscope than to write a general prescription applicable to all the earth's millions. But it represents the difference between the automatic action (if any) of a cheap patent medicine and the painstaking diagnosis and treatment of an outstanding medical specialist.

The informed astrologer never ceases to cry out against the "boiler-plate horoscope," that astrological monstrosity which seemingly has learned only of the months and knows nothing of years, days, hours or minutes. Anybody born when Sun is in Aries or Taurus or whatnot has the same appearance, character and fate. Similarly the transits prevailing each day affect the whole of creation alike. These horoscopic cure-alls have brought real astrology, most painstaking of sciences, into understandable disrepute among those who from ignorance regard them as representative of the ancient Science of the Stars. But no one is more bitterly contemptuous of this degradation of one of the grandest arts known to man, than is the competent practitioner of astrology. The difference is that between the AstrologER (the correct term) and "AstroloGIST" (popular word having no dictionary sanction). The latter term may well be used to include the astrological charlatans, the extent of whose knowledge appears to end with the ability to recite the verse beginning "Thirty days hath September."

The native looking for a position should therefore pay no attention whatever to newspaper or magazine advice assuring him that "this is a good day to secure a job." To know if it is really a good day and exactly what period of a "good day" is best, he must compare the transiting Sun and Moon with his own natal positions and then having arrived at a satisfactory hour, narrow it down to an exact minute by transiting Midheaven and Ascendant positions.

Reference should be made to Chapters X and XI where the method for determining the current major influences is given. These always constitute the main "atmosphere" prevailing, and nothing can be done about them if they are adverse except to wait until they have disappeared. This may involve a delay of months, or even years, so that in most of the affairs of life it is quite impracticable to defer action until they are wholly or largely good. They set the bounds, so to say, of the possibilities open to the native at a given time of success or failure, but they do not ordain either success or failure. Within this major framework all kinds of constructive effort may take place. It is only the *scale* of the success which is determined by the major directions. Success may be very great when these are mainly favorable. But small, relative successes are possible even when the progressions are largely adverse. As noted in a previous chapter, this appears to be Hitler's method. He tries to catch the "Grade A" major periods whenever they are available. But if events force him to move under "Grade B" or "Grade C" major influences he takes care to select only "Grade A" minor influences for the inception of his warlike projects. And this he (or anyone else) can readily do because, while the major movements of planets and angels extend over years and months, the minor movements of some of them cover only weeks, days, hours and even minutes.

For huge advances we need the aid of the most important favorable directions to key points in our natal charts. Blessed is he who can start a business, apply for a job or ask for a raise in salary, when the progressed Moon trines his natal Sun. And particularly if Sun is in good aspect to Moon in his birth horoscope. But that particular progression comes only once in 14 years and lasts about 3 months. A sextile (not quite so good but still helpful) of progressed Moon to Sun occurs at varying intervals twice in 28 years. Obviously one can hardly plan one's future in detail based on aspects so very infrequent.

Yet it is not impossible to plan at long range to take full advantage of any unusual aggregation of good progressions falling over a given period. These may be figured out a lifetime in advance if desired and the native may build his future on a sound astrological basis by directing his efforts so that they may, so far as possible, culminate during one of the highly favorable periods. This is not quite so difficult as may appear. The aspects themselves will automatically mould existing circumstances so that they tend to bring their greatest good into the life at the zenith of the favoring period. Yet by working with them, with eyes open to the manner in which their influences are operating, incomparably greater results are procurable. The old adage, "Nature unaided fails," though not entirely applicable to the progressed horoscope, is true in a measure. The tide, "taken at its flood" may wash us in to shore, but we shall get there far more speedily and efficiently if we do a little rowing on our own hook.

Letting the major directional framework, therefore, come "as is," seeing that we cannot do otherwise without perhaps waiting an indefinite length of time, we should select a day to apply for our new job when Moon transits sextile or trine.

(a) A planet in the sixth house of the natal horoscope, providing such planet is not in bad aspect to Moon natally (if good, so much the better), and providing it has more good aspects than bad. Also providing that it is not afflicted with more bad aspects than it has good by progression.

(b) If no planet possesses these qualifications then take planet which rules sign on cusp of sixth house, subject to same qualifications and conditions.

(c) If this too is not available, take Mercury, normal ruler of sixth house and therefore of employment. Same conditions applicable.

(d) If Mercury has to be passed up for like reasons, take any good planet in Virgo. Same conditions.

(e) If none of previous four suggestions can be carried out try a planet in tenth house or ruling tenth house, or take Midheaven itself. Observe same conditions on all these alternatives.

(f) If there is still failure to find the ideal planet, the second house occupants may be similarly experimented with, second house ruler or Venus.

(g) Sun, Moon or ruler of Ascendant are about the last chances. It is most unlikely, however, that the native will not find some planet possessing the needed requirements and without drawbacks, before he has gone this far down on the list.

Having selected the planet, ascertain within which hours the transiting Moon makes a sextile or trine aspect to it. Allow an orb of 1-1/2° each way. The aspect is stronger when separating than when forming. As Moon moves from a little less than 12° to a little more than 15° per day such aspect will last from 5 to 6 hours in all cases, even when Moon is moving at its fastest.

Make sure that Sun is not making an adverse transit to the planet selected or this is likely to frustrate the good effect of Moon. Also be sure that while it transits sextile or trine your good planet, Moon does not make a square or opposition to some other planet in your natal chart or a conjunct to a malefic (Pluto, Neptune, Uranus, Saturn) or to the South Node. However if Moon is natally in good aspect to any of the four malefics, its conjunct by transit will not hurt, but watch out for the conjunct South Node and for all squares and oppositions.

Having steered clear of all these, we next narrow down the time to within a minute or two by taking the transiting Midheaven and Ascendant. This is done by the same method as in setting up a natal horoscope. From the ephemeris note down the Sidereal Time for noon of the selected day. From the Table of Houses for the place in which the native is living (*not* the birthplace, if this is somewhere else), choose a Sidereal Time which falls within the favorable transiting period of Moon to the planet you have decided upon. Give preference to the latter rather than the earlier half of the period. Remember that the Sidereal Time at noon bears the same relation to the Sidereal Times listed in the table of houses as 12 noon bears to any time on the clock.

Thus on June 22nd, 1941 the Sidereal Time at Noon is 6-1-6. If the native resides in New York we add the customary 50 seconds for the 5 hours difference between New York and Greenwich (England) time. Whatever the difference this must be added (or subtracted in Eastern longitudes). Be careful of the astrologer's latest pitfall, Daylight Saving Time. Make the necessary 1 hour correction or your calculations will be worthless. Then if you desire to know what the Sidereal Time will be at 3 P.M., June 22nd, 1941, merely add 3 hours plus 50 seconds, plus 30 seconds (the 10 seconds per hour sidereal correction for the 3 hours elapsed since noon) and you have 3 hours, 1 minute, 20 seconds to add to the Sidereal Time at noon. Thus:

$$6 - 1 - 6$$
$$50$$
$$3 - 0 - 0$$
$$\underline{30}$$
$$9 - 2 - 26$$

Now refer to your Table of Houses for New York and take the closest Sidereal Time you can find to 9-2-26. This proves to be 9-1-53, at which moment the Midheaven is in 13° Leo and the Ascendant in 5° Scorpio 53. There will be a slight correction for the 33″ difference, but to all intents and purpose we may say 6° Scorpio are rising and 13° Leo on the Midheaven. This might or might not be what we wanted. Let us take a concrete instance.

Supposing the planet we had selected was Jupiter in 8° Aquarius, and we had picked on June 22nd because on the afternoon of that date Moon would transit in trine that degree. As a matter of fact June 22nd, 1941 falls on Sunday, so unless we could see our future employer at his home or, by some special dispensation, get a Sunday interview at his office, we would have to pass up that day in favor of some other. This is of no consequence, however, as we are only using the day to illustrate the method.

We find that Sun in about 1° Cancer makes no adverse transit to anything natal and in fact is sextile Mercury in 0° Taurus. So far so good. If we could get a good Midheaven or Ascendant aspect to Jupiter, our selected planet, that would be ideal. However the range the Moon transit trine Jupiter allows us is only from about 6.5° Gemini to 9.5° Gemini, which journey is covered from about 10 a.m. to 4 p.m. As Sidereal Time at noon is 6-1-6, Sidereal Time at 10 A.M. would be approximately 4-0-0 (allowing for small time corrections) at 10 A.M. and 10-0-0 at 4 P.M. At 4-24-55 Sidereal Time, Midheaven is in 8° Gemini and Ascendant in 11° Virgo 10. This would give us a clock time of 10:25 A.M. and is the only good Midheaven aspect available during the chosen period. If Ascendant in 11° Virgo 10 is in no bad aspect to anything natal, this time immediately becomes a possibility, assuming that we can arrange for an interview then. If Ascendant does cast a bad aspect we have to abandon the Midheaven and see if we can get a good aspect of the Ascendant. Between 4-0-0 and 10-0-0 Sidereal Time, Ascendant moves from about 6° Virgo 12 to 17° Scorpio 15. Obviously the only trine it could cast to Jupiter in 8° Aquarius is from 8° Libra which it reaches at about 6-42-0 Sidereal Time. This is approximately 12:42 P.M. Sun Time. (Don't forget to correct to Clock Time and to allow for Daylight Saving Time, if in effect). Midheaven at that moment is in 10° Cancer. If we find Midheaven casts no bad aspect to any natal point we then have our second possibility.

If a bad aspect is cast in either case we have to do our work again, selecting a second choice planet for our Midheaven or Ascendant aspect—perhaps a third or a fourth choice. If we cannot get either of these angles to throw a favoring ray to the planet to which Moon has its good aspect (and it is not often possible) then we take as good a substitute as the horoscope affords. If we can arrange so that Midheaven throws a trine or sextile to one planet and Ascendant to another, that is fine, and with our good Moon transit we may feel we have done as well as possible and proceed to arrange for our interview with the confidence that only one versed in the astrological laws can know, when he has taken full precautions to select the most auspicious time.

CHAPTER XIII

THE INTERVIEW

Objections invariably present themselves to students of vocational astrology who hear for the first time of the importance of beginning an interview regarding a position at a given minute. "How in the world can that be done?" is their unspoken inquiry. How can one be certain that the prospective employer will make an appointment for the time indicated as being best for the applicant? If he can be induced to make it for that time, how can there be any assurance that he will not be tied up with something else and keep the applicant waiting until the auspicious moment has passed? Also what constitutes the beginning of an interview—the exact time the applicant appears at the employer's place of business—when he is admitted to the presence of the employer—or when the conversation begins?

Attention will be given to all these points and it may be said at the outset that in practice these difficulties turn out to be far less than in theory. The author of this book (who is also in a prosaic wholesale business having nothing to do with astrology) has found it perfectly possible to arrange affairs so that important business interviews were started at exactly the moment he desired. Occasionally, but not very often, circumstances frustrated this but if the matter to be discussed was of sufficient importance an excuse for deferring its consideration could usually be presented and a later time set, already figured out for just such a contingency. As a matter of fact all should not be staked on one time—the native should have several satisfactory periods already chosen. It is not more difficult to alter a suggested appointment for astrological reasons than it is to change it for ordinary physical ones. The other person need not be given the real reason or any reason for that matter. The time suggested is simply not convenient and the native counters with a suggestion of his own—or another and another, if need be.

It is true we cannot well "play horse" with a prospective employer, who usually reserves the right to set the time for the interview and will make short work of the applicant if the latter starts boggling about it. However, such difficulties are not insurmountable. If the application is made by letter (which also should be started and mailed under "right" aspects), a time or several times may be diplomatically suggested. If the employer chooses one of these the native should be on hand well ahead of time. Some employers seem to feel it absolutely necessary to keep an applicant sitting on a bench in an ante-room for half-an-hour or so before they will deign to see him.

But assuming this hurdle has been surmounted and the applicant is sitting across from the great man's desk ready to be interviewed, how can one insure that at exactly the right minute and second, the interview will begin?

Well, fortunately Nature is not quite so exacting as that. It does not have to be at exactly a given minute or second. The Midheaven and Ascendant remain approximately on the same degree for about 4 minutes. And there is an "orb" of about a degree and a half either way, that gives a further latitude of approximately 12 minutes more (6 minutes each way from the exact moment). Thus a total "possible" period of 16 minutes is available and with a little *finesse* on the applicant's part he should be able to direct the conversation into the proper channel within this time range. He should however try to delay it until *after* the culminating minute rather than to have it commence before. As previously stated, separating aspects are stronger than those just forming which is fortunate, as it is usually easier to delay a business conversation than to start it prematurely. There are always other things to talk about, even to a prospective employer, than the immediate business in hand and—here is the point to bear in mind—the interview begins at the exact moment the native (not the employer) either broaches the subject which has brought him there or answers the interviewer's first question. However, the native should take the initiative in order to come fully under the sway of the astrological influences he has selected. It is *his* planetary party, so to speak, and he loses something of the full effect of the aspects if the other person starts the ball rolling.

Merely to announce his name does not mark the "birth" of the interview, unless at the same time he states his business. But if he says, "I am John Smith. You wrote me to come in about a position," the die is cast and the interview has begun at whatever time he uttered the last nine words of the sentence. If he glances at his watch as he enters the "presence," and finds he needs to stall for a few minutes before the desired time arrives, this should not be too difficult. A remark about the weather, the size of the building or almost any

casual thing which occurs to him may hold the fort for the oppor-
tune moment. It is, of course, rather more difficult to create chit-chat
when one is applying for a job than if the meeting concerns some
other business matter, but with a little intelligent handling of the
situation it is by no means impossible.

The question may arise, will the prospective employer resent
this loquacity on the part of one applying for a job? That, of course,
depends upon how it is done. If the native doubts his own ability in
this direction he might try getting the employer to do the talking.
There is a danger here, however; the latter may talk past the fateful
moment or he may switch to the subject in hand too soon. With the
16 minute leeway there should not be much hazard here. The native's worst peril is that the phone may ring and the employer be
tied up in a lengthy conversation.

But it must not be forgotten that within this entire 16 minute
period, the native's current aspects are good—exceptionally good,
in fact, otherwise he would not have selected that particular time.
Unlucky "breaks" such as the above are therefore really not due to
happen and probably will not happen. At least that has been the
author's experience, and he has used these "selected times" in his
own business and advised others regarding their use, for years. If
the temporary aspects are good and the major framework not too
bad, things move along like a charm. Everything goes as hoped. The
other person says just the right thing—you say just the right thing.
When you leave you have no regrets—no looking back to think,
"Why did I say that? Why didn't I say this? What a bad slip I made
there! Why did I pass up that marvelous opening he gave me?" and
so on.

An excellent example of how almost unbelievably perfect results may be obtained in face of the most unpromising circumstances may here be given, as it is in the author's own experience of
only a few months ago. It does not concern an interview for a position but something even more vital—the shutting off of supplies
needed to carry on a business, because of shortages caused by defense priorities. With dwindling stocks available the writer decided
to make a 600 mile trip and plead his case with the source of supply
in the hope of being tided through the emergency. As several hundred other buyers all had the same idea at about the same time and
there was nothing like enough to go around, the situation was
pretty desperate. It was made more so when the concern in ques-

tion, upon learning of the proposed visit, first sent a special delivery letter, then a telegram and finally made a long distance call urging the writer not to come. The tenor of all the communications was the same: "You are wasting your time. We can do nothing for you."

The writer, who has his fair share of fixed signs besides an abiding faith in the efficacy of a properly selected astrological time, ignored the warnings and went anyway. But first he carefully chose a time when the transiting Moon was trine Sun, trine natal Moon and conjunct Mars. All three of these aspects were good because natal Moon is trine Mars natally. It is also trine Sun in the natal chart. A better transit could hardly be imagined for the purpose desired. Sun rules those in position to grant favors. Mars governs controversies and antagonism. Moon is part ruler of the particular product on which the shortage exists.

Narrowing down the time by Midheaven and Ascendant aspects it was possible to obtain at 8:57 Clock Time on the morning of February 19th, 1941 a sextile to the natal Ascendant from the Midheaven and a trine to natal Saturn, the business planet, from the Ascendant. This set up is almost incredibly good, more particularly as the time, about 9 A.M., is the logical one for such an interview.

At 8:57 A.M. on the dot, the writer walked into the office of the official on whom the fate of his business depended and plunged into conversation regarding the shortage. Several hours later he left, having gained everything he requested without a solitary exception. His business associates were surprised beyond measure, but the writer, having from lengthy experience the utmost faith in astrology, was not surprised.

Obviously one's case has to be good or no amount of good aspects will suffice. It is useless to rely on even the best influences to obtain a position for which one is not qualified. But given proper qualifications, the ability to present them in convincing form, and a position available in which they can be used, the clinching factor in this writer's firm belief is the right astrological influence under which to make the bid for the job.

CHAPTER XIV

FROM THE EMPLOYER'S SIDE

Every Personnel Director should possess some knowledge of vocational astrology. It would help him immeasurably in placing the right people in the right jobs. Records of previous employment, references, high school and college credits, are all good rule-of-thumb guides but they lack the precision of an astrological analysis of character, talent and ability. It will no doubt seem ridiculous to say it and may provoke scornful laughter, but there should be an astrological division in every Personnel Department. It should be directed by the most competent astrologer procurable, whose own chart should conclusively demonstrate that he has the qualifications for so exacting a position. In a large institution he should be assisted by a suitable staff.

This will be done one day, of course. Certain moving picture producers are known to have their astrological advisers. Hitler is reported on very good authority to have a board of five, besides being a very able astrologer himself. We shall get around to it in course of time as we have got around to so many other reforms in business which once were sneered at as the dreams of idealists and visionaries.

Most employers require an applicant to state his birthdate. Even without the time certain facts of value can be gleaned from the sign positions and aspects of the planets. But with a little knowledge of astrology a very good guess at the rising sign may be made from the personal appearance, mannerisms and interests of the native. Scientific rectification, of course, requires correction also by important events of the life, but even without these a clue can often be obtained which, in light of later information, proves very close to accuracy in the rising sign determined upon.

As each rising sign contains six modifying "faces" (sets of 5° each), slightly differing from each other, a further narrowing down is possible. In the absence of exact information the native may be judged as to rising sign by observing him closely, providing one has a fair working knowledge of the general appearance conferred by each sign.

It must be emphasized that the popular notion that the birth

month marks the sign the native is born under, and that his appearance conforms to the Sun sign, is the rankest of astrological heresy.
Only if the birth took place around sunrise (when Sun sign and Ascendant are the same) is this generally true. A native might be born
with Sun in Taurus and Libra rising and look no more like a Taurean
than does Hitler, who has that particular combination, which does
not mean that many Taurus characteristics are not present, but they
form the deeper, rather than the more observable layers of the character.

As a matter of fact, Hitler's face is somewhat more Taurean
than would ordinarily be the case with a native who had Sun in Taurus and Libra rising, for the reason that in his chart Venus (ruler of
both Libra and Taurus) also appears in Taurus where it is very
strong. Besides this, another planet, Mars, is there. None of these aspects the Ascendant in any way and the Ascendant is the prime factor in personal appearance. An aspecting planet, particularly from
Sun sign, will modify it in some degree and if from Sun sign will
give the latter a prominence it might not otherwise possess. A Sun
sign containing three or more planets, however, is always likely to
show out a little in the personal appearance even though none of
them aspects Ascendant, but it will not usually upset the characteristic expression of the ascending sign.

Thus President Roosevelt has Virgo rising. Sun, Mercury and
Venus are in Aquarius, making no Ascendant aspect. Uranus, ruler
of Aquarius is almost exactly on the rising degree, bringing out all
the characteristics of the powerful Aquarius and almost, but not
quite, swamping out the negative Virgo.

Yet the birdlike look which astrologers associate with Virgo is
still there, and Mr. Roosevelt's handsome, domed Aquarian head,
nevertheless contrives to retain a certain birdlike expression peculiar to Virgo. His quick, emphatic movements and his habit of toss-
ing his head in punctuation of his sentences are all very reminiscent
of the Mercurial Virgo.

In the main, however, it is reasonably safe to sum up the salient
sign characteristics of a native by studying him, and mentally classify him as dominated largely by one or other of the 12 great zodiacal signs. This is, of course, assuming that it is not possible to have a
proper horoscope cast, which is always the only true scientific
method to employ.

With a view to helping personnel directors and employers as

well as others to whom such knowledge would be valuable, to size up astrologically those applying to them for positions or with whom they have business dealings in other ways, a brief description is here given of certain striking characteristics each sign confers. The author has, in his own business, hired and trained hundreds of traveling salesmen and sales executives by applying the rules herein given—and has rejected thousands ore. Only a brief summary can be given, but the emphasized points have been found to be very peculiar to the particular zodiacal type in each case. Some of the points, so far as is known, are not included in "orthodox" astrological classifications but are based on the writer's own long continued observation.

Aries – ♈

The nose in this type is nearly always long and rather pointed, with a sort of hump in the middle, sloping down into a valley and then rising slightly again at the end. Eyes unusually piercing. Native quite likely to appear to be staring you out of countenance without any intention of doing so. Adam's apple (in the male) prominent. Manner rather abrupt and impatient. Talk advancement to this type—possibility of his having subordinates of his own to order about (Aries loves this). Will usually respond better to this than to talk of money. Very ambitious and wants to be at the head of something. Fine when he can put over his projects with a rush. Not so good (in absence of fixed signs) when persistence called for.

Taurus – ♉

Look for long lobe of ear, usually present. Hands and feet rather undersized for build. Thick neck. "Bulldog" look. Firm chin. Advancement talk not nearly so appealing to him as talk about money. Has excellent money sense and can usually make it, if not for himself then for others. Not so good as Aries at originating ideas but better at carrying them out. Bulldog tenacity. Equable temperament when not crossed but a fierce and implacable opponent when aroused.

Gemini – ♊

Almost always tall, thin, rangy. Large hands and feet. Fine, expressive eyes. Often underweight. The "flyer" type. Clever at repartee—a born "wisecracker." Will try to wisecrack his way out of embarrassing situations and quite at a loss if unable to do so, as he often can. Curious about things rather than people. Dexterous with his hands; good mentality but divided energies. Tries to do too much at one time but in his own Gemini field is unexcelled. Not overstrong on system and method but very good improviser.

Cancer – ♋

Broad shoulders, tapering lower limbs. Eyes sometimes appear sleepy but Cancer is quite wide awake. Very sensitive and home-loving. Great respect for tradition and desires to be a "somebody" in the community. Likes to talk about *his* children, *his* home, *his* automobile, *his* hobbies. Bitingly sarcastic when annoyed. Dislikes "scenes." Desires what he thinks is proper respect paid him by those he doesn't know well. A worker until he achieves what he wants, then sometimes becomes insufferably lazy. Tenacious and apparently very sure of himself, but not always able to "take it" if misfortune comes. Reliable worker.

Leo – ♌

Large nose with spreading nostrils very typical. Lion-like head with mane of hair (baldness often comes in middle life as with all the fiery signs). Pleasant, open face. Frank manner. Conversation often interlarded with immense amount of unnecessary detail. Very trustworthy. Seldom dishonest. Lover of children and a social "lion." Dignified manner, condescending to subordinates; the ruling rather than the leading type.

Virgo – ♍

Usually rather small features; bottom of face has "pinched in" look, giving resemblance to bird. Very alert in manner. Have trick of following people with their eyes even when sitting down quietly. Curious about people primarily, things secondarily. Finicky about food. Sometimes faddy over health, either using medicines to excess or eschewing them altogether. Best detail workers (Capricorn second best). Seldom forget any routine duty but dislike to make decisions.

Libra – ♎

Well modeled features, regular and usually pleasing. Particular about personal appearance. Often part hair in middle. Slender to middle age, then sometimes (but not always) put on flesh. Very good judgment and fine artistic sense. Nearly always have good taste. Humane in their personal contacts though in case of a character such as Hitler (Libra with Taurus Sun) this would not prevent extreme cruelty as a matter of policy.

Scorpio – ♏

Strongest sign in the zodiac. Powerful features. Nose curved and large or on the Taurus order but longer. Ear-lobes often very fleshy. "Penthouse" eyebrows. Formidable appearance. Undaunted fighters with enormous staying power. Can be broken but not bent. Excellent for difficult and dangerous assignments.

Sagittarius – ♐

Equine look. Long face. Teeth usually prominent. Sagittarius women have a way of sitting or standing pigeon-toed. The men wind their legs around the chair and appear to be trying to tie them in knots. Very tall; expressive eyes, usually dark. Sometimes Spanish type. Athletic. At their best when full trust is placed in them. Strong religious sense, though not necessarily church-goers.

Capricorn – ♑

Hooked nose and chin. Sometimes flat "goatish" looking face. Usually no ear lobes. Suspicious look. Watery eyes. Scant hair. The "Cassius" type (lean and hungry look). Very capable and hard working. Tremendous respect for the old and established. Dislike innovations. Great worriers. Long lived though constitution not strong and they have many illnesses. Get results by nagging methods, though higher type does it diplomatically. Find fault with most things and are easily irritated, but very staunch when real misfortune befalls. Fine business people. Good executive types but not too easy to get along with.

Aquarius – ♒

Good looking, attractive, friendly. Very up-to-date and intelligent. Decisive but carry through without upsetting people. Reliable workers but would rather play. Sense of duty keeps them on the job, and also the necessity of money to gratify their somewhat expensive tastes. Well liked wherever they go and usually envied for something or other. Possess all-around ability and one of the most desirable of signs.

Pisces – ♓

Fishlike appearance, though often good looking in a rather dreamy way. Small "Cupid's bow" mouth. Small hands and feet. Limbs so short they are almost "fins." Chin close to shoulders with short, thick neck. Prominent eyes. Happy-go-lucky disposition. Philosophical under misfortune which often alternates with amazing good luck. Not seldom end up well-to-do without quite knowing what happened. Lower types addicted to drink, drugs or curious habits. Higher types have great creative imagination, far ahead of their day and generation.

Above are very sketchy outlines intended mainly as an aid to identifying the types. It must not be supposed that all of the pleasant or unpleasant characteristics are present in every person in whom the sign is most prominent. There are a hundred or more factors in each horoscope to be taken into account in appraising character.

It is suggested that the applicant's birthdate be secured (an easy thing to do) and that the rising sign be approximately arrived at by study of the appearance and mannerisms as sketched out above. Such a speculative horoscope is not likely to be accurate but if it is anywhere near so it will give some clue to the native's abilities and the things he is best fitted for.

If an accurate horoscope can be procured the employer has a most reliable guide for placement and advancement of the native in the way most advantageous to both.

CHAPTER XV

HOROSCOPES OF THE SUCCESSFUL
(Foreword)

In the example horoscopes which follow and on which detailed analyses are given, names have been suppressed to avoid embarrassment to the individuals concerned. They have been selected because in each case these natives are happy in their chosen fields and consider themselves successful in what they are doing. They are also regarded as successful by those who know them. In each case the native believes in astrology and admits having received the utmost benefit by following its guidance.

Horoscopes of great or international figures have purposely not been used for these exhaustive analyses for two reasons. Firstly because the "one in a million" success is of little use as an example to the other 999,999 who aim at only modest success and would perhaps be happier in attaining that than in the fierce limelight which beats about the ultra-successful. Secondly the natal charts of these world figures have been analyzed and super-analyzed *ad nauseam*, and it is the aim of this work, so far as possible, to avoid duplicating existing material. In the brief analyses which follow in a later chapter, some such celebrities have been included, in order to demonstrate striking horoscopic positions or aspects.

The reader is recommended to study these horoscopes and analyses without the feeling that they inevitably indicated that the natives would be successful or would follow these particular lines. They did not. They furnished a background of certain ability, talents, willpower—they also supplied plenty of friction and drawbacks. Others born with closely similar horoscopes may have made greater or less use of the opportunities their astrological equipment provided. The natal chart indicates trends only. The native has great free will in using or ignoring the sidereal and planetary aids with which he has been provided. True, we can probably always find something in the natal chart which has impelled the individual to follow this or that type of work, even though sheer accident, chance or luck may outwardly seem responsible. But we may, and often do, find some magnificent position or aspect which bears every mark of the ideal occupation for the native, totally ignored or followed only as a hobby or sideline.

Yet the planets do their best. So long as a native is in the wrong occupation everything seems to conspire against his success. In desperation, perhaps, he is forced out of an unpromising career into something which develops amazingly for him and which years later, when he learns something of astrology, he finds was the natural outlet for his talents and energies. Retrograde, but well placed or aspected planets, seem to act in that way. The good they indicate comes into the life after a series of false starts or mediocre success in lines indicated by other planets connected with the occupational houses, but poorly indicated.

Students sometimes express surprise that often there are many bad aspects as well as good ones in successful horoscopes. Yet why should there not be? Bad aspects—squares, oppositions and malefic conjunctions or parallels—bring difficulties, defeats, antagonisms, even misfortunes. Yet on these hard foundations some of the most solid edifices of achievement have been erected. The very good horoscopes—many trines, sextiles, benefic conjunctions and the like—give great ease of accomplishment in certain directions, and those directions are by all means to be sought out and followed. Yet if unleavened by any bad aspects at all, the native will be almost too successful—and unless the horoscope indicates a very strong character in other ways, his success may go to his head. He may live life without ever fully understanding it. Nature must have use for suffering and adversity—they are so omnipresent in her works. There is nothing desirable about them in themselves. They are there to be overcome, and in the overcoming something is added to character and ability which perhaps could be put there in no other way.

So no one should look at the horoscope of a John D. Rockefeller or a Henry Ford with the thought, "How could he help making a success? Look at the natal chart he has." Many a little business man or bookkeeper may have a better chart than either of them in certain ways. But these notables extracted every ounce of the possibilities of their good aspects and used their bad ones to gain experience. The lesser fry may have as great potentialities, but they will not make the sacrifices their charts call for, will not think their problems through intelligently, will not strive mightily to find out what they are best fitted for. The wonderful guide furnished by astrology is at the behest of all. Yet it is ignored, laughed at, treated with contempt by the very people, too often, who need it most.

The student is begged to take astrology seriously. It will be incredible to our enlightened descendants a century hence or less, that we could have committed the folly of allowing such menaces to the human race as Hitler to have a virtual monopoly among the world's rulers, of this greatest of sciences, while those who fought to preserve liberty and civilization turned their backs on it.

It is supposed among the so-called educated to indicate great strength of mind to condemn astrology out of hand, to term it nonsense, to look down one's nose at those who presume to believe in it. Yet which takes the greater strength of character—to follow the lead of the uninformed who parrot the phrase "Astrology is bunk" without the slightest first-hand knowledge—or to proclaim publicly, "I have studied Astrology. I believe in it because I can do no other, without ignoring the evidence of my own senses"?

There are probably many more educated than uneducated people who believe that "there is something in Astrology." Its practitioners boast of a distinguished group of great thinkers including Sir Isaac Newton, the famous astronomers Kepler and Camille Flammarion, and at least one of the Popes. True enough there is a "lunatic fringe" in the astrological movement as in every other. Wild-eyes fanatics make impossible claims, sensational predictions and ridiculous statements they claim are based on the science of the stars. Charlatans exploit popular credulity at profit to themselves. Reputable astrologers regard these fakers as some renowned physician might look on the activities of an advertising quack. They fiercely resent being classified with the dregs of an ancient and honorable profession. One of the best astrological books of recent months is the work of an Oxford M.A. Many astrological writers hold scientific and literary degrees from front rank Universities.

And there is evidence that the Universities themselves will not forever maintain their aloofness to this key science, so badly needed to implement their educational efforts. Some years ago a leading midwestern University invited the author to deliver a lecture on Vocational Astrology and according him a respectful and intelligent hearing.

These facts are emphasized because unless the reader is free from preconceived prejudice and will earnestly follow the path his horoscope maps out for his success, he is not doing justice to himself. Yet no one knows better than the author, who took up the study of astrology in a spirit of the utmost hostility because challenged to know what he was talking about before he attacked it, how hard prejudice dies.

An understanding examination of the example charts which follow, in the light of the information which has preceded, should convince the reader that Vocational Astrology has an immense field of usefulness before it, the surface of which has been barely scratched.

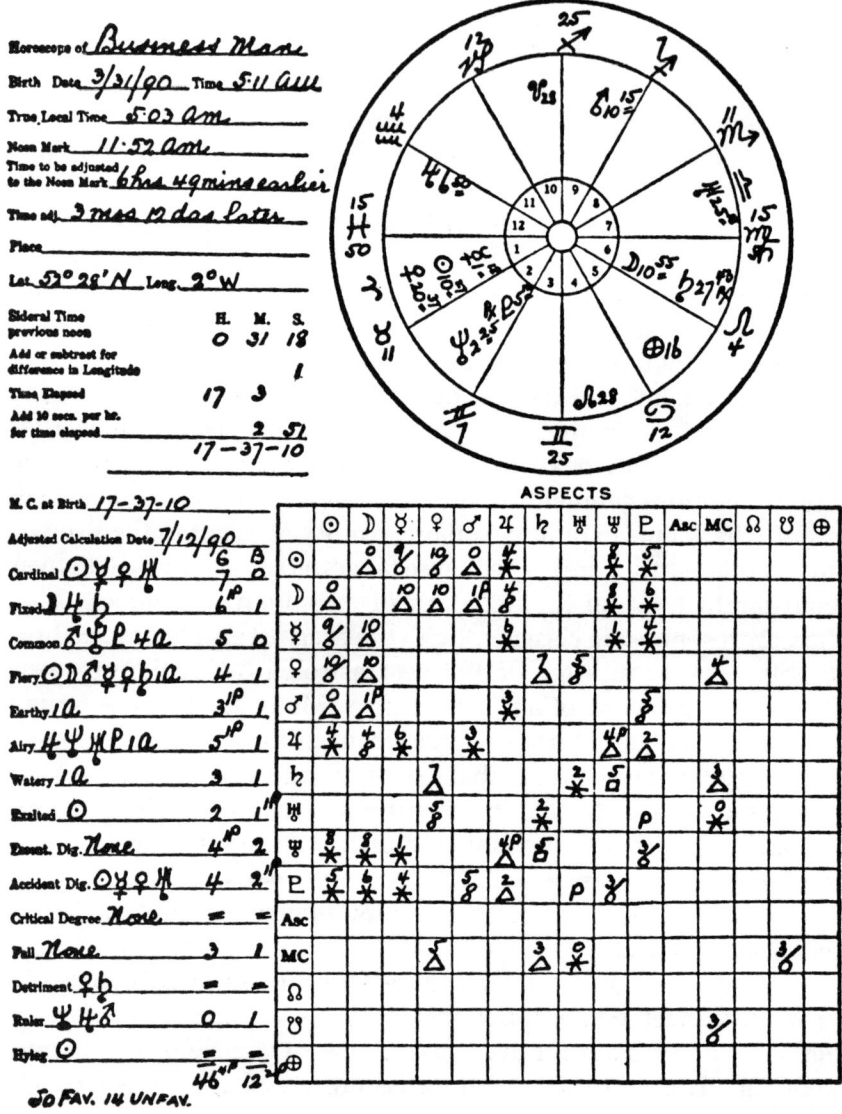

CHAPTER XVI

HOROSCOPES OF THE SUCCESSFUL
(Continued)

1. A Successful Businessman

This is the horoscope of a man engaged in a highly specialized wholesale business in which he is generally regarded as having been very successful. He is known nationally in his own particular trade circles as very expert in his line, one so difficult and hedged about with technical hazards that no direct competition exists and he has a virtual monopoly of the field.

Starting 30 years ago as Sales Correspondent in a somewhat similar business he worked his way through nearly all departments including road selling. His big "break" came when, after 7 years' experience, a wealthy individual in another city, desiring to start a similar business, offered him the position of General Sales Manager. Success was instantaneous and the new business flourished until hit by the post-war depression of 1921. In this year the native withdrew and organized his own Company, obtaining ample financial backing with small difficulty. The Company prospered until the Hoover depression of 1932-33 when bank closings and general conditions forced it to the wall. It was rescued by outside capital which had faith in the native and placed him in position to continue, though only at the expense of losing financial control and a cutting of one-half of his income. In the past seven years, after many setbacks, the native has again built up a solid structure and, though far from the size attained in the prosperous 'twenties, his business has made considerable headway and his income substantially increased. New difficulties, however, are crowding about him due to defense priorities and other troubles created by the war. He expresses confidence in his ability to overcome them as he has overcome those of the past.

There are some unusual features here, fully reflected in the horoscope. The native has followed one steady line for 30 years. We would expect to find Saturn concerned, as this planet rules not only business itself (the occupation) but is concerned with anything very much prolonged. Sure enough Saturn is in the sixth house (employment) and in close trine (very good) to the Midheaven (occupation). The Midheaven itself has 3 good aspects—one of them (from Uranus) exact. Uranus is co-ruler with Moon of the particular type of business in which the native is engaged.

But the Midheaven has one fly in its otherwise clean ointment. That bugbear of all horoscopes, South Node, is in conjunction. Now South Node is a sort of lesser Saturn so far as malignancy is concerned. It does not govern anything, as Saturn does, but sends out a similar type malefic radiation on a smaller scale. It stops short of wreaking the actual ruin which Saturn delights in when in bad aspect or without aspect, but it can do pretty considerable damage for all that.

It is South Node that is responsible for the native's repeated setbacks. Only the major ones have been cited but there are many minor ones attributable to this South Node influence. Yet the native has weathered them thus far, due to the remarkable phenomenon of 50 good aspects and positions against only 14 bad ones. Some of these are quite exceptional as Sun with 7 favorable aspects, exalted, and with not a single affliction, also strong in the angular first house. Moon is almost as good, with 7 favorable against 1 unfavorable. And to add the final touch of good fortune, Sun is exact trine Moon.

There is one curious lack, however, for a good business horoscope—the almost total dearth of earthy (practical) signs. This group is represented by only one minor angle. This has worked out in a rather significant fashion, and must be considered in connection with the overwhelming fiery signs which contain 6 planets and an angle—100% over average. Fiery signs confer intuition, long range vision and an almost uncanny ability, when very prominent, to pierce below the surface and play a "hunch" successfully.

The native is in a business so "impractical" that no one else will have anything to do with it. Yet he has sustained himself by it for 30 years—20 of them heading his own concern. His fiery signs showed him possibilities and methods of operation no "level headed" business man with a horoscope full of earthy signs could see. His "hunches" rarely fail and he possesses a strange sort of prophetic faculty as to outcomes which his associates rely on without understanding. He is also a firm believer in astrology, which has helped him immeasurably.

The amazing aspected Sun has brought him much help from those in better position than himself, and in many cases unsought. Sun rules influence and the influential, and his career has been greatly furthered in such ways. A badly afflicted Sun rules out aid of this kind—the native has to do everything for himself and if his Ascendant is well aspected makes a very good job of it.

The unusual nature of his occupation—one with which the public at large is little acquainted and about which many misunderstandings exist even in trade circles has several indicators. Neptune and Uranus together rule the unusual; Pluto governs the exclusive—that of which only one exists. Thus Pluto rules death, and a man can die but once. Under Pluto's government are dictators, and one dictator to a country (and now one to many countries) makes dictatorship a very exclusive profession. In individual horoscopes Pluto, like Uranus and Neptune, may have no good effects even when well aspected if the native is of the "backward" type. Everyone, however, responds to his bad aspects. These three planets seem to call for a certain above-average level of intellect or spirituality before their good side can manifest. Consequently it has to be determined, not from the horoscope alone but from some knowledge of the native and his background, whether or not the good aspects of this trio of "advanced" planets should be considered or ignored.

They may safely be taken where the native is an intelligent (not merely credulous) believer in astrology—where he has faith in the reality of a directive power in Nature—or even where he is only willing to concede that there is something "behind the scenes" and that the visible workings of the Universe do not constitute its sole reality. Many planets in fiery signs supply this realization as a matter of course. A large number in the watery group will do it in lesser degree. Earthy signs when preponderant mitigate against it. Airy signs may lead to such a conclusion from sheer hard thinking the matter through, but except for Aquarius, which has occult leanings, do not contribute to deep beliefs. Some knowledge of the native's background and an estimate of his degree of evolutionary advancement, apart from what the horoscope shows, is therefore desirable in attempting to evaluate the planets Pluto, Neptune and Uranus from the standpoint of their good indications. In practice astrologers usually take them at face value where the client's own horoscope is under examination. Obviously he has some faith in the reality of the unseen or he would not be consulting them. But even here the degree of intelligence is to be considered. Blind, unreasoning faith is not necessarily the hallmark of advancement in evolution.

In the horoscope now being analyzed it is evident that these planets may be taken into full account. Neptune conjunct Pluto in the second house (money) clearly shows the unusual and exclusive nature of the money-making abilities. Both planets are within orb (5°) of the third house (mind) and exercise powerful influence upon it. They give the same out-of-the-ordinary slant to the mental processes. Uranus in exact sextile the Midheaven gives the final touch to this *flair* for the unusual in business and money-making activities. It is a fact that throughout the native's entire career he has never been successful in any line or occupation of a routine or well-understood nature. In merchandising, he has to devise methods which have never occurred to others. Even his business correspondence dispenses with the customary formalities and is attention-compelling by its staccato statements of fact and its keen appraisement of essentials. Irrelevancies are brushed aside, original points of view developed, and in every department he contacts, the native's efforts are surrounded with an aura of Pluto-Neptune-Uranus. As a result the native is running what might be termed a "one-man show," which it would be difficult, if not impossible, to carry on without him.

In this case, Saturn, though trine Midheaven is entirely subordinate as a business indicator to Uranus, though the latter is only sextile. Uranus makes an exact aspect where Saturn's is nearly 3° out. Uranus is strong by house, being angular (seventh) where Saturn is in a weak cadent house (sixth). Uranus, while not exalted or dignified by sign is at least not in any disability, while Saturn is in its detriment in Leo. Saturn is sextile Uranus which is very good for both, yet Uranus has taken the lead in coloring the native's business life with Saturn only as runner-up. Saturn, however, has played no consequential part in aiding the native, even though inferior in importance to Uranus. Its influence is plainly seen in the tenacity with which the native has followed one line of business for 30 years. Only once during the entire period (and then for only 30 days) did he take a flyer at something else—accepting a position as Credit Manager for a large cereal house (Saturn, ruler of grains and cereals). The native spent the most unhappy month of his life during this period, which followed his decision to leave the road because of the lack of home life. Within 30 days, with Uranian suddenness and unexpectedness the great opportunity heretofore described had opened up, without any kind of effort on his part, and he was back again in the Uranian field where he so obviously belonged.

Here is a case where the Uranus sextile Midheaven (exact) took precedence over all other business indicators in the horoscope. Had the native consciously selected his field instead of being pushed into it by circumstances, themselves the product of the strong indicators, he might have made a choice even better than the course charted by Uranus.

Sagittarius is on the Midheaven, with Jupiter, ruler, in Aquarius on the cusp of the twelfth house but still retaining influence on the eleventh (hopes, wishes and ambitions) as it is not yet out of orb of the eleventh and its presence in Aquarius, eleventh house sign, adds greatly to this influence. The native has always felt a strong attraction to the occupations governed by Jupiter and Sagittarius, especially advertising, writing for publication and the publishing business. The presence of his co-ruler Mars in Sagittarius and the powerfully aspected Jupiter (6 good, 1 bad) has reinforced this attraction. The South Node in Sagittarius and in the tenth house has, however, heretofore prevented this from being more than a sideline in his life. Advertising material is a tremendous factor in his business and he has always written such copy himself, relying on no outside agencies, and only in minor measure on assistants. He has written for magazines and newspapers and has had little difficulty in getting his material accepted. The perfect Mercury (5 good aspects, no bad, and strong in an angle—also nearest planet to Ascendant) shows writing ability. He also has been a prolific writer of sales manuals and bulletins and trade copy of various kinds. He edits and publishes in the interests of a semi-religious organization of which he is an officer, a small monthly magazine.

The interesting question is, if the native had selected his vocation consciously, as a result of an analysis of the horoscope, could he have made a greater success and (more important) would he have lived a happier life? The answer is, probably yes. Though in this case the horoscopic influences were so strong that they virtually pushed him into his career, the general rule is that greater success always follows deliberate choice based on knowledge rather than in blindly following what appear to be the lines of least resistance.

Furthermore, this type of horoscope is rather rare. Often the occupational indicators are so confused and conflicting that the native drifts from one thing to another, never quite finding himself, and ends up in some secondary occupation, which the horoscope may indeed show as a possibility but on which the influences sneer rather than smile.

The native could in all probability have developed into quite a successful writer, had he also taken into account his powerful Pluto-Neptune-Uranus cast of mind and have written along entirely original and unusual lines. He might have made a success in the advertising business, by the same methods—the out-of-ordinary. As he is still a comparatively young man, retaining plenty of energy, there is a not remote possibility that he may yet exploit that particular side of his occupational possibilities, which thus far he has barely scratched.

The malevolent interference of South Node in Sagittarius and in the tenth must not be overlooked. Probably the sidetracking of Sagittarian occupations and concentration on things indicated by the Uranus-Midheaven sextile were astrologically brought about by this horoscopic killjoy. Yet one compensating advantage of South Node in tenth house is that in consequence North Node must be in the fourth house which governs outcomes, and also the latter years of the life. The frequent setbacks South Node has caused have been mentioned earlier, but North Node in a curious and at times almost uncanny fashion has guided the outcome even of the most unpromising situation to a satisfactory conclusion.

The native could have been born with a horoscope which might have taken him much farther, but he might have fared much worse. He is happy in his work, with a keen zest for life and an understanding of what it means, which goes far to compensate him for the minor annoyances and irritations of his bad aspects. And so he is cited as an example of a successful business man—not wealthy—not outstanding (except in his own circle)—not yet with his future fully assured. But satisfied with his chosen work, still ambitious and with plenty of *joie de vivre* left, and if success consists in having these things, therefore successful.

Twenty Years After

The native retired from his wholesale commodity business several years ago after being in it for 38 years and in the same line for others ten additional years (Saturn trine Midheaven). He has turned to good account the unafflicted Mercury (five favorable, no unfavorable aspects) and formed his own publishing company (Jupiter, six good aspects, one adverse; Mars in Sagittarius, four good, one bad, Mars being a life ruler).

He has written and successfully marketed several "best sellers," all along unconventional and original lines (Neptune and

Pluto on cusp of third house; Neptune, five good, three bad; Pluto, four good, three bad). Both Neptune and Pluto are sextile Jupiter. The "small monthly magazine" he edits and publishes which likewise deals with Uranus-Neptune affairs is still small in size but very much greater in circulation and influence than when the original reference to it was made. It now has an international circulation and is quoted in periodicals as far off as Indian and New Zealand.

The Neptune-Jupiter sextile has also given his activities, and more especially those of the organization with which he is connected, a very great amount of favorable publicity via TV and radio. He has had both his own program and scores of interviews by invitation. Now in his seventies he is as active as at any period of his life and with the benefic Leo in the fourth house (declining years) and the excellent Mercury governing Gemini on the fourth house cusp, this protective activity may reasonably be expected to continue well into old age.

CHAPTER XVII

HOROSCOPES OF THE SUCCESSFUL
(Continued)

2. A Successful Clubwoman

The Clubwoman is a peculiarly American phenomenon, the product—and a healthy one—of the more ample leisure which the labor-saving devices of this generation permit to its womenfolk. It is an outgrowth of the gregarious instinct among women which, in less sophisticated times, expressed itself in the sewing circle, the prayer meeting and the "coffee-klatsch." But it also expresses, and in much greater measure, the desire to be of service to the world.

"Clubwomanism," if such a term is permissible, is now one of the country's major "industries," rating respectful notice from pulpit and press. Its keynote was ably summed up in an address given by a well known clergyman at the Triennial Convention of the General Federation of Women's Clubs, attended by 6000 women representing a membership of two million throughout the country. He termed it "the very genius of women at work for themselves and with themselves to strengthen America and to help build a better world."

The horoscope selected is that of a woman peculiarly fitted for this type of endeavor, possessing the requisite leisure to follow such avocation. She is happy in this work and because of the special nature of the horoscope has advanced in it without any ambitious effort of her own. She has volunteered her service freely and gladly to those particular branches which interested her, but has made no attempt whatever to advance herself in office in any of the several clubs with which she has been associated. Yet preferment has come to her unsought and even undesired. Her interest is in the work itself and in no way in the limelight of office.

At present she occupies the presidency of a large and active literary society, is past president of another leading club and district chairman of the Art Section of the Federation. She is a member of several other clubs and a landscape artist of merit. In the past she has held numerous offices and directorships in other women's clubs, some of them political. She is well liked and enjoys a wide circle of friendships.

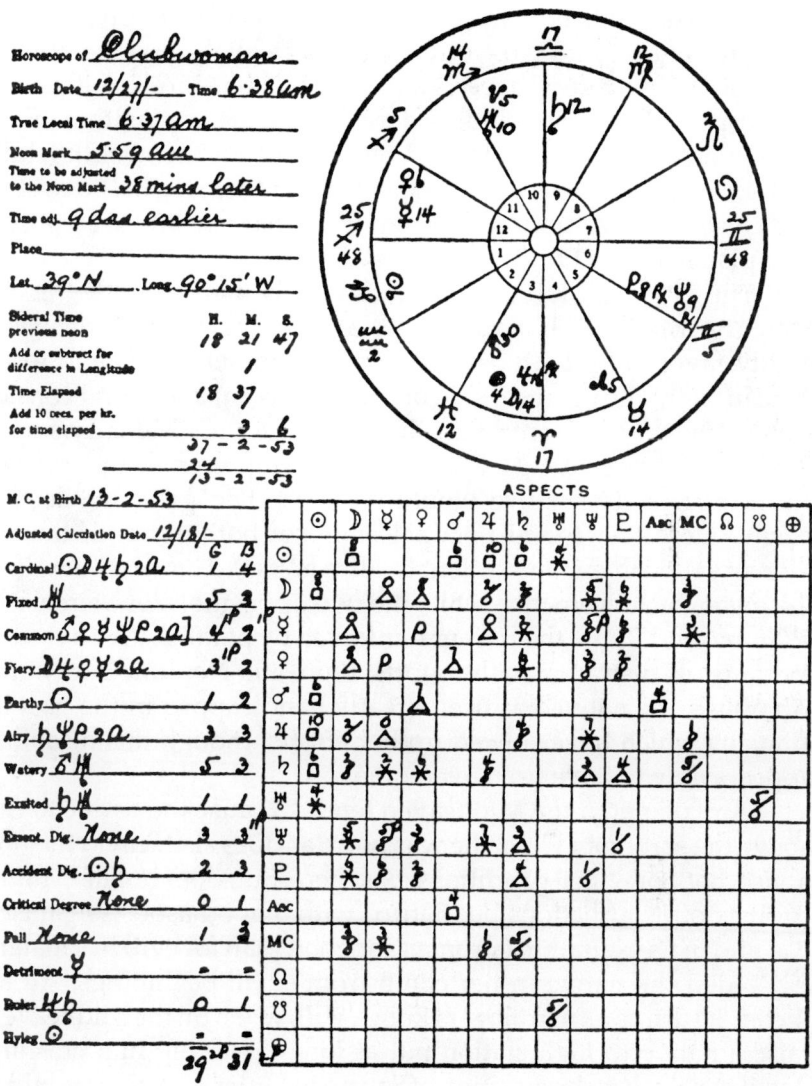

The horoscope shows the very earnest and sincere Sagittarius rising—a sign possessing great altruism and desire to be of use. Sun is in the capable Capricorn and Moon in Taurus, which delights in leadership. The heavily afflicted Sun (4 bad aspects, 1 good) has been of little help to the native in providing influence from those in higher station to push her forward—such as was so prominent in the business man's horoscope. The native has risen entirely by her own efforts and by favor found with her equals, especially with friends. Moon's 5 good aspects against 3 bad ones are significant in this respect, the good including a trine to Venus, well within orb of the eleventh house (friends) and on the cusp of the twelfth (clubs and societies). Moon is also in exact trine to Mercury in the twelfth and close conjunct Jupiter, the ruler. It also has a sextile to Neptune, club planet and to Pluto.

The Literary Club presidency is clearly marked in the Moon-Mercury trine, which also denotes a good mentality. Mercury is highly favored by both benefics, being parallel Venus and exact trine Jupiter. The practical side of the mind is enhanced and considerable power of concentration shown by the close Mercury sextile Saturn. The airy element (mentality) is well represented by 3 planets and 2 angles. The native would have reached great intellectual heights were it not for the poor placement by both sign and house of Mercury (detriment and cadent twelfth house). This sets bounds to the mental achievements, while the two oppositions of Mercury to Neptune and Pluto, the former reinforced by parallel, give a certain measure of frustration to the efforts. Pluto and Neptune both in the 6th house, the native has been greatly handicapped in the past by ailments which have slowed up her efforts, though this disability appears now to have been overcome.

Any planet in the Midheaven tends to cause the native to rise above the station in which he was born, as does also Sun in the first house, both of which conditions exist here. Sun does not help much because of its afflictions but Saturn with 5 good aspects against 3 bad and in its exaltation (stronger for good than for evil) has materially aided the native in her climb from small beginnings. An afflicted Saturn as all astrologers know, will, when on the Midheaven, raise a native to high station but at long last bring him crashing down to ruin. It is this position of Saturn in Hitler's horoscope which astrologers claim is the ultimate hope of civilization to be rid of him and his system. [Saturn in tenth square Venus (4) square Mars (4) parallel Mars, against only one light sextile Uranus (7).]

In our clubwoman's chart, however, no such catastrophe is to be feared, as the good far outweighs the bad in this key occupational planet.

Many years ago when clubwork was probably the farthest thing from her mind, an astrologer stated that there was considerable evidence in the natal chart that prominence would be achieved in political and social work. At that time the native's interests lay in wholly other directions and it hardly seemed possible either to her or her family that such a changed state of affairs could come about.

But horoscopic indicators, when powerful enough, have a way of coming into their own, and in due season the astrologer's opinion was justified by events. Greater successes in this field lie before the native if she takes full advantage of the wider possibilities the horoscope permits. But man has freewill and it is strictly up to her.

Twenty Years After

The possibilities indicated in the closing paragraph of the foregoing delineation have come to pass in full measure. The planet Saturn exalted in Libra sextile Venus has extended the art interests into a far wider field. Now recognized as one of the outstanding women artists of the area she was awarded last year by a jury of art experts from out-of-town, a citation and subsequently first prize of $200 for the best pastel of the season.

The four good aspects of Venus coupled with the twelfth house position of both Venus and Mercury (institutions) have been astrologically responsible for her taking a major part in organizing a Women Artists Society (of which she became first President) with a distinguished and respected membership.

This is a good example of a horoscope, the potentialities of which have been in large measure fulfilled in spite of considerable number of adverse aspects which at times have placed formidable obstacles in the way.

HOROSCOPES OF THE SUCCESSFUL
(Concluded)

3. A Successful Secretary

The native has been connected with one concern virtually her entire business life (17 years). She was hired as an extra typist for temporary work only but, showing efficiency and intelligence far above the average, she was retained as stenographer, later being promoted to secretarial work to which much later were added the duties of office manager. Eventually she became Secretary to the President of the Company and recently, while continuing to retain this position, was also elected Secretary-Treasurer and a Director of the concern.

Ample leadership is shown by 4 planets, including the ruler, Uranus and Moon in cardinal signs. There is great tenacity of purpose and considerable willpower, as evidenced by Sun, Mercury (mind planet), Jupiter and all 4 angles fixed. The natural Aquarian friendliness is reinforced by 3 planets common, including the subordinate ruler, Saturn. The native is a double Aquarian, having both Ascendant and Sun there. Moon in Capricorn gives shrewd business sense. Mercury exalted in Aquarius, coupled with adequate airy signs, supplies quick, alert intelligence. Moon conjunct Ascendant is also indicator of a responsive mind.

The native's long service with one Company is shown out by the same indicator as in the case of the Business Man's horoscope (Chapter XVI) by Saturn trine Midheaven. She has excellent taste and a real *flair* for artistry in clothes. Venus is exalted in Pisces with an almost exact sextile Uranus and trine Neptune. These two planets confer an original idea of design and ornament so pronounced that her milliner recently offered her a partnership if she would come into the business with him, an offer promptly refused for reasons which will be made manifest further on.

An indefatigable worker, the native supplements her income by work as spare time Secretary to a journalist and by specialized routine editorial work. Jupiter trine Mars in second house, though light, shows this particular source of income. Jupiter rules journalism and Mars in second gives good earning power. Mars seldom holds on to his accumulations however. The native also has Saturn in the second. This planet is the exact antithesis of Mars and is quite thrifty. The native is a curious mixture of thrift and extravagance, following out the indications of both these second house planets. Her employers have sufficient confidence in the former quality to leave a good deal of routine buying in her hands, and have never

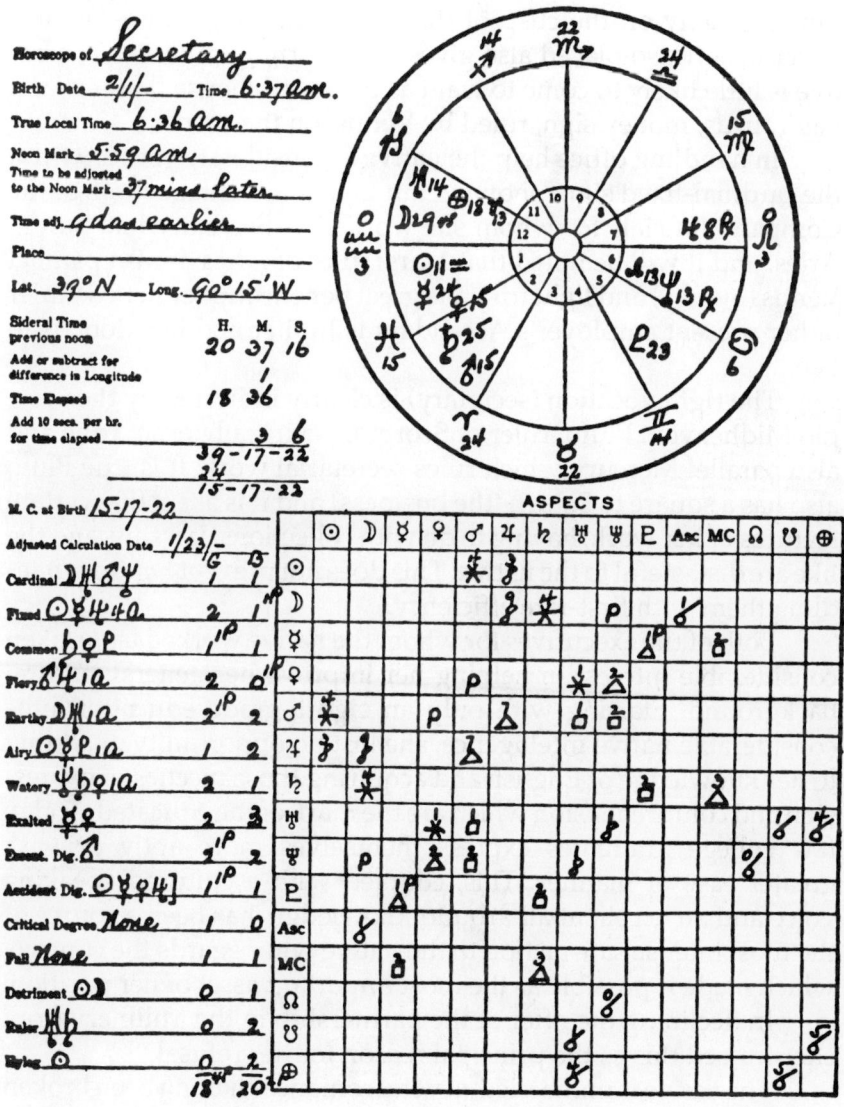

found occasion to criticize her for paying too much. Yet should some particular article of feminine adornment especially appeal to her she is likely to cast financial discretion to the winds and spend the painful savings of several months in an afternoon. The Saturnine thrift shows out in the fact that even here she will invariably obtain the best possible value for her money.

The "clothes complex" is indicated by the excellently placed Venus exactly on the cusp of the second (money) house. Venus, lesser benefic, so placed also gives good earning capacity. The native is little likely to come to want as the fourth house (latter years) has Taurus, money sign, ruled by Venus, on the cusp.

In handling office help the native is considerate yet very firm, the cardinal-fixed signs showing out to best advantage. Both of the Company officials for whom she worked as Secretary had Sun in Aries, and it will be noted that Mars, ruler of Aries, is also parallel Venus (money) and light trine the great benefic Jupiter in Leo. Ruler of her present employer's Ascendant is Jupiter and his Moon is in Leo.

The right vocation (secretary) is clearly indicated by the Scorpio Midheaven. Pluto, ruler of Scorpio, is virtually exact trine and also parallel Mercury which rules secretarial work. It is true Pluto also has a square to Saturn (the business) and it is a fact that certain features of her work, having to do with collections, lawsuits and the like are distasteful to the native. This does not prevent her from handling them with first-rate efficiency.

Both of the executives for whom the native worked have taken considerable interest in helping her improve her general cultural background. Starting with only an eighth-grade education plus considerable native intelligence, she lost no opportunity of adding to her knowledge of English and acquiring those niceties of expression and comprehension which are the mark of the educated. Today few college graduates express themselves more aptly or with greater ease of manner. This, coupled with a cultured speaking voice and an excellent all-around knowledge, has been a source of the most intense satisfaction to the native who regards the contacts which made it possible as the most important asset of her position.

In declining the offer of the partnership in the Millinery firm, she stressed this as the principal reason for her refusal.

The native is unmarried, several romances having been broken up by her parents because of difference in faith. Sun, co-ruler of marriage, is in close opposition to Jupiter which rules religion. Mars, the other marriage ruler, is in very close square both to Uranus, which shatters when in bad aspect and Neptune which frustrates. Neptune is also ruler of the Church of which the native is a communicant and which frowns on mixed marriages. Neptune, however, is also in nearly exact trine Venus and absolutely exact conjunct North Node. The native is devout in her religion both in belief and practice. The religious house (ninth) has Libra on cusp and is therefore governed by Venus which, however, is close sextile Uranus, though trine Neptune. While adhering to all the rites and customs of her belief (Neptune) the native has a considerable *flair* for the occult (Uranus) and feels that it enables her to understand her own faith better because of the light it casts on otherwise obscure teachings.

With all the order and method of her many fixed signs, the native retains the fun-loving Aquarian disposition, and at times is somewhat incomprehensible to her more staid acquaintances and even to her own family. The two odd planets Uranus and Neptune, almost exactly opposite each other, add this curious quirk to the character which at base, however, is well grounded and down to earth. The native is far from being the stodgy secretary of novels and movies. She is athletic (Mars strong) and has captained a softball and basketball team, plays an excellent contract bridge game and lives a thoroughly rounded out life.

She is likely to rise much higher, both in business and social life.

Twenty Years After

The native is still associated with the same enterprise, completely reorganized and in a different type of production. Her thinking and general outlook has continued to mature, the excellent Mercury, exalted, parallel and almost exact trine Pluto having fulfilled its promise. The reasoning powers and the capacity for well-considered judgments have broadened and deepened with the years, so that her opinions and counsel are always given weight whenever expressed.

This good all-around horoscope has bright assurance for the latter years, as Taurus is on the cusp of the fourth house that rules the culminating period of the life. There is no planet in the house but the exalted Venus in Pisces rules Taurus and therefore stands for the house ruler. It has two very close good aspects, one of which is a trine to the ruler Uranus. Aside from a parallel to Mars, not of much consequence, there are no afflictions to Venus. A fortunate augury for comfort and security in the years to come.

CHAPTER XIX

HOROSCOPES OF WORLD FIGURES

1. A President of the United States
2. A Dictator
3. A Prime Minister of Great Britain

In this and the two following chapters abridged horoscopes and short vocational delineations are given of the following outstanding characters, each a typical representative of his chosen line of endeavor:

1. A President of the United States.
2. A Dictator
3. A Prime Minister of Great Britain
4. An Oil Millionaire
5. A Financier
6. A Pioneer in Medical Research
7. A Playwright
8. An Artist
9. An Inventor
10. A USSR Dictator
11. A Vice-President of the United States
12. A Governor of New York

Attention is drawn only to the most significant features of the chart. It is recommended that the student set up the horoscope in each case in detail, calculating all aspects, positions, etc., and then make his own full delineation based on the astrological laws set forth in earlier chapters.

1. Franklin D. Roosevelt
President of the United States

Uranus almost exactly on the Ascendant, coupled with Mars and Moon in tenth—6 of the 10 planets high up in the chart and another on the ascending angle—mark a character of great power, almost certain to rise in life. Jupiter in virtually exact trine Uranus from his own house, the ninth, Jupiter also being trine Ascendant, Neptune having similar trines from ninth, precipitates foreign affairs most forcefully into the life.

The native gains much from these powerful aspects and positions—the third term was probably due to them—yet Saturn on cusp of ninth square Sun and Venus, and South Node near the Midheaven, constitute a major threat from this same source.

Mr. Roosevelt's strong Mercury, exalted in Aquarius, rules both Ascendant and Midheaven. His tenth house Mars trines Mercury exact. There is no "Presidential Horoscope." Thousands of other natives born with closely similar horoscopes did not become Presidents of the United States. They might, and many of them probably did, become Presidents of Companies, organizations, societies, or other institutions. Mars and Moon both in tenth, Mars being exact trine to ruler, gives enormous drive which, if the balance of the horoscope is reasonably favorable, can hardly fail to lift the native high in his field, whatever it may be.

Note Moon is also very strong—essentially dignified in Cancer. Venus is conjunct Part of Fortune. The President is a wealthy man. Sun also conjoins Part of Fortune. All are in fifth (investments). Venus rules second, both normally (Taurus) and because Libra, other sign of Venus, is on second cusp. Yet there are bad afflictions from Saturn in its fall. The native has, however, nearly twice as many good aspects as bad ones.

Sun is nearly trine Midheaven—another testimony of advancement. Moon is exact sextile Saturn, cutting down some of the latter's malignancy. The native battled his way to health (Mars trine Mercury exact) against the terrible affliction of infantile paralysis (Mercury in sixth parallel Neptune and exact square Pluto in detriment). The astrological odds were against him in spite of Mercury's excellent sign position.

The balance was doubtless turned by the terrific array of planets in fixed signs—7 of them.

The almost total lack of planets in cardinal signs may seem puzzling in the horoscope of the leader of the country. It explains a good deal that is mysterious in the President's actions. It is known that he waits for public opinion to crystallize before taking action—then he shapes his course accordingly. With many cardinal signs, he would be far ahead of it and seek to mould it. Advisers probably play a far greater part in the President's life than is generally known.

A man can rise without cardinal signs, if other aspects favor, but others will have a great deal to do with his policies. An explanation of the prominent part played by the "Brain Trust" and other

FRANKLIN D. ROOSEVELT

ADOLPH HITLER

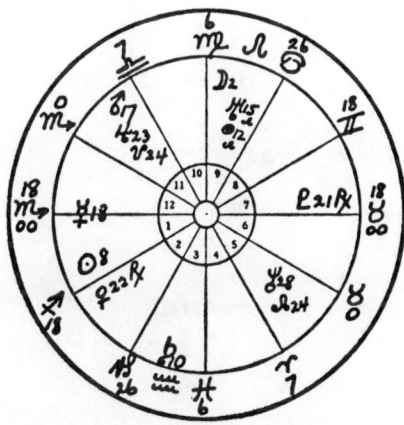

WINSTON CHURCHILL

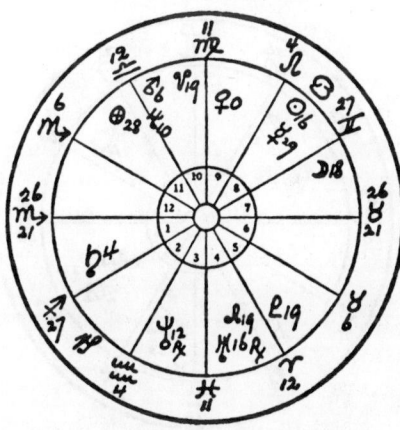

JOHN D. ROCKEFELLER, SR.

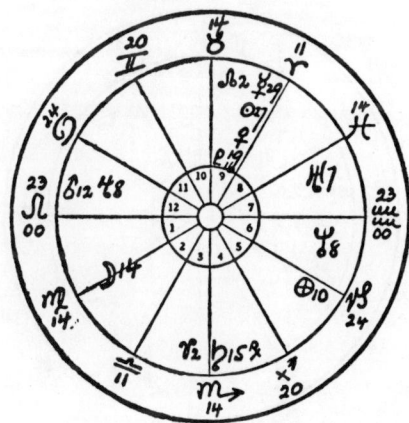

J. P. MORGAN, SR.

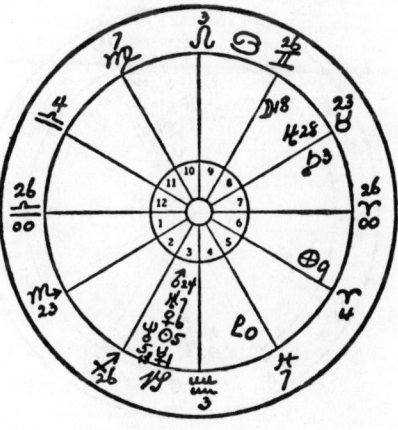

LOUIS PASTEUR

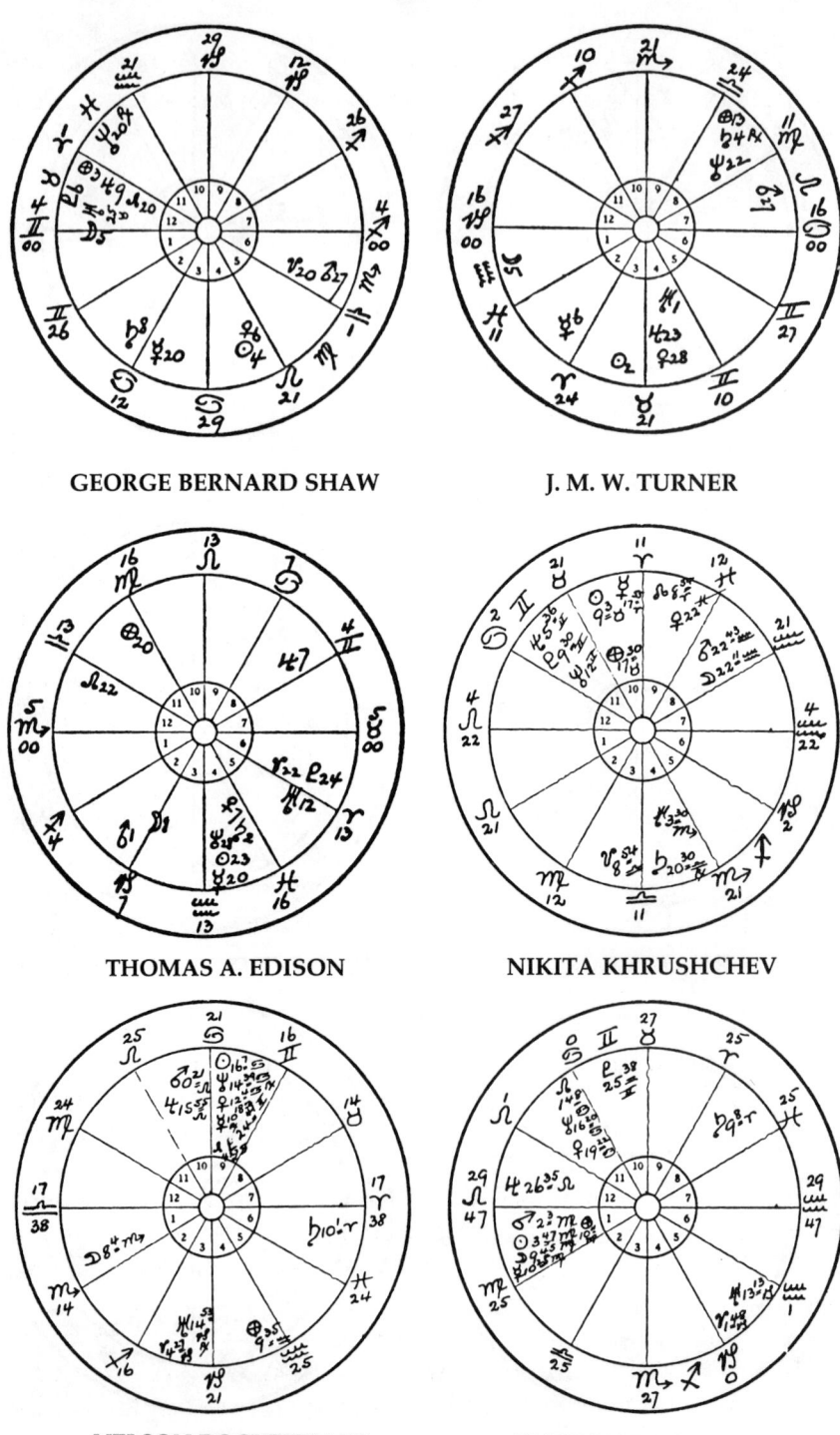

GEORGE BERNARD SHAW

J. M. W. TURNER

THOMAS A. EDISON

NIKITA KHRUSHCHEV

NELSON ROCKEFELLER

LYNDON B. JOHNSON

trusted "New Dealers" is seen in the 4 common angles plus 2 planets in common. They make the President likable and approachable without noticeably weakening the formidable effect of the fixed signs.

This horoscope will well repay the most intensive study and analysis.

2. Adolph Hitler
Dictator of Nazi Germany

In the horoscope of a nation's ruler, particularly of one whose word is so absolute as that of the German fuehrer, the houses, signs and planets assume a national significance and are to be interpreted not merely with reference to the private affairs of the individual but of the nation whose destiny is bound up with his.

It is interesting, therefore, to note that the terrific opposition felt for Hitler's ideas all over the civilized world is expressed in his natal chart in as full a measure as the greatest stickler for astrological consistency could ask. The seventh house (public enemies) and the sign Libra (normal to seventh house) are the ones we would expect to find involved, and they are the most prominent factors in the chart. The former contains 4 of the 10 planets (40% of the whole as against an average of 8-1/3%). The latter is the ascending sign and also contains the powerful Uranus. This appears in the twelfth house (secret enemies). In the house of death (the eighth) which has played so great a part in the fuehrer's bloody career, are Pluto, planet of death and Neptune, which so often makes its appearance in lethal matters. Earth, which marks the source from which the greatest material accumulations come, is, significantly enough, in the sign Gemini (writings) and in the house of mortality. Hitler's entire income is said to be derived from the sale of millions of copies of his book, *Mein Kampf*, which preaches woe, destruction and death to all who oppose him. Significant, too, is North Node in the ninth (publications).

It is said that Hitler's great ambition was to be an artist and that he still cherishes the hope that his later years may be devoted to this peaceful occupation. Those in position to judge state that he has some talent along artistic lines, though far from a genius. Venus (art) is strong in its own sign (Taurus), though retrograde, which would push this possibility into the future. There are other reasons why Hitler may never realize it, one being the square of Saturn to Venus

(4° of orb), the other the exact conjunct Mars. Libra, the Ascendant, is the most artistic of signs and although it has been disparagingly said that Hitler was a housepainter and paperhanger "and not a very good one," the horoscope shows that he *was* probably a very good one.

The extraordinary placement of Mars and Venus, planets of war and peace respectively, in the identical degree and sign and in the seventh house, both square Saturn and with no other aspects, is an omen of hope for the world. While the benefic Venus gives Mars (war) every aid and comfort, at long last Saturn will smash down the whole evil structure.

In starting his various drives, Hitler, who is said to be a most competent astrologer or very well advised, seems to set great store by good aspects to his Moon-Jupiter position in 7°-8° Capricorn. These planets are unafflicted and, while neither is well placed by sign, he evidently regards them as the best offset he has to his malignant Saturn, as they are in the Saturnine sign Capricorn. That his judgment has been amazingly good is shown by the uncanny success of his belligerent enterprises. German thoroughness and planning, of course, technical efficiency, years of preparation, ruthless execution letting nothing stand in the way—all these were present and the other side had little to oppose them with except steadfastness and courage. But they were present in the last World War in as great measure relatively speaking, and the other side had still less at the outset. What is the missing factor which has made the German war-machine thus far so nearly invincible? We say it is the fuehrer's knowledge of astrology.

His enemies concede him a superb sense of timing. From whence does this come? No human being, not even a Hitler, can by ordinary standards be sure of not making one false guess when planning moves which bring in so many bewildering factors. We know of no way it can be done, other than by expert use of astrology. Saturn will wear Hitler down at last, but it may be a very long last if he continues to stay out of Saturn's realm by staking everything on Uranian blitzkriegs and surprises. No planet can function if not given material to work with. Saturn needs lengthy periods of time and, preferably, orthodox, routine-like methods, long established and well understood. Time fights against him, it is true, but he is doing a remarkable job of ducking and keeping out of its way. That, with all his cunning, he has miscalculated the ultimate eventuality is shown by Mercury opposition Ascendant, exact.

To later readers of this book the outcome of the war and Hitler's fate may no longer be the mystery it is as these words are penned. But whatever that outcome and that fate may be, in the convinced opinion of the author, Saturn will be (astrologically) the greatest contributory factor.

3. Winston Churchill
Prime Minister of Great Britain

In perfect contrast to Hitler, Mr. Churchill's Mercury is exactly on the Ascendant. This brilliant meteor of British politics has been soldier, writer, statesman and is now leader of the British people in their most hazardous period since England became a nation. His Ascendant is Scorpio, most unyielding of all the signs. His mind (Mercury) is also cast in the Scorpio mould, and Pluto, ruler of Scorpio, is in Taurus and opposing the Ascendant (3° orb). Four planets and 2 angles fixed exactly equal Hitler's 4 planets, 2 angles in the same constitution. He cannot boast of the same showy leadership as Hitler who has 4 planets, 2 angles in cardinal signs against Churchill's scant 3 planets and no angles. Hitler calls for loyalty to Hitler as leader—Churchill to Britain as country. We have seen no word of demand from him for loyalty to himself, though this is magnificently bestowed without being asked, by his embattled people.

One does not deliberately train to become a Prime Minister, President of the United States or Fuehrer. These are positions to which men are called (or, in the case of the last named, force themselves). Looking at a natal chart, no matter how good, one cannot say at the child's birth, "This is the horoscope of a President or Prime Minister." Others born at approximately the same time and place will have similar horoscopes. A superbly muscled young man with a powerful constitution may or may not choose to exploit his physical perfection by becoming a prizefighter or athlete. He has the equipment. What he chooses to do with it may depend upon his own choice or upon external circumstances over which he may have little control. Similarly the horoscope shows possibilities; and the greatness or littleness of the soul behind, will determine to what extent they are used. Winston Churchill, born to the purple, son of a leader of the House of Commons, educated at Harrow and Sandhurst, could hardly have failed to make some kind of a mark unless he had an extremely bad horoscope. As a matter of fact he has a very good one and has exploited its possibilities well-night to the utmost.

His success as a soldier is shown by Mars (war) conjunct Jupiter and sextile Venus. As a writer his Jupiter sextile Venus from Libra (sign of Venus) to Sagittarius (sign of Jupiter) points to outstanding recognition. These planets, being in each other's signs are in what is called "mutual receptivity," greatly adding to their power. As a statesman Sun sextile Saturn (2° orb) and Sun in the strong first house, amply accounts for his long stay in politics. Yet Sun square Moon, though rather light (6°), has threatened his prestige many times and is likely to threaten it again.

The harrowing threat from abroad is plainly shown out by Uranus in ninth house (foreign affairs) opposition Saturn (5°). It is not strong, but strong enough to cause plenty of trouble. England's worries on the sea are aptly typified by Neptune (sea) opposition Jupiter foreign affairs planetary ruler, and in Libra (strife). Jupiter itself is almost on top of the snarling South Node. Yet Neptune conjoins North Node—a good luck token for the British Navy.

With Venus in second house (money) Churchill could hardly be anything but well off, and all the aspects of Venus contribute to this happy state of affairs. Churchill is said by his intimates to be "enjoying the war hugely." With Mars conjunct Jupiter in the eleventh house (hopes, wishes and ambitions) this is understandable. Sagittarius in which he has his Sun, is humane, as is Virgo where Moon is posited. There is, however, nothing especially humane about Scorpio, nor about Taurus where his ruler Pluto appears. His co-ruler Mars is in Libra, a gentle sign when left alone but vicious when blended with Mars.

This most historic character will certainly leave a profound impress on both British and international history, but wars have proved graveyards of many great reputations, and Mr. Churchill will need every resource his fine heritage and splendid background provide him to escape all of the lurking pitfalls his natal chart indicates as probably lying before him.

CHAPTER XX

HOROSCOPES OF WORLD FIGURES
(Continued)

4. An Oil Millionaire
5. A Financier
6. A Pioneer in Medical Research

4. John D. Rockefeller, Sr.
Oil Millionaire

Again Scorpio is rising, and the ruthlessness with which the native crushed competition in the days during which he was building up his oil empire required this hefty sign for its full expression. Mars, co-ruler of Scorpio, is in the tenth, occupational house, very close sextile Saturn in first. This gives terrific drive in business matters. The planets are so arranged as to give the native aid in almost anything he does connected with his material affairs. Mars is in the tenth conjunct Jupiter; Jupiter is sextile Saturn. Mercury, ruler of tenth, is trine Ascendant, also sextile Mars. Very seldom do the planets and signs so conspire together to smooth a business path.

At that it was not all smooth. South Node in tenth not far from Midheaven subjected him to tremendous public criticism, though it in no way affected his steady progress to millionairedom.

It is interesting to trace the astrological correspondences which can be found every step of the way along this native's monumental career. At 16 he became an assistant bookkeeper, a Scorpio occupation. On the cusp of the sixth (employment) is Taurus, money sign, ruled by Venus which is in Scorpio. This was for a commission house, a business ruled by Saturn. Venus is square Saturn (4° orb), and weak in Scorpio. The native earned $50 for the first three months of his employment, after which he was advanced to $25 per month. Even for those days these were "starvation" wages.

As evidence that an insignificant start under the worst aspects may lead to great things, the native somehow managed to save enough in three years to buy a partnership in a produce firm. He was no longer an employee and his poor employee aspects (which by incredible self-sacrifice he used for good) disappear from the picture henceforth. He was never an employee again. The first foundations of his career were, however, from employment and from money earned in employment. In this regard, Virgo, employment sign, on the Midheaven, and Taurus, money sign, on the employment house are most significant.

He became a partner, and the Moon occupying the seventh (partnership) house took over. Taurus is on the cusp but a planet in any house except the first always takes precedence of the sign. In the first only when within 5° of the Ascendant, and not always then if the rising sign be fixed. The connection between the employment and the partnership, the one leading to the other is, however, clearly indicated by the same sign, Taurus, being on the cusp of both the sixth and the seventh.

Rockefeller made a good investment in his partnership. In the fifth house (investments) is his ruler, Pluto, almost exact sextile Moon in seventh. Moon also trines Jupiter in partnership sign, Libra, and in tenth (business) house—a perfect setup. It is, too, trine Neptune and its one bad aspect, a square Uranus is insufficient to upset this congeries of good ones. Four years later he and his partner were able to invest $4,000 in an infant oil refining business. Here Neptune, ruling oil, trine Moon, also ruling oil, the former being in Aquarius, the sign of new processes, clearly marked the path the native traveled.

Why was Uranus, then, so quiescent, with its close square Moon? Why did it not upset things or at least bring about some kind of difficulty? Doubtless all was not such plain sailing as a bald narration of the facts would indicate, but astrologically the power of a malefic to harm is largely nullified by a conjunct Leo. Uranus here conjoins within 3° and its efforts by square to frustrate the trines and sextiles are in consequence almost impotent. North Node in fourth is a consolation prize for having South Node in tenth. It smiles on "outcomes," no matter how unpromising the beginnings may be, as evidence Rockefeller's pitiable starting wage which developed into hundreds of millions.

Eight years more saw Rockefeller and his partners (he had another one by then) doing 20 percent of all the oil refining business in Cleveland, chief oil refining city of the United States. He organized a million dollar corporation (enormous for those times), holding more than 25 percent of the stock himself. Jupiter (ruling Sagittarius on cusp of second) sextile Saturn (ruling Capricorn intercepted in second) was beginning to tell. He was on his way.

It has been mentioned in a previous chapter that Pluto governs the exclusive. Its sextile Moon is of great moment in this chart. It is virtually exact and Pluto is in the investment house. Moon is Rockefeller's co-ruler due to Sun in Cancer. Pluto is the other ruler (Scorpio rising). Pluto rules monopoly and Rockefeller was perhaps the first great monopolist in America. By a series of shrewd moves Rockefeller induced the railroads to grant huge rebates to his Company and other refiners who were members of an association he formed, while at the same time they placed penalties, or "drawbacks" as they were called, on all oil shipped by non-members. By this method he forced 21 out of 26 competing refiners to sell out to Standard Oil, his new Corporation.

South Node came charging forward with full malignancy, causing a storm of public indignation which forced the railroads to withdraw their agreement, but it was too late. The object had already been achieved and Standard Oil owned the Companies. Here it may be seen how a malefic influence may work adversely but not sufficiently so to upset stronger benefic influences. The same would apply of course on the other side, were the malefics in the superior position.

A few years more saw the native controlling 90 percent of the country's oil refineries.

It is not practicable to pursue his career at further length here, but in spite of many legal difficulties due to Leo on cusp of ninth (law) ruled by Sun square Pluto, ruler of seventh (litigation) square Saturn and the aforesaid South Node in tenth, no significant damage ever resulted to the native. He was reputed at his retirement to be the richest man in the country.

A word may be said regarding his enormous benefactions, reaching upwards of half a billion dollars. Charity is ruled by the twelfth house, Jupiter and Neptune. There is no planet in the twelfth so Pluto and Mars assume primary rulership as Scorpio is on the cusp. Mars trine Jupiter, Pluto sextile Neptune and North Node in Pisces (twelfth house) signify his great hearted generosity in this respect—surely of so much benefit to the human race that a grateful public may well consign to oblivion the memory of hard dealings of the native's earlier life, when all was fair in business as in war.

5. J. P. Morgan, Sr.
International Financier

This native, born with the regal Leo rising and his ruler, Sun, exalted in the leadership sign Aries along with 3 other planets, was fortune's favorite from his first cry.

Exactly on cusp of second (money) house is Moon within 1° of exact sextile of Saturn. On cusp of tenth is money sign, Taurus. Highest in the chart stands benefic North Node. The native was born to money, received every educational and cultural advantage money could provide, and from his earliest manhood was an important figure in the banking and financial world. His ninth house (foreign matters) contains no fewer than 4 planets and North Node, and all his life his affairs constantly involved foreign countries. He was even educated at the University of Gottingen in Germany.

His financing of many railroads is shown by Libra (ruler Venus) on cusp of third (transportation), Venus being in ninth, a coruler in general of railroads, steamship lines and other institutions out of which the Morgan millions were garnered. Even the U. S. Government was beholden to him when, in 1895, he supported a tottering Treasury reserve by furnishing over $60,000,000 in gold. Mercury rules U. S. and is close conjunct native's Sun (gold). Sun is conjunct Venus.

Pluto, planet of monopoly, is also conjunct Venus which is not good for Venus but excellent for Pluto. By itself Venus, which is not over-strong, could not have accounted for Morgan's wealth, but the unexcelled (for money) position of Moon needed little reinforcement from the normal money planet.

Highest planet in the horoscope is Mercury conjunct North Node conjunct Sun (too close for eloquence, but the native was not famous for this), with no afflictions. The native's keen intellect overpowered all others in his field. He was a generous giver, his co-ruler, Mars, being in the twelfth house (charity) and Jupiter, planet of benevolence, being also there. Moon rules sign on twelfth cusp (Cancer) and its paramount monetary influence has already been stressed.

Last, but supreme over all, is the main aspect which made J. P. Morgan the financial wizard of his generation and perhaps of all time. Moon, whose stellar role in his financial affairs dwarfs everything else in the horoscope, is exact trine his Midheaven. Money was his business, and a fortunate business it was. True Saturn opposes

Midheaven but a planet opposing its own sign or house has much of its malefic effect removed by the "throw-over" effect of opposite signs. Morgan built up his business the hard Saturnine way regardless of all the advantages of his environment and training. The country is indebted to him for the magnificent art collection left to the Metropolitan Museum of Art. That his judgment of art was not always of the best the Venus in detriment of conjunct Pluto position seems to show; but as a very rich man he could command the opinion of experts and could afford to be wrong sometimes.

He followed the natural lines of the horoscope, doing those things for which the horoscope best fitted him, hence his natal chart is ideal for vocational study.

6. Louis Pasteur
Great Medical Research Worker

Of all the horoscopes we have selected for vocational analysis this one is the most staggering to the imagination. No fewer than 6 planets are in the third house (mentality) and in the sign Capricorn. This is 60 percent of the whole. Allowing 10 planets for twelve houses, but taking into account that Mercury and Venus stay close to Sun and frequently are found in the same house, this is still far above the normal horoscope. The author does not recall, out of hundreds of students who have passed through his classes, a single one with 6 planets either in a single sign or house. Eight of the 10 planets also are in earthy signs.

To add to the potency of the third house, if an addition were needed, Moon is in the third house sign, Gemini. Here is a native who is obviously a mental genius, with a mind equipped to tackle almost any task requiring the most intense study and concentration. A lesser character than Pasteur might not be able to stand the terrific strain of so many planets in the mind house and might have cracked, becoming some kind of a psychopathic case. Pasteur, however, could not only "take it," he could use it. The well balanced Libra Ascendant doubtless aided him. Even so, his tastes appear to have been a trifle peculiar. Thus at 16, when preparing for college in a school away from home, his health broke down and he begged to be sent home. His father was a tanner of hides, a peculiarly Saturnine occupation. Young Pasteur with so many planets in Saturn's sign, Capricorn, and itself trine nearly all of them, assured his instructors that if he could only smell the tannery once more he would soon be well. With most people the reverse would be the case.

Pasteur scrupulously, if unconsciously, followed his natural tendencies as indicated by the natal chart. His first money was earned as a teacher of mathematics (Saturn, ruler, in Taurus, money sign). Capricorn's insatiable appetite for work is well known. With almost his entire horoscope one gigantic Capricorn, Pasteur might be expected to exemplify this *in excelsis*. He did. "Throughout his entire life," reads a biographical sketch, "work was his constant inspiration." Capricorn is tremendously ambitious. No sign places a higher premium on success. It is not, therefore, surprising to find him writing to his sisters, "These three things, will, work and success, between them fill human existence." That he had plenty of will is shown by 2 planets and 2 angles in fixed signs which together with the tyrannous Capricorn, which has all the tenacity in the world of its own, gave him his full share of the first quality on his list. His favorite words, said to be the last words he uttered, were, "*Il faut travailler:* It is necessary to work." The perfect Capricorn native, in life or death.

The curious way in which the various researches which interested him and commanded his absorbed attention match up with the third house indicators may be briefly pointed out. One of his earliest researches was into the nature of a certain acid, involving examination of two types of crystals. Acids and crystals are ruled by Saturn and Saturn's sign Capricorn. Later he delved into the mysteries then surrounding diseases of beer and wine, both under the general rulership of Neptune in third house. Beer comes under Saturn, being made with grain, and partly under Moon (fermentation). Moon is in third house sign, Gemini. Wine is ruled by Venus in third house. In 1864 Pasteur announced his atmospheric germ theory (germs ruled by Moon).

The uniqueness and originality of Pasteur's discoveries are shown by Uranus, planet of originality, in the third. The ferocious energy with which he pushed his researches are amply accounted for by Mars (energy) in third. Mars is exalted in Capricorn. The fame they brought him is attributable to Sun in Capricorn in third; the money to Venus in Capricorn in third.

Earth is in sixth. His material accumulations came almost wholly from his work in connection with health and disease (sixth). However, Pasteur remained poor by choice. Mars ruling second trine Jupiter in money sign, Taurus within 4° brought him a competence and might have brought him much more had he wished. He was, however, indifferent to money. Pluto, co-ruler of second is close square Jupiter. It has been pointed out that Pluto does everything exclusively. Indifference to money certainly renders one exclusive in that sense. It is not a general trait.

Pasteur lived long (to 73) as might be expected with so many planets in the long lived Capricorn. He might have lived much longer had he not so unmercifully driven himself all the days of his life. He died peacefully (Jupiter in eighth house). He was a devout Catholic to the last. (Moon, part ruler of ninth, religion, in eighth, death). He was one of the most useful personages ever to live on this planet and all humanity owes him a debt of gratitude. He was born with a horoscope enabling him to perform the especial type of work which it was his life's mission to follow successfully. Had he known of astrology or believed in it he could have died knowing that he had utilized to the full the magnificent sidereal heritage with which he was endowed at birth.

CHAPTER XXI

HOROSCOPES OF WORLD FIGURES
(Concluded)

7. A Playwright
8. An Artist
9. An Inventor
10. A Dictator
11. A Vice-President
12. A Governor

7. George Bernard Shaw
Playwright

This whimsical genius who has added so much to the gaiety of nations was born with Gemini rising and Moon almost exactly on the ascending degree. Sun is in Leo and Mercury, the ruler, in Cancer. All three constitutions are therefore well represented.

As we might expect, Mr. Shaw has Mercury in the third house (writings). Everything he writes or has written since his youth up has found a ready market. It is not surprising therefore to find the ninth house (writings which are published) with Capricorn on the cusp and Saturn, ruler of Capricorn, in the second house (money). Saturn is sextile Pluto in the money sign, Taurus, and exact within 2°. Jupiter squares Saturn closely and Jupiter also rules published writings, but Jupiter also is close sextile Venus, money planet, and sextile Sun (5° orb). Mercury (writings) rules sign on cusp of money house, Gemini, and is sextile Uranus (5°) in the money sign, Taurus. The native is wealthy and has a pronounced money sense, as we would expect, with Saturn in the second. Saturn also rules Capricorn, Midheaven sign, and the native is equally canny in all affairs having to do with his profession Saturn is in Cancer (detriment), which perhaps steered Mr. Shaw away from business and into the writing world as otherwise he has a very good business horoscope. Four planets and two angles Cardinal give exceptional leadership ability, though the rising Gemini is not a leadership sign and Moon, also rising, is a bit uncertain on decisions. Mr. Shaw does presume to state his opinions in a very determined way as though he were the arbiter of the world's destinies. As, however, he does not have to follow them up with any particular action they are not likely to involve him in any serious difficulties, even when they turn out to be wrong—as they sometimes do.

The old gentleman is not nearly so set in his ways as he has contrived to make the world think. He has only two planets, neither of them of first importance, in fixed signs—and no fixed angles. At heart he is just feeling his way and hoping for the best like others who do not put up such an omniscient front. While undoubtedly a genius of sorts, Mr. Shaw has sold the world a bill of goods at a price possibly higher than the merchandise is really worth, as the natal chart fails to show the supernal wisdom of the ages which the native is so fond of impressing upon the world that he possesses. Sun is essentially dignified in Leo and Neptune in Pisces. Saturn, however, is in detriment in Cancer, Uranus in fall in Taurus, and Pluto in detriment in same sign. Mars is also in its detriment in Libra. The native has almost worked miracles with a horoscope which, in spite of many aids to success, did not furnish him with the equipment usually found in the natal charts of those who climb high.

Yet Mr. Shaw writes very clever, entertaining plays. He exploits fields from which more orthodox writers would shy away in horror. Who but Shaw could make so grotesque a fantasy as *Pygmalion* acceptable, not merely to the highbrow but to the lowbrow public? The story is an impossible one but the playwright by his art gives it not merely possibility but probability—and more plausibility.

The hookup of the tenth, occupation, with the ninth, published writings, is obtained by Capricorn appearing on the cusps of both houses and Saturn, ruler common to both, in the money house. The unusual style of writing, so unique that a word "Shavian" has been coined to express it, is amply accounted for by Mercury, exact trine the potent Neptune, which not only is essentially dignified but is also the highest planet in the chart.

For all his native shrewdness, Shaw is a humanitarian at heart. His twelfth house contains 3 planets, North Node and Part of Fortune. He is much more "solitary" than would appear on the surface. A filled twelfth house gives a deep sense of retrospection and this one is reinforced by Neptune in Pisces, twelfth house sign. Shaw must do a lot of pulling himself up by the roots to find out what makes him grow. Is Shaw as satisfied with Shaw as he claims to be? The generally benefic nature of the planets and aspects concerned with the twelfth indicates the answer to be yes, in the main. A couple of undersized flies in the ointment: Jupiter square Saturn and Mars, cuspal ruler, in detriment, may occasionally cause him to temper his self-satisfaction with a trifle of doubt but on the whole Shaw highly approves of Shaw.

His lengthy tale of years is attributable to Pluto, lethal ruler, sextile Saturn (2°). The latter planet bestows long life when hooked up favorably with death factors. Jupiter rules Sagittarius on cusp of eighth (death) house, and its fine trine Venus has already been commented on. This is another contributory factor. Jupiter's square Saturn is not bad, as no benefic can wreak great harm, especially when other aspects counterbalance. Gemini, however, is not an especially strong sign constitutionally and Shaw has taken excellent care of himself or, with Mars and South Node in sixth, he could hardly have contrived to go the long route of 84 years and still find himself in the excellent physical shape in which he is reported to be. He is helped by a strong Sun in a strong sign, Leo.

His astonishing success in everything to do with the theater (fifth house) is borne out by Sun virtually exact sextile Moon. This "lucky" aspect has been a great protector to the native throughout his entire career.

The "lesson" of this chart to the student is that high success and world reputation may be wrested from a horoscope far from perfect in its endowments, by a soul great enough to make use of what it finds to hand without crying over what it lacks.

Bernard Shaw probably does not believe in Astrology. So far as we know nobody has had the temerity to ask him; though, as he has publicly stated he has no belief in an after life, he would hardly regard the Science of the Stars as worthy of his consideration. But Bernard Shaw is one of millions of living proofs of the truth of astrology. He exemplifies his horoscope in every conceivable way, but has done better with it than most of the millions of his fellow beings contrive to do with theirs.

8. J. M. W. Turner
Famous English Landscape Painter

The greatest of England's landscape artists, who won the praise of that most exacting of art critics, John Ruskin, came of the humblest beginnings. He was the son of a barber and strong attachment between him and his father existed to the latter's death. As would be expected Libra, art sign, and Venus, art planet, are very powerful. Venus is essentially dignified in Taurus conjunct Jupiter (5°) trine Neptune, which gives magnificent creative imagination. The landscapes in which Turner excelled are indicated as his specialized type of work by Saturn (land) exalted in Libra (art). Capricorn, an earthy sign, is rising and 4 of 9 planets are in earthy signs. (Note: Position of Pluto is not given owing to remoteness of the birth date). Saturn is highest planet in the chart. Part of Fortune shows source of the wealth. It is placed in Libra.

The curious impressionistic nature of Turner's paintings is the source of much of their charm. A sort of haze over his landscapes, unusual in the style of painting of his day, puzzled contemporary critics who, not seeing the countryside in that way, were at a loss to understand why Turner should. Many years after his death the theory was advanced that Turner was myopic and, his short sight not being corrected by glasses, that was the manner in which scenes appeared to him. The horoscope bears out the explanation. Sun and Moon jointly rule the eyes. A close affliction between the two will often indicate deficient vision when an important planet is in one of the so-called nebulous spots, afflicted by a malefic. One of these nebulae is in 28° Taurus, termed the Pleiades.

In Turner's natal chart, his co-ruler, Venus, is in that exact degree, with Mars in Leo practically exact square Sun is also close square Moon (3°). Venus is also afflicted by conjunct Uranus (3°). The myopic theory of Turner's style of painting is therefore in all probability the correct one.

This native could never learn to speak the English language correctly in spite of the cultural contacts he was able to make by the high esteem in which his work was held. Mercury (speech) opposition Saturn (2°) demonstrates this incapacity. He lived to a great age (Capricorn rising—Saturn exalted in Libra in eighth and trine Moon within 1°) but his closing years were marred by some loss of his mental faculties. (Three planets in fourth—latter years—all afflicted by Mars; also Uranus afflicting Venus and Jupiter in fourth).

The second decan of Capricorn which the native has rising bears this description: "If not too rash and headstrong native achieves great honors and rises to wide fame."

Turner was not too rash and headstrong.

9. Thomas A. Edison
Inventor

Inventions and discoveries are ruled by Uranus and its sign, Aquarius. Neptune also takes a hand as it governs that which is secret, and inventors must tear from Nature her secrets by hard experimentation, study and thought.

Consequently we are not surprised to find that Edison has Sun, Mercury (mind planet) and Neptune all in Aquarius, and Uranus in Aries which rules the brain. The redoubtable Scorpio is rising. All 4 angles are fixed, 3 planets including Sun and Mercury are fixed. Moon is in the tenacious Capricorn together with the ruler, Mars, who is exalted there. Four planets are cardinal but only 2 common. The native had a will of iron and a capacity for work which wore his assistants down to shadows. The horoscope is in every way outstanding and the native, like other great characters of history, has capitalized on every talent with which it provided him.

Still again we find the native's occupation indicated by an indirect significator. There is no planet in the Midheaven. Leo is on cusp, ruled by Sun, but Sun is in the inventive Aquarius conjunct Neptune (5°), conjunct Mercury (3°), and all are trine Pluto in 24° Aries, the trines being very close. Pluto's exclusiveness is again in evidence. There was only one Edison. His methods and his business were utterly exclusive to himself. And Pluto is in the sixth house (service). It is, too, conjunct South Node and it is Edison's ruler (Pluto governs Scorpio rising). It probably accounts for his deafness, though usually the twelfth house and Mercury are involved in this affliction. North Node is in twelfth and Edison often termed his deafness a blessing with which he would not part, as it enabled him to concentrate without using up energy in shutting out the noises of a clamorous world.

The native never valued money, apart from the greater opportunities for service it provided. His indifference to it is shown by the two benefics square one another exact (Venus square Jupiter). Mars, which in good aspect in the second and unafflicted gives enormous earning power, is sextile Venus (6°), sextile Saturn (2°), sextile Neptune (3°), sextile Sun (8°), trine Pluto (7°), sextile Ascendant (4°). There are no afflictions. After that nothing any other planet could do was of the least consequence in preventing Edison from becoming a millionaire—and never giving it a second thought.

Edison had advanced and very unorthodox religious ideas,

bordering on the occult (North Node in occult twelfth house). His Part of Fortune is in the sixth sign, which in its larger sense rules service to the race, and in the eleventh house—hopes, wishes and ambitions. What he made materially from his work was all he ever could have hoped for, but his real reward was in the transcendent service he was able to render his fellow-men.

10. Nikita Khrushchev
Dictator

One of the most outstanding features of the Russian premier's natal chart is the impressive group of airy (mental) signs. Khrushchev is a deep thinker, a clever planner and an ingenious maneuverer. He is seldom or never caught napping and can out-think and out-guess most of his opponents. His mind planet, Mercury, is the most elevated in the horoscope. It is in the tenth house and Khrushchev's major occupation is and has been since his peasant day—*thinking*.

The benefic Leo conjoins his Midheaven, which is ruled by an unafflicted Mars with a close trine to Saturn and a sextile to Mercury. The fierce nature of the personality is shown by a virtually exact conjunction of Mars and Moon, both in the lethal eighth house. The man has risen to power over the dead bodies of his enemies. He himself has so far borne a charmed life, with both Moon and Mars among the best indicators in the chart.

But Uranus governs Aquarius on the cusp of the eighth. It opposes Sun and squares Ascendant. While subordinate to the planet and luminary actually in the house, it must one day have its inning. It is to be doubted if Uranus, in spite of its violent reputation when afflicted, will take precedence over the two highly favorable significators in the house itself. Also Uranus is in Scorpio, its exaltation sign, which tend to mitigate its adverse side.

The native's commanding position in the world is shown by Sun in the tenth but it will be noted that Sun has two afflictions and no good influences and this eminence can hardly be considered as for the world's good. The eleventh house—hopes, wishes and ambitions—contains three planets with favorable aspects aggregating six and unfavorable four. But added to the favorable showing is Mercury ruling the intercepted Gemini—three to one favorable—bringing the total to nine favoring and five adverse.

This does not tell the whole story, however. The tenth house cuspal sign is Taurus, and its ruler Venus is exalted and with no aspects of any kind, good or bad. This leaves Venus entirely free to express its own benefic nature and gives to the eleventh house an overwhelming preponderance of good—for Khrushchev, if not for anyone else. Add to all this the helpful influence of Mars and Moon in Aquarius, normal eleventh house sign, and in spite of the bad Uranus, the Aquarian ruler, the house is so enormously favorable that it completely accounts for the fantastic heights to which this native has risen. He could hardly have held ambitions at any time in his life for place and power higher than he has achieved.

It is rather rare that a ruling planet is exalted and with no aspects at all, and Venus must be credited (or should it be debited?) with aiding Khrushchev's climb from obscurity to mightiness. He is having his troubles, of course, but with twenty-one good aspects to thirteen bad ones (60%-40%) and with Saturn trine Moon and trine Mars, with Midheaven sextile Neptune sextile Pluto conjunct Leo, he is not likely to be unseated for a long time, if ever.

His remarkably good Venus in the ninth house (dealings with other nations) seems to show that he really is anxious to keep the peace, which Venus governs, in spite of his tough Martian talk. The possibility that he will be ousted eventually does not seem to be great. His fourth house (latter years of life) contains an exalted Saturn and is ruled by Venus (Libra on the cusp). The one possibility is the afflicted Uranus, but this planet, also exalted, does not seem strong enough to overturn the favoring indicators.

If he does fall at last it is likely to be through bad judgment in old age—Saturn opposition Mercury—but it does not seem that the world should bank on it. And his successor may not have an exalted, unaspected Venus in the ninth house.

11. Lyndon B. Johnson
Vice President of The United States

The tremendous drive and magnetic personality of this statesmanly figure is amply demonstrated by the striking aggregation of planets and luminaries in his first house.

With the ruling Leo on the Ascendant, the Sun is in conjunction with the rising degree and Sun, of course, governs Leo. Even in closer conjunction is the vigorous Mars, while Mercury, the co-ruler and mind planet, is also in the first (personality) house almost exact conjunct Moon. This last position denotes a very fine, clear mind, fully supported by the totally unafflicted Mercury with five good configurations.

The remarkable rise of this rugged individualist is astrologically accounted for by the almost perfect distribution of the planets by constitution—four cardinal, five fixed (including the angles), five common (including Sun and Moon). Leadership, determination, diplomacy, all are present in good measure. His life history shows that he has made utmost use of these talents. None has been buried in the earth.

Analysis of the elements, as is usually the case where the constitutions are well balanced shows a more uneven distribution. Fiery signs governing the intuitions and the religious sense are adequate, watery signs (emotion and feeling) measurably so but, surprisingly, the airy group, representing the mentality, are scant, only Pluto and the Descendant appearing in this division. Anyone who sells Lyndon Johnson's mentality short on that account, however, will be making a serious mistake. His magnificent Mercury and a beautifully aspected Pluto in Mercury's sign Gemini, and the most elevated planet in the chart, plainly demonstrates the high grade quality of the mind.

What is indicated by the lack of planets in the airy division is the wide diversification of the mental interests that many airy planets confer. Mr. Johnson is interested mentally in comparatively few things but his exceptional Mercury and five fixed signs demonstrate how one-pointedly he can concentrate on these interests. Politics have all along been his first love. He comes of a politically minded family and his early ambition was some day to be a United States Senator, a distinction he achieved at 40.

The tenth house is the house of Government, and Pluto, well aspected, the thing one can do better than most other people. Its position in this house speaks as clearly as if stated in language, of the achievements in this field of Lyndon Johnson.

The many planets in Virgo, the health sign, and its position in the first house (the body) have taken their toll. An appendicitis operation manifested the adverse influence of the Mars-Ascendant conjunction. The 1955 heart attack the very lose conjunct of Mars with Sun, ruling the heart. The Ascendant also governs this organ.

Johnson's horoscope shows 34 good aspects to 16 adverse—a ratio on the favoring side of more than two to one. From State Administrator for Texas of the National Youth Administration at 27, to

Congressman at 28, to re-election at 32, to Naval Lieutenant Commander at 33, to U. S. Senator at 40 and Minority Leader at 44. Finally—or is it finally?—Vice President at 52. Twenty-five years to reach the top—almost.

Will the "almost" be transcended? A meteoric career such as this certainly indicates the high favor of the astrological "gods," but Lyndon Johnson assuredly cooperated with his fine horoscope to the last possible influence. For the ultimate achievement, the Presidency, the ruler Mercury or Sun up in the Midheaven would almost set the seal of certainty on such a possibility and without such assistance it seems hazardous to indulge in fiat forecasts. Saturn is badly afflicted and in fall and may forbid the highest office.

But with Pluto up there and so well aspected together with the powerful personality of the native himself, if he can stand the continuous strain of office without his health giving way, there might be a remote chance Pluto, slowest moving planet in the Solar System and therefore of great power, may outwit Saturn.

Johnson's grandfather announced to his neighbors the birth of the future Vice-President with the words, "A United States Senator was born this morning—my grandson." The old gentleman fell short in his prophecy. A United States Vice-President was born that morning—a President ... perhaps!

12. Nelson Rockefeller
Governor of New York

A very acute summing up of the character of this distinguished political leader is in a biography which declares "Nelson Rockefeller is not a humble man." With Sun, five planets and all four angles in cardinal signs and only one in a common sign, his horoscope certainly says amen to that. The rather overdone term, "Born Leader" certainly fits him. In spite of the great things he has achieved, aided astrologically by seven of his ten planets up in the Midheaven or close to it, the cardinal group is definitely too full. The Libra Ascendant should be helpful in what might otherwise be a somewhat arrogant personality.

Fixed signs contain Moon and two planets, sufficient backing for the formidable cardinal division.

But the outstanding phenomenon of the chart to an informed astrologer must be the impressive ninth house. Rockefeller is known to be a deeply religious man; the breadth of his thinking, his munificent charities and his long range vision are here set forth in striking array. His role in organizing the United Nations was not a small one and his interest in developing the poorer areas of Latin America is well known. The ninth house, governing foreign affairs has bulked large in Nelson Rockefeller's life.

Yet in spite of a success that has been phenomenal his horoscope in some respects is a difficult one. He is said by those who know him to be a complex character and with Sun, Jupiter, Uranus and Neptune all closely aspecting the Ascendant, this cannot be doubted.

His great inherited wealth is indicated by Taurus on the cusp of the eighth house, ruled by Venus trine Moon and conjunct Sun; also by Jupiter trine Saturn. His ascent in the political world by Jupiter in the tenth. It is astrologically recognized that Sun conjunct Midheaven, if reasonably well aspected tends to raise the native to high positions. In this chart not only Sun but the ruler Venus is almost as elevated.

Interestingly enough Pluto is entirely without aspects and rules his second (money) house. Pluto is normally considered to be a malefic and there is no doubt that it rules death and general upsets. It is named (correctly) after ancient Pluto, god of the nether regions. Another god Pluto was, however, the deity that conferred immense wealth, hence our term "plutocracy." In very good aspect he is said to bestow more abundant riches than even Jupiter but there is the condition that the native must be far ahead of average in intellect and vision. It would seem that Nelson Rockefeller would qualify.

Does the natal chart show presidential possibilities? Yes, undoubtedly, but that does not mean a certainty. In a contest the influences natal and progressed of each contestant have everything to do with the outcome. This was well illustrated in the National Presidential Election of 1960. Nixon's natal horoscope was slightly better than Kennedy's but the latter's progressed aspects were considerably better than Nixon's. To complicate the matter further, on the day of election Kennedy's aspects were terrible but Nixon's fairly good.

After three evenings of close study and the weighing of these decidedly conflicting influences the present author gave a close decision to Kennedy, based on his better progressions. Interviewed by the Press he stated that in his opinion Kennedy would "squeak through by the narrowest popular margin ever given a National

President." The newspapers carried this, several days before the election and it proved to be so accurate that this again was carried as news.

Therefore unless and until Nelson Rockefeller decides to stand for President and until his opponent's birth time and progressions on election day are known, it would be hazardous to forecast that this ultimate prize would come to him.

But his horoscope, if it does not say yea, does not say nay.

CHAPTER XXII

AND FINALLY—

It will be evident to those who have studied this book that Vocational Astrology is no kindergarten subject to be picked up in a day. Simple in fundamentals, its ramifications are almost endless. Allowing wide latitude of choice, it nevertheless sternly bars certain vocations as obviously unfitted to a native; shakes its head doubtfully at others; bestows an indifferent glance on still another set, but beams all over in ecstatic approval when the right choices are finally reached.

These choices may be several. Even in the natal charts of the most successful there are usually indicators which if followed might have taken them to the top *via* an altogether different ladder than that which they actually elected to climb. There is, in fact, a school of thought (non-astrological) which holds that a really successful person in any line, no matter how specialized, could have been equally successful in anything else he had set his mind to. They except of course such vocations as call for special physical development. Astrologers are not likely to agree with them. If all the energy wasted in trying to teach music to children without a spark of musical talent had been used to analyze their horoscopes and arrive at what they were best fitted for, both the children and the neighbors would have benefited immeasurably.

Yet it would be a false conclusion to state that Edison *had* to be an inventor, Shaw a playwright, Turner a painter or Hitler a dictator. There were other things these natives might have done and done well, still reaching heights of fame and affluence far above the crowd. True astrology will not hearken for a moment to the claptrap which so circumscribes the fate that a man is born to be and do this, that or the other and nothing besides. Perhaps the very greatest figures who so influence the destiny of the world that had they not been born all events would have been changed, do have their ordained work mapped out for them. But where shall we draw the line? If Edison had not lived these words might be penned by the light of an oil lamp instead of by electric light. Or they might not—perhaps someone else would have found a suitable filament by now.

On the other hand, the world might not have been so very different a place had George Bernard Shaw not honored it with his presence. It probably would be a much more comfortable place had Mr. Hitler succeeded in getting the art education he wanted and left political agitation alone.

Who shall say? These speculations take us into the realm of advanced metaphysics and really have no place in this work except as a partial answer to the fallacy, "I'm bound to be what the horoscope says I shall be." We earnestly hope no student will approach the subject from that hopeless angle, otherwise this book has been written in vain. We *must* act on the theory that we have freewill, and this implies freedom of choice of a vocation. The ineffectual leaning back and waiting for fate to do something for one, so characteristic of an excess of common signs, has ruined many promising careers. Some modern Hogarth might well limn the wretched down-and-outers parading up and down the "Market Streets" of any large city and give this picture the title, "They Waited for Something to Happen." Something always does happen, of course, to those who wait long enough. Everyone has an eighth house.

The student is urged to take the vocational indicators in the horoscope seriously and it is believed that he will never find them to let him down. A vast specialized field exists for vocational guidance by astrology, and a field of the greatest helpfulness. It is not too early for parents to have a child's horoscope examined by an expert in this work immediately after birth—at least before he starts to school—so that his training may proceed along lines exactly in harmony with what the horoscope shows as his natural vocational bent.

There are no "hopeless" horoscopes. Even in the natal charts of those who are pointed to as overtowering successes in their particular professions, there are often afflicted malefics, weak benefics, squares, oppositions and detriments. Always there is South Node somewhere, to put his blight on whatever he touches. Yet elsewhere in the world are those with charts approximately the same who have made only mediocre successes where their astrological counterparts are up in the top brackets. And there is no one, however exalted, who could not in some way have done better, had he been guided by the indicators of his natal chart.

It is unfortunate that one has to point to a character like Hitler for evidence of the truth of this assertion. He is, however, the one outstanding world figure known to use astrology in every important decision he makes. The general staffs of Britain and our own country are copying and trying to improve upon Hitler's own novel military methods. There is, therefore, nothing out-of-the-way in suggesting that his astrological methods might be followed by all with equally effective results. The rain of heaven falls alike upon both just and unjust, as do the influences of the heavens. Why permit only the unjust to apply them and secure the benefit of knowing how they work?

The true student of Astrology is always a student. He may obtain his "instructor's rating," may set up in professional practice and even have his astrological conclusions reported by the Associated Press. Regardless of this, he continues to learn while he teaches. No day goes by that he does not add something to his store of astrological knowledge. Everyone he meets is an experimental subject. He notes here a Leo trait, there a quirk of Sagittarius, a touch of typical Aries dominance, the quiet humor of a Libra or the wisecrack of a Gemini. He may have no idea of the date or time of birth of any of them, but by their ways he knows them. Life is never dull for the astrologer so long as he has people to watch. And if there is none around he can go back to his own self-examination, which perhaps teaches him even more.

One day, at long last, the ancient and honorable science of Astrology shall be restored once more to the position of dignity and respect it occupied in the remote past. Emperors and Kings, Statesmen and Popes were glad to make it their study and to encourage its exponents. Then came the charlatans who turned it into a racket, and it fell in the social and intellectual scale until, a couple of generations ago, none was so poor to do it reverence. The efforts of such great astrologers as Leo, Sepharial and others who devoted their lives to study and research gradually started to tile the balance in the other direction, until, today, there is a recrudescence of interest among the educated very heartening to those who love and believe in the science and work for its restoration to intellectual favor.

Meantime the public continues to buy the astrological lucubrations to be found in the Ten Cent Stores, and to deposit pennies in weighing machines for a card giving not only the weight but the horoscope. Perhaps this kind of astrology will always be with us, but it adds immeasurably to the task of those who labor for a restored science of the stars to have to overcome the prejudices roused in the thinking by these popular fallacies.

In the final analysis, only by his own hard study and experiment, constant watching of results, and associating them with their appropriate natal influences, can the student arrive at the absolute certainty of the truth of Astrology which never again can be shaken. That is indeed a happy outcome for it furnishes him with a sure guide for the remainder of his life which will, if he follows it sincerely, never fail him. Whether he will acquire this certainty to the full depends largely upon what kind of fourth house he possesses—the house of "outcomes."

Here's hoping he has a good one.

MEANING OF THE SYMBOLS USED

SIGNS

Aries	♈
Taurus	♉
Gemini	♊
Cancer	♋
Leo	♌
Virgo	♍
Libra	♎
Scorpio	♏
Sagittarius	♐
Capricorn	♑
Aquarius	♒
Pisces	♓

PLANETS

Sun	☉
Moon	☽
Mercury	☿
Venus	♀
Mars	♂
Jupiter	♃
Saturn	♄
Uranus	♅
Neptune	♆
Pluto	♇

OTHER SYMBOLS

Dragon's Head (Moon's North Node)	☊
Dragon's Tail (Moon's South Node)	☋
Part of Fortune	⊕
Midheaven	M.C. or MC

ASPECTS

Sextile (60°)	Favorable	∗
Trine (120°) V	Very Favorable	△
Square (90°)	Unfavorable	□
Opposition (180°)	Very Unfavorable	☍

POSITIONS

Conjunction (0°)	☌
Parallel (0° of declination)	P

APPENDIX B

SOME EXPLANATIONS

(1) Throughout this work, as in most astrological books and delineations, Sun and Moon are referred to as planets, which of course they are not. The correct term for either of these bodies is "luminary" or "light."

It is inconvenient and cumbersome, however, when considering Sun and Moon together with the planets to keep differentiating them by use of the above terminology. The practice has therefore developed of including Sun and Moon under the generic term "planets" together with the rest.

(2) Conjunctions and Parallels are not "Aspects" but "Positions." They are loosely referred to sometimes as aspects for the same reason that Sun and Moon are often referred to as "planets."

(3) Figures in parentheses occurring after the listing of an aspect or position indicate how far from exact such aspect or position is.

Thus Sun trine Moon (5°) or (5) shows that this trine is within 5° of exactness. "Within orb" of 5° is the technical term.*

---

* *The Unit System of Judging Planetary Influences*, by Charles E. Luntz (Philadelphia: David McKay Publishing Co.), is a standard reference work dealing with the strength of the various aspects, positions, exaltations, etc.

APPENDIX C

PLANETARY INDEX OF OCCUPATIONS

A

Accessory Makers, Toilet ♀
Accountants ☿
Acoustic Experts ☿
Actors ♀
Actuaries ☿
Advertising Agents ♃
Ad-Writers ♃
Airplane Mechanics ♅
Aldermen ♃
Amusement
  Concessionaires ♀
Anaesthetists ♆
Appraisers ♃
Architects ☿

Armament Makers and
  Workers ♂
Army Officers ♂
Artists ♀
Art Museum Curators ♀
Assayers ♂
Astrologers ♅, ♆
Authors ☿
Automobile Manufacturers
  and Dealers ♅
Automobile Mechanics ♅
Automobile Racers ♅
Aviators ♅

B

Bakers ☽
Bankers ☉
Bank Tellers ☉
Barbers ♂
Bath House Proprietors ☽
Beach Life Guards ♆
Beauty Parlor Operators ♀
Bee Keepers ☿, ♀
Boat Owners ☽
Bond Salesmen ♃

Bookbinders ☿
Bookkeepers ☿
Boxers ♂
Brewers ☽
Brewery Workers ☽
Bricklayers ♄
Builders ♄
Bus Drivers ☿
Butchers ♂
Buyers ☿

C

Cabbage and Cauliflower
  Growers ☽
Capitalists ♀, ♃
Carpenters ♂

Candy Manufacturers ♀
Cap and Hat Makers ♂, ♀
Chiropractors ♅
Clairvoyants ♅, ♆

Cashiers ♀, ♃
Cemetery Associations ♇
Cemetery Lot Salesmen ♄
Cheese Manufacturers ☽
Chemists ♅
Chicken Fanciers ☽
Chinaware and Glassware
  Manufacturers ☽
Chiropodists ♃

Dairies ☽
Dairy Farmers ☽
Death ♇
Dentists ♂
Department Heads ☉
Detectives ♅
Dictators ♇
Dietitians ☿
Diplomats ☿
Directors, Entertainment ☉

Editors ☿, ♃
Efficiency Experts ♄
Electrical Appliance Manu-
  facturers and Dealers ♅
Electricians ♅
Embalmers ♇
Engineers ♅

Farmers ♄
Farm Hands ♄
File Clerks ☿
Filling Station Owners ♅
Financiers ♃
Firemen ♂

Clergymen ♃
Clerks ☿
Clock and Watch Makers ♄
Coal and Ice Dealers ♄
Conductors, Street-car ☿
Confectioners ♀
Contractor ♄
Correspondents ☿
Cosmeticians ♀

D

Directors, ☉
Distillers ♅
Doctors ☿
Doctors (of Divinity) ♃
Doctors (of Law) ♃
Doctors (of Literature) ♃
Doctors (of Philosophy) ♃
Dressmakers ♀
Dry Goods Stores ♀

E

Engravers ♀
Entertainers ♀
Entertainment Directors ☉
Errand Boy ☿
Excavators ♄
Exclusive, The ♇
Executives ♂

F

Fishermen ☽
Fish Market Proprietors ♅
Florists ♀
Foremen ☉
Furniture Manufacturers and
  Dealers ♀

Garage Proprietors ♅
Gardeners ♄
Gin Manufacturers ☉
Glassware and Chinaware
  Manufacturers ☽
Gold, Workers in ☉
Governesses ☿

G

Grain Dealers ♄
Grocers, Retail ☿
Grocers, Wholesale ♃
Guards ♂
Guides ♃
Gun Makers ♂

Hairdressers ♂, ♀
Handwriting Experts ☿
Hardware Manufacturers
  and Dealers ♂
Hat and Cap Makers ♂, ♀
Healers ☿
Healers, Faith ♅

H

Heart Specialists ☉
Hides, Dealers in ♄
Horse Trainers ♃
Hotel Keepers and Workers ♀
Household Help (Female) ☽
House Painters and
  Paperhangers ♀

Illustrators ♀
Implement Makers ♂
Impresarios ☉
Information Clerks ☿
Instructors ☿
Instrument Manufacturers
  and Dealers ♅

I

Interior Decorators ♀
Interpreters ☿
Inventors ♅
Investment Bankers ☉
Iron and Steel Workers ♂

Jewelers ☉
Jockeys ♃

J

Judges ♃
Jugglers ☿

Laborers ♄
Landscape Gardeners ♀
Lawyers ♃
Leather Goods Manufactur-
  ers and Dealers ♄
Lecturers ☿, ♅
Life Insurance Salesmen ♇

L

Laundry Proprietors and
  Workers ☽
Lighting Specialists ♅
Liquor Dealers ☽
Locksmith ♂
Lumberjacks ♂

M

Machinists ♂

Maids ♀

Mail Carriers ☿

Mechanics ♂

Medical Men ☿

Melon Growers ☽

Merchandise Managers ☿

Messengers ☿

Metal Workers ♂

Metaphysicians ♅

Midwives ☽

Milkmen ☽

Milliners ♀

Mind Readers ♆

Miners ♄

Money Lenders ♀

Monks ♄

Motormen ♅

Movie Theater Owners ♅

Moving Picture Producers ♅

Mushroom ☽

Musicians ♀, ♆

N

Naval Officers ♆

Nerve Specialists ☿, ♅

Night Watchmen ♄

Night Workers ♄

Notaries Public ☿

Nuns ♄

Nurses ☽

O

Obstetricians ☽

Occultists ♅

Occult Writers ♆

Office Help ☿

Oil Well Operators ♆

Oil Workers ♆

Orange Growers ☉

Orators ☿

P

Painters, House ♀

Paperhangers ♀

Paper Manufacturers ☿

Park Keepers ☉

Peach Growers ♀

Playground Directors ☉

Plumbers ♄

Poets ♆

Policemen ♂

Politicians ☉

Poultry Raisers ☽

Priests ♄

Printers ☿

Perfume Manufacturers ♀

Pharmacists ♆

Photographers ♀

Physicians ☿

Plastic Artists ☽

Prison Guards ♆, ♂

Private Investigators ♆

Psychotherapists ♅

Publications, Writers for ♃

Publishers ☿, ♃

Pugilists ♂

Pursers ♀

R

Racing Stable Owners and Workers ♃
Radio Announcers ☿, ♅
Radio Manufacturers and Dealers ♅
Real Estate, Dealers in ♄

Recorders of Deeds ☿
Reporters ☿
Research Workers ♅
Restaurant Proprietors and Workers ☽
Retail Grocers ☿

S

Sailors ☽
Salesmen ☿
Scientists ♅
Secretaries ☿
Sextons ♄
Shoe Manufacturers and Dealers ♃
Shoe Workers ♃
Singers ♀
Social Secretaries ♀
Social Service Workers ♅
Society Editors ♀
Soldiers ♂

Speakers ☿
Sporting Goods Manufacturers and Dealers ♃
Spotlight Operators ☉
Stationers ☿
Stenographers ☿
Stock Exchange Workers ☉
Stock Raisers ♂
Stock Speculators ☉
Storekeepers ☿
Street-car Conductors ☿
Surgeons ♂

T

Tailors ♀
Tanners ♄
Tavern and Taproom Owners and Helpers ☽
Theater Owners and Managers ☉
Throat Specialists ♀
Time Keepers ♄
Tombstone Makers ♄

Teachers ☿
Telegraphers ♅
Telephone Operators ☿, ♅
Tellers ♀
Train Conductors ☿
Traveling Men ☽
Treasurers ♀
Trial Lawyers ♃
Typists ☿

U

Underground Workers ♄

Undertakers ♄, ♇

V

Vocational Specialists ♄

W

Waiters and Waitresses ☽
Walnut Growers ☉
Wardens ♆
Watchmen ☽
Whale Hunters ♃
Wholesale Grocers ♃

Women's Apparel Manufacturers and Dealers ♀
Woolen Merchants ♃
Wrestlers ♂
Writers ☿

X

X-Ray Workers ♅

APPENDIX D

PLUTO
(With some notes on Neptune and Uranus)

A great deal has been learned about the vocational influence of this Planet during the past twenty years. Reasoning by analogy and then observing how closely the facts conformed to the reasoning has led to the conclusions expressed in this chapter.

Thus it was established soon after Pluto was discovered that it undoubtedly governed physical death, that it did, in fact, take precedence over Mars, which had never been regarded as quite answering the question of planetary death rulership. It was also quickly recognized that Pluto ruled modern dictators, totalitarian governments, all-out war (not small wars or the individual combats world wars include, which are in the domain of Mars). Other unhappy products of the present age—organized crime, gangsterism, even the wholesale juvenile delinquency that has flourished since 1930 when Pluto's existence was first verified—trace to this planet's influence.

It is well known that the discovery of a "new" planet (new to the world but not to the universe) marks a decided quickening of everything the planet influences. Uranus, discovered in 1781, definitely marked the beginning of the industrial age. It was in 1781 that James Watt obtained his patent covering a device for driving machinery by steam power. There had been crude mechanical contrivances prior to that but the birth from this tiny but important beginning of modern industry took place in the year Uranus appeared on the scene. Reference to the occupations listed under Uranus in Chapter III will show that almost all of them were unknown prior to the planet's discovery.

Even the esoteric rulerships of Uranus have brought modernization in these fields. Thus Astrologers, Occultists, Faith Healers and Clairvoyants come in part under the dominance of Uranus and in part under Neptune. Certainly these occupations have been with the race since earliest times, but they have been pursued scientifically and with the research system of modern technique only since Uranus revealed himself. Discovery of Neptune sixty-five years later enhanced these precise methods still further.

In 1846 August Leverrier announced the discovery of Neptune which rules oil as applied to industrial use. (Oil for lighting is governed by Moon). Eleven years later the first oil wells were sunk in Rumania and two years after that in the United States. Interestingly enough it was irregularity in the motion of Uranus that led to the discovery of Neptune, almost as though the former was trying to give a clue to the fact that the latter existed. While this may only be a poetic fancy, it is an astrological fact that the two planets are co-rulers of a number of the same things and seem to have influences largely in common with each other.

The facts regarding Uranus and Neptune are cited as supporting analogous facts respecting Pluto. Analogies are useful in constructing theories, but theory is not fact, and facts must never be distorted to make them conform to theories that have been built around them. But if, as is now known, Pluto rules death and the monstrous things recorded above when in adverse aspect or without aspects, then the favorable things he governs must bear some relationship in an opposite way to the unfavorable. This is always the case with the Sun, Moon and planets. Their bad side invariably is contrastingly opposite to their good side.

To demonstrate this by a few examples: Sun well aspected indicates dignity; badly aspected, boastfulness. Jupiter alone or in favorable aspect, abundance of good; unfavorable, abundance of trouble. Saturn well influenced, thrift; alone or badly influenced, miserliness. Uranus with good configurations, originality; alone or badly configurated, eccentricity.

The rulerships of Pluto alone or badly aspected can be summed up in two words. THE EXCLUSIVE. Death is certainly the most exclusive thing that can happen to an individual and it can occur only once in a lifetime. A dictator has to be exclusive. There can be only one of him or he is no longer sole dictator. Organized crime usually traces to one "big shot" who dominates the organization. Juvenile delinquency, of the vicious kind almost unknown in former years, seems to be an exclusive product of the present generation.

So if Pluto afflicted or by its own malefic self rules the harmful exclusive, surely Pluto well favored by the aspects must govern the helpful exclusive. Observation ranging over a period of 30 years, shows that it does. This was suspected even 20 years ago when the first edition of this book appeared. The statement made then in listing occupational rulership was this:

"It is hazardous at present to use Pluto as a significator of occupation." That statement has been allowed to stand in the present edition, but with a supplementary footnote.

Even then the listing gave as one of Pluto's rulerships, "The Entirely Exclusive." It can now be enlarged to read, "Things one can do better than most others in his circle." This gives us an important new vocational element for exploration. The traditional rules as set forth in this book will certainly not be affected but a new factor is introduced to augment them. This can only be employed, however, if Pluto has more and stronger good aspects than adverse, and if it is in some way connected beneficently with the Midheaven, tenth house, Capricorn, Saturn or one of the vocational indicators. Otherwise it is of no occupational value.

What this means in practice (assuming it can be used) is that the native has some exceptional talent in a certain direction that should be utilized in the occupation, whatever it is. The function of a helpful Pluto is to pinpoint a particular adroitness that considerably exceeds the prevailing average and that can bring the native into special prominence by his unusual ability in this direction.

The special faculty need not be original—that is the function of Uranus. It may be some ability that has been known since the dawn of time. It is exclusive not as against all the world (although that occasionally happens as in the case of Edison and Ford) but as contrasted with the abilities of others in the limited circle of the native's associates or of the professional or industrial group which he is affiliated.

The nature of the special skill may be determined by the following house positions of Pluto:

1st	All-around efficiency,
2nd	Exceptional money sense.
3rd	Unusual skill in expression of ideas.
4th	Very shrewd real estate appraisal ability.
5th	Investment sagacity.
6th	Keen judge of human nature.
7th	Diplomatic skill.
8th	(Pluto's own house) Able executor.
9th	Impressive farsightedness.
10th	Unique business or professional talent.
11th	Remarkable capacity for making friends.
12th	Unwonted breadth of outlook.

All of these special and unique powers are *adaptable* to the occupation but do not *indicate* the occupation. They are usable whatever this may be and if Pluto is good enough to rely on in these respects, great thought should be given as to how they best may be applied.

It should first be ascertained, however, that Pluto has sufficient strength on the favorable side to make its help possible. Reliance on an adverse or indifferent Pluto can only bring disappointment, In such a case forget him (or her, as Pluto is a feminine planet) and trust to your really good planets aided by your own constructive thought and intelligent action to bring you such success as your horoscope shows is possible for you.

Which is usually far greater than those astrologically uninformed would regard as attainable.

STAY IN TOUCH

On the following pages you will find listed, with their current prices, some of the books and tapes now available on related subjects. Your book dealer stocks most of these, and will stock new titles in the Llewellyn series as they become available. We urge your patronage.However, to obtain our full catalog, to keep informed of new titles as they are released and to benefit from informative articles and helpful news, you are invited to write for our bi-monthly news magazine/catalog. A sample copy is free, and it will continue coming to you at no cost as long as you are an active mail customer. Or you may keep it coming for a full year with a donation of just $5.00 in U.S.A. and Canada ($20.00 overseas, first class mail). Many bookstores also have *The Llewellyn New Times* available to their customers. Ask for it.

Stay in touch! In *The Llewellyn New Times'* pages you will find news and reviews of new books, tapes and services, announcements of meetings and seminars, articles helpful to our readers, news of authors, advertising of products and services, special money-making opportunities, and much more.

The Llewellyn New Times
P.O. Box 64383-Dept. 387, St. Paul, MN 55164-0383, U.S.A.

• • •

TO ORDER BOOKS AND TAPES

If your book dealer does not have the books and tapes described on the following pages readily available, you may order them directly from the publisher by sending full price in U.S. funds, plus $1.50 for postage and handling for orders *under* $10.00; $3.00 for orders *over* $10.00. There are no postage and handling charges for orders over $50.00. UPS Delivery: We ship UPS whenever possible. Delivery guaranteed. Provide your street address as UPS does not deliver to P.O. Boxes. UPS to Canada requires a $50.00 minimum order. Allow 4-6 weeks for delivery. Orders outside the U.S.A. and Canada: Airmail—add retail price of book; add $5.00 for each non-book item (tapes, etc.); add $1.00 per item for surface mail.

FOR GROUP STUDY AND PURCHASE

Because there is a great deal of interest in group discussion and study of the subject matter of this book, we feel that we should encourage the adoption and use of this particular book by such groups by offering a special "quantity" price to group leaders or "agents."

Our Special Quantity Price for a minimum order of five copies of *How to Use Vocational Astrology for Success in the Workplace* is $44.85 cash-with-order. This price includes postage and handling within the United States. Minnesota residents must add 6.5% sales tax. For additional quantities, please order in multiples of five. For Canadian and foreign orders, add postage and handling charges as above. Credit card (VISA, Master Card, American Express) orders are accepted. Charge card orders only may be phoned free ($15.00 minimum order) within the U.S.A. or Canada by dialing 1-800-THE-MOON. Customer service calls dial 1-612-291-1970. Mail Orders to:

LLEWELLYN PUBLICATIONS
P.O. Box 64383-Dept. 387 / St. Paul, MN 55164-0383, U.S.A.

Prices subject to change without notice.

SPIRITUAL, METAPHYSICAL & NEW TRENDS IN MODERN ASTROLOGY
edited by Joan McEvers

This is the first book in the Llewellyn New World Astrology Series. Edited by well-known astrologer, lecturer and writer Joan McEvers, this book pulls together the latest thoughts by the best astrologers in the field of Spiritual Astrology.

She has put together an outstanding group of informative and exciting topics.

- Gray Keen: Perspective: The Ethereal Conclusion
- Marion D. March: Some Insights into Esoteric Astrology
- Kimberly McSherry: The Feminine Element of Astrology: Reframing the Darkness
- Kathleen Burt: The Spiritual Rulers and Their Practical Role in the Transformation
- Shirley Lyons Meier: The Secrets behind Carl Payne Tobey's Secondary Chart
- Jeff Jawer: Astrodrama
- Donna Van Toen: Alice Bailey Revisited
- Philip Sedgwick: Galactic Studies
- Myrna Lofthus: The Spiritual Programming within a Natal Chart
- Angel Thompson: Transformational Astrology

0-87542-380-9, 288 pgs., 5-1/4 x 8, softcover $9.95

PLANETS: THE ASTROLOGICAL TOOLS
edited by Joan McEvers

This is the second in the astrological anthology series edited by respected astrologer Joan McEvers, who provides a brief factual overview of the planets.

Then take off through the solar system with 10 professional astrologers as they bring their insights to the symbolism and influences of the planets.

- Toni Glover Sedgwick: The Sun as the life force and our ego
- Joanne Wickenburg: The Moon as our emotional signal to change
- Erin Sullivan-Seale: Mercury as the multi-faceted god, followed with an in-depth explanation of its retrogradation
- Robert Glasscock: Venus as your inner value system and relationships
- Johanna Mitchell: Mars as your cooperative, energizing inner warrior
- Don Borkowski: Jupiter as expansion and preservation
- Gina Ceaglio: Saturn as a source of freedom through self-discipline
- Bil Tierney: Uranus as the original, growth-producing planet
- Karma Welch: Neptune as selfless giving and compassionate love
- Joan Negus: Pluto as a powerful personal force

0-87542-381-7, 380 pgs., 5-1/4 x 8, illus., softcover $12.95

Prices subject to change without notice.

FINANCIAL ASTROLOGY
edited by Joan McEvers
Favorably reviewed in the *Wall Street Journal* by financial expert Stanley W. Angrist! This third book in Llewellyn's anthology series edited by well-known astrologer Joan McEvers explores the relatively new field of financial astrology. Nine respected astrologers share their wisdom and good fortune with you.

Learn about the various types of analysis and how astrology fine-tunes these methods. Covered cycles include the Lunar Cycle, the Mars/Vesta Cycle, the 4 1/2-year Martian Cycle, the 500-year Civilization Cycle used by Nostradamus, the Kondratieff Wave and the Elliott Wave. Included topics are:
- Michael Munkasey: A Primer on Market Forecasting
- Pat Esclavon Hardy: Charting the U.S. and the NYSE
- Jeanne Long: New Concepts for Commodities Trading Combining Astrology & Technical Analysis
- Georgia Stathis: The Real Estate Process
- Mary B. Downing: An Investor's Guide to Financial Astrology
- Judy Johns: The Gann Technique
- Carol S. Mull: Predicting the Dow
- Bill Meridian: The Effect of Planetary Stations on U.S. Stock Prices
- Georgia Stathis: Delineating the Corporation
- Robert Cole: The Predictable Economy

0-87542-382-5, 368 pgs., 5-1/4 x 8, illus., softcover   **$14.95**

THE HOUSES: POWER PLACES OF THE HOROSCOPE
edited by Joan McEvers
This volume combines the talents of 11 renowned astrologers in the fourth book of Llewellyn's anthology series. Besides compiling all this information into a unified whole, Joan McEvers also contributes her viewpoint and knowledge to the delineation of the 12th House.

Each house, an area of activity within the horoscope, is explained with clarity and depth by the following authors:
- Peter Damian: The 1st House and the Rising Sign and Planets
- Ken Negus: The 7th House of Partnership
- Noel Tyl: The 2nd House of Self-Worth and the 8th House of Values and Others
- Spencer Grendahl: The 3rd House of Exploration & Communication
- Dona Shaw: The 9th House of Truth and Abstract Thinking
- Gloria Star: The 4th House of the Subconscious Matrix
- Marwayne Leipzig: The 10th House of the Life's Imprint
- Lina Accurso: The 5th House of Love
- Sara Corbin Looms: The 11th House of Tomorrow
- Michael Munkasey: The 6th House of Attitude and Service
- Joan McEvers: The 12th House of Strength, Peace, Tranquillity

0-87542-383-3, 400 pgs., 5-1/4 x 8, charts, softcover   **$12.95**

THE ASTROLOGY OF THE MACROCOSM
edited by Joan McEvers

The fifth book in Llewellyn's New World Astrology Series, *The Astrology of the Macrocosm* contains charts and articles from some of the world's top astrologers, explaining various mundane, transpersonal, and worldly events through astrology. It will help you gain insights into the global arenas of politics, social organization, and cultural analysis. It is the perfect introduction to understanding the fate of nations, weather patterns, and other global movements.

Featured are noted astrologers Nick Campion, Carolyn W. Casey, Steve Cozzi, Jimm Erickson, Charles Harvey, Jim Lewis, Richard Nolle, Marc Penfield, Nancy Soller and Judy Johns. Topics include ingress charts, cycles, Astro*Carto*Graphy, cultural and mythological evolution, the chart of England, weather forecasting and more. Charts and diagrams expand and illustrate most of the articles.

0-87542-384-1, 480 pgs., 5-1/4 x 8, softcover **$14.95**

ASTROLOGICAL COUNSELING: The Path to Self-Actualization
edited by Joan McEvers

A very prominent, yet rarely discussed astrological topic, is that of the role between the counselor and the counseled. *Astrological Counseling*, the sixth book in Llewellyn's New World Astrology series, explores the challenges for today's counselors, and gives guidance to those interested in seeking a counselor to help them with their own personal challenges. Editor Joan McEvers has enlisted the help of ten top astrologers to discuss this important subject.

Bill Herbst, Donna Cunningham, Gray Keen, Donald L. Weston, Susan Dearborn Jackson, Ginger Chalford, Maritha Pottenger, David Pond, Doris A. Hebel and Eileen Nauman are this volume's featured astrologers. Their articles cover such topics as co-dependency, psychotherapy, reading the body, healing wounded spirits, personal counseling, business counseling, medical counseling, and more.

There are more people consulting with astrologers than there are devoted astrological students. This book helps both groups understand the needs of the modern counseling client.

0-87542-385-X, 368 pgs., 5-1/4 x 8, softcover **$16.95**

INTIMATE RELATIONSHIPS
edited by Joan McEvers

Explore the deeper meaning of intimate relationships with the knowledge and expertise of eight renowned astrologers. Dare to look into your own chart and confront your own vulnerabilities. Find the true meaning of love and its place in your life. Gain new insights into the astrology of marriage, dating, affairs and more!

In *Intimate Relationships*, the seventh book in Llewellyn's New World Astrology Series, eight astrologers discuss their views on romance and the horoscope. The roles of Venus and the Moon, as well as the asteroids Sappho, Eros and Amor, are explored in our attitudes and actions toward potential mates. The theory of affinities is also presented wherein we are attracted to someone with similar planetary energies.

Is it a love that will last a lifetime, or mere animal lust that will burn itself out in a few months? The authors of *Intimate Relationships* will help you discover your natal attractions as well as your fatal attractions.

0-87542-386-8, 298 pgs., 6 x 9, softcover $14.95

THE WEB OF RELATIONSHIPS
edited by Joan McEvers

The astrology of intimacy has long been a popular subject among professional astrologers and psychologists. Many have sought the answer to what makes some people have successful relationships with one another, while others struggle. *Web of Relationships* examines this topic not only in intimate affiliations, but also in families and friendships, in this eighth volume of the Llewellyn New World Astrology Series.

Editor Joan McEvers has brought together the wisdom and experience of eight astrology experts. Listen to what one author says about the mythological background of planets as they pertain to relationships. Discover how past life regression is illustrated in the chart. Consider the relationship of astrology and transactional analysis.

Web of Relationships explores the karmic and mystical connections between child and parent, how friends support and understand each other, the significance of the horoscope as it pertains to connections and much more. Each chapter will bring you closer to your own web of relationships and the astrology of intimacy.

0-87542-388-4, 240 pgs., 6 x 9, softcover $14.95

Prices subject to change without notice.

HORARY ASTROLOGY
by Anthony Lewis
This new book delves deeply into the heritage and the modern applicability of the horary art. Author Anthony Louis is a practicing psychiatrist, and he brings the compassion and erudition associated with his field to this scholarly textbook.

Written beautifully and reverently in the tradition of William Lilly, the book translates Lilly's meaning into modern terms. Other features include numerous case studies; tables; diagrams; and more than 100 pages of appendices, including an exhaustive planetary rulership list, planetary key words and a lengthy astrological/horary glossary. Dignities and debilities, aspects and orbs, derivative houses, Arabic parts, fixed stars, critical degrees and more are explored in relation to the science of horary astrology. Worksheets supplement the text.

0-87542-394-9, 600 pgs., 6 x 9, softcover   **$18.95**

PREDICTION IN ASTROLOGY
by Noel Tyl
No matter how much you know about astrology already, no matter how much experience you've had to date, you'll be fascinated by *Prediction in Astrology*, and you'll grow as an astrologer. Using the Solar Arc theory and methods he describes in this book, the author was able to accurately predict the Gulf War, including the actual date it would begin and the timetable of tactics, two months *before* it began. He also predicted the overturning of Communist rule in the eastern bloc nations nine months in advance of its actual occurrence.

Tyl teaches through example. You learn by *doing* astrology, not just thinking about it. Tyl introduces Solar Arc theory in terms of "rapport" measurements, which you begin to do immediately, without paper, pencil, or computer, dials, or wheels. Just with your eyes! *You will never look at a horoscope the same way again!*

Tyl, in his well-known, very special way, also gets personal. He presents 30 Aphorisms, the keenest of maxims, the most practical of techniques, *to create predictions from any horoscope.* And as if this were not enough, Tyl then presents 20 Aphorisms for *Counseling.* Look for Tyl's "Quick-Glance" Transit Table, 1940-2040, to which you can refer more quickly than a computer. The busy astrologer will use this Appendix every day for many years to come.

0-87542-814-2, 360 pgs., 6 x 9, softcover   **$14.95**

Prices subject to change without notice.

HOLISTIC ASTROLOGY: THE ANALYSIS
OF INNER AND OUTER ENVIRONMENTS
by Noel Tyl
When an individual's life does not reflect what is expressed in his or her chart, it doesn't mean the chart is wrong! Holistic astrology demands that the horoscope be related to the life as it is lived by the individual, that we take into consideration environmental as well as planetary influences.

This landmark study of astrology and parental influences, generational differences, defense mechanisms, and the patterns of environmental pressures provides incisive techniques for becoming better astrologers/analysts. Here are clues to the meaning of anxiety, a new look at communication and points of view, and a new understanding of Pluto and Neptune. Learn practical and effective counseling techniques, the dynamics of loving, and the significance of the sexual profile. Ten case studies demonstrate the practical application of this method. Original, creative, human—and hopeful.

0-9356200-00-1, 363 pgs., hardcover **$15.95**

THE PRINCIPLES AND PRACTICE OF ASTROLOGY
by Noel Tyl
Seven volumes of the most complete course of instruction in astrology ever published. These important source books will open horizons and expand your knowledge and understanding of astrology as never before.

0-87542-803—ASPECTS & HOUSES IN ANALYSIS

0-87542-805—THE EXPANDED PRESENT

0-87542-807—ANALYSIS & PREDICTION

0-87542-808—SPECIAL HOROSCOPE DIMENSIONS

0-87542-809—ASTROLOGICAL COUNSEL

0-87542-810—ASTROLOGY-MUNDANE, ASTRAL, OCCULT

0-87542-811—TIMES TO COME

Order by number, softcover **$3.95 each**

THE NEW A TO Z HOROSCOPE MAKER AND DELINEATOR
by Llewellyn George
This is a new and totally revised edition of the text used by more American astrologers than any other—135,000 copies sold. Every detail of: How to Cast the Birth Chart—time changes, calculations, aspects & orbs, signs & planetary rulers, parts of fortune, etc.; The Progressed Chart—all the techniques and the major delineations; Transits—how to use them in prediction; also lunations and solar days. Rectification. Locality Charts, a comprehensive Astrological Dictionary and a complete index for easy use. It's an encyclopedia, a textbook, a self-study course and and a dictionary all-in-one!

0-87542-264-0,600 pages, 6 x 9, softcover. **$12.95**

Prices subject to change without notice.

THE LLEWELLYN ANNUALS

Llewellyn's MOON SIGN BOOK: Approximately 400 pages of valuable information on gardening, fishing, weather, stock market forecasts, personal horoscopes, good planting dates, and general instructions for finding the best date to do just about anything! Articles by prominent forecasters and writers in the fields of gardening, astrology, politics, economics and cycles. This special almanac, different from any other, has been published annually since 1906. It's fun, informative and has been a great help to millions in their daily planning. **State year $4.95**

Llewellyn's SUN SIGN BOOK: Your personal horoscope for the entire year! All 12 signs are included in one handy book. Also included are forecasts, special feature articles, and an action guide for each sign. Monthly horoscopes are written by Gloria Star, author of *Optimum Child*, for your personal Sun Sign and there are articles on a variety of subjects written by well-known astrologers from around the country. Much more than just a horoscope guide! Entertaining and fun the year around. **State year $4.95**

Llewellyn's DAILY PLANETARY GUIDE and ASTROLOGER'S DATEBOOK: Includes all of the major daily aspects plus their exact times in Eastern and Pacific time zones, lunar phases, signs and voids plus their times, planetary motion, a monthly ephemeris, sunrise and sunset tables, special articles on the planets, signs, aspects, a business guide, planetary hours, rulerships, professional astrologers directory and much more. Large 5.25 x 8 format for more writing space, spiral bound to lay flat, address and phone listings, time zone conversion chart and blank horoscope chart. **State year $6.95**

Llewellyn's ASTROLOGICAL CALENDAR: Large wall calendar of 48 pages. Beautiful full color cover and full color inside. Includes special feature articles by famous astrologers, and complete introductory information on astrology. It also contains a Lunar Gardening Guide, celestial phenomena, a blank horoscope chart, and monthly date pages which include aspects, Moon phases, signs and voids, planetary motion, an ephemeris, personal forecasts, lucky dates, planting and fishing dates, and more. 10 x 13 size. Set in Central time, with fold-down conversion table for other time zones worldwide. **State year $9.95**

Prices subject to change without notice.

Llewellyn's Astrological Services

There are many types of charts and many different ways to use astrological information. Llewellyn offers a wide variety of services which can help you with specific needs. Read through the descriptions that follow to help you choose the right service. All of our readings are done by professional astrologers. The computer services are set up on Matrix programs and the interpretations are tailored to your needs. Remember, astrology points out potentials and possibilities; it will serve as your resource guide. Only you can decide what is right. Astrology should help you guide your life, not control it.

If you have never had a chart reading done before, we suggest that you order the Complete Natal or the Detailed Natal Service. We encourage informative letters with your request so that our astrologers can address your needs more specifically. All information is held strictly confidential. Be sure to give accurate and complete birth data: exact time, date, year, place, county and country of birth. Check your birth certificate. *Accuracy of birth data is important.* We will not be responsible for mistakes made by you! An order form follows the descriptions of Llewellyn Astrological Services.

Personalized Astrology Readings

These chart readings are done by professional astrologers and focus on your particular concerns. Include descriptive letter.

APS03-119 Simple Natal: Your chart calculated by computer in whatever house system stated. It has all of the trimmings, including aspects, midpoints, Chiron and a glossary of symbols, plus a free book! We use Tropical/Placidus unless you state otherwise. Include full birth data. . . . $5.00

APS03-101 Complete Natal: Our most thorough reading. It not only gives you the computer chart and detailed reading, but also interpretation of the trends shown in your chart for the coming year. It is activated by transits and focuses on any issue you specify. Include full birth data and a descriptive letter. $125.00

APS03-500 (3 months) **APS03-501** (6 months) **APS03-502** (1 year) **Transit Forecasts:** These reports keep you abreast of positive trends and challenging periods. Our reports can be an invaluable aid for timing your actions and decision making. Reports begin the first day of the month you specify. . . . . $15 (3 months), $30 (6 months), $50 (1 year).

APS03-105 Progressed Chart With Transits: Your birth chart is progressed by techniques to determine what it says about you now. Use this reading to understand the evolution of your personal power. Provides interpretation of present and future conditions for a year's time with a special focus as stated by you. Include descriptive letter. $85.00

Prices subject to change without notice.

APS03-102 Detailed Natal: Complete natal chart plus inter-pretation with the focus on one specific question as stated by you. Learn about aspects of your chart and what they mean to you. $65.00

APS03-110 Horary Chart: Gives the answer to any specific question. This is divination at its best, Should you marry? Will you get a new job soon? Give precise time of writing letter. $50.00

APS03-503 Personality Profile Horoscope: Our most popular reading! This ten-part reading gives you a complete look at how the planets affect you. It is an excellent way to become acquainted with astrology and to learn about yourself. Very reasonable price! $20.00

APS03-114 Compatibility Reading: Determines compatibility of two peo-ple in an existing relationship. Give birth data for both. $75.00

Personal Services Order Form

Remember to include all birth data plus your full name for all reports.
When you order the Simple Natal Chart, you'll receive a 25% discount on any one additional computer report, a 35% discount on any second report, and a 50% discount on any additional report.

Service name and number_____

Full name (1st person)_____

Time_____ ☐ a.m. ☐ p.m. Date _____Year_____

Birthplace (city, county, state, country)_____

_____

Full name (2nd person)_____

Time_____ ☐ a.m. ☐ p.m. Date_____Year_____

Birthplace (city, county, state, country)_____

_____

Astrological knowledge: ☐ Novice   ☐ Student   ☐ Advanced
Please include letter describing questions on separate sheet of paper.

Name_____

Address_____

City_____State_____Zip____

Make check or money order payable to Llewellyn Publications.To charge your order use ($15 min.) Visa, MC or Am. Exp. (circle one).

Account Number_____Exp. Date_____

Day Phone_____Signature_____

Mail this form and payment to:
Llewellyn's Personal Services, P.O. Box 64383-387, St. Paul, MN 55164-0383
Allow 4-6 weeks for delivery.

Prices subject to change without notice.